Structural Dynamics and Economic Growth

Ever since Adam Smith, economists have been preoccupied with the puzzle of economic growth. The standard mainstream models of economic growth were and often still are based either on assumptions of diminishing returns on capital with technological innovation or on endogenous dynamics combined with a corresponding technological and institutional setting. An alternative model of economic growth emerged from the Cambridge School of Keynesian economists in the 1950s and 1960s. This model – developed mainly by Luigi Pasinetti – emphasizes the importance of demand, human learning and the growth dynamics of industrial systems. Finally, in the past decade, new mainstream models have emerged incorporating technology or demand-based structural change and extending the notion of balanced growth. This collection of essays reassesses Pasinetti's theory of structural dynamics in the context of these recent developments, with contributions from economists writing in both the mainstream and the Cambridge Keynesian traditions and including Luigi Pasinetti, William Baumol, Geoffrey Harcourt and Nobel laureate Robert Solow.

RICHARD ARENA is Professor of Economics at the University of Nice-Sophia Antipolis, France, where he is Director of the Institute of Human and Social Sciences. He is also the managing editor of the *Revue d'Économie Industrielle*.

PIER LUIGI PORTA is Professor of Economics at the University of Milano-Bicocca, Italy, and a visiting fellow of Wolfson College, Cambridge. He is also the Editor-in-Chief of the *International Review of Economics*.

Structural Dynamics and Economic Growth

Edited by

Richard Arena and Pier Luigi Porta

CAMBRIDGE UNIVERSITY PRESS
Cambridge, New York, Melbourne, Madrid, Cape Town,
Singapore, São Paulo, Delhi, Mexico City

Cambridge University Press
The Edinburgh Building, Cambridge CB2 8RU, UK

Published in the United States of America by Cambridge University Press, New York

www.cambridge.org
Information on this title: www.cambridge.org/9781107015968

First published 2012

A catalogue record for this publication is available from the British Library

Library of Congress Cataloguing in Publication Data

Structural dynamics and economic growth / edited by Richard Arena,
Pier Luigi Porta.
p. cm.
ISBN 978-1-107-01596-8 (Hardback)
1. Economic development. 2. Sustainable development. 3. Pasinetti, Luigi L.–Political and social views. I. Arena, R. (Richard) II. Porta, Pier Luigi. III. Title.
HD82.S84577 2011
338.9–dc23

2011025054

ISBN 978-1-107-01596-8 Hardback

Contents

Figures

Table

Contributors

WILLIAM J. BAUMOL is Professor of Economics and Academic Director of the Berkley Center for Entrepreneurial Studies at New York University, and Professor Emeritus at Princeton University. Professor Baumol has written some 40 professional books and 500 articles. He holds eleven honorary degrees and has been elected to three of the United States' leading honorific societies, including the National Academy of Science, as well as to the world's oldest honorary academic society in Italy, the Accademia Nazionale dei Lincei.

HEINRICH BORTIS is Professor of Political Economy at the University of Fribourg, Switzerland, where he teaches economic theory, history of economic thought and economic history. He is the author of numerous articles and books, including *Institutions, Behaviour and Economic Theory* (Cambridge University Press 1997; translated into Ukrainian 2007 and into Russian 2009).

DAVIDE GUALERZI teaches political economy in the Department of Economics at the University of Padua, Italy. He received his PhD from the Graduate Faculty, New School for Social Research, New York. He has taught at the University of Pisa and was Assistant Professor of Economics at Bard College, New York, as well as Visiting Professor at UBA (University of Buenos Aires), and Visiting Scholar in the Department of Economics, New School for Social Research, New York. He has served as a consultant to several Italian and international institutions. His research is in the fields of political economy, growth and structural change, consumption theory, urban and regional development. His latest book is *The Coming of Age of Information Technologies and the Path of Transformational Growth* (2010), a long-run perspective on the late 2000s' recession.

PETER D. GROENEWEGEN is Emeritus Professor of Economics at the University of Sydney and a well-known scholar of the history of economic thought. He is a distinguished fellow of the History of Economics

Society and an honorary life member of the European Society of the History of Economic Thought. His published works include the definitive biography of Alfred Marshall, a series of edited economic classics, some of them in English translation, three volumes of collected essays, an edition of Turgot's major economic writings in English translation, and a history of Australian economics. He is currently completing a volume on 'minor' Marshallians dealing with ten students of Marshall and their role in spreading the 'economic organon'.

HARALD HAGEMANN is Professor of Economic Theory at the University of Hohenheim, Stuttgart, Germany. He is also a life member of Clare Hall, University of Cambridge. In the academic year 1999/2000 he was Theodor-Heuss-Professor at the Graduate Faculty of Political and Social Sciences at New School University, New York. He has taught at the universities of Bremen and Kiel, the Free University of Berlin, and as a Visiting Professor at the Universities of Bologna, Linz, Nice, Paris I Pantheon-Sorbonne, Strasbourg and Sydney. His research covers growth and structural change, technological change and employment, business cycle theory and the history of economic thought. He is President of the European Society for the History of Economic Thought (ESHET).

GEOFFREY HARCOURT is a graduate of the universities of Melbourne and Cambridge. He taught for half his working life in Adelaide and the other half (with overlaps) in Cambridge, where he has spent part of every decade since the 1950s. He is Visiting Professorial Fellow (2010–2013) at the School of Economics at UNSW (and Emeritus Reader in the History of Economic Theory, Cambridge (1998), Emeritus Fellow, Jesus College, Cambridge (1998) and Professor Emeritus, Adelaide (1988)). He is the author and/or editor of 25 books, including 9 volumes of selected essays and more than 240 articles and/or chapters in volumes. With Prue Kerr, in 2009 he wrote an intellectual biography of Joan Robinson.

ÖNDER NOMALER is Assistant Professor in the Department of Industrial Engineering and Innovation Sciences at Eindhoven University of Technology. In 1993, he received his BSc degree in Industrial Engineering at the Middle East Technical University (METU) in Ankara. In 1996, he received his MSc degree in Economics at the same university, where he also worked as research and teaching assistant for two years. He earned his PhD in Economics in 2006 at Maastricht University. His research interests include economic growth and international trade, innovation and technological change, evolutionary modelling, agent-based simulation modelling, bibliometrics, scientometrics and infometrics.

LUIGI L. PASINETTI is a leading member of the second generation of Cambridge Keynesians. He was Reader in Economics and Official Fellow of King's College, Cambridge up to the mid-1970s, then Professor of Economic Analysis (now Emeritus) at the Università Cattolica del Sacro Cuore, Milan. A student of Piero Sraffa and Richard Kahn, he developed one of the first rigorous mathematical formulations of Ricardo's theory of value and distribution. Along with them, as well as Joan Robinson, he was one of the prominent members on the Cambridge (UK) side of the Cambridge capital controversy. His contributions to economics include developing the analytical foundations of neo-Ricardian economics, including the theory of value and distribution, as well as work in the line of Kaldorian theory of growth and income distribution. He has developed the theory of structural change and economic growth, structural economic dynamics and uneven sectoral development. His most recent book is *Keynes and the Cambridge Keynesians* (Cambridge University Press, 2007).

MARIO POMINI is Associate Professor of Economics in the Department of Economics and Management at the University of Padua, Italy. His main research interests lie in the areas of philosophy of social sciences, economic methodology and the history of economic thought. He has published many articles on the recent history of Italian economic thought, with particular reference to the Paretian tradition.

ROBERTO SCAZZIERI is Professor of Economic Analysis at the University of Bologna. He is also Senior Member of Gonville and Caius College and life member of Clare Hall, University of Cambridge. His research interests cover the theory of production, structural economic dynamics, the economic theory of institutions and organisations, the epistemology of economics, and the history of economic analysis. He has contributed scholarly papers in the above research fields and has published a number of books, including *A Theory of Production* (1993), *Production and Economic Dynamics* (Cambridge University Press, 1996), co-edited with Michael Landesmann, *Markets, Money and Capital* (Cambridge University Press, 2008), co-edited with A. Sen and S. Zamagni, *Capital, Time and Transitional Dynamics* (2008), co-edited with H. Hagemann, and *Fundamental Uncertainty* (2011), co-edited with S. Marzetti Dall'Aste Brandolini. He was awarded the St Vincent Prize for Economics, 1984 and the Linceo Prize for Economics, 2004.

ROBERT M. SOLOW is a leading theorist on economic growth. He started to specialise in economics immediately after the Second World War at Harvard University under Wassily Leontief. He then moved to MIT, where he was appointed Professor of Economics in 1958. In 1979 he served as President of the American Economic Association. In 1987 he was awarded the Nobel Prize in Economic Sciences for his contributions to the theory of economic growth, and in 1999 he was honoured with the National Medal of Science – one of only seven economists ever to have won that distinction. Since 2000 he has divided his time between MIT and the Russell Sage Foundation in New York, where he is the Foundation's only permanent fellow.

MOSHE SYRQUIN is Professor of Economics in the Department of International Studies at the University of Miami. He obtained his undergraduate degree from Bar-Ilan University in Israel and a PhD in Economics from Harvard University. He has been a visiting professor at various universities and institutes, including Harvard, Rice, Toronto, Ancona, the Catholic University of Milan, the State University of Milan at Bicocca, and ICER (International Centre for Economic Research) in Turin. He has co-authored and edited 6 books and written more than 60 papers in professional journals.

BART VERSPAGEN holds the chair of International Economics at Maastricht University and is Professorial Fellow at the United Nations University institute UNU-MERIT, Maastricht. He has a PhD from UNU-MERIT and Maastricht University, and previously held the chair of Economics of Innovation and Technological Change at Eindhoven University of Technology. He is also a visiting professor at the TIK Institute at the University of Oslo. His research interests include economic growth and the relationship to innovation and technological change, evolutionary modeling of economic processes, microeconometrics of innovation and innovation indicators.

TAKASHI YAGI is Professor in the School of Political Science and Economics at Meiji University, Japan. He studied economics at the School of Political Science and Economics, and at the Graduate School of Economics, Waseda University. He became an assistant professor at Gunma University in 1993, a professor in 2003, and moved to Meiji University in 2009. He has had visiting appointments at Wolfson College and the Faculty of Economics, Cambridge (1999–2000) through a fellowship from the Ministry of Education of Japan, and at the Centro Sraffa of the University of Rome 3 (2003) through the Piero Sraffa Fellowship. His research interests are in Sraffian economics, post-Keynesian economics, capital theory and distribution, structural dynamics and economic growth, and input–output analysis.

Introduction: structural dynamics and contemporary growth theory

Richard Arena and Pier Luigi Porta

1 The scope of growth theory today

The essays collected in this volume address the role of structural dynamics in the context of the current state of the theory of economic growth. Given the many extensions and ramifications of contemporary growth theory, it would seem far too ambitious an undertaking, within the space of an introductory essay, to attempt a comprehensive survey. Instead, our more modest purpose here is to draw attention specifically to developments in the study of structural dynamics. Over the past four or five decades, the theory of economic growth has made enormous progress. Much as in other fields of scientific enquiry, this progress tends to take the form of cumulative knowledge acquisition and formation clustered around a few lines of research. Even so – and notwithstanding the emergence of an overarching and powerful analytical framework – other less well-explored lines of research tend to survive and coexist.

In their introduction to the *Handbook of Economic Growth* (2005, p. xi), Aghion and Durlauf note that 'interest in economic growth has been an integral part of economics since its inception as a scholarly discipline'. In fact, one of the few undisputed facts in the history of the discipline is perhaps that what is at the heart of political economy through the Modern Age (sixteenth to eighteenth centuries) is a focus on aggregate *wealth*. Defining the *nature* of wealth, as well as suggesting *ways to increase* aggregate wealth and to improve its quality, is foremost among the questions addressed by the political economy of the modern age.

The editors are extremely grateful to a large number of colleagues and scholars who have cared to discuss and advise on the project of this book. Much of the work has been done in Cambridge, where the Marshall Library of Economics and Wolfson College have provided the ideal setting for working on the project. In particular they wish to record an obligation to Dr Stephanie Blankenburg, both for invaluable scientific advice and for generous practical help and assistance.

Together with the issue of income distribution, wealth certainly remains the principal problem of classical political economy, especially from Adam Smith onwards. That is why Adam Smith wrote an *Inquiry into the Nature and Causes of the Wealth of Nations*, rather than a treatise on the *principles* of political economy.

Through the modern age political economy can be described as a long series of endeavours to solve what is sometimes called the 'mystery' of economic growth (Helpman, 2004).

In ancient times, wealth would be regarded as instrumental in happiness. With the onset of the modern age, wealth gradually turned into an end in itself, or rather, the end of economic policy, and it was economic policy that emerged as the driving force of economic thought: that is, in fact, the age termed by Schumpeter (1954), when 'the consultant administrators and the pamphleteers' turn into pioneers of economic thought and analysis.

The above transformations took place primarily during the sixteenth and seventeenth centuries and extended well into the eighteenth century. They entailed a transition from an idea of possessive *acquisitiveness*, based on commerce in a zero-sum game (mercantilism), to one of *productivity*, based on primary production and on circulation (physiocracy), to approach, as a further step, a line of thinking concerned with *creativity* founded on learning and on human and social capital, with the rise of the British Classical School. The novelty of this latter approach lies in the much larger space given over to the analysis of the motivations underlying action and institution-building. This strand of reasoning is typically personified in Adam Smith, the unwitting 'founding father' of the Classical School of political economy, although it can be shown that his contribution could hardly be fully understood independently of other currents of the Enlightenment.[1]

The editors of the *Handbook of Economic Growth* argue, furthermore, that 'this ancient lineage is consistent with growth economics representing one of the most active areas of research in economics in the last two decades', although (more surprisingly) 'this activity followed a relatively long period of calm in the aftermath of the seminal theoretical and

[1] While it used to be common procedure to associate Smith's analysis with the Smith–Ricardo–Marx line of descent (emphasizing distribution) or with the Smith–Marshall or even the Smith–Walras–Pareto strand (emphasizing allocation and equilibrium), it is nowadays more common to see Smith as a child of the Enlightenment movement, and in particular of the cross-fertilization of the Italian and Scottish Enlightenment. The latter interpretation places particular emphasis on economic growth, knowledge and learning, and on institutions.

empirical work by Robert Solow on the neoclassical growth model. Solow's research set the growth research agenda for over 25 years' (ibid.). Extended periods of 'calm' were, indeed, a feature of the development of political economy throughout the nineteenth and part of the twentieth centuries, as political economy had turned into an allocative discipline. So much so that William Baumol, in a well-known scholarly treatment of the topic (itself a 'classic'), speaks of the *magnificent dynamics* of the Classics. If we are still keen, to the present day, on 'those older dynamic systems', Baumol (1970, p. 13) writes, it is 'simply because, although imperfect, they represent an approach of which there are few recent examples'. As indicated, after the Classical period economics did, in fact, focus largely on resource allocation rather than extended reproduction over time, and the analysis of long-run economic dynamics remained 'out of focus' for quite a long time, with some notable exceptions, among which Schumpeter's *Entwicklung* of 1912 is the best known. In retrospect, this period can also be considered one of prolonged 'incubation' that paved the way for a new avenue of research on economic dynamics. The new start was the product of a whole set of ideas, easily retrievable from a range of well-documented sources, with Solow's 1956/57 model playing a pivotal role in the process. Remarkably enough, however, one finds again Keynes at the source of the initial inspiration. It was in fact Roy Harrod who, as early as 1939, in an attempt to extend the implications of Keynes's *General Theory* to the long run, stressed the importance of concentrating the dynamic economic analysis on the novel concepts of the 'rates of change' of macroeconomic magnitudes. He presented his ideas more extensively in a series of lectures which he delivered at the London School of Economics immediately after the war, and then published in his *Towards a Dynamic Economics* (1948). Meanwhile, the appearance of an independently written contribution by Evsey Domar (1946), more mathematically framed but less complete, led the growth literature to couple their two names as authors of the Harrod–Domar macroeconomic model of growth, which was to become well known. It was from this model that originated the contributions to economic growth of the Post-Keynesian Cambridge economists.[2]

[2] During the 1960s and early 1970s several contributions analyzed the main features of the newly emerging growth theory. We may single out Hahn and Matthews (1964) and Sen (1970) as core historical references. In both cases it was openly acknowledged that it was Roy Harrod who had originally blazed a trail in the field. L. Pasinetti clearly sketched out this genealogy of Cambridge Keynesian contributions, from Harrod to Kaldor, in his book on *Growth and Income Distribution* (1974). It was, however, Solow's 1956/7 model that played a pivotal role in the process of bringing to evidence the way to insert the Harrod–Domar model into mainstream neoclassical economics.

With a view to his pivotal role, Solow's remarks on the latter-day achievements of economic growth theory, read today, are of particular interest. His reflections rightly occupy the opening pages of the *Handbook* (pp. 3–10). To start with (including in the abstract to this contribution), Solow's 'Reflections' (Aghion and Derlauf, 2005, pp. 3–10) express 'surprise at the lack of attention both to multisector growth models and to multi-country models with trade and capital flows'. The '*basic*' neoclassical model of growth is still alive – 'astonishingly'! Solow proudly observes – and in good shape after some 50 years: the '"endogenous growth" models of Romer and Lucas and their many successors are, in fact, entirely neoclassical' (ibid.). On the positive side, Solow stresses that 'progress, in theory and in practical analysis, has come mainly from extending the basic model at the edges' (ibid.). Thus, in his view, 'the territory of growth' has not merely expanded but has done so 'to include more topics in what used to be border areas'. However, '[t]his is not exactly the same thing as "endogenizing" these borderline topics'. Indeed, prominent among the extensions are treatments of 'the influence of background forces like "institutions" on the evolution of technology or total factor productivity. Some of it is in the mood of the "New Growth Theory" but not all of it. Much of it just wants to be explicit about background forces without trying to absorb them into the model' (ibid.).

These are perceptive observations from one of the greatest contemporary masters of economic growth theory. They are all the more interesting as they also touch on a core concern of economic thinking today that goes well beyond the analysis of economic growth, namely the relationship between economics and other disciplines.[3] Regarding growth theory in particular, it is not always clear where the line should be drawn between endogenizing as wide a range as possible of explanatory factors into a unifying analytical framework and a more explicit treatment of background forces.

In the current context, it is of some interest to stay with Solow for a little longer, as he proceeds 'to contemplate a few of the territories into which the theory has not expanded' (ibid.: 4). First among these are

[3] George Stigler once spoke of economics as 'the imperial science' (e.g. Stigler, 1984). For a constructive approach to the issue of interdisciplinary studies, see the recent collection of papers, edited by Arena *et al.* (2009), where it is acknowledged that interdisciplinary studies are justified when they provide the multiplicity of tools and perspectives necessary to tackle specific problems. It is hardly surprising that a large number of breakthroughs in current economic theory appear to have been achieved via tweaks and bridgings at the edges. Cf. also Coase (1977).

'multisector growth models'. As Solow points out, 'Luigi Pasinetti has written extensively on the sort of structural changes to be expected along a trajectory, arising from such inevitable factors as differing income elasticities of demand for different goods' (ibid.). The solid realism of Solow's timely remark is confirmed also by the fact that this is the *only place* where Pasinetti's name – undoubtedly the greatest economist to have focused attention on structural dynamics today – finds mention in the entire two-volume *Handbook* of some 1,800 pages (see in particular Pasinetti, 1981).

Pasinetti's analysis has put an increasing emphasis through his own work on the role of institutions as background forces and significant constraints. For a proper study of institutions Pasinetti has introduced an important 'separation theorem' in his recent book (Pasinetti, 2007, Chapter ix). This emphasis on the role of institutions is bound to call attention, in particular, to the links between economic theory and economic history. It is precisely the intriguing and relevant progress and proliferation of growth theory which brings into focus the question of the relationship between theory and history. Over past decades, the studies of economics and economic history have largely drifted apart. We are now at a stage where *connections* are being rediscovered. In Solow's view, the emphasis on institutions, in particular, opens up 'the possibility – about which I am now more optimistic than I once was – of connecting up growth theory with the problem of economic development, in which issues of institutional change are clearly central' (ibid.: 6).

Not surprisingly, Solow here refers to a number of leading contributors to the new endogenous growth theory, such as Daron Acemoglu, Avner Greif and Alberto Alesina. It is interesting, however, to see how Solow comes back, in a roundabout way, to the issue of 'imperialism', adding that his own 'prejudice' is that 'there may have been a premature tendency to assimilate growth and development, abetted by the vogue of cross-country regressions' (ibid.). Indeed, he finds it reasonable to suggest that a 'detailed analysis of institutions is probably a better method than cross-country regressions'. Such recent extensions of growth analysis sometimes produce a 'breathtaking broad sweep' such as 'the story-line proposed by Daron Acemoglu and colleagues'. Though – as Solow readily admits – 'much of it has the ring of truth' and it is 'irresistibly fascinating', 'I must confess nevertheless to a certain scepticism about firm conclusions at this level of generality, especially when they bear on "ultimate" causality' (ibid.).

This all sits well with Solow's views expressed in Szenberg's (1992) collection of self-portraits of outstanding economists some years ago, where Solow emphasized that 'it does economics no good to be too ambitious'. In particular, 'economics is foreclosed from a Theory of Everything' and 'not just because it is all so complicated but for deeper reasons'. 'Pretty clearly' – Solow explains – 'economic behaviour depends on the nature of social institutions (...). Believers in an economic Theory of Everything would say "Okay, but then we just have to include the choice of social institutions as an endogenous process".' That is precisely what is happening today in large swathes of current political economy. 'I think' – Solow argues – 'the response is wrong, not just hard to carry out, but wrong. Social institutions are not chosen, they evolve' (p. 272).

We very much agree with Solow when he notes that 'economics should not take itself too seriously' (ibid.). This is a point of the utmost significance. As we argue in this introduction, the relevance of structural dynamics today is closely related to the question of the relationship between economic theory and economic history, at a time when the imperialist dream of current political economy acquires a distinctive flavour of *Übermenschlichkeit*. Ways of doing economic history are, no doubt, changing. However, pretending to abolish the border between economic theory and economic history would result in foreclosing a whole territory of reciprocal interaction.

2 Two building blocks of the contemporary analysis of economic growth

We now turn to a more thorough consideration of our argument, and to discuss the question of whether, and if so how, following Solow's contribution to balanced growth, the contemporary theory of economic growth has come to include structural change in its agenda. We distinguish three main stages of the development of economic growth during the last fifty years.

A *first stage* consisted of the development of *optimal growth* models. These models (in particular by Cass, 1965, but also by Koopmans, 1965 and onwards) were credited in the literature with paying greater attention to the nature of the microfoundations of the theory of growth, but above all with advances in transitional dynamics that facilitated the use of numerical simulations and, eventually, econometric calculus. These achievements did, however, also facilitate the tendency 'to assimilate growth and development, abetted by the vogue of cross-country regressions', as pointed out by Solow above. These models did not, therefore, in any real sense, face up to the problems of structural change from an analytical standpoint. Moreover, optimal growth models are by their very nature normative and thus rather ill-equipped to tackle the empirical features of structural change. As Solow observed, 'it seems to me foolish to interpret as a descriptive theory what my generation learned from Frank Ramsey to treat as a normative theory, a story about what an omniscient, omnipotent, and nevertheless virtuous planner would do' (Solow, 1997, p. 12).

A *second stage* corresponded to the emergence of *endogenous growth theory* that allows for an explicit treatment of innovations and a better analysis of their *structural* effects. Innovations here are mostly considered to be *incremental*, as, for instance, by Ethier (1982) and Romer (1990). In this line of enquiry, intermediate goods owned by specialized productive units contribute to the division of labour and to productivity increases in final goods production. Thus, the new intermediate goods modify the *organization and degree of specialization of the productive structure* of the economy: Romer (1990), for instance, differentiates between research, intermediate and final goods sectors, and to this limited extent, some notion of *structural analysis and change* is implicitly recognized without, therefore, making this a core point of the analysis. Aghion and Howitt (1992) introduce the possibility of addressing *radical* or (general-purpose technology) (*GPT*) innovations combining, in neo-Schumpeterian fashion, different forms of obsolescence with 'creative destruction'. New products can appear in addition to older ones, but they can also replace these. Over time, all technologies eventually become obsolete and are replaced by successors. Such new technologies are the product of recent innovations that, due to their GPT characteristics, increase productivity at the macroeconomic level. In this kind of model, radical innovations and structural change are therefore closely linked to the emergence of new goods and technologies.

Such advances by endogenous growth theory, and in particular the more convincing attempts by its neo-Schumpeterian branch to inscribe structural change on its agenda, should not, however, distract from certain analytical limitations of contemporary endogenous growth theory – for instance, the enduring role of the representative consumer guided by constant preferences (notwithstanding the occasional introduction of some form of structural dynamics) and the use of *ad hoc* assumptions formally required to generate externalities and, in this way, to account for the relevance of different forms of returns to scale (see e.g. Arena and Raybaut, 2003, Arestis *et al.*, 2007 or Salvadori, 2003). Moreover, the possibility of multiple equilibria reinforces the importance of uneven economic change over time, in particular where a wider range of different types of innovation is taken into account (e.g. Amable, 1996).

3 The present state of structural dynamics

If these first two stages of recent developments in modern economic growth theory have paid only relatively scarce attention to structural dynamics, it is also the case that the *idea of structural dynamics* has never ceased to intrigue economists of all straits, and to captivate their interest and intellectual curiosity. This section focuses on a *third* stage in the development of contemporary growth theory post-Solow, and on the ways in which structural change has made an appearance in, as well as been addressed by, this comparatively recent literature.

Cristina Echevarria (1997) can certainly lay claim to having put structural change back on the agenda of recent growth analysis. Rather than simply ignoring differing existing contributions to the theory of structural change, she distinguishes two traditions of thought on structural change, and highlights their different views on the relationship between changes in the sectoral composition of the national product, on the one hand, and aggregate growth, on the other. Specifically, she argues that a first perspective – which she labels 'the neoclassical view' – held that structural change, understood as the evolution of the sectoral composition of national output, was a relatively 'unimportant by-product of growth' (Echevarria, 1997). The second view – attributed to 'scholars associated with the World Bank, including Baumol *et al.* (1989), Chenery and Syrquin (1975), Kuznets (1971), and Rostow (1971)' – made an original and divergent contribution in that it argued 'that growth is brought about by changes in sectoral composition' (Echevarria, 1997: 431).

Echevarria goes on to propose a kind of synthesis of both approaches based on the idea that the sectoral composition of national output affects per capita income growth rates as well as the structure of economic growth. She also provides a synthesis of the previously mentioned stages of the contemporary theory of economic growth by developing the methods of dynamic general equilibrium (including the use of a collective utility function) within the framework of a Solovian model of sustained growth. The real innovation of her paper consists, however, in the introduction of three different consumption goods demanded by agents on the basis of non-homothetic preferences, namely primary goods, manufacturing goods and services. Each consumption good is produced with different factor intensities, that are compatible with different exogenously given sectoral rates of technological change. This diversity of sectoral productivities affects the change over time of the sectoral composition of national output, and thereby the growth rate of the economy. In Echevarria's model, the equilibrium path has an asymptotic limit in which labour in the three sectors remains constant, while capital in all the three sectors, i.e. total capital, investment and consumption of manufactured goods, grows at the same rate. Therefore, if the proportion of inputs allocated to each sector is constant, the consumption of manufactured and primary goods and of services grows at different rates, in line with diverse forms of technical change as well as, partially, the overall increase of capital. While relative prices compensate for lower or higher growth, the proportions between the three goods or sectors change at a constant rate in real terms. Asymptotically, one sector tends to dominate the whole economy while the two other goods or sectors proportionally decline, although they grow in absolute terms. Structural change therefore is an explicit and core part of the analysis, even if the long-run implication is that it will eventually 'vanish' to make space for the 'neoclassical view' of an asymptotic steady-state equilibrium.

As Ngaï and Pissarides (2007) observe, Echevarria (1997) inspired a wide response, among this in particular Laitner (2000). Laitner's model admits the existence of non-homothetic preferences as one possibility. Consequently, he locates the origin of structural change on the demand-side of the economy. In Laitner's model, structural change is due to the operation of Engel's law and its impact on the economy-wide saving rate. An increase in the average propensity to save follows naturally from an increase in per capita income due to sufficiently pronounced technical progress. Other than in some endogenous growth models, Laitner does not explain an increase in the propensity to save by recourse to collective utility functions and optimization, but he considers the implications of Engel's law for financial variables.

He argues that while abnormal thrift may lead to higher income levels (as in Solow's framework), causality can run the other way round: a higher standard of living can lead to a higher saving rate. In Laitner's model, there are not three but only two goods, an agricultural and a manufacturing good, both of which are consumption goods. Household saving follows the stages of life-cycle behaviour with overlapping generations. Each household lives for two periods, is identical to all others born at the same time, and takes prices as given. While young households will save all labour earnings, retired households will deplete all wealth. This pattern will not vary over time even if incomes change, while the composition of consumption depends on changes in income. On the production side of the economy, aggregate effective labour supply depends on the number of young households and current technology. Finally, the economy is seen to undergo a shift from an initial specialization in agriculture to devoting more and more labour to manufacturing production.

Notwithstanding differences in the detail of their respective analyses, Echevarria, Laitner and, according to Ngaï and Pissarides (2007), Caselli and Coleman (2001) and Gollin *et al.* (2002), all conceptualize some form of structural change within a two- or three-sector economy with non-homothetic preferences, thus locating the origin of structural change in long-run changes in consumer tastes.

A different type of approach has been pioneered by Kongsamut *et al.* (2001, KRX for short). Their originality is twofold: first, KRX reshape Echevarria's distinction between two views on structural change ('neoclassical' and 'scholars associated to the World Bank'). The neglect of structural change in the neoclassical view or, in KRX's terminology, the dominance of 'balanced growth models', is now justified by the compatibility of these models with the 'Kaldor facts' regarding economic growth. KRX remind us that Kaldor emphasized the constancy, roughly speaking, of the growth rate of output, the capital-output ratio, the real interest rate, and the labour income share over time, in particular in the case of the long-period behaviour of the US economy. These 'stylized facts' are taken to provide sufficient justification for the regularities assumed by balanced growth theory and, consequently, for treating the study of structural change as secondary. Kaldor's 'stylized facts' can be found in Kaldor (1961/1989: 230–231). From this, it quickly becomes evident that KRX's interpretation has a distinct 'reductionist' flavour that is rather different from Kaldor's own perception. In fact, Kaldor specified these 'stylized facts' in a paper prepared for the Corfu meeting of the International Economic Association in August 1958, and developed the idea in the context of what Marglin and Schor (1992) refer to as the 'golden age of capitalism', i.e. the period 1945–1970 characterized by historically exceptionally high sustained growth rates and low rates of unemployment in leading Western economies.[4] Moreover, Kaldor (1961/1989: 231) remarked that 'none of these "facts" can plausibly be "explained" by the theoretical constructions of neoclassical theory'.

Second, KRX argue that the 'Kuznets facts' cannot possibly be ignored, that is, 'the massive reallocation of labour from agriculture into manufacturing and services that accompanies the growth process. This reallocation process, often called "structural change", has been documented by authors such as Clark (1940), Kuznets (1957) and Chenery (1960)' (ibid.: 869). KRX do not refer to Echevarria's scholars

[4] Very recently, Jones and Romer (2009) brought out what they called 'the New Kaldor Facts'.

'associated with the World Bank', but note that 'the macroeconomics and growth literature, which makes heavy use of balanced growth models, generally disregards the dramatic sectoral reallocation of labour experienced by all expanding economies. In contrast, there is a literature on structural change that ignores the Kaldor facts, in part because it focuses on a longer time period for which these facts may not apply (e.g. Baumol (1967), Pasinetti (1981), Park (1995), Echevarria (1997) and Laitner (2000))' (ibid.).

Much as Echevarria earlier, KRX propose their own synthesis of both these views in the form of a model that integrates the main features of balanced growth and the dynamics of structural change in a macroeconomic trajectory described by a 'generalized balanced growth (GBG) path' (Kongsamut *et al.*, 2001). This path features a constant real interest rate, constant relative prices, a constant aggregate labour income share, a constant growth rate for capital and aggregate output, a constant capital-output ratio, and time-varying sectoral growth rates and employment shares in three different sectors that are similar to those of the Echevarria model. The employment share declines in agriculture (which replaces Echevarria's sector of 'primary goods'), rises in services (as in Echevarria's model), and is stable in manufacturing (again, as in Echevarria's model). The rates of change of the factor shares of both agriculture and services converge to zero in the long run. As the economy grows, the importance of these sectors declines and the economy converges to a standard balanced growth path.

Not unlike in a balanced growth model, the economy here features transitional dynamics that are reminiscent of the stability properties of the one-sector neoclassical growth model. What ensures the existences of the GBG growth path in the KRX model is a restriction imposed on the value of agent endowments with services and agricultural goods. Without this restriction, the economy can still converge asymptotically to the GBG path, provided deviations from the restricted endowment value are not too pronounced. The introduction of different sectoral production functions and rates of technical progress implies that the relative prices of the different sectoral goods will vary over time. This, in turn, requires the imposition of constraints on the GBG path stability that are far more complex and difficult to interpret. Thus, within this framework structural change can be handled only in specific and limited ways, that exclude, for example, cases in which there is a wide variety of forms of technical progress.

Still more recently, Ngaï and Pissarides (2007) have provided an analytical framework which they consider an improvement over both of the previously mentioned approaches. Thus, they are, for example, critical of the approach developed by Echevarria (1997), Laitner (2000) and Caselli and Coleman (2001) for deriving structural change on the basis of a unique *ad hoc* assumption of non-homothetic preferences. In the case of the second approach, mentioned above, their criticisms are mainly directed at Kongsamut *et al.* (2001) and Foellmi and Zweimuller (2005). With regard to Kongsamut *et al.* (2001), Ngaï and Pissarides object to the fact that they have obtained their results 'by imposing a restriction that maps some of the parameters of their Stone–Geary utility function onto the parameters of the production functions, abandoning one of the most useful conventions of modern macroeconomics, the complete independence of preferences and technologies' (Ngaï and Pissarides, 2007, p. 429). In the same vein, they criticize Foellmi and Zweimuller (2005) for having obtained 'their results by assuming endogenous growth driven by the introduction of new goods into a hierarchic utility function' (ibid.). Ngaï and Pissarides argue that, by contrast, their own 'restrictions are quantitative restrictions on a conventional CES utility function that maintains the independence of the parameters of preferences and technologies' (ibid.). Moreover, their model considers structural change in the context of a real diversity of technical change, expressed in the form of different sectoral growth rates of total factor productivity that imply shifts in industrial employment shares over long periods of time. This diversity is shown to be compatible with the constancy of the economy's aggregate ratios. Ngaï and Pissarides's model includes various consumption goods and a single capital good supplied by a 'manufacturing' sector. Production functions are assumed to be identical across all sectors except for their rates of total factor productivity growth, and each sector produces a differentiated good that enters in the CES utility function. Under specific assumptions concerning the elasticity of substitution across final goods, the relative size of total factor productivity growth rates and the intertemporal elasticity of substitution in the utility function lead to *structural change* combined with a constant aggregate capital-output ratio and a balanced growth path. Finally, their approach essentially derives structural change from a 'technological' explanation mainly based on different rates of sectoral total factor productivity growth. This differs from the so-called 'utility-based' explanations 'which require different income elasticities for different goods and can yield structural change even with equal TFP growth in all sectors' (Ngaï and Pissarides, 2007, p. 430). Ngaï and Pissarides also emphasize the compatibility of their approach with the results of Baumol (1967) regarding the distinction between 'progressive' and 'stagnant' sectors, as well as the main long-run evidence, provided by Kuznets (1966) and Maddison (1983), to show the decline of agriculture's employment share, the rise and then fall of the manufacturing share, and the rise of the service share.

Interestingly, the literature just reviewed does not appear prominently in Aghion and Durlauf's (2005) *Handbook of Economic Growth*, where the theme of uneven sectoral growth surfaces only towards the end of a long paper on 'Accounting for cross-country income differences' by Francesco Caselli, an expert on structural transformation (ibid.: 679–741). Among the papers in the present volume, Moshe Syrquin takes notice of this literature and refers to Kuznets, Baumol or even Solow.

It is also worth mentioning Daron Acemoglu's recent *Introduction to Modern Economic Growth* (2009) in this context. Acemoglu's ambition is to develop a *general* theory (or at least a general view) of growth and development as unified phenomena. It is in that context that structural dynamics makes its appearance under 'Structural change and economic growth', the opening chapter of part VII of his book, devoted to the larger theme of 'economic development and economic growth' (ibid.: 697–724).

Acemoglu takes on board much of the literature discussed above and referred to as the *third* stage of contemporary growth theory and its treatment of structural change. Thus, regarding the 'Kaldor facts' as a synonym for balanced growth, he discusses Kongsamut *et al.* (2001), noting that 'they assume that production functions in different sectors are identical' (Acemoglu, 2009, p. 703) but that this assumption is 'useful for isolating the demand-side sources of structural change' (p. 699).

At the same time, so Acemoglu argues, KRX badly neglect the supply-side of the economy. He then praises Baumol (1967) for its emphasis on uneven growth resulting from different sectoral growth rates due to different rates of technological progress. In Acemoglu's view, the main requirement is, however, to bring together both sides of the economy (demand *and* supply), something he regards as having been achieved by Acemoglu and Guerrieri's two-sector model of constant growth equilibrium path (CGEP) (2008) on one side and on the other side by other suggestions relating to the 'demand-side' proposed in Acemoglu (2009– see section 20.1 and exercise 20.17 in Chapter 20). 'My first purpose,' Acemoglu explains, 'is to show that there are more subtle and compelling reasons for supply-side nonbalanced growth than those originally emphasized by Baumol'. In particular it is 'factor proportion differences across sectors combined with capital deepening [that] lead to non-balanced economic growth' (Acemoglu, 2009, p. 703; see also p. 705). Concerning the supply-side of non-balanced growth, Acemoglu and Guerrieri's 'richest set of dynamics' (Acemoglu, 2009, p. 714) is based on some conditions on the form of the household utility (ibid.: 712), of the transversality condition (ibid.: 711) (namely, rather restrictive demand conditions) and is finally based on the case of an elasticity of substitution between capital and labour less than one (namely, a supply condition), which is said to be empirically validated (see Acemoglu, 2009, pp. 709–710 for the analytical explanation; and Acemoglu, 2009, section 15.6 in Chapter 15 for the empirical discussion). If these conditions are simultaneously respected, the asymptotic growth rate of the model converging to the CGEP is determined by the asymptotically dominant sector, namely the one which is growing more slowly (Acemoglu, 2009, p. 712). Moreover, 'this model based on technological sources of non balanced growth is also broadly consistent with the Kaldor facts as well as the Kuznets facts' (ibid.: 714). This attempt is then combined with a purely demand-side one (section 20.1 of Chapter 20) assuming a rather abrupt consumer type of aggregation, generalized Cobb–Douglas production functions and an exogenous and Hicks-neutral technical progress (Acemoglu, 2009, p. 723).

Acemoglu also addresses the question of the sources of industrialization, making use of a wide range of models. The Acemoglu–Zilibotti model (1997) is presented as a refinement of Rosenstein–Rodan's big-push idea. The Matsuyama model (1992) – a two-sector model based on non-homothetic preferences in consumption and on learning-by-doing in manufacturing – is credited with formalizing the view (widely shared by historians) that agricultural productivity is the prime mover of economic growth. By contrast, the contribution made by Ngaï and Pissarides (2007) is rather played down as simply providing a modern version of Baumol's original idea. Chapter 21 of Acemoglu's book devoted to 'structural transformations and market failures in development' (ibid.: 725–775), explores a number of issues, ranging from finance to demography, urbanization and dualism. For our purposes, the most interesting section within this chapter is section 21.4, which discusses growth strategies and the role of imitation-innovation processes, based on Acemoglu *et al.* (2006). In section 21.7, Acemoglu concludes the chapter on a triumphant note, but shuns the idea of providing a unified model of structural transformation and market failures in development, arguing that this kind of ambition would lead 'to a framework that is complicated, whereas I believe that relatively abstract representations of reality are more insightful. Moreover the literature has not made sufficient progress for us to be able to develop a unified framework. Instead I provide a reduced-form model intended to bring out the salient common features of the models presented in this chapter' (Acemoglu, 2009, p. 765). Nevertheless, he maintains that we can 'approximate the growth process with an increase in the capital-labour ratio of the economy' (p. 765), suggesting that the Solow model should retain its role as a useful benchmark and starting point for growth analysis, that can be filled out with more recent insights from the analysis of structural change, as essentially complementary pieces of the jigsaw.

Despite their substantial differences, it is clear that the models we have looked at in the previous and especially in the present sections can be included in what might best be labelled the post-Solovian view on balanced growth and structural change. This view contrasts with Pasinetti's view of structural change to which many of the chapters in this volume refer. Core disagreements between these two views concern the persistence, within the post-Solovian approach, of a balanced growth framework, its use of sectoral production functions and of a macroeconomic utility function, as well as the approach to institutions.

4 The role of institutions in structural change

The *institutional* aspects of the analysis of growth and structural change have gained increasing significance. Examples include parts of the so-called 'new comparative economics' (Djankov *et al.*, 2003), as well as the contributions by authors such as Acemoglu, Douglass North and Dopfer, among others, who have increasingly focused their analyses on institutional design and on the politics of institutional change.

If standard neoclassical growth theory still took institutions to be exogenously determined, to date the new endogenous growth theory is often seen to 'endogenize' or absorb multidisciplinary insights on the analysis of institutions into its unifying analytical and methodological framework. Others have advocated a less 'imperialist' approach whereby the analysis of the role of institutions in the economy should arise from a more genuinely inter- and multidisciplinary perspective and method, making use not only of insights gained in other disciplines but also of some of their tools of analysis. In this sense, scientific progress will take place at, and emerge round, the 'edges' of a number of disciplines.

Starting with contemporary endogenous or post-Solovian economic growth theory, institutions, such as the law and property rights, and regulation, for example on taxation and competition, frame the environment and the inter-individual arrangements within which decisions are made. They primarily contribute to shaping micro-level incentive structures. Institutions are, therefore, exogenous in the sense that they are a part of economic 'fundamentals', but they are also seen to contribute to explaining economic growth endogenously.

Pasinetti's approach to growth and structural change, discussed in various contributions to this volume, substantially departs from this perspective on how to take account of institutions in economic analysis.

A first point of difference concerns the interpretation of the 'Kaldor facts'. According to Pasinetti, Kaldor never interpreted these 'facts' as an empirical justification for the construction of a theory of balanced growth: 'Kaldor, who often repeated in his own words Keynes's phrase – ["When the facts change, I change my mind"] – used to begin many of his works with an accurate list of "stylised facts", that needed to be explained, as he repeatedly stressed (Kaldor, 1961); the term "stylised facts" meaning some empirical regularities that were sufficiently general and persistent, so as to capture some objective features of reality' (Pasinetti 2005b, pp. 837–48, see also Pasinetti, 2007, pp. 219–20). In other words, Pasinetti regards the 'Kaldor facts' as a specific application of the Cambridge idea of 'reality (and not merely abstract rationality) as the starting point of any economic theory' (ibid.: 10). The foundations of economic dynamics should not be located in an *a priori* conception of agent rationality, even if this provides a logically coherent framework. Rather, such foundations must be based *from the start* on some kind of 'stylization' or 'typification' of 'facts' (see Arena, 1991).

Beyond this appeal to realism, a second point of contention refers to what, in his latest book, Pasinetti calls 'the separation theorem' (Pasinetti, 2007, p. 274). This states that 'we must make it possible to disengage those investigations that concern the foundational bases of economic relations – to be detected at a strictly essential level of basic economic analysis – from those investigations that must be carried out at the level of the actual economic institutions' (ibid.: 275). Analyses of the former type consider fundamental economic relationships that can be uncovered independently of specific behavioural patterns and institutional settings. This level of investigation, which Pasinetti calls 'natural', allows the determination of economic magnitudes 'at a level which is so fundamental as to allow us to investigate them independently of the rules of individual and social behaviour to be chosen in order to achieve them' (ibid.: 275). In Pasinetti's view, this stage of analysis identifies the domain of pure economic theory and should be kept distinct from 'a second stage of investigation, which concerns how the economic magnitudes are actually determined, within the bounds and constraints of the institutions characterising the economy at the time it is investigated' (ibid.).

We first consider the stage of 'pure economic theory'. At this stage, in accordance with Pasinetti's emphasis on 'reality' as a starting point, 'the focus is on those objective elements of reality that have a high degree of persistence through time. The relationship between these elements should be studied carefully and through an exercise of abstraction organized in a logically coherent theoretical framework. The result, as yet, will not reach an all-comprehensive theoretical framework, but it will provide an essential – and in this sense, a general – economic theory' (Pasinetti, 2005b, p. 846). A core concept of 'pure economic theory' is the notion of the 'natural system' (Pasinetti, 1993, Chapter VIII). This notion is incompatible with the 'exchange paradigm' – central, of course, to the neoclassical tradition – in which the basic analytical reference is to a pure exchange model: given a set of individual and arbitrary endowments, individual agents maximize their utilities by exchanging the goods with which they have been endowed on the basis of a set of equilibrium prices simultaneously determined in the market. By contrast, Pasinetti's view of structural change is based on an alternative model, the pure production model. At the heart of this model 'is the technological process of production, with division and specialisation of labour. Prices and costs arise from the fact that each individual specialises in producing only one (or even a fraction of one) good or service' (Pasinetti, 2007, p. 19). The basic production model does not require any assumptions about specific agent behaviours and deals only with those elements of the analysis that are sufficiently persistent over time to abstract from the behaviours of economic agents.

To arrive at a 'full economic analysis', a second stage of 'institutional analysis' is required that now necessitates some conceptualization of the economic agent. This stage of the analysis addresses a range of hypotheses about individual and social behaviours, and consequently introduces different institutional settings and related forms of organization. This is warranted because a real economic system is a much more complex entity than the essential, objective and coherent core of the logically interconnected elements represented by the *natural* system. *Real* economic systems are subject to various mutable and sometimes unpredictable events that cannot be ignored.

Pasinetti's approach to structural change consequently clearly contrasts with contemporary mainstream theory of economic growth. Two main considerations stand out. First, Pasinetti stresses that his approach is *macro-* not *micro-*founded. He refers to the Cambridge tradition that 'always avoided starting from subjective behaviour (or preferences) and from the study of single individuals. The Cambridge economists, from Keynes to Sraffa, showed very clearly that the behaviour of the economic system as a whole is not reducible – except under very restrictive conditions – to the sum of its single individual parts. This does *not* mean a denial of the role of microeconomics as a field of economic investigation, but it *does* mean the impossibility of explaining crucial economic phenomena on the sole basis of microeconomic behaviour' (Pasinetti, 2005b, p. 844, see also Pasinetti, 2007, pp. 227–8). Moreover, for Pasinetti, trying to capture with simple rationality assumptions the complexity and variety of reality seems an impossible task. Such complexity and variety are compatible with *various* forms of rationality embedded in different institutional settings.

If a natural system free from any institutional constraints is conceivable, one may wonder why this would not also be true for the analysis of economic behaviour. In Pasinetti's theory of pure production, human beings are, above all, agents who learn – from experience but also from social communication and interaction with other agents (Pasinetti, 1981, p. 22). This is why, in his latest book, Pasinetti contrasts two 'social philosophies', corresponding to the pure exchange and the production models. 'It might also be said that the theoretical choice that is implied in the formulation of the pure exchange model springs, so to speak, from a particular "social philosophy", that relies on each individual's self-interest as the basis of rational behaviour. . . . By contrast, the pure production model springs from another particular way of looking at society, that through division of labour stresses the necessarily *cooperative aspects* of any organised society' (Pasinetti, 2007, pp. 10–11). This opposition, however, leads one to question the idea that natural systems are entirely independent from any form of economic rationality. Is it not the case that the pure production model implicitly presupposes an assumption of cooperative individual rationality, also required by social learning? According to Pasinetti, the answer is clearly in the negative. His theory of structural change is not based on any kind of behavioural assumption. The concept of natural system is based on the 'production paradigm', but, strictly speaking, does not rely on any *a priori* notion of individual rationality about learning or cooperative behaviour. It is a theory of the *structural macro*-constraints any productive system must address in order to ensure that all its labour is fully employed and all income is spent. These constraints are summed up by 'a single truly macroeconomic relation', the aggregate condition of full employment and of full expenditure (Pasinetti, 2007: 283, 285) which is not microfounded at all.

The second main consideration that places Pasinetti's approach at a distinct distance from dominant mainstream growth theory concerns the fact that a natural system is not a stable equilibrium model: 'Note now that the fulfilment of condition (13) [i.e. the above aggregate condition on employment and expenditure] by no means entails an automatic self-adjusting process. The spontaneous forces operating behind it are in fact tending to make it *not* satisfied' (ibid.: 285–286). In accordance with Kaldor's views on capitalist instability, the natural system exhibits 'normative properties' (Pasinetti, 2007, p. 296) but their probability of realization strongly depends on the nature of the institutional environment of the economy. This is why Pasinetti always defended the prevalence of 'disequilibrium and instability (not equilibrium) as the normal state of the industrial economies' (Pasinetti, 2007, p. 229). It also explains why Pasinetti's central condition has not been easily amenable to standard stability analyses *per se*. To consider stability in Pasinetti's framework of *natural* structural change it is, first, necessary to realize that the probability of reaching a stable system that respects 'condition (13) (just retrieved) permanently is extremely low because of the complexity of the main movements affecting the structure of the economy and the absence of their coordination' (Pasinetti, 2007, p. 286). Second, it is also necessary to interpret Pasinetti's central condition as a *normative relation* which economic policy should strive to attain through specific macroeconomic decision making. This is not far removed from Kaldor's views on the Harrodian 'knife-edge' problem.

Pasinetti's central condition is not the only normative condition to emphasize within the theory of structural change. For instance, monetary policy may require the definition of other normative conditions (concerning, for instance, the quantity of money or the level of interest rates) within the *institutional* context of economic growth. But it is the only condition that it is possible to define within a framework of the natural part of structural change, which is also why it is accorded such a central place in Pasinetti (2007).

Our remarks on the stability issues mainly go to highlight the perhaps core difference between Pasinetti's and the post-Solovian approaches to structural change: basically, while for the latter structural change always remains a step towards balanced growth, even if this step can last for a very long time, Pasinetti's approach persistently emphasizes disequilibria and instability as the 'normal' state of affairs. This core difference is not surprising at all. Solow's concept of balanced economic growth never inspired positively Pasinetti's conception of structural dynamics. From this perspective, if we had to choose the name of an economist who inspired the latter, we would certainly refer to Roy Harrod (see Pasinetti, 1974, Chapter VI, part 1 and Chapter IV, Part 6). First, one of the features of Harrod's model is the independent determination of the actual and the natural growth rates and therefore the long-lasting possible divergence of actual from natural growth. Therefore, in Harrod's as well as in Pasinetti's economic theory, the economy has no inherent tendency to reach full employment. Second, in both authors, growth is generally unstable: we are reminded how this instability is probable in Pasinetti's dynamics; in Harrod it is related to the so-called knife-edge problem, that is, the type of relations existing between the actual and the warranted rates of growth.

In addition, and by way of concluding this section, it should be pointed out that, over and above Pasinetti's unique distinction between the natural and the institutional level of the analysis of structural change and economic growth, based on his three core building blocks of analysis – consumption, technology and employment – his emphasis on learning processes opens the way to a perhaps useful cross-fertilization between the theory of structural dynamics and evolutionary approaches to economic theorizing in the future.[5]

5 The contributions in this volume

The first part of this volume, entitled 'Structural dynamics: past and present', is concerned with the analysis of some links and connections between 'old' and 'new' approaches to the theory of economic growth, meaning by that the Classical approach and its relationship with structural dynamics as developed in the Cambridge School and in the post-Solovian approaches.

The volume opens with a brief presentation of the issues by Peter Groenewegen. He focuses on the classical background of structural dynamics and, more generally, contributions to the theory of structural dynamics in the tradition of classical political economy, including a somewhat critical emphasis on Pasinetti's approach. As an outstanding scholar of Turgot's and Marshall's contributions, among others, Groenewegen provides a highly perceptive analysis of the stages theory of growth and its potential scope, on the one hand, and of the long-run impact of demand factors on the economy, on the other. He argues that any comprehensive theory of structural dynamics ignores the stages theory, used by both Turgot and Adam Smith, at its peril, and calls for explicit attention to be paid to insights from classical political economy regarding the long-run role of demand forces in the economy. Under both aspects, Groenewegen observes, omissions, indeed 'minor omissions', can be detected in Pasinetti's own account of the classical sources of his own analysis.

5 See, for example, Loasby's (1999) masterly treatment of evolutionary theory with a particular focus on knowledge and institutions. Structural dynamics should be understood as a proper theoretical setting for a theory of learning.

Mario Pomini's chapter straightforwardly addresses the task of placing the analysis of structural dynamics in historical perspective, with a view to drawing out similarities and differences with some of the recent literature on endogenous growth. Pomini provides a fully fledged and balanced analysis of the analogies and differences between linear growth models of both the Pasinetti and the von Neumann types, on the one hand, and the Romer–Lucas approach to endogenous growth theory, on the other. His historical account of post-von Neumann growth theory is illuminating and comprehensive. Interestingly, Pomini concludes that the relationships between growth and income distribution, highlighted in contemporary growth theory, emphasize the overlap rather than the gaps between the analyses of structural dynamics and endogenous growth. However, while the latter approach embarks more boldly on the development of a *theory* of knowledge, the former appears to be concerned almost exclusively with the *effects* of economic change. Pomini would definitely prefer a 'pure knowledge' model over a 'pure labour' model.

In his chapter, Moshe Syrquin, a long-standing scholar of structural analysis, opts to return to Kuznets in order to bring out the meaning and effectiveness of the notion of structural transformation. He is puzzled by the fact that in modern growth economics so many virtually complementary paths seem to ignore or even avoid each other. Syrquin is adamant that even prior to Pasinetti's contribution 'a no less significant and influential program of research on growth and structural change was underway'. He refers to Simon Kuznets, in particular, but does not overlook important contributions made by those based in Cambridge, albeit mostly outside 'the inner circle' of Cambridge economics, such as Richard Stone's 'programme for growth'. Beyond these references, Syrquin provides a comprehensive account of the origins of the analysis of structural dynamics and transformation, with its roots in post-war theories of growth and economic development. He is inclined to follow in the footsteps of Kuznets as regards the latter's reluctance to make a distinction between growth and development, but is nevertheless forced to admit that this distinction is very much alive and well in contemporary dynamic analysis (see Acemoglu, 2009, especially Part VII). Syrquin is critical of Pasinetti, whose approach he regards as a kind of bloodless creation. By emphasizing links with what he sees as an outdated notion of economic classicism, Syrquin suggests a reading of Pasinetti as a mainly defensive contribution that delivers only insufficiently on the promise to build on Adam Smith, takes an almost paradoxical turn with the analysis of a pre-institutional 'natural system', and remains surprisingly silent on the sources of technical change. Notwithstanding the occasional harshness of his train of argument, Syrquin's analysis is not devoid of overall sympathetic overtones and, above all, of constructive suggestions. In fact, he seems to want to urge Pasinetti to go the distance and cross roads with Kuznets, but is not necessarily confident in the realism of this avenue.

Next, Önder Nomaler and Bart Verspagen discuss the applicability of the analysis of structural dynamics. They explore a concrete example of an application of structural dynamics as an approach to knowledge flows between science and technology. Pasinetti's notion of vertically integrated sectors plays a central role in their analysis. The authors start from the current presumption that the number of 'science references' per patent can be considered as 'a standard way of quantifying the impact of science on technology'. At close inspection, however, this measure implies unrealistic assumptions and appears radically inadequate for the analysis of knowledge flows. It is only through the use of vertical integration, as an essential tool for analysis in this case, that it becomes possible to construct a patent citation flow table that provides substantial information on the net knowledge supply by individual sectors (see also Dopfer, 2005 and Loasby, 1999).

The first part of this volume is aptly concluded with a masterly contribution by William Baumol, who takes Pasinetti's theory of structural dynamics as his point of departure. This acknowledgement of the originality and significance of an approach to the analysis of structural change, that emerged in the context of post-war economics at Cambridge, in the UK, is all the more striking since Baumol himself is among the pioneers of research into structural dynamics. He generously credits an early partnership between Pasinetti and Spaventa (1960) with having achieved a breakthrough for the analysis of structural dynamics. As we know, this partnership was discontinued and Pasinetti went on to pursue and develop this line of research on his own. In Baumol's view, however, it was the Pasinetti and Spaventa paper, in particular, that put the analysis of structural change on a new footing. Baumol then develops an attractively simple model of his own, which evolves around the relationship between economic growth, institutions, and the role of 'productive' (rather than 'redistributive') entrepreneurs. While Baumol takes on board much of endogenous growth theory (and in particular its approach to endogenizing the role of institutions), he also seems to remain at a certain critical distance with regard to the often mechanical undertones of this literature, pointing, in his own model, to the possibility of multiple time paths. Baumol's perceptive analysis concludes on an upbeat note that emphasizes the role of the entrepreneur. His contribution should probably be read together with those by Pasinetti and Solow at the end of this volume; Baumol's chapter points at a positive and potentially uncontroversial, constructive way of working at structural dynamics through the twenty-first century.

Part II of this volume collects core contributions that analyze the role and development of theories of structural change and economic growth from the vantage point of Cambridge economics in the post-war period.

Geoffrey Harcourt opens the discussion. He considers Pasinetti's contribution to structural dynamic analysis to be one of the most important products of the Cambridge School of Economics, as it developed in post-war decades. Harcourt discusses some core characteristics of Pasinetti's overall scientific work, paying special attention to structural dynamics. His main concern, however, is to emphasize the Keynesian traits of Pasinetti's analysis. For – he argues – in fact all through his career Pasinetti himself has stressed the 'natural links of Keynesian developments, on the one hand, to our classical forebears, on the other'. Harcourt's contribution in that sense is itself an important one, as it is fully borne out by Pasinetti himself, in particular in his most recent publication (Pasinetti, 2007).

Heinrich Bortis undertakes to outline the main strands and core features of Cambridge Post-Keynesianism. In his view it is mainly through the work of Pasinetti that we can find the appropriate perspective together with the appropriate tools for a unified view of the Cambridge Keynesians. As is well known, many scholars have argued that Piero Sraffa's work cannot easily be integrated with that of J.M. Keynes, and Sraffa can be regarded as a student of Keynes in only a very specific and limited way. Bridging the differences between their respective intellectual and scientific orientations was regarded as a core task for Post-Keynesians, by Joan Robinson, among others. In Bortis's view such a synthesis has actually been achieved, at the level of fundamental pure theory, by Pasinetti. He argues that Pasinetti's theory advances 'a coherent set of principles bringing together the classical view of value and distribution ... and the Keynesian vision of employment and output determination, through the principle of effective demand'. His chapter sets out to make this point in more detail, situating itself in a history of analysis perspective of the Keynes-and-the-Classics type.

Davide Gualerzi's contribution takes its cue from Pasinetti's remark that there is a 'great need for a theory of consumers' decisions, both private and public, in a dynamic context' and 'the theory of consumers' behaviour which is offered to us by the textbooks of current mainstream economics is insufficient and inadequate for dynamic purposes' (Pasinetti, 1993, p. 107). More specifically, Gualerzi compares Pasinetti's approach to Amartya Sen's capabilities theory. His analysis is valuable beyond this comparison in that it reopens the door to re-interpreting the theory of consumption along 'classical lines'. Interestingly, Gualerzi also draws from recent developments in the theory of consumption as an 'entrepreneurial' activity, by both economists and historians.[6]

Harald Hagemann's chapter highlights similarities and differences between some of the major contributions to the literature on structural dynamics. He pays particular attention to prominent lines of analysis in the context of recent developments in the theory of production. Hagemann's diagramme usefully summarizes his view of the intellectual genealogy of what amounts to 'a modern analysis of Ricardo's machinery problem'. Pasinetti's analysis is highlighted and its 'stronger Smithian flavour' perceptively emphasized. The thrust of Hagemann's analysis also leads him to focus on one of the vital issues in the modern theory of technological progress, namely, the fact that productivity growth cannot be analyzed at the industry level due to inter-sectoral spillovers. Among a range of approaches relevant to studying this question, Hagemann focuses on Hicks, Loewe, and Pasinetti.

As argued above, the concept of a *natural economic system* is central to Pasinetti's analysis. Roberto Scazzieri's chapter discusses the intellectual sources of Pasinetti's natural system as the basis for a proper understanding of the basics of structural dynamics. In Scazzieri's view we are confronted here with a fully fledged theory of economic history that can superficially be taken to parallel Hicks's contribution which goes under that title, but in fact it is very different in both content and tendency. Pasinetti's model is singled out mainly for its normative properties. A good deal of attention is given to the study of relative prices and income distribution as perhaps the most relevant field of application of the concept of a natural economic system. Scazzieri's chapter perceptively pinpoints overlaps and differences with comparable contributions, among which he considers (besides Hicks) Baumol, Loewe, von Neumann, Herbert Simon, Negishi, Hishiyama, and Quadrio Curzio.

Finally, Takashi Yagi takes up the discussion of the meaning and the analytical role of Pasinetti's dynamic standard commodity, defined as a composite commodity for which labour productivity grows at a rate equal to the 'standard' rate of growth of productivity of the entire system (see Pasinetti, 1981, 1993). Yagi combines Pasinetti's analysis with John Hicks's insights on the measurement of income and capital. His exercise produces the concept of 'effective wage curve' with an important role to

[6] Interesting examples include Bianchi (1998) and de Vries (2008). It should be remarked that, in constructing his argument, Gualerzi makes use of Walsh (2003).

play in the analysis of changes in production structures, prices, and distribution.

Structural dynamics as a field of research today appears to be wide open to new and stimulating developments. An important message from the contributions to this volume certainly is that Pasinetti's approach in particular, if carefully studied and considered, is set to become one of the possible reference points for a different political economy. It is the Keynesian mode of reasoning that comes round full circle. The inadequacy of *laissez-faire* philosophy, which Keynes had highlighted, is brought to bear also upon a *theoretical* fallacy, so common nowadays: the inability to distinguish between theoretical premises and institutional assumptions. Through a distillation of fundamental concepts and premises, Pasinetti's approach opens up the Keynesian framework to the structural challenges of the twenty-first century. Robert Solow, despite fully acknowledging the need for structural analysis, remains (as he writes) 'a bastard Keynesian'. And he adds (p. 522, this volume): 'Joan Robinson intended that label as a devastating insult, to make the bastard Keynesians ashamed of their origins and of their actions. But I rather like the label and I adopt it cheerfully. I am sure that if I were a Freudian I would be a bastard Freudian; and if I were a Marxian I would be a bastard Marxian; and so I am indeed a bastard Keynesian.'

That is why the book closes with the final confrontation between Pasinetti and Solow on structural dynamics and labels structural dynamics itself as the *unfinished revolution*.

6 The future of structural dynamics

Before reflecting on Robert Solow's and Luigi Pasinetti's contributions to this volume, as well as their possible implications for the future of structural dynamics, we would like to focus here on Pasinetti's recent 'road map' for a Keynesian Revolution (Pasinetti, 2007). Apart from providing a concise restatement of the perhaps best known approach to structural dynamics, this suggests important links and extensions for future analysis.

Among the core features of the Cambridge approach to structural dynamics is a new emphasis on the study of inequality and income distribution. Although this had certainly not disappeared from contemporary growth theory, neither was the study of income distribution particularly central to it. One aspect of the classical inspiration of much of the recent analysis of structural dynamics has precisely to do with the fact that a focus on the links between growth and income distribution is among the prominent well-known characteristics of the classical tradition in political economy. Thus one of the advantages of structural dynamics appears to be its ability to include in a unified framework both a realistic and a rich perspective on knowledge and technical progress, while at the same time keeping the significance of income distribution well in sight. This is an important side of the theory, although we have not made it the object of a special investigation in the above treatment.

Concerning possible links and extensions, in a recent contribution on happiness in economics, Pasinetti discusses the issue of happiness in the classical economists and their acknowledged shift from happiness to wealth (see Pasinetti, 2005a). Here, Pasinetti acknowledges that, with their concentration of attention on the production of wealth, classical political economists did narrow the scope of economic analysis at the same time that they managed to keep their horizon wide open to a whole range of factors in their explanation of the actual workings of any given economic system. Pasinetti adds that 'a classically inspired framework is favourable to the adoption of theories which are conceived from the outset in a dynamic setting. These kinds of theories would consider novelty, creativity, and human learning not as a perturbation of a (statically conceived) equilibrium but as the essence itself of the basic movements of modern economies for which human beings must face the task of continuous adaptation' (Pasinetti, 2005a, p. 341). An important consequence of the proposed approach is that 'we do not need to adhere to the widespread neoclassical view that economics is all about means, not ends. We should not fear to go straight – as indeed Keynes did (1936) – to discussing ends and social goals: not only as regards full employment (the centre of Keynes's work), but also as regards an equitable distribution of income and wealth, and social justice in the determination of wages, prices, rates of interest. Within this line of analysis, appropriate notions of "common good" and of "public happiness" emerge, in my view, as more easily compatible with Classical analysis than with any type of economic analysis suggested by the utility-dominated approach to economics' (Pasinetti, 2005a, pp. 341–342). The above remarks suggest that the scope and significance of the Cambridge School go well beyond what perhaps happens to be commonly thought. Structural dynamics, as a research field today, could hardly be treated without having recourse to the work of the Cambridge School, such as it is discussed, for instance, by Pasinetti in his recent book (2007).

We should further note, in fact, that it is precisely in the field of institutional analysis that a whole host of recent contributions has points in common with the legacy of the Cambridge School, such as it is embodied in Pasinetti's contribution. However, the recent proposal by Acemoglu and Robinson that institutions themselves may come under the domain of individuals' rational choices (rather than setting limits to those choices) follows a different line of enquiry from Pasinetti's attempt to identify a level of investigation *independent* of particular behavioural assumptions (see, for example, Acemoglu and Robinson, 2006, p. 19).

A last possible extension we would like to mention is the relation between structural dynamics and business cycles. This issue was raised in Chapter X of Pasinetti (1981) as well as in Chapter 7 of Pasinetti (1993). Moreover, as early as 1960, Pasinetti had stressed the gap between corresponding macroeconomic theories of economic growth and cyclical fluctuations (Pasinetti, 1960). Since that date, mainstream economics has tried to reduce the gap between both of these analytical fields and to build a unique theory of equilibrium cyclical growth based on dynamic stochastic general equilibrium. Its advances are substantial and contributed to the emergence of the *New Neoclassical Synthesis*. However, this New Synthesis literature is presently distinct from the Neo-Solovian structural change literature. What Pasinetti stressed in his 1981 and 1993 books is that a structural change model may strongly help to focus on the sectoral or disaggregated effects of business cycles. Now, it is sufficient to observe the empirical features of the 2008 crisis to understand that its real aspects and effects strongly differ in the respective sectors of capital goods, information goods, luxury goods or the car industry, for instance, and this is even more true if one considers different countries. Therefore it will be crucial to focus on these relations between business cycles and structural change; after all, Goodwin and Kaldor – both eminent business cycle theorists – were also Cambridge economists!

According to Mark Blaug, it must be acknowledged that Pasinetti 'has veered away from the Sraffian camp with his own approach to growth theory' (Blaug, 2009, p. 234). In our view, it is definitely *not* a matter of veering away from the Sraffian camp; it is rather a matter of making *full sense* of the Sraffian approach.[7] A recent contribution by Vivian Walsh makes a similar point by treating structural dynamics as a significant off-shoot of the Cambridge School with its own specific characteristics and leading to what Walsh calls 'Pasinetti's and Sen's enriched classicism'. It is a perspective that, differently both from other strands of the Cambridge School and from the neoclassical tradition, is squarely centred on Adam Smith (Walsh, 2003, pp. 371–378). Indeed, Vivian Walsh has a point when he writes that Pasinetti 1981, 'together with Pasinetti 1993 offers a striking example of a major effort to construct a rich, Smithian edifice upon classical (Sraffian) foundations' (ibid.).

[7] P.L. Porta made the same point in a review to Roncaglia's book on the Sraffian schools. Cf. Porta (2003), pp. 600–601.

Epilogue

Robert Solow and Luigi Pasinetti must have the final word in our concluding comments. As it appears from the above, a confrontation between Solow and Pasinetti remains the best way to get at the root of the problem of growth in economics and, in particular, to highlight the difficult life (to say the least) of structural dynamics as an approach within the context of contemporary growth theory in economics and in political economics alike.

This is done by publishing here in the closing section of the book – on 'structural dynamics: the unfinished revolution' – an adapted and revised version of the exchange between the two authors recently delivered at the Accademia dei Lincei in Rome. The insertion of this extract, which mainly concerns Pasinetti's 2007 book, might appear somewhat surprising. However, during the preparation of the present volume, when asked to contribute, both Solow and Pasinetti felt that their exchange could be the best way to emphasize how different analytical foundations can generate divergent views as well as a common interest in structural dynamics. They suggested to the editors to publish these successive comments in the present volume, each comment being expanded with a special addendum specifically devoted to the issue of structural dynamics. It is important also to make crystal clear that, as argued in this introduction, especially in the previous section, the issue of structural dynamics cannot be treated in isolation from a more general position about economic theory considered as a whole. This is the real gist of our argument here.

As mentioned above, Solow's chapter confirms his time-honoured criticisms of the Cambridge School. He has no misgivings in accepting the label of 'bastard Keynesian', a term used by Joan Robinson to describe more or less what others would more politely call the 'neoclassical synthesis'. On the contrary, in his contribution he takes the opportunity to extol the virtues of 'bastard Keynesianism' as a sensible approach to macroeconomics, embodying a sort of Aristotelian *via media*, that steering clear of the dangerous extremes of a return to some form of libertarianism, on the one hand, and of radical Keynesianism, on the other.

At the same time, Robert Solow openly acknowledges, once again very forcefully, the significance of Pasinetti's analysis of structural dynamics, 'on essentially how to extend the study of macroeconomic dynamics to incorporate the structural changes', a point he takes up in his addendum to the present volume. Even so, Solow refuses to accept the implications

Pasinetti attaches to structural dynamics as a *method* of analysis, and maintains that this 'most interesting and exciting' part of Pasinetti's contribution should be kept apart, as much as possible, from the 'unfinished Keynesian revolution as a drama of some kind'.

As Pasinetti points out in his rejoinder, while Solow's common-sense 'bastard Keynesianism' leads him to concede that capitalist economies are 'never paths of continuous full employment', he never radically departs from this ideal situation: to Solow, it is reasonable, 'as a matter of historical fact ... to describe those paths as fluctuations around a trend, with most of the time the fluctuations contained within fairly narrow bounds'.

As argued by Pasinetti, in the neoclassical synthesis 'Keynes's theory is regarded as the leading model of short-run economic fluctuations, while claiming that, in the long-run, when the ocean is "flat again", neoclassical general equilibrium theory comes back to rule the roost' (2007, p. 231n). This is entirely incompatible with Pasinetti's own research programme and has, for him, 'a sense only in the context of economic dynamics of the *proportional* type' (ibid.). Pasinetti consequently re-establishes the link between the Keynesian approach to disequilibrium and the theory of structural dynamics (a perspective we have discussed in the previous section).

What this debate demonstrates is perhaps brought out in Pasinetti's final words, which emphasize the significance of structural dynamics as an issue in economic theory today. In particular, structural dynamics is not just a matter of a more detailed analysis. As Pasinetti puts it in his afterword in this volume, 'the structural dynamic approach is not merely complementary to the one-sector approach. It goes much beyond complementarity'.[8] In our view, the contributions gathered in this volume provide an extremely effective example of important issues fully retaining their relevance, even if the vagaries of 'normal science' sometimes lead us astray onto more esoteric and often less realistic paths. Last but not least, two great masters take the profession to task by refocusing attention on the essentials at the close of this volume.

[8] Pasinetti makes the point by reference to his 'pure production model'. As he writes in Pasinetti (2007, p. 21), 'the pure production model springs... from another (alternative) social philosophy so to speak, that through division of labour, stresses the necessarily cooperative aspects of any organized society.... On this, the fulfilment becomes necessary of a macroeconomic condition, which concerns overall effective demand'. This is 'the all-embracing effect of overall demand', also discussed in his afterword to this volume (cf. also Pasinetti, 2007, p. 285).

REFERENCES

Acemoglu, D., 2009, *Introduction to Modern Economic Growth*, Princeton University Press.

2006, *Economic Origins of Dictatorship and Democracy*, Cambridge University Press.

2003, 'Why not a Political Coase Theorem? Social Conflict, Commitment, and Politics', *Journal of Comparative Economics*, **31**, 620–652.

Acemoglu, D., Aghion, P., Zilibotti, F., 2006, 'Distance to Frontier, Selection and Economic Growth', *Journal of the European Economic Association*, **4**, March, 37–74.

Acemoglu, D., Guerrieri, V., 2008, 'Capital Deepening and Nonbalanced Economic Growth', *Journal of Political Economy*, **116**, 3, 467–498.

Acemoglu, D., Johnson, S., Robinson, J.A., 2002, 'Reversal of Fortune: Geography and Institutions in the Making of the Modern World Income Distribution', *Quarterly Journal of Economics*, **117**, 4, 1231–1294.

Acemoglu, D., Robinson, J.A., 2006, 'Persistence of Power, Elites and Institutions', CEPR Discussion Papers 5603.

Acemoglu, D., Zilibotti, F., 1997, 'Was Prometheus Unbound by Chance? Risk, Diversification and Growth', *Journal of Political Economy*, **105**, 4, 709–754.

Aghion, P., Durlauf, S.N., eds., 2005, *Handbook of Economic Growth*, Amsterdam: Elsevier.

Aghion, P., Howitt, P., 1992, 'A Model of Growth Through Creative Destruction', *Econometrica*, **60**, 2.

1998, *Endogenous Growth Theory*, Cambridge, MA: MIT Press.

Amable, B., 1996, 'Croissance et cycles endogènes induits par les innovations incrémentales et radicales,' *Annales d'Economie et statistiques*, **44**, 91–110.

Arena R., 1991, 'De l'usage de l'histoire dans la formulation des hypothèses de la théorie économique', *Revue Economique*, **42**, 2, March, 395–409.

Arena, R., Dow, S., Klaes, M., eds., 2009, *Open Economics, Economics in Relation to Other Disciplines*, London and New York: Routledge.

Arena, R., Raybaut A., 2003, 'Neo-Schumpeterian Versus Neo-Kaldorian Approaches, Two Different Views on Knowledge, Learning and Cyclical Growth', in Hagemann, H., Seiter, S., eds., *Growth Theory and Growth Policy*, London: Routledge.

Arestis, P., McCombie, J., Vickerman, R., eds., 2007, *Growth and Economic Development*, Cheltenham: Edward Elgar.

Atkinson, A.B., 2009, 'Factor Shares: The Principal Problem of Political Economy', *Oxford Review of Economic Policy*, **25**, 1, Spring, 3–16.

Baranzini, M., Harcourt, G.C., eds., 1993, *The Dynamics of the Wealth of Nations. Growth, Distribution and Structural Change. Essays in Honour of Luigi Pasinetti*, New York: St Martin's Press.

Baumol, W.J., 1970, *Economic Dynamics: An Introduction*. Third edition. New York: Macmillan(First edition 1951).

1967, 'Macroeconomics of Unbalanced Growth: The Anatomy of Urban Crisis', *American Economic Review*, **57**, 415–426.

Baumol, W., Blackman, J.S., Wolf, E.N., 1989, *Productivity and American Leadership*, Cambridge, MA: MIT Press.

Bianchi, M., ed., 1998, *The Active Consumer. Novelty and Surprise in Consumer Choice*, London: Routledge.

Blaug, M., 2009, 'The Trade-Off between Rigour and Relevance: Sraffian Economics as a Case in Point', *History of Political Economy*, **41**, 2, 219–247.

Bruni, L., Porta, P.L., eds., 2005, *Economics and Happiness. Framing the Analysis*, Oxford University Press.

Caselli, F., Coleman II, W.J., 2001, 'The U.S. Structural Transformation and Regional Convergence: A Reinterpretation', *Journal of Political Economy*, **109**, 3, 584–616.

Cass, D., 1965, 'Optimum Growth in an Aggregative Model of Capital Accumulation,' *The Review of Economic Studies*, **32**, 3, 233–240.

Chenery, H., Syrquin M., 1975, *Patterns of Development, 1950–1970*: Oxford University Press.

Coase, R., 1977, 'Economics and Contiguous Disciplines', reprinted in *Essays on Economics and Economists*, 1994, University of Chicago Press, pp. 34–46.

David, P.A., Thomas, M., 2003, *The Economic Future in Historical Perspective*, Oxford University Press.

de Vries, J., 2008, *The Industrious Revolution. Consumer Behaviour and the Household Economy, 1650 to the Present*, Cambridge University Press.

Djankov, S., Glaeser, E., La Porta, R., Lopez-de-Silanes, F., Shleifer, A., 2003, 'The New Comparative Economics', *Journal of Comparative Economics*, **31**, 595–619.

Dopfer, K., 2005, ed., *The Evolutionary Foundations of Economics*, Cambridge University Press.

Dosi, G., 2000, *Innovation, Organisation and Economic Dynamics. Selected Essays*, Cheltenham: Elgar.

Echevarria, C., 1997, 'Changes in Sectoral Composition Associated with Economic Growth', *International Economic Review*, **38**, 2, 431–452.

Ethier, W., 1982, 'National and International Returns to Scale in the Modern Theory of International Trade', *American Economic Review*, **73**, 389–405.

Foellmi, R., Zweimuller, J., 2002, 'Structural Change, Engel's Consumption Cycles and Kaldor's Facts of Economic Growth', Institute for Empirical Research Economics, Zurich.

Friedman, B., 2005, *The Moral Consequences of Economic Growth*, New York: Knopf.

Gollin, D., Parente, S., Rogerson, R., 2002, 'The Role of Agriculture in Development', *American Economic Review (Papers and Proceedings)*, **92**, 2, 160–164.

Grossman, G.M., Helpman, E., 1991, *Innovation and Growth in the Global Economy*, Cambridge, MA: MIT Press.

Hahn, F., Matthews, R. C. O., 1964, 'The Theory of Economic Growth: A Survey', *Economic Journal*, **74**, 296, 779–902.

Harcourt, G.C., 2006, *The Structure of Post-Keynesian Economics: The Core Contributions of the Pioneers*, Cambridge University Press.

Harrod, R., 1948, *Towards a Dynamic Economics*, London: Macmillan.

1939, 'An Essay in Dynamic Theory', *Economic Journal*, 14–33.

Helpman, E., 2004, *The Mystery of Economic Growth*, Cambridge, MA: Harvard University Press.

Jones, C., Romer, P., 2009, 'The New Kaldor Facts: Ideas, Institutions, Population, and Human Capital', *American Economic Journal: Macroeconomics*, **2**, 1, January, 224–245.

Kaldor, N., 1989, *Further Essays on Economic Theory and Policy*, ed. by F. Targetti and A.P. Thirlwall, London: Duckworth.

1961, 'Capital Accumulation and Economic Growth', in Lutz, F.A., Hague, D.C., eds., *The Theory of Capital. Proceedings of a Conference Held by the International Economic Association* (Corfu Conference, 1958), London: Macmillan, pp. 177–222.

Kongsamut, P., Rebelo S., Xie D., 2001, 'Beyond Balanced Growth', *Review of Economic Studies*, **68**, 4, 869–882.

Koopmans, T., 1967, 'Objectives, Constraints and Outcomes in Optimal Growth Models', *Econometrica*, **35**, 1, 1–15.

1965, 'On the Concept of Optimal Economic Growth', *Pontificiae Academiae Scientiarum Scripta Varia*, **28**, 225–300.

Kurz, H.D., Salvadori, N., 2003, *Classical Economics and Modern Theory. Studies in Long-period Analysis*, London: Routledge.

Kuznets, S., 1971, *Economic Growth of Nations: Total Output and Production Structure*, Cambridge, MA: Harvard University Press.

1966, *Modern Economic Growth: Rate, Structure, and Spread*, New Haven, CT: Yale University Press.

Laitner, J., 2000, 'Structural Change and Economic Growth', *The Review of Economic Studies*, **67**, 3, July, 545–561.

Loasby, B.J., 1999, *Knowledge, Institutions and Evolution in Economics*, London: Routledge.

Lucas, R.E., 2008, 'Ideas and Growth', NBER Working Paper. 14133, June.

Maddison, A., 1983, 'A Comparison of Levels of GDP Per Capita in Developed and Developing Countries, 1700–1980', *The Journal of Economic History*, Cambridge University Press, **43**, 1, 27–41.

Marglin, S., Schor, J., eds., 1992, *The Golden Age of Capitalism*, Oxford: Clarendon Press.

Matsuyama, K., 1992, 'Agricultural Productivity, Comparative Advantage, and Economic Growth', *Journal of Economic Theory, LVIII, 2, Dec.*, 317–34.

Ngaï, L.R., Pissarides, C.A., 2007, 'Structural Change in a Multisector Model of Growth', *American Economic Review*, **97**, 1, 429–443.

North, D.C., 2005, *Understanding the Process of Economic Change*, Princeton University Press.

1990, *Institutions, Institutional Change and Economic Performance*, Cambridge University Press.

Offer, A., 2006, *The Challenge of Affluence. Self-Control and Well-Being in the United States and Britain since 1950*, Oxford University Press.

Pasinetti, L.L., 2007, *Keynes and the Cambridge Keynesians. A Revolution in Economics to be Accomplished*, Cambridge University Press.

2005a, 'Paradoxes of Happiness in Economics', in Bruni, L., Porta, P.L., eds., *Economics and Happiness. Framing the Analysis*, Oxford University Press, pp. 336–343.

2005b, 'The Cambridge School of Keynesian Economics', *Cambridge Journal of Economics*, **29**, 6, 837–848.
1993, *Structural Economic Dynamics. A Theory of the Economic Consequences of Human Learning*, Cambridge University Press.
1981, *Structural Change and Economic Growth. A Theoretical Essay on the Dynamics of the Wealth of Nations*, Cambridge University Press.
1974, *Growth and Income Distribution. Essays in Economic Theory*, Cambridge University Press.
1960, 'Cyclical Growth and Fluctuations', *Oxford Economic Papers*, reprinted in Pasinetti, L.L., 1974, *Growth and Income Distribution: Essays in Economic Theory*, Cambridge University Press, pp. 54–85.
Pasinetti, L.L., Spaventa, L., 1960, 'Verso il superamento della modellistica aggregata nella teoria dello sviluppo economico', *Rivista di Politica Economica*, **50**, 3–35.
Porta, P.L., 2003, 'Review' of A. Roncaglia's *Piero Sraffa: His Life, Thought, and Cultural Heritage*, *History of Political Economy*, **35**, 3, 598–602.
Rodrik, D., 2007, *One Economics, Many Recipes. Globalization, Institutions and Economic Growth*, Princeton University Press.
Romer, P., 1990, 'Endogenous Technological Change', *Journal of Political Economy*, **98**, 5, Part 2, S71–S102.
Rostow, W., 1971, *Politics and the Stages of Growth*, Cambridge University Press.
Salvadori, N., ed., 2003, *The Theory of Economic Growth. A 'Classical' Perspective*, Cheltenham: Elgar.
Schumpeter, J.A. (1954) *History of Economic Analysis*, Oxford University Press.
Sen, A.K., 1999, *Development as Freedom*, Oxford University Press.
ed., 1970, *Growth Economics*, Harmondsworth: Penguin.
Solow, R., 1997, 'Is There a Core of Usable Macroeconomics We Should All Believe In?', *American Economic Review*, **87**, 2, 230–232.
Stigler, G.J., 1984, 'Economics: The Imperial Science?', *Scandinavian Journal of Economics*, **86**, 3, 301–313.
Szenberg, M., ed., 1992, *Eminent Economists. Their Life Philosophies*, Cambridge University Press.
Walsh, V., 2003, 'Sen After Putnam', *Review of Political Economy*, **15**, 3, July, 315–394. (Sen's reply, 'Walsh on Sen After Putnam', **17**, 1, January 2005, 107–114, contains perceptive remarks on the Pasinetti model as well.)
2000, 'Smith After Sen', *Review of Political Economy*, **12**, 1, January, 5–25.
Wrigley, E.A., 2004, *Poverty, Progress and Population*, Cambridge University Press.

Part I

Structural dynamics: past and present

1 Structural change: some historical aspects of Pasinetti's work with special reference to classical economics

Peter D. Groenewegen

1 Introduction

My chapter for this book offers a number of brief observations on some historical aspects of Pasinetti's work on structural change with special, but not exclusive, reference to classical economics. In turn, these observations deal with the following. The first observation in Section 2 of the chapter notes Pasinetti's staunch and long-established practice of acknowledging the inspiration in his work offered by past economists, especially by the classical economists from the Physiocrats to Ricardo and Marx. In Section 3, Pasinetti's prefacing of theoretical work with the requisite history of previous thought on the subject enables comment on his book's deliberate policy of placing the theory of structural change within a broad historical context (Pasinetti 1981, introduction). Among other things, its introduction highlights the historical context in which economic analysis had come into being with the *modern* world characterised by experiment and science, a remark worthy of some historical observations in itself.

Pasinetti's surprising omission of any real reference to the classical four stages theory developed in the eighteenth century by Turgot and Smith is the subject of Section 4 of the chapter. A fourth and final observation is made in Section 5, designed to discuss other significant references to the literature made in Pasinetti (1981), which go beyond the classical economists. It will include some comments in particular on Pasinetti's peculiar treatment of Marshall in this context. A final section presents some conclusions.

2 The classical inspiration of Pasinetti's theory of structural change

My first observation is to note the fact (as earlier I had the pleasure of doing in my contribution to Pasinetti's *festschrift* (Baranzini and Harcourt 1993, pp. 45–70)) that Pasinetti frequently commenced volumes of his theoretical work with a survey of the history of economic thought relevant to these contributions. Thus Pasinetti's very influential formulation of the Ricardian system, with its emphasis on determining distributive shares in a growing economy (Pasinetti 1960), is the opening chapter for his collected essays on *Growth and Income Distribution* (Pasinetti 1974). When introducing his major theoretical contributions, including those on structural change (Pasinetti 1977, 1981), Pasinetti carefully provided the historical background of the foundations on which he built his own analysis of production, structural change and economic growth. These introductions invariably contrasted the classical tradition, in the main exemplified by the work of Ricardo, with the post-1870s marginalist tradition. In a more detailed historical framework (Pasinetti 1986), he developed this theme further by examining the theory of value as a source of alternative paradigms in economic analysis. These alternative approaches are reflected in the classical labour model focusing on production, and the pure exchange or pure preference model which came into its own in the post-1870 marginalist period (Groenewegen 1993, p. 45).

A similar observation can be made on the introduction to Pasinetti's R.C. Mills Memorial Lecture (Pasinetti 1993, pp. 297–9), which likewise pays tribute to classical economists and later predecessors of his work on structural change, technical progress and growth. Pasinetti's theoretical writings therefore do not stop with a brief and polite bow in the direction of the work of predecessors by way of acknowledging their insights. They use that work as a crucial starting point by which to focus on the essential aspects of the problem to be analysed. This statement in itself connects directly with my second observation.

3 The historical context of Pasinetti's conception of structural change

My second observation arises from illustrating the quality of Pasinetti's historical introductions by looking at those he provided for his *Lectures on the Theory of Production* (Pasinetti 1977, Chapter 1) and for his theoretical essay, *Structural Change and Economic Growth* (Pasinetti 1981).

Pasinetti's *Lectures on the Theory of Production* commence with a 'brief historical excursus' taking up the whole of the first chapter. The opening section paints that history on very broad lines, starting with the hunter/gatherers of primitive society, moving on to the agricultural revolution (dated 8000 BC) before introducing the Industrial Revolution of the eighteenth century. All this is covered on one page (Pasinetti 1977, p. 1).

After briefly defining both flow and stock concepts of wealth, Pasinetti uses the remainder of the chapter to investigate key elements in the analytical development of the theory of production starting with the mercantilists. Mercantilists saw wealth as a zero-sum game, a given stock, so that one nation's gain in wealth was another nation's loss. Pasinetti then mentioned the major critiques of this position, first by the Physiocrats, then by Adam Smith and the English classical school; finally, by Marx. This historical argument is elaborated by a more detailed examination of the dynamic models of production of Quesnay, Ricardo and Marx. Marginalist theory is portrayed basically as a retrogression to the mercantilist's static world, with wealth simply treated as a given endowment of resources (Pasinetti 1977, p. 4). Exceptions are noted: Walras and his 'original formulation of production coefficients' (p. 26) and Wicksell's analysis of the production function (Section 5.3). Surprisingly, Marshall is excluded from these exceptions, despite his very long Book IV on Production in the *Principles of Economics* with its insights into dynamic aspects and, occasionally, issues of structural change. Pasinetti's historical survey closes with a brief section (Pasinetti 1977, p. 32) noting the twentieth-century return of inter-industry production analysis by Leontief and Sraffa.

Pasinetti's 'essay' on *Structural Change and Economic Growth* (Pasinetti 1981) has a more sophisticated historical introduction. Its focus is man-made progress, through experiment and science, critical intellect and organised production, inducing a process for 'unprecedented increase in material wealth' (Pasinetti 1981, p. 2). In a seemingly expanding world, as discovery assisted by technical progress in navigation increased man's possibilities in voyages by sea, trade became a static starting point for such increase. Industry followed suit, improved as it was by scientific progress, division and specialisation of labour, invention and new utilisations of energy sources and materials. Unlike the static phenomena of exchange and trade, improvement in industrial production required dynamic change in the structure of society (Pasinetti 1981, pp. 2–3). As implied by the factors explaining industrial improvement, Adam Smith is depicted as the first economist of the new production economics and the growth it entailed. David Ricardo continued this intellectual development by distinguishing *scarce* commodities from those capable of steady reproduction. He then concentrated his analysis almost exclusively on the second category (Pasinetti 1981, pp. 5–8). Pasinetti's omission of the French eighteenth-century pioneers in this context is surprising: only Quesnay's *Tableau économique* is mentioned briefly as an early reproduction model, highly critical of mercantilist thought (Pasinetti 1981, pp. 4–5).

As was the case in the earlier *Lectures on the Theory of Production*, marginalist economics is depicted once again as switching attention to *scarce* goods in fixed supply, with their distribution under competitive conditions geared to maximising welfare. Pasinetti describes the tremendous success of marginalism as 'baffling', particularly given the analytical weaknesses of its marginal productivity theory. Production, technical progress, growth and structural change were not part of their analytical framework, and not really put back on the economists' agenda until the 1930s (Keynes, Kalecki, Harrod, Domar, Sraffa, Leontief and even Marshall's theory of the firm as improved by Sraffa's criticism). Yet the classical economists, especially Smith, Ricardo, J.S. Mill and Marx, had possessed all the key elements for a dynamic theory of an industrial economic system, where emphasis was placed on fully reproducible commodities. In this sense, reviewing change over time in the nature of the perceived economic problem permitted Pasinetti to focus attention on an earlier classical problem of economic growth, technical progress and structural change.

Some further emphasis needs to be given to Pasinetti's strong association of the emergence of economics as a science seeking to explain the origins of wealth, with the scientific revolutions taking place in the sixteenth, seventeenth and eighteenth centuries. The intellectual circles in which Petty operated (analysed in detail in Aspromourgos 1996, especially Chapters 2 and 4) show the importance for the early development of economics of such scientific revolutions. Petty as economist needs, of course, no introduction. It is equally well known he was also described as one of the founders of classical political economy in the work of Marx (1971, p. 52) together with his contemporary, Boisguilbert, in France. Later, the enlightenment, with its further emphasis on science and experiment, produced the founders of modern economics, once again in both France (Quesnay and the Physiocrats, Turgot) and in Britain (Hume, Adam Smith). The integration of economic discourse with general scientific discourse is an important aspect of the development of economics, fully recognised in Pasinetti's (1981, pp. 1–2) brief introductory statement to his structural economics and unfortunately, but quite understandably, not really developed there. However, this remark, explicitly recognising the important association between science, experiment and the emergence of economics, is a clear indication of the concise excellence of his historical excursions (and see Pasinetti 1993, pp. 297–8 for further remarks on Adam Smith and the industrial revolution in Britain).

One further point can be made here. As shown by these examples, looking at his predecessors is for Pasinetti a step in advancing knowledge, by resurrecting abandoned but still highly relevant problems. A genuine dynamic economics was missing from the marginalist literature. Reformulating an agenda of dynamic economics required appreciation of the classical economists whose work revealed they were fully aware of the tremendous importance of growth and structural change for increasing human welfare through a progressing economy, partly the result of the scientific revolution of which the founders of that classical economics were such an important part.

4 Pasinetti and the classical four stages theory

My third observation notes briefly that Pasinetti's historical introduction to *Structural Change and Economic Growth* (1981) virtually ignored the classical four stages theory, developed by Smith in Glasgow and by Turgot in France. The significance of this theory as a view of progress was retrieved during the 1970s by Ronald Meek and Roberto Finzi in particular. The theory conjectured that human society proceeded naturally and successively from the hunting to the pastoral to the agricultural stages to reach a commercial or capitalist stage of general industrial development. (Only rough hints acknowledging the existence of such a theory are visible on the first page of Pasinetti's earlier *Growth and Income Distribution*, as mentioned briefly at the start of Section 2.) Pasinetti's omission of the four stages theory is all the more surprising because its development by Smith and Turgot as a *materialist* theory of progress fits in particularly nicely with a dynamic theory of production and structural change, where the causes for change are internalised in the model of progress it embodies.

Although the essentials of the four stages are well known, a quick summary of its basic contents may be useful to some readers of this chapter. The theory argued that in the natural course of human progress, society's manner of producing its subsistence changed fundamentally in four different stages: from the original first stage of hunter/gatherers it changed to a society of shepherds and pastoralists (stage 2), then to agriculture (stage 3) before reaching the fourth and highest stage of a commercial and industrial society. This was not simply a view of the historical evolution of the manner in which mankind gained its subsistence (the materialist base), the theory also examined associated progress in property relations, class structure, methods of government and law (or aspects of the superstructure, as Marx was to call them). Furthermore, this development was seen as *natural* by its protagonists since each stage, sooner or later, necessarily induced the changes required to effect the coming of the next stage. Observable deficiencies in the prevailing mode of producing subsistence in time generated a shift to its natural successor, which heralded the next stage.

Thus it was eventually realised that the uncertainty of food supply from the hunt could be removed by the more certain access to food from maintaining a flock of animals as a herd. Similarly, the uncertainty of securing adequate food and water for the flocks of nomadic shepherds encouraged settlement at fertile places, slowly stimulating agriculture as a means of securing more certain food supplies for man and beast. Surplus product from agriculture in turn enabled the development of both a manufacturing and a trading sector, thereby paving the way to the greater variety of goods secured through commercial and industrial society as the highest stage of human development. It is easily shown that each successive stage involved more complex property relations and more advanced produced means of production. Higher rates of capital accumulation were implicit when shifting from stage to stage: from the simple implements of the hunt, to the capital accumulation process first involved in the gathering of a herd, then in settling and later purchasing land and acquiring the necessary implements for its cultivation, and ultimately to that required for the development of towns, the natural situation for encouraging the growth of industry and commerce. The last two activities in particular generated enormous capital accumulation of their own, essential for their effective development. These in turn complicated both property and class relations, and enhanced the need for the protective powers of government.

From this perspective, the four stages theory embodied not only a theory of progress but a theory of growth dependent on capital accumulation, increased specialisation and division of labour, and structural change. Aspects of this part of the process were particularly clearly depicted in Turgot's *Reflections on the Production and Distribution of Wealth*. Its concise text can be interpreted as a brief treatise on the transformation of agricultural to capitalist/commercial society (cf. Groenewegen 1983, pp. 332–6). It is therefore difficult to grasp why Pasinetti failed to mention the four stages theory explicitly in the historical introductions to his analysis of both the theory of production and his theory of growth and structural change. His failure to mention Turgot's work despite its significant contributions to the classical view on these topics is particularly surprising. In short, this observation suggests that Turgot's and Smith's four stages theory made a major classical contribution to the theory of growth and structural change which Pasinetti's historical introductions ought to have specifically acknowledged. Both of these introductions, in my opinion, would thereby have been 'historically' enriched, even if it is fully realised that space may not have easily been found for a discourse on the four stages theory in what were, after all, brief historical introductions to major contributions in economic theory.

5 Pasinetti, and Ricardo's and Marshall's economics

As suggested earlier, the post-1870 marginalist economists are generally treated in Pasinetti's historical introduction as economists whose analysis stands in major contrast to that of the classical school. The basic difference between these schools of thought which Pasinetti emphasises was that classical economics treated production as an essential element of the whole of their economics while the new marginalist economics treated the subject essentially from the perspective of a pure exchange economy (Pasinetti 1981, pp. 8–9). Pasinetti (1977, p. 26) did recognise that some of the marginalist economists dealt with aspects of production in their work. Examples he gave include Walras and his stress on fixed coefficients of production as an essential feature of his economics, while he considers Wicksell to be one of the first economists to use a production function explicitly (Pasinetti 1977, pp. 26–32). Of course, Wicksell was not the only economist of his generation to do so. As Whitaker (1974) has shown, Marshall used equations akin to production functions in unpublished manuscript notes on growth and distribution, written circa 1880. Wicksteed (1894, p. 4) made product an explicit function of the necessary agents of production, which he gave the form

$$P = f(a, b, c \ldots\ldots\ldots)$$

where P is product, and a,b,c,... are the requisite agents of production. For both Wicksteed and Wicksell, production functions were introduced as part of their marginal productivity-based theories of distribution. For Marshall, the production function became the organising mechanism for treating production as a whole in his *Principles of Economics*, as is clearly visible in the treatment of the subject in its Book IV (Marshall, 1920). This deals with the analysis of production by way of a discussion of the four agents of production which Marshall identified, that is, labour and nature (land) as original agents of production, capital and organisation as man-made agents, in which organisation of production was treated in terms of adaptation of the division of labour, economies and diseconomies of scale, the advantages of large and small firms.

Pasinetti suggests (1981, p. 9 note 7) that Marshall was in fact not a straightforward adherent of the new marginalist economics, but a hybrid 'neoclassical' who used both the marginal method for his economics and some insights of classical economics. As Dobb (1924, 1955, p. 6) recognised long ago, this had made Marshall's economics neoclassical in the full sense of the word, that is, something which modified classical doctrine by introducing alien, modern features in order to improve the rigour of the analysis. These peculiarities of Marshall's work are recognised by Pasinetti in arguments designed to restrict and modify the classical credentials which Marshall's economics claimed to have (Pasinetti 1981, pp. 139–41). In the context of this chapter, this aspect of Pasinetti's historical perspective needs further examination.

A note in Pasinetti's book on structural change (1981, p. 9 note 7) referred to Marshall and his economics as follows:

> Alfred Marshall's *Principles of Economics* represents a case of its own. Marshall, deeply imbued by the English pragmatic tradition, was never really able to turn his attention away from production: he clearly felt it was practically too important to be neglected or minimised. He tried a compromise. He did accept marginal analysis, but he attempted a reconciliation with the Classical economists ... No wonder that he has always been eliciting hostility from the purists of marginalist economic theory. (Pasinetti 1981, p. 9 note 7)

In the context of a discussion of 'the determination of relative prices and physical quantities in a dynamic context', Pasinetti (1981, pp. 138–42) returns to the matter of distinguishing marginalism from classical economics. In this section, Pasinetti analyses their disparate attitudes to this problem as well as that of the neoclassical economists (by whom he seems to mean Marshall). Ricardo had drawn attention to the distinction between *scarce* (or non-reproducible) commodities and *produced* commodities (or those commodities reproducible without limit or constraint). Ricardo's analysis, generally speaking, ignored the first type of scarce commodities and confined attention to the second type of readily reproducible commodities. According to Pasinetti, the marginalists did exactly the opposite. They analysed scarce commodities and charged the classical economists, especially Ricardo, with neglecting demand in their explanations of value. Ricardo, it is true, had analysed the value of readily reproducible commodities in terms of cost of production only. Moreover, Ricardo argued, under certain simplifying assumptions, cost of production of a commodity could be fully captured in relative terms by the quantity of labour required for its production.

Marshall, Pasinetti went on to argue, avoided both the marginalist perspective and that of the classical economists. When confronted with the question of whether utility or cost of production determined value, he proposed a famous compromise in terms of supply and demand or, to put it in other words, that both cost of production and utility determined value. Marshall expressed the argument neatly in terms of an analogy based on a pair of scissors. Both blades are essential for the act of cutting even if, when one appears to be cutting, the other blade seems to be held still. Likewise in the market, when in the short run the structure of production is given and constant, demand is the main factor responsible for determining prices. In the long run, when market fluctuations are ignored, the influence of demand may be ignored, and it is correct to speak of normal price as governed by cost of production (Pasinetti 1981, pp. 140–1; Marshall, 1920, pp. 348–9).

Pasinetti credits Marshall with a superb understanding of Ricardo and classical economics on two grounds. First, Marshall, like Ricardo, concentrated on industrial commodities or, in Ricardo's words, on those commodities reproducible without restraint. Second, when focusing on cost of production, Marshall, like Ricardo, concentrated on long-term, normal, considerations which abstracted from fluctuations in supply and demand. This way of putting the argument, Pasinetti argued, is misleading. It implies that demand has no role to play in the long run (Pasinetti 1981, pp. 140–1).

As Pasinetti had already demonstrated in his work on structural change, cost of production (embodied in a specific technology) determines relative prices. Demand determines the relative quantities of the commodities which are to be produced, in order to eliminate either excess production or shortages of particular commodities. Ricardo never grasped, or discussed, the second part of the problem. Marshall, however, failed to bring out this important aspect of demand even though it was implied in (static) supply/demand equilibrium analysis, where prices and quantities were simultaneously determined.

However, Pasinetti (1981, pp. 140–1) emphasises that Marshall's work contains a major error with respect to this type of analysis. He implied that demand has no role to play in long-run analysis on grounds similar to those of Ricardo. Like Ricardo, by concentrating on the proposition that long-term normal (natural) prices depend on cost of production, he ignored the influence of demand in determining the quantities to be produced. Emphasis in Marshall's analysis of the *Principles* was too much on the problem of determining value, or relative prices. He failed to discuss the amount to be produced in the light of changes in long-term demand as influenced by population changes, changes in tastes and other influences on consumption decision making, particularly changing levels of income. Such long-term demand factors determine the structure of production in the sense of the relative composition of firms as producing units in terms of the commodities they manufacture. The closest Marshall came to this problem was when he pontificated on the possibilities inherent in rising living standards (income per head) on standards of life, that is, the socially desirable consumption pattern of the working class in particular.

Now it is interesting to note that this part of the problem of production was not ignored by one of the founders of classical economics, François Quesnay. His model of the circular flow, or *Tableau économique*, was also a very simple example of input–output analysis capable of presenting a highly stylised portrait of the French economy in the mid-eighteenth century or, as was more frequently the case, a highly stylised representation of what that French economy could be like if its economic structure was better balanced. Pasinetti was fully familiar with this model, including its input–output implications. These were outlined in his *Lectures on the Theory of Production* (1977), in a section of its introductory chapter devoted exclusively to François Quesnay as the author of the *Tableau économique* (Pasinetti 1977, pp. 5–8). At the end of this section, Pasinetti translated the data of the *Tableau* into a double-entry table linking inputs and outputs (Pasinetti 1977, Table 1.1, p. 7). The output of the agricultural sector in this table forms the inputs for the manufacturing sector (wage goods, raw materials) and of the landlords by way of their consumption. Likewise, manufacturing output provides inputs for the agricultural sector (new equipment and its replacement) and consumption for the landlords (manufactured luxuries). The landlords as consumers have a crucial role in keeping the economic structure balanced, by spending their income (the productive surplus from the agricultural sector or net product in Quesnay's terminology) to purchase the surplus output (relative to next year's production requirements) from both the manufacturing and the agricultural sectors. Aggregate demand is maintained at the requisite level by the spending pattern of the (non-producing) landlords. Although the *Tableau* was not explained in value terms, generally speaking, Quesnay's analysis provided a brilliant picture of the quantitative relations of production in an agricultural kingdom.

In the context of the specific omission of long-term demand factors by both Ricardo and Marshall, it is interesting to note that some versions of the *Tableau économique* explicitly showed that the landlords as the dominant class were also crucial in determining the structure of industry by the pattern of their demand. If this was more than proportionally directed to agricultural produce, it stimulated the agricultural sector, hence setting the scene for a growing economy from the exclusive surplus producing properties of the agricultural sector. These were summarised in the evocative phrase, the benefits of *luxe de subsistence*. If landlords directed an undue proportion of their spending (effective demand) to the manufacturing sector (incapable of producing a surplus on Quesnay's assumptions), the economy would eventually decline as the surplus produced by the agricultural sector became smaller in relative terms. Patterns of class demand thereby had consequences in terms of the quantity of commodities produced in the long run.

It is well known that Marx adapted and improved the growth implications of Quesnay's *Tableau économique* in the models of simple and expanded reproduction prepared for the second volume of *Capital* (a summary is provided in Pasinetti 1977, pp. 19–24).

6 Concluding remarks

What conclusions can be derived from the argument of the previous four sections? Most generally, they indicate the importance of classical economics for the development of Pasinetti's dynamics of growth and structural change. Pasinetti often gained great insights by explicitly comparing the successes of the classical analysis of economic dynamics with the performance of the early generations of marginalist economists on these issues. My observations on these historical introductions here and there noted some minor omissions in Pasinetti's accounts. These included his failure to draw attention to Sir William Petty's life and work as an example of the association between innovative economics against a backdrop of innovative science and experiment (in Section 3 above); and the development of a four stage growth theory by Smith and Turgot as an instance of long-run structural change analysis he ought to have explicitly mentioned (in Section 4 above). Likewise, Section 5 indicated that the use of production functions was more widespread than Pasinetti's introduction to his *Lectures on the Theory of Production* (1977) suggested, though this section also praised his critique of both Ricardo and Marshall (as neoclassical hybrid) in ignoring the problem of long-term determination of quantities in their work by their failure to consider a long-run role for effective demand. For both of them, as Pasinetti clearly indicated, long-run analysis was confined to demonstrating the crucial role of cost of production in determining natural, or long-run normal, prices. They ignored the major role of demand in explaining industrial structure, even though, during the second half of the preceding century, this problem had been quite systematically analysed in Quesnay's *Tableau économique*, a model during the nineteenth century only really appreciated by Marx, who used its underlying idea in developing his own models of simple and expanded reproduction. As had others done before him (in particular Leontief and Sraffa), Pasinetti fully recognised the implications of these contributions for examining the dynamics of structural growth. It is to the commemoration of Pasinetti's 1981 contribution in particular that this chapter is devoted.

REFERENCES

Aspromourgos, A. (1996), *On the Origins of Classical Economics*, London: Routledge.

Baranzini, M. and Harcourt, G.C. (eds.) (1993), *The Dynamics of the Wealth of Nations. Growth, Distribution and Structural Change*, New York: Macmillan, St Martin's Press.

Dobb, M.H. (1924, 1955), 'The Entrepreneur Myth' in Maurice Dobb, *On Economic Theory and Socialism*, London: Routledge and Kegan Paul, pp. 3–15.

Groenewegen, P. (1983), 'Turgot's Place in the History of Economic Thought: A Bi-centenary estimate', *History of Political Economy*, **15**(4) Winter, 585–616, reprinted in Groenewegen, P. (2002), *Eighteenth Century Economics. Turgot, Beccaria and Smith and their Contemporaries*, London: Routledge, Chapter 19.

(1993), 'Marshall on Ricardo', in Baranzini, M. and Harcourt, G. eds., *The Dynamics of the Wealth of Nations. Growth, Distribution and Structural Change*, Houndsmill, Basingstoke: Macmillan, pp. 45–70.

Marshall, A. (1920), *Principles of Economics*, eighth edition, London: Macmillan.

Marx, K.H. (1971), *A Contribution to the Critique of Political Economy*, London: Lawrence and Wishart.

Pasinetti, L.L. (1960), 'A Mathematical Reformulation of the Ricardian System', reprinted in Pasinetti, L.L. (1974), *Growth and Income Distribution. Essays in Economic Theory*, Cambridge University Press, pp. 1–28.

(1974), *Growth and Income Distribution. Essays in Economic Theory*, Cambridge University Press.

(1977), *Lectures on the Theory of Production*, Basingstoke: Macmillan Press.

(1981), *Structural Change and Economic Growth*, Cambridge University Press.

(1986), 'Theory of Value – A Source of Alternative Paradigms in Economic Analysis', in Baranzini M. and Scazzieri, R. eds., *Foundations of Economics*, Oxford: Blackwell, pp. 409–31.

(1993), 'Technical Progress and Structural Change', 17th R.C. Mills Memorial Lecture (17 August 1993), in Groenewegen, P., ed. (2004), *Australian Economic Policy, Theory and History. R.C. Mills Memorial Lectures 1958–2003*, Sydney: Faculty of Economics, University of Sydney, pp. 295–306.

Turgot, A.R.J. (1963) *Reflections on the Production and Distribution of Wealth*, New York: Ashley edition, reprinted by Augustus M. Kelley, pp. 5–6, 43–56.

Whitaker, J.K. (1974), 'The Marshallian System in 1881: Distribution and Growth', *Economic Journal*, **84**, March, 1–17, reprinted in Wood, J. C., ed. (1982), *Alfred Marshall. Critical Assessments*, Volume III, London: Croom Helm, pp. 508–26.

Wicksteed, P.H. (1894), *An Essay on the Co-ordination of the Laws of Distribution*, London: Macmillan.

2 Structural dynamics in historical perspective

Mario Pomini

1 Introduction

Owing to a number of factors, some internal to economic theory – such as the attempt to extend the results of the *General Theory* (Harrod 1939) from the short to the long period – others external – resulting from the new economic and social conditions in the period following the Second World War – in the 1950s and 1960s the theory of growth once again occupied a central position in economic reflection, at the expense of the theory of the economic cycle in vogue between the two wars. The theoretical contribution of Pasinetti occupies a special place in this renewed interest in the factors that determine the long-period trends of the economy; it was put forward in 1965 and then definitively located in the main text of 1981, *Structural Change and Economic Growth*, probably one of the most important contributions of the Cambridge School to dynamic analysis.

The aim of this study is to analyse Pasinetti's contribution in a historical perspective, the purpose being to compare it with the recent literature on endogenous growth. A few decades after its initial formulation, it is now possible to see how Pasinetti's inquiry is part of a wider research programme which aims to establish the conditions and possibilities of dynamic macroeconomics. From this point of view, his model can be considered a fundamental stage in the evolution of a research programme which we can define as 'linear dynamic macroeconomics'. From the analytical point of view, the essential characteristic of this approach to macroeconomic dynamics consists in assuming a linear relation between the accumulated factor and the product, therefore abandoning the neoclassical viewpoint of scarcity. This line of reflection began with von Neumann's study of 1937, but was given decisive impetus by the Keynesian Revolution via Harrod's model. Pasinetti's endeavour was to extend these two important models in an original direction. Recently, this research programme has received new impulse within the theory of

The author would like to thank Prof. Meacci for useful comments on a previous draft.

endogenous growth (Lucas 1988; Romer 1986), since one of its distinctive features is the abandonment of the traditional assumption of the decreasing marginal productivity of the accumulated factor. It is therefore interesting to analyse how Pasinetti's work can be considered in the light of the latest developments, in order to bring out the similarities but also the substantial differences that remain.

2 From statics to dynamics in the theory of the general economic equilibrium

As historiographical research has shown (Ingrao and Israel 1987, Weintraub 1985), at international level the 1930s represented an important maturation phase for the theory of general economic equilibrium (GEE), the effects of which were to be fully expressed in the following two decades. Following Koopmans (1957, p. 57), we can say that in purely mathematical terms, but with considerable repercussions also from the interpretative point of view, the GEE theory followed two completely different paths which can be associated with the names of Wald and Leontief. Thanks to the work of the Hungarian mathematician Wald, the GEE theory lost its elementary nineteenth-century analytical form of a process of constraint maximisation, taking on a richer mathematical configuration which was to lead to its complete axiomatisation in the 1950s. The work of Wald is important because it introduces some topics, such as that of monotony, decrease and convexity, which were to constitute the analytical instruments for all subsequent research. This axiomatic turning point, aimed at maximum generalisation of the Walrasian model, was to lead to the fundamental theorems of existence formulated in the 1950s (Ingrao and Israel 1987, Chapter X).

There is a second path, however, again in the context of the mathematics of the GEE, which was followed, perhaps with greater success in terms of application results: the application of linear space mathematics to economic problems, which subsequently became linear programming. This analytical tool provides a very different point of view from which to observe the interdependences between markets, undoubtedly much less refined than the axiomatic approach in mathematical terms, but with the advantage of being immediately borne out by empirical experience. Leontief's work on sectoral interdependences opened the way for activity analysis, which was to become, also in view of the need for planning imposed by the war, an important strand of research, with significant repercussions also in the field of the GEE. Even more important within this framework, since it relates to the dynamic part, is von Neumann's contribution of 1937.

Of these two currents, the first emphasising the axiomatic point of view and the second linked to linear space mathematics, it was the latter that had a considerable influence on the theoretical debate in the period following the Second World War in Italy, replacing the Paretian tradition which relied on functional calculus (Amoroso 1940; La Volpe 1936).[1] The axiomatic approach never took root among the Italian economists of the period; on the one hand there were no mathematicians or physicists interested in economic matters or in their formalisation, and on the other this approach offered little stimulus for those who were interested in dynamic analysis. By contrast, the analytical techniques connected with linear programming were widely discussed and analysed (Napoleoni 1965). The reference text for the Italian debate was not Debreu's essay *Theory of Value* (1959), published in the Cowles Foundation's series of monographs, but rather another essay published the previous year by the Rand Corporation, *Linear Programming and Economic Analysis*, by Dorfman *et al.* This important monograph, in particular Chapter 13, 'Linear programming and the theory of general equilibrium', contributed to defining the general terms of the discussion on the GEE. In Italy it was above all Claudio Napoleoni who undertook the task of initiating new reflection on the themes of general economic equilibrium outside the marginalist tradition and coherently with activity analysis. Napoleoni's approach, strongly rooted in von Neumann's, links with two characteristic aspects of Italian reflection on the GEE in the period prior to the Second World War: the need to perform the analysis at a disaggregate level and the search for a dynamic approach. We will see how these two essential traits also characterise the reflection of Pasinetti, albeit in a completely different theoretical context. Napoleoni and Pasinetti were the two authors who in the period after the Second World War relaunched dynamic macroeconomic analysis on a new basis in Italy, following different analytical paths but with the same basic scientific purpose of returning to the classic fundamentals.

3 Pasinetti's research programme

The approach to structural dynamic analysis constitutes for Pasinetti the result, and perhaps the compendium, of a precise programme of research which was developed and expanded over a long period. It was

[1] The theory of general economic equilibrium constituted a lively field of research for the generation of post-Paretian economists, who sought to dynamise the GEE equations in various directions. Amoroso (1940) attempted to apply the motion equations of rational mechanics. La Volpe (1936) approached the problem in intertemporal terms.

outlined in definitive form right from the outset, in an essay of 1960 written jointly with Spaventa and entitled, significantly, 'Verso il superamento della modellistica aggregata nella teoria della sviluppo economico'. In this essay the two economists clarify the new coordinates for a dynamic analysis that aims to break free of the straitjacket of Keynesian aggregate analysis, but without relapsing into neoclassical individualism. The starting point is recognition of the centrality of dynamic analysis:

Contemporary economic analysis is for the most part essentially dynamic: the economic phenomena are considered in their evolution over time; and the process of development of the system has been placed at the centre of the analysis. This approach is fairly recent. (Pasinetti and Spaventa 1960, p. 1749)

While formalisation of the dynamic phenomena is the new challenge for economic theory, and also for economic policy, Pasinetti and Spaventa are very critical of the aggregate models deriving from the Harrodian approach, both neoclassical and Keynesian-inspired, since both have the same basic defect: that of proposing completely unrealistic aggregate models far removed from the concrete economic reality. For the two young economists, a dynamic analysis based on the concept of stationary state and an aggregate model is unsatisfactory and can be considered at most an exercise in style preliminary to a real scientific analysis. On the contrary:

We must acknowledge the continuous changeability of reality, and therefore renounce rationalisation of the evolution of reality as a process that occurs in a continuous equilibrium between aggregate variables of uncertain significance: we must try to establish the factors that determine the changes, analyse them and investigate whether laws exist governing the occurrence of the changes. There is no doubt in our opinion that, unless we wish to deny the very function of economic analysis, this second route must be attempted.

This choice involves the adoption of an analysis method different from the one followed so far. It is evident that, for the purpose of analysing the position, not necessarily balanced, of the individual variables and parameters, an analysis in aggregate terms is no longer sufficient since, due to its nature, it conceals the very subject of the research. Technical progress, productivity, consumption, investment, are no longer sufficient to define the economic system in a dynamic research. We must go beyond this, and find out what lies behind the façade of these aggregate expressions. In short, the research must be formulated in disaggregate terms. (Pasinetti and Spaventa 1960, p. 1770)

For Pasinetti and Spaventa, aggregate dynamic analysis, while highlighting important aspects of economic development such as the accumulation of capital or the distribution of income, remains on the surface, since it is unable to analyse the driving forces of long-period economic dynamics, both those on the demand side and those on the supply side. The uni-sector scheme must be replaced by disaggregate analysis where the reference unit consists of the single sector. This need is all the more urgent because the analytical model does not have solely theoretical purposes but aims to be a guide for traditional economic policy operations based on increased public spending. In carrying out their project, Pasinetti and Spaventa reject neoclassical analysis because it is completely static. Disaggregate analysis, however, based on the traditional theory represented mainly by the von Neumann model, is also unsuitable for the purpose, for the same reason. The ambitious project of grounding disaggregate dynamic analysis on new bases was achieved in the 1960s by Pasinetti, leading to the development of new conceptual tools suited to the problem to be tackled. The fundamental analytical result is the study of 1965 which, despite subsequent additions, remains the fundamental text on the matter.

4 The criticism of the von Neumann model

The von Neumann approach constituted the reference point for the debate in Italy on the disaggregate dynamic models outside the neoclassical framework. It was authoritatively supported by Claudio Napoleoni, according to whom it deserved a very important place in the history of economic thought. He devoted a long article in *La Rivista Trimestrale* (1963) to a detailed illustration of it, highlighting its most innovative analytical elements, in addition to those of an interpretative character.

For Napoleoni, the von Neumann model constituted the general paradigm of a genuine dynamic analysis outside marginalism because it permitted, first, the logical inconsistencies in the Walrasian theory of capitalisation to be overcome. As the debate in Italy (Garegnani 1960; Graziani 1965; Napoleoni 1965) had highlighted, the Walrasian equations relative to the production of new capital goods were contradictory with respect to the condition of equality of the rate of return on the individual capital goods. This contradiction no longer had any reason to exist in von Neumann's perspective since all goods, and therefore also capital goods, were considered reproducible. Second, the latter perspective could be considered the formalisation closest to the classical approach based on the concept of surplus and on the idea of the circular flow of income, which for Napoleoni were principles better suited to interpreting the capitalist economic reality. This did not mean that von Neumann's model had no shortcomings, which concerned in particular the exclusion of consumption and exogenous treatment of technical progress, but these were points indicating the direction for development of the research programme. This project, however, was not carried out by Napoleoni who, towards the end of the 1960s, preferred to turn his attention to the work of Marx.

Pasinetti's position, meanwhile, which we find stated in definitive form in the appendix to the sixth chapter of his book (1965), 'A criticism of the von Neumann type of dynamic model' is quite different. Pasinetti also recognises that von Neumann's approach constitutes the most notable attempt to construct a dynamic analysis outside the marginalist paradigm, but he immediately identifies its fundamental limitations which make a profound revision necessary. The most unsatisfactory aspect is the fact that, intentions notwithstanding, it is substantially a static model, a model in which time has no essential role. The dynamic characteristics of the system are defined once and for all via the matrix of coefficients and the only interesting problem is to verify whether it is possible to determine a balanced growth path. Pasinetti's criticism therefore concentrates on the fact that the models à la von Neumann are formally dynamic, since they contain differential equations, but substantially static, since they pay inadequate attention to the effects of technical progress, which leads, by definition, to a continuous modification of the production coefficients. For Pasinetti, the central hypothesis of an equilibrium growth rate, although very convenient at the analytical level, is not borne out by empirical experience.

> But such an assumption, convenient though it is mathematically, has clearly nothing to do with the real world. It means omitting deliberately what has been singled out as the basic force responsible for the dynamism of a modern society, namely the process of learning which goes on, both on the technical and the demand side. (Pasinetti 1965, p. 680)

The criticism also extends to the normative aspects of the model. For Pasinetti it cannot even be affirmed that the growth path is a path that has optimality characteristics, on either the demand or the production side. On the demand side, consumers change their habits as income grows, increasing their consumption of certain goods and reducing that of others, thus randomising the relation between the growth rate of the system and a growth configuration that is optimal for the consumers. On the production side, the system is in a continuous state of transformation, tending to decrease the weight of the goods that obstruct economic growth via a process of substitution.

To conclude, for Pasinetti the advantages of the von Neumann model are outweighed by its limits, which consist substantially in the rigidity of the basic analytical scheme. This conclusion was shared by other Italian interpreters (Graziani 1965). To achieve a disaggregate dynamic analysis, a different path had to be taken, passing through Harrod's Keynesian dynamics without abandoning the multisector perspective. To obtain this result Leontief's model had to be reappraised with a dynamic slant.

5 From Leontief's model to the dynamics of the vertically integrated sectors

Having set von Neumann aside, Pasinetti turned to the other reference model for multisector analysis, that of Leontief's sectorial interdependences, but here, if possible, the difficulties were even greater for dynamic analysis. Although analysis of the sectorial interdependences had the advantage of possessing a solid empirical grounding, it was by definition a static approach where the coefficients of production measured moment by moment the economic relations between the sectors of the economy. To give Leontief's scheme a genuine dynamic content, two problems had to be overcome: the first was represented by the heterogeneity of the industrial structure and the second derived from the need to introduce an intertemporal mechanism able to sustain the dynamic path over time. The solution to the first problem was found in a return to the classical school's approach, which postulated the centrality of the labour factor, while the second problem was solved by extending Harrodian dynamics to several sectors. Pasinetti could rightly affirm that his approach comprised numerous research traditions, all with the common denominator of being unconnected with marginalism.

Pasinetti devoted the sixth chapter of the 1965 text to detailed examination of how his structural dynamics model can be considered a natural extension of Leontief's, where the central notion is no longer that of industry but the dynamically more coherent notion of vertically integrated sectors. For Pasinetti, the table of sectorial interdependences and the matrix of vertically integrated sectors constitute two different ways of looking at the same economic system: the first from a static point of view, the second from a dynamic point of view. The differences consist only in how economic relations are classified, but it is possible to switch from one to the other by means of linear algebraic transformations: the production coefficients of a vertically integrated sectorial model are a linear combination of the production coefficients of the corresponding input–output model.

The usefulness of the notion of vertically integrated sectors appears to its full extent in the field of dynamics – it permits reduction of the complex network of relations between sectors to one single element: the vertically integrated labour coefficient. In the new theoretical scheme all the intermediate stages are eliminated and each production process can be expressed via the use of a certain amount of labour. It can thus be seen why this procedure is essential for achieving dynamic analysis: while the input–output table is continuously modified over time, in the new scheme the vertically integrated relations remain intact and what is seen is only the variation in the quantity of the primary factor, labour, applied to each sector. As Pasinetti wrote:

> Concluding and summarising, we may say that, at any given point of time, a very definite relation exists between the static input–output model and the model presented in the previous pages through a fully specifiable matrix of coefficients. Considered at a very given point of time, the input–output model is more analytical – it has much more to say about the structure of an economic system. However, as time goes on, and the conditions of production and consumption change, the inter-industry relations break down. ... In this way the static input–output and the dynamic vertically-integrated systems appear as mutually complementary and completing each other. Inter-industry relations, referring to any particular point of time, present a cross-section of the vertically integrated variables, whose movements through time express the structural dynamics of the economic system. (Pasinetti 1965, p. 677)

Pasinetti then observes that the notion of vertically integrated sectors is not new in the history of economic thought. It was already outlined in Smith and was fully applied in Sraffa's notion of sub-system, but the originality of Pasinetti's contribution is his dynamic interpretation (Porta 1998).

This analytical invention alone is not sufficient, however, since the problem of determining the dynamics of the system remains open. Pasinetti adopts Harrod's Keynesian approach, which is based on the linear relation between the production factor and the product obtained. In Harrod's model the accumulated production factor is capital and economic dynamics are determined by the fact that the production variations are the result of demand variations. In Pasinetti's model, by contrast, economic dynamics are linked to variations in labour: both on the demand side, via variations in tastes, and on the supply side, via analysis of the effects of technical progress.

In short, these two elements, the notion of vertically integrated sectors and that of technical progress, in the form of a reduction of the labour contained in the production processes, constitute the essential ingredients of Pasinetti's linear dynamic scheme.

6 Some characteristics of structural dynamics

What is the specific contribution of structural dynamics to the linear dynamic approach? To answer this question it is expedient briefly to summarise some analytical aspects of Pasinetti's proposal. Following a Ricardian-type approach, Pasinetti sets out to develop a general model, assigning only a secondary role to historical and descriptive aspects. He aims to develop a theory that remains neutral with respect to the institutional organisation of society, concentrating his attention on the natural or primary characteristics that enable a system to grow, exploiting all its possibilities. This project results in the *pure production model*, as Pasinetti called his approach in order to distinguish it from the neoclassical approach centred on the phenomenon of exchange.

In this multisector pure production model there is one single production factor, labour, which is allocated from the outset among the individual production sectors, each of which is characterised by its own technology expressed by the coefficient of production. Given these characteristics, the end price of the goods is proportional to the labour coefficient, a theory which was dear to the classical school. The prices formed in this way in turn determine the exchanges that occur in the economy so that the end products are then shared between the end uses of the demand. In this simplified economy we find the Keynesian theory that the volume of production is determined by the intensity of global demand.

Moving to the dynamic analysis, this is greatly simplified in analytical terms by the fact that not only is production of the end good proportional to the labour performed but, via the notion of vertically integrated sectors, one single unit of the final good corresponds to each sectorial production unit. In symbols, the following relation applies:

$$\dot{K} = \dot{Y} \tag{1}$$

where the dot above the variable indicates the derivative with respect to time, hence the variation in the production capacity is exactly equal to the variation in demand. If, like Pasinetti, we relate (1) to the linear production scheme in labour, we obtain an equilibrium relationship in terms of production coefficients for the creation of capital goods and variation in the demand for consumer goods:

$$a_{k_i n} = g a_{in} \tag{2}$$

where g is the growth rate of the population, $a_{k_i n}$ is the coefficient of demand for new investments and a_{in} is the coefficient of demand relative to the same sector. Condition (2) is a condition of dynamic equilibrium of the Harrod–Domar type, one for each sector, on the basis of which each new additional sectorial investment must be equal to the corresponding demand, multiplied by the population growth rate. When this condition is satisfied, the economy achieves the increase in production capacity necessary to maintain full employment. On this assumption, only the physical quantities evolve over time, while prices, which depend only on the conditions of technology, remain constant.

In relation (2) we are still in the field of sectorial dynamics; to switch to structural dynamics, we must consider how the coefficients of labour (at rate ρ) and demand (at rate r) are modified over time following the innovations brought about by technical progress or via a change in consumer tastes (Engel's law). If the two variation rates are identical, the economic system moves, expanding the various sectors in the same proportion, so that its structure remains constant over time, as in the traditional models of exogenous growth. If the rates are different, as normally happens, the structural dynamics constituting the specific focus of interest of Pasinetti's analysis will emerge. If the coefficient of demand is constant, the conditions of equilibrium for each sector become the following:

$$a_{k_i n} = (g + \rho) a_{in} \tag{3}$$

The economic meaning is immediate: each sector separately and the economic system as a whole grows at a rate which is the sum of the population growth rate and the rate of technical progress. Since (3) is relative to one single sector, in the economy considered as a whole we have n dynamic equations, each of which is characterised by an equal population growth rate but a different demand growth rate. In order for the system, which starts from a condition of equilibrium, not to diverge from it, the variations of one sector must be off-set in the opposite direction by those of other sectors, according to an analytical condition that links the coefficients of the system and which Pasinetti calls the multisector equation of Harrod:

$$\sum_{i=1}^{n} a_{ni} a_{in} + \sum_{i=1}^{n} a_{nk_i} a_{in} + (g + \rho) \sum_{i=1}^{n} a_{nk_i} a_{in} = 1 \tag{4}$$

The system indicated by (4) incorporates a macroeconomic condition: for the economy to maintain full initial employment, variations in demand must be off-set by variations in potential production. System (4) represents a series of sectoral conditions, one for each sector. Each sector grows at a rate which is the sum of the population growth rate and technical progress. The structural dynamics emerge when the demand growth rates and the sectoral variation rates in technical progress are different. This is a situation in which nothing can be taken for granted: the composition of the demand varies, as does, under the effect of technical progress, the structure of production. To determine the breadth and effect of these variations, it is necessary, according to Pasinetti, to abandon the abstract model and refer to empirical analysis.

In structural dynamics each individual sector can be in equilibrium, i.e. the increase in production capacity is absorbed by the demand, but the system as a whole is not in equilibrium. In fact, the system is constrained by a condition that requires the various production transformations to be such that they maintain full initial employment: if some sectors lose labour because of reductions in the labour coefficients due to technical progress, the unemployed workers will find employment in new sectors. This process of continuous intertemporal distribution of the workers among sectors is not, however, a spontaneous process that can be left to market forces. On the contrary, it requires the creation of a planning organisation that draws up a long-term strategy to compensate for the chaotic market forces. In Pasinetti (1965), economic policy requirements derive from the fact that the evolution of the economic system is determined by structural dynamics, the negative effects of which on the labour factor can be controlled via a shrewd policy of public investments.

7 From the pure labour model to the pure knowledge model. A comparison between Pasinetti's approach and NGT

Each phase of a research programme must tackle the challenges resulting from the new prospects that emerge in the course of scientific progress. In the case of linear macroeconomics the new stage is represented by the theory of endogenous growth which developed in the second half of the 1980s. It is therefore interesting to compare these new views with the theory of structural dynamics, in order to highlight the similarities and the differences.

At first sight it may seem that there is little in common between the theories of endogenous growth and structural dynamics as put forward in the 1960s. The former emphasises the role of the endogenous and institutional factors able to explain economic growth, primarily the decisions of firms to invest in research and development, whereas, as we have seen, in Pasinetti's model the learning activity underlying technical progress is completely exogenous, determined by an involuntary aptitude for learning which is typical of human nature. Upon closer analysis, however, at least two relevant similarities emerge that point to both theories being the expression of the same research programme: the linear structure of the basic scheme and dealing with the difficulties inherent, in a multisector context, in the notion of capital and, more generally, of production factor. However, these analytical affinities, albeit important, do not fill the gaps that remain between the two approaches; in short, we can say that in the recent literature there has been a transition from Pasinetti's pure labour model to a pure knowledge model.

As Jones and Manuelli observed in a long review article (1997), above and beyond the various mechanisms involved, growth in the long period is possible because a linear relation exists between the accumulated factor, in this case knowledge, and the end product:

In terms of key features of the environment that are necessary to obtain endogenous growth there is one that stands out: it is necessary that the marginal product of some augmentable input be bounded strictly away from zero in the production of some augmentable input which can be used to produce consumption. (1997, pp. 78–79)

The essence of the problem, in an intertemporal context in which the usual representative agent maximises his utility, is the fact that it is necessary to appropriately define the conditions in terms of technology, and therefore on the supply side of the economy, so that the profitability of the accumulated factor is not annulled by the growth process. What the new model will achieve is in many ways some sort of modification of the traditional aggregate function of production which goes in the required direction of annulling the effect of the decreasing returns. If, alongside the accumulable factor, there are other factors essential to production, then the global production function will present increasing returns to scale, a circumstance well known in the literature of the 1960s. As has been noted in particular by Solow (2000), in many of the new models endogenous growth is obtained via *ad hoc* hypotheses on the production function which allow the required result to be obtained. If the marginal product of the accumulated factor does not have unitary elasticity with respect to the product, the model tends towards an explosive solution, or long-period growth is annulled.

This common Harrodian root is very evident in the first wave of the new models, represented mainly by the contributions of Romer (1986) and Lucas (1988), but it is also apparent in models seemingly distant from it, for example that developed by Grossman and Helpman (1991) in which innovation is achieved via the production of new goods. Above and beyond the complexity of the model in which there are three interacting sectors, the long-period growth is determined by the production function of innovations, which is as follows:

$$\dot{n} = \frac{1}{a} nl \tag{5}$$

where l represents the number of researchers employed, n the number of patents taken out, and lastly a the coefficient of labour relative to the research sector. As can be noted, the basic assumptions are not very far from those of Pasinetti, since the number of new inventions produced, with the consequent birth of new sectors of the economy, is a linear function of the number of skilled workers employed in the research sector. We could even say that, using his categories, the models of endogenous growth with product differentiation also fall within the institutional variations of the more general pure labour model, the only difference being that all the other sectors depend subordinately on the research sector.

Since this assumption of linearity, which underlies the reasoning, is very drastic and very far from the general neoclassical approach, it is interesting to consider the lengthy justification offered by the two authors:

> Equation [5] represents a production function for blueprints. We also need to specify the link between research activity and the accumulation of general knowledge capital. In principle, we might want this specification to incorporate lags in the dissemination of knowledge. We might also want to allow for general nonlinear relationship between investment in research and the knowledge stock that accumulates as a consequence. Such a nonlinear specification would be appropriate if the marginal contribution of a particular project to general knowledge were a function of the prevailing state of knowledge. The process of knowledge accumulation might be characterized by increasing returns, for example, if important complementarities existed between different ideas ...
>
> We choose, however, to concentrate our attention in the main text on a formulation that ignores these potential complications. Our specification posits an immediate contribution by each R&D project to the stock of knowledge capital, and makes this contribution independent of the aggregate amount of R&D undertaken in the past. We take the knowledge capital stock to be proportional, at every moment, to the economy's cumulative experience in R&D. (Grossman and Helpman 1991, p. 58)

In this passage Helpman and Grossman highlight the two central elements that led them to abandon the assumption of decreasing returns in the accumulated factor. The first is of an analytical character and consists in the fact that without it, endogenous growth is quite simply impossible. This is not merely a matter of reducing the analytical difficulties, but rather of obtaining a positive growth rate also in the long period. The second, no less important, has to do with the nature of knowledge as an economic good: its acquisition does not obey the law of decreasing returns; on the contrary, it may even fall within that of increasing returns.

The relationship of linearity between the accumulated factor and the product that characterises the model of endogenous growth has a second aspect that is worth highlighting. In the 1970s the multisector neoclassical models were abandoned because they suffered from serious logical inconsistencies. The general result of the theoretical debate was that an inverse monotone relationship between the quantity of capital and its marginal product did not exist. This relation was valid only in the uni-sector case, which, however, explained little. This incoherence in logic was completely overcome in the theory of endogenous growth, since this assumed that no variable relation existed between the return of the factor and the available quantity of it. The marginal productivity of capital is constant, being determined solely by the fact that the production function is linear and independent of the stock of accumulated factor. Hence the debates on the notion of capital as a production factor, rather than being forgotten, as Pasinetti (2000) observed, have been eliminated via specific assumptions on the production function. In this regard, one may wonder to what extent a linear production function in which there is no possibility of substitution between the individual factors is neoclassical. In this way, new perspectives also emerged that linked with previous research traditions. In particular the classic theme of the relation between the distribution variables and the rate of growth re-emerged, which was not taken into consideration in the traditional Solovian model. In the new models economic growth comes to depend directly on the profit rate, this time defined according to technology, exactly as in the reflections of the authors of the classical school (Kurz and Salvadori, 1998). In short, therefore, both the structural dynamics of Pasinetti and the theory of endogenous growth share the same analytical roots, which lie in the linear dynamics of Harrod and even before that, in a multisector context, in the model of von Neumann.

The fundamental difference between the two approaches resides in the conceptual reference framework and, basically, in what they aimed to achieve. Over time Pasinetti remained loyal to his idea of the centrality of labour for analysis of economic relations, considering satisfactory the hypothesis put forward in the 1960s according to which technical progress is a form of Marshallian externality embodied in labour. Consequently, in the scheme of structural dynamics all sectors have the same importance; what counts is realising that the differences between the pace of growth and variation in demand create perennial instability which lays the premise for intervention by the state. We can therefore say that Pasinetti is more interested in the effects of economic change and how to provide the means to mitigate its negative aspects rather than in identifying the causes that produce it.

The new theory of growth changed research direction, returning to the problem of the factors that determine economic growth. To overcome the Solovian approach, two indications were followed: the scheme of scarcity and decreasing returns was abandoned and attention was focused mainly on the social mechanisms of production and dissemination of new knowledge. The accumulation of knowledge, and with it technical progress, no longer derives from the application of labour but is determined by the resources that society allocates to it. Above and beyond the number of sectors into which the economy is divided, which can also be very important, it has a hierarchical structure in which the long-period dynamics depend on what happens in the research sector, the real driving force behind the system. The theory of endogenous growth therefore proposes a series of variations on what we could call a model of pure knowledge, where a secondary role is assigned to labour. This shift of attention from the labour factor to the knowledge factor represents the important new aspect in development of the linear dynamics research programme.

8 The role of profit in the process of economic growth

A distinctive feature of the new theory of growth is indubitably the emergence of the connection between economic growth and the distribution of income, which reprises a theme proper to the classical tradition. It may therefore be of interest to compare the role performed by the distribution of income, particularly profit, in endogenous growth models and in Pasinetti's approach.

As we have seen, the essential property of endogenous growth models is the absence of decreasing returns to capital, this being the only factor to be accumulated, and therefore the tendency of the profit rate to be constant over the long period. In this context, the limit to growth derives only from the presence of non-accumulable factors, primarily natural resources. This conflicts with the traditional neoclassical model, where the profit rate tends to decline as capital grows relatively to labour. In the stationary state, the profit rate and wages are determined endogenously because they are prices which must respect equilibrium conditions.

There is a huge variety of such models where accumulation of the productive factor occurs under a regime of constant returns. In the simplest case, represented by the so-called *AK* model (Rebelo 1991), the balance between investments and savings on the one hand and the steady state condition on the other univocally determines the relation between the profit rate and the growth rate, which can be expressed as follows:

$$g = \frac{\dot{K}}{K} = sA - \delta \qquad (6)$$

where s is the saving rate and δ represents the capital amortisation share. Equation (6), albeit simple, shows the main novelty contained in recent models which is represented by the fact that a direct relation is determined between the remunerability of the accumulated factor A and the growth rate g, thus resuming an approach well rooted in the history of economic thought and which can be considered characteristic of the classical school.[2] Since profit is maintained constant as accumulation proceeds, the economy's growth rate will show no tendency to decline. Second, the link between growth and the propensity to save is re-established: in the long period an economy that allocates a greater share of resources to the process of accumulation can record higher growth. Lucas' (1988) model, in which physical capital is replaced by human capital, has the same basic structure, and the growth rate of the economy depends on the productivity of the sector that accumulates human capital, such productivity being assumed constant.

The consequences of relation (6) are profound for the neoclassical theory of functional distribution. As the marginal productivity of the accumulated factor is constant, recourse can no longer be made to the principle of substitution to explain the determination of prices and hence income distribution between the factors. The equilibrium prices lose their characteristic of being indexes of scarcity. Thus one of the central assumptions of the neoclassical vision no longer holds. On the other hand, in (6) profit is determined by technological relations with an over-favourable formulation of the production function. The typical neoclassical element remains linked to the fact that the distribution variable important for growth, profit, is determined exogenously by technology. As observed by Kurz and Salvadori (1998, p. 85), while in the traditional neoclassical theory growth was determined exogenously and income distribution was endogenous, in the new perspective the direction of the causality changes: growth becomes an endogenous fact, while the mechanisms that oversee the functional distribution of income are exogenous and therefore to be determined.

Pasinetti reaches a similar conclusion, although he gives a different interpretation of it consistently with his model, in which the ultimate source of economic growth is labour. Moreover, determination of the profit rate was a problem left unresolved in his 1965 PhD thesis, and it was treated thoroughly only in his 1981 book. In Chapter VII of *Structural Change and Economic Growth*, Pasinetti addresses the problem of defining, within a 'natural' economic system, the elements determining the 'natural' profit rate. Identifying the forces that define the profit rate is not a secondary concern in the theory of structural dynamics, which also comprises capital goods.

Pasinetti's approach replicates von Neumann's model insofar as it has the existence of profit depending on economic growth. In a 'natural' system undergoing growth, part of the surplus must be used to increase

2 This equation is very similar to the Cambridge equation, in which the accumulation rate depends upon the rate of profit and the capitalist's propensity to save.

productive capacity. From this it follows that the rate of profit on the capital invested in a certain production sector must be equal to the rate of growth of the corresponding sector, which in its turn depends on two components: the rate of population growth plus that sector's growth rate of demand. However, since the system is in dynamic equilibrium, increased demand must be matched by an equal increase in productive capacity. In a certain sense, profits must be used to finance long-period investments – that is, to pay the wages of the workers employed to produce new capital goods.

Hence, in both Pasinetti's view and that of endogenous growth theory, there is a nexus between the profit rate and economic growth. However, in structural dynamics the role of the distributive variables is reversed: it is not profit that determines growth, as in the classical approach; rather, it is the dynamics of the system that impose a natural profit rate which is consequently entirely exogenous because it is 'determined' by technology conditions. If there were no economic growth, the profit rate would also be null, according to an argument typical of linear models. In his 1993 essay, *Structural Economic Dynamics: A Theory of the Economic Consequences of Human Learning*, Pasinetti extended his conclusions by shifting his attention from the accumulation of capital to technical progress. In a pure labour economy without capital goods, long-period growth depends mainly on the acquisition, accumulation and diffusion of knowledge. Harcourt (2006) has accordingly pointed out: 'So Pasinetti, as with Kaldor, is the source, rarely acknowledged, of the conceptual basis of neoclassical endogenous growth theory that has been developing over the past twenty years and more' (p. 130).

To conclude, in Pasinetti as in models of endogenous growth, the profit rate occupies a position of prime importance. The common feature is that in both cases the profit rate is determined exogenously by the technology conditions. Different, however, is the theoretical frame of reference. In the new theory of endogenous growth, the pace of capital accumulation, given constancy of profits, is governed by the formation of saving, so that Say's law holds. In Pasinetti's natural system, which is instead rooted in the Keynesian tradition, the long-period dynamic is determined by the intensity of the evolution of demand that regulates the pace of production of new capital goods.

9 Concluding remarks

It has been observed that Pasinetti's structural dynamics constitutes one of the most interesting developments of Sraffa's analysis and, in general, one of the most important results of the Cambridge School

(Roncaglia 2005). This judgement, albeit correct, is reductive and does not take account of other important aspects which we have endeavoured to highlight here. Pasinetti's contribution, in its original version as in its subsequent developments, also constitutes an important stage in the research programme of linear macroeconomics which, having begun with von Neumann, developed after the Keynesian Revolution.

While in the 1960s the debate centred substantially on the problem of stability, with the marked contrast between the classical and the neo-Keynesian schools, Pasinetti developed an original approach, fully recovering the conceptual elements typical of the classical tradition, and primarily the centrality of the labour factor. To do so, he developed new conceptual tools, such as the notion of vertically integrated sectors, which, by reducing the complex relations between the production sectors to labour alone, opened the way for genuine dynamic sectorial analysis. His model was therefore a step forward with respect to those of von Neumann and Leontief, but above all of Harrod, again within the framework of a linear dynamic approach in which the production side played a dominant, albeit no longer exclusive, role.

The same analytical set-up also underlies the theory of endogenous growth. Following the same linear analytical scheme, the key factor was identified no longer in labour and in its ability to transform the world but in the importance of social knowledge as an independent production factor. The linear scheme permitted, on the one hand, the traditional criticisms of the production function to be overcome, while on the other, recognition of the central role of the production of knowledge induced economic reflection to address the problem of the causes of economic growth, rather than its effects. While Pasinetti defined his model as a pure labour model, the reference model for the new literature can be defined as a pure knowledge model, where it is openly recognised that the crucial point for analysing the long-period dynamics is the fact that not all sectors are on the same level and that the knowledge-producing sector is the decisive one. The contrast between these two perspectives, as often happens in economic theory, points up the different underlying visions, one centred, as in the classical approach, on the labour factor and the more recent one centred on the knowledge factor. This may be one of the elements that helps explain why the theory of endogenous growth has rapidly gained ground, while structural dynamics has remained an interesting theory but with fairly limited effects.

REFERENCES

Amoroso, L. (1940), 'The Transformation of Value in the Productive Process', *Econometrica*, **8**, 1, 1–11.

Baranzini, M. and Harcourt, G.C. (eds.) (1993), *The Dynamics of the Wealth of Nations*, London: St Martin's Press.

Debreu, G. (1959), *Theory of Value: An Axiomatic Analysis of Economic Equilibrium*, New Haven, CT: Yale University Press.

Dorfman, R., Samuelson P. and Solow, R. (1958), *Linear Programming and Economic Analysis*, New York: McGraw-Hill.

Garegnani, P. (1960), *Il capitale nelle teorie della distribuzione*, Milan: Giuffrè.

Graziani, A. (1965), *Equilibrio generale ed equilibrio macroeconomico*, Naples: Edizioni Scientifiche Italiane.

Grossman, G. and Helpman, E. (1991), *Innovation and Growth in the Global Economy*, Cambridge, MA: MIT Press.

Harcourt, G.C. (2006), *The Structure of Post-Keynesian Economics*, Cambridge University Press.

Harrod, R.F. (1939), 'An Essay in Dynamic Theory', *Economic Journal*, **49**, 193, 14–33.

Ingrao, B. and Israel, G. (1987), *The Invisible Hand: Economic Equilibrium in the History of Science*, Cambridge, MA, MIT Press.

Jones, L.E. and Manuelli, R.E. (1997), 'The Sources of Growth', *Journal of Economic Dynamics and Control*, **21**, 1, 75–114.

Koopmans, T. (1957), *Three Essays on the State of Economic Science*, New York: McGraw-Hill Book Company.

Kurz, H. and Salvadori, N. (eds.) (1998), *Understanding 'Classical' Economics: Studies in the Long-Period Theory*, Cambridge University Press.

La Volpe, G. (1993) [1936], *Studies on the Theory of General Dynamic Economic Equilibrium*, Houndmills, Basingstoke: Macmillan. First published as *Studi sulla teoria dell'equilibrio economico dinamico generale*, Naples: Novene.

Lucas, R. (1988), 'On the Mechanics of Economic Development', *Journal of Monetary Economics*, **22**, 1, 3–42.

Salvadori, N. (2003), *The Theory of Economic Growth. A Classical Perspective*, Cheltenham: Edward Elgar.

Meacci, F. (ed.) (1998), *Italian Economists in the 20th Century*, Cheltenham: Edward Elgar.

Napoleoni, C. (1963), 'La teoria dell'equilibrio economico generale secondo von Neumann', *La Rivista Trimestrale*, **3**, 590–621.

(1965), *L'equilibrio economico generale*, Twin: Boringhieri.

Pasinetti, L. (1965), 'A New Theoretical Approach to the Problems of Economic Growth', in *The Econometric Approach to Development and Planning*, Amsterdam, North-Holland, pp. 571–686.

(1981), *Structural Change and Economic Growth: A Theoretical Essay on the Dynamics of the Wealth of Nations*, Cambridge University Press.

(1993), *Structural Economic Dynamics: A Theory of the Economic Consequences of Human Learning*, Cambridge University Press.

(2000), 'Critique of the Neoclassical Theory of Growth and Distribution', *Banca Nazionale del Lavoro Quarterly Review*, **53**, 383–433.

Pasinetti, L. and L. Spaventa (1960), 'Verso il superamento della modellistica aggregata nella teoria dello sviluppo economico', *Rivista di Politica Economica*, **15**, 1751–1781.

Porta, P.L. (1998), 'Structural Analysis in Retrospect. A Note On Luigi Pasinetti's Structural Economic Dynamics', *Storia del Pensiero Economico*, **35**, 43–60.

Rebelo, S. (1991), 'Long-Run Policy Analysis and Long-Run Growth', *Journal of Political Economy*, **99**, 3, 500–521.

Romer, P. (1986), 'Increasing Returns and Long-run Growth', *Journal of Political Economy*, **94**, 5, 1002–1037.

Roncaglia, A. (2005), *The Wealth of Ideas: A History of Economic Thought*, Cambridge University Press.

Solow, R. (2000), 'The Neoclassic Theory of Growth and Distribution', *Banca Nazionale del Lavoro Quarterly Review*, **53**, 349–381.

von Neumann, J. (1945) [1937], 'A Model of General Equilibrium', *Review of Economic Studies*, **13**, 1–9.

Weintraub, S. (1985), *General Equilibrium Analysis: Studies in Appraisal*, Cambridge University Press.

3 Two approaches to the study of structural change and economic development: Kuznets and Pasinetti

Moshe Syrquin

1 Introduction

Most of the chapters in this book can be seen as elaborating or interpreting the contribution to the theory of structural dynamics of Luigi Pasinetti in his celebrated book *Structural Change and Economic Growth* (1981) and in related endeavors. These chapters share a common methodological outlook and reflect a common discourse community.

All through the period when Pasinetti's structural dynamics approach was being developed, and even prior to that, a no less significant and influential program of research on growth and structural change was underway. I refer to Kuznets' study on Modern Economic Growth for which he was awarded the 1971 Nobel Prize in economics. The main elements are already hinted at in Kuznets' 1930 study on *Secular Movements in Production and Prices* and became his main project from the late 1940s, culminating in the publication of the ten long articles in *Economic Development and Cultural Change* (1956–1967) and the monographs on *Modern Economic Growth* (1966) and on the *Economic Growth of Nations* (1971).

The two approaches would seem to have developed almost orthogonally with very little cross-referencing. The extent of these non-intersecting developments is nicely illustrated in two key recent publications on structural change. In the massive three-volume Elgar collection on *The Economics of Structural Change* (Hagemann *et al.*, 2003), Kuznets' lone entry appears only in Volume 3 on 'Patterns and empirics' in the part devoted to 'Decomposing economic growth: historical perspectives'. In the recent bibliometric survey on structural change (Silva and Teixeira, 2008), Kuznets does not even appear in the table of 'most

This chapter was originally prepared for a special session at an ESHET conference (Porto, May 2006) to mark the twenty-five years of Luigi Pasinetti's book *Structural Change and Economic Growth*. A different version appeared in *Structural Change and Economic Dynamics* (Syrquin, 2010).

cited authors in the literature of structural change' that refers to 'articles gathered from all the issues of *SCED* from vol. 1 (1991) up to vol. 18 (1) (2007).'[1]

Pasinetti refers to Kuznets in his 1993 study but only as part of a group of non-theoretical gatherers of data that includes Leontief, a reductionist view for which he was chided by Malinvaud in his 1995 review (see below).

While apparently addressing similar issues and using the same terminology I will argue (but leave the full argument and documentation to another occasion) that they are very different endeavors, with different, almost non-overlapping aims and methods. Here I further argue that the very precise aims and methods of the Pasinetti approach were not designed to serve as a theoretical framework for the study of economic development and that this is not always recognized. For the study of economic development the relevance of the structural dynamics approach appears to be limited, a point not always acknowledged.

Following a discussion of how Kuznets and Pasinetti conceive of structural change as a key ingredient in the process of economic development I conclude with some observations on the main issues that would have to be considered in a re-evaluation of the Kuznets approach today.[2]

2 What is 'structural change'?

There are many uses of the concepts of structure and structural change in economics. Some of them have a clear meaning while others are vague or worse.[3] The most common use refers to long-term persistent changes in the composition of an aggregate. In development and in economic history, structural change usually refers to the relative importance of sectors in the economy, to changes in the location of economic activity (urbanization), and to other concomitant aspects of industrialization jointly referred to as the *structural transformation*. A broader measure

[1] Some signs of change are beginning to emerge; references to Kuznets can now be found in various growth-related studies, such as Metcalfe (2003), who sees Kuznets as a pioneering precursor of the evolutionary approach, and Acemoglu (2008), who acknowledges an inability to offer 'a framework that can do justice to Kuznets's vision ... largely because the current growth literature is far from a satisfactory framework that can achieve this objective.'

[2] In this chapter I draw from several of my publications, with Hollis Chenery or alone, including 1988, 1989, 1993, 2006, and 2008.

[3] Machlup (1963) is still the best source for the various ways in which the terms have been used and abused in economics.

also considers changes in institutions by which structural change is achieved.[4]

As a cursory review of the Elgar collection (Hagemann *et al.*, 2003) makes clear, structural change also appears in various other approaches more or less akin to those of Kuznets and Pasinetti. One major approach can best be described by what it is not rather than what it is. The common elements in this approach are the rejection of equilibrium and of systematic maximization by agents, and the common label identifying them as Schumpeterian and/or evolutionary. These studies would often, but not always, refer to structural change as a byproduct of the evolution of the system, but mostly present a concept of structure which, while more encompassing, is less adapted to the economy-wide balance which figures so prominently in Kuznets and Pasinetti, whose contrast is the focus of this chapter.

Two brief digressions

a. ***Sectors***. In much of the literature on history and development, structural change refers to sectors of economic activity. One of the early skirmishes in the field focused precisely on the issue of our ability (or lack of it) to clearly differentiate among the various occupations in terms of sectors of economic activity (Bauer and Yamey, 1951). Sectors can simply represent lines of activity with no clear identity other than the ordinal indicator ($x_1, x_2, x_3, \ldots$) but otherwise undifferentiated for practical or theoretical purposes. This is the case with much of the theoretical literature on growth (a prototype would be the von Neumann model). At the other end of the spectrum in some of the development literature we have models, mostly not well formalized, where identity (of sectors) is destiny. A generic example is the staples approach where the characteristics of the dominant staple determine the fortunes of the economy.[5] In between we find most of the applied literature on growth and development in which structural change does not always figure prominently but sectors intermittently do.
b. ***Terminology***. Structural change has been the common term used to denote the changing composition in economic activity in the development literature and in economic history. While the term also

[4] But see Morris and Adelman (1988), and Acemoglu *et al.* (2002). North (1981) interprets structural change in economic history as institutional change, but almost completely omits shifts in the structure of production and factor use.

[5] See Hirschman (1977) for a very broad ranging view of staples, and Findlay and Lundahl (1994) for a more recent and more formal presentation.

appears in the title of Pasinetti's 1981 book, there has been a subtle differentiation in terminology since then. In the works of Pasinetti and kindred scholars we do find the term 'structural change' but embedded now as part of the 'structural dynamics' of an economic system, this being taken to be more theory based. 'Structural dynamics' studies can be found in the *Cambridge Journal of Economics*, in the *Economic Journal*, and primarily in *Structural Change and Economic Dynamics*, the journal specially created in 1990 to provide a receptive place for this approach. A Google search for 'structural dynamics' shows that most of the entries continue to refer to engineering applications. In this chapter, with the exception of direct references to Pasinetti, I will continue using 'structural change'.

3 Why care?

Both Kuznets and Pasinetti (and the traditions that relate to them, which, while not homogeneous, I continue to treat as such) stress the inevitability of structural change and remark or bemoan the lack of attention to it in the major theoretical works in the field.

But even if structural change is everywhere and always a concomitant of growth, there may still be a question of whether it has to be modelled.[6] Models are abstractions; it is not immediately obvious that any change is model-essential. The argument for considering it must be that otherwise we would miss something essential. As we shall see, while their analyses of the proximate sources of structural change are not too different, their rationale for its study, other than because it is there, is.

For Kuznets, and more generally in economic history and development, growth and structural change are strongly interrelated. Once we abandon the fictional world of homothetic preferences, neutral productivity growth with no systematic sectoral effects, perfect mobility, and markets that adjust instantaneously, structural change emerges as a central feature of the process of development and an essential element in accounting for the rate and pattern of growth. It can retard growth if its pace is too slow or its direction inefficient, but it can contribute to growth if it improves the allocation of resources by, for example, reducing the disparity in factor returns across sectors or facilitating the exploitation of economies of scale.

An important motivation for Kuznets' studies was the fact that structural change is a conflictive process that requires individual and

[6] A question posed by Sen and others at the Varenna conference. See Pasinetti and Solow (1994).

societal adaptations and, especially in the early stages of development, a large reallocation of population from rural traditional places to modern urban ones. These changes require mechanisms for conflict resolution. Kuznets regarded the State as having often been the arbiter among group interests and a mitigator of the adverse effects of economic change.

In Pasinetti's synthesis of the classical and Keynesian approaches, structural change poses a continuous challenge to the stability of the system. There is an ever-present tendency toward unemployment owing to the structural dynamics of the economy. Fear of technological unemployment appears to be an important consideration.

For Pasinetti, structural dynamic analysis requires new tools and, accordingly, he carries out the discussion in terms of vertically integrated sectors whereby all value can be traced back to labor. The normative component is an essential part of the analysis to be conducted, Pasinetti emphasizes, for the 'natural economy' at the pre-institutional stage. This, one of the most puzzling elements of the approach, is discussed further below.

4 Structural change in models of growth and development

Kuznets was among the few who did not adopt the distinction between growth and development. He documented and analyzed the processes of structural change over time in the advanced countries and showed it to be an integral part of the overall process of Modern Economic Growth. If development is growth with structural change then of course there is no other type recorded, or, as Pasinetti strongly argues, possible. In most of the literature, however, the two are treated as almost separate disciplines.

While formal theories of growth ignored structural change, this was not the case with most of the vast empirical and theoretical literature on economic development. Here, the process of development is usually portrayed as going beyond just growth, incorporating at a minimum structural changes and at times considering also social, political, and institutional transformations.

Models of growth

The original growth models were one-sector dynamic extensions of the Keynesian model and an outgrow of its concerns. By definition they ignored structural change, even in the multisectoral versions which continued to focus on balanced growth solutions.

In the last decade some formal models have attempted to replicate the basic patterns of structural change by modifying some of the usual assumptions in standard growth models.[7]

The main departures from the standard presentations that may lead to unbalanced growth have been, on the *demand side*, the introduction of non-homothetic preferences by positing Stone–Geary preferences (Echevarria, 1997; Kongsamut *et al.*, 2001), or by assuming 'hierarchies of needs' in consumption (Stokey, 1988). On the *supply side* the main innovation has been allowing for differential productivity growth. This was the core of Baumol's 1967 contribution to the 'macroeconomics of unbalanced growth' in which he assumed the rates of productivity growth to be exogenous. Modern versions of Baumol's hypothesis include Ngai and Pissarides (2006) and Acemoglu's presentation in his book (2008) where it is shown that Baumol's results can arise endogenously from the combination of different capital intensities and capital deepening in the aggregate.

These are most welcome developments, especially when accompanied by empirical implementation. However, their intended domain of application is still limited to only the early stages of development. Acemoglu's frank assessment is telling. I quote extensively from his excellent presentation:

> Behavior along or near the balanced growth path of a neoclassical or endogenous growth economy provides a good approximation to the behavior of relatively developed societies. But many salient features of economic growth at lower incomes or at earlier stages of development are not easy to map to this 'orderly' behavior of balanced growth ...
>
> [W]e have not offered a framework that can do justice to Kuznets's vision ... largely because the current growth literature is far from a satisfactory framework that can achieve this objective. In this light, the distinction between economic growth and economic development can be justified by arguing that, in the absence of a unified framework or perhaps precisely before we can develop a unified framework, we need to study the two aspects of the long-run growth process separately. Economic growth, according to this division of labor, focuses on balanced growth, ... approximating the behavior of relatively developed economies. Economic development, on the other hand, becomes the study of structural transformations, and the efficiency implications of these transformations, at the early stages of development. (Acemoglu 2008, pp. 693–694)

But even if structural change was not incorporated in the key theoretical models of growth, it would be very inaccurate to claim that structural

[7] The following is based (lifted, really) from the essential text by Acemoglu, certainly to become the standard reference for models of growth and development. I mention only some of the newer studies beginning with the earlier ones. For further references see Acemoglu (2008).

change has been absent from the economic literature of developed and, especially, developing countries. This applies to both empirical and theoretical studies, as long as we refrain from adopting a narrow conception of what 'theory' is. We turn now to a sample of those studies.

Some early studies relevant for development

Arguably the most important contribution to the early development literature was Lewis' (1954) model of dualistic development (and its neoclassical variant in Jorgenson, 1961). Development was seen as a gradual replacement of traditional by modern sectors and techniques – structural change fueled by capital accumulation in the expanding modern sector. Other approaches going back to Marx stressed the composition of capital or of demand (consumption and investment) as crucial.

Fisher and Clark (see Syrquin, 1988 for references) focused on sectors of economic activity, the former to draw attention to 'growing points' in the economy and the latter to point out the association of level of development with structure. Kuznets embedded this in a more comprehensive approach. He regarded structural shifts as a requirement for the high rates of growth and in turn saw the changes in economic structure as requiring

> shifts in population structure, in legal and political institutions, and in social ideology. [Not] all the . . . shifts in economic and social structure and ideology are *requirements*, [but] . . . *some* structural changes, not only in economic but also in social institutions and beliefs, are required without which modern economic growth would be impossible. (1971, p. 348)

An additional group of studies, that includes some very congenial to Pasinetti's concerns and to his approach, are the computable general equilibrium models, neoclassical or not. Multisectoral economy-wide models of the 1950s' and 1960s' vintage were primarily consistency models built around input–output relations or optimization exercises of the linear and non-linear programming type. Those models were particularly well suited to put forward a structuralist message not too dissimilar to Pasinetti's, of low or no substitution in consumption and production, rigidities, and often an implied corollary of the necessity of planning. In the mid-1970s, input–output and programming models began a transformation into price endogenous models that could mimic the working of the price system in a market economy. These models owed a great deal to two major, not quite neoclassical, precursors: Johansen's (1960) multisectoral growth model and Stone's Cambridge Growth Project, whose first publication dates from the same period

(Stone and Brown, 1962). Computable general equilibrium (CGE) models reintroduced substitutability, endogenized prices, and provided a more thorough specification of income flows, taking as a point of departure a more or less disaggregated social account matrix (SAM).

Applied CGE models in development start from a Walrasian framework, neoclassical in spirit, but invariably abandon some of the strong assumptions of the neoclassical model and introduce a variety of structural features that leads to less flexibility, to lower speeds of adjustment, and to sector or agent-specific characteristics that highlight the importance of disaggregation and the prevalence of gaps in returns across the system. At the extreme of the structuralist end of the spectrum we find a group of models close in spirit to the models of the 1950s, though dressed up in CGE garb this time, that see themselves hailing not from Walras but from KKK (Keynes, Kalecki, and Kaldor).[8]

Of the early studies of unbalanced growth only Baumol's 1967 paper on differential productivity growth is cited by Pasinetti as a relevant model of growth. Differential productivity growth has long been an important factor in studies of transformation in the economic history literature. Jeff Williamson, among others, has featured it as a prime determinant of structural change in advanced and in less developed countries. One important example would be his joint study on third-world city growth (Kelley and Williamson, 1984).

The contributions of Kuznets are presented in the next section.

5 Kuznets and Pasinetti

Following a brief illustration of the work of Kuznets on growth and the structural transformation I present a more extensive interpretation of the applicability of Pasinetti's structural dynamics approach to the study of economic development.

Kuznets and the study of Modern Economic Growth

During the 1930s there were two interesting and totally independent developments which presaged the break between growth and development.[9] One was the von Neumann model of growth and the second

[8] See Taylor (1990) for a collection of such models.

[9] At the time Schumpeter was not much present in growth or in development. Kuznets (1940) wrote a very harsh review of *Business Cycles* even while praising it as a 'monumental treatise.' The Kuznets–Schumpeter chapter remains to be written. An insightful preview of this epic interaction appears in Perlman (2001).

was the publication of Kuznets' *Secular Movements in Production and Prices*. Von Neumann's was an elegant, parsimonious representation of equilibrium in a multisector expanding economy. It took more than a decade for it to be translated and interpreted in the economic literature and another decade to be appreciated as a complete exposition of duality, minimax, etc. It became the canonical multi-sectoral balanced growth model.

Kuznets started his comprehensive project on the economic growth of nations not much before 1950; however, already in his earlier studies in the late 1920s he showed interest in growth and structural shifts. His 1930 book on secular trends looks at long-term movements in production and prices in many products in six countries. He first notes that the global 'modern economic system is characterized by ceaseless change ... a process of uninterrupted and seemingly unslackened growth' (pp. 1, 3); yet at the sectoral or national level the picture is less uniform: leadership among nations shifts over time and, within a nation, leading sectors are continuously replaced as retardation inevitably reaches former leaders. Kuznets contrasts the secular retardation at the sectoral level 'with our belief in the fairly continuous march of economic progress' (p. 5) and asks, why not balanced growth? The answer combines demand effects and technological change: progress of technique makes new goods available (tea, cotton, radios) but eventually demand reaches saturation, the pace of technical change slackens, new goods emerge, as does, possibly, competition from younger nations. With this general retardation come shifts in the relationship between capital and labor, in the distributive process, in the character of the market, in the type of business organization, and in the roles of industry and agriculture. Here, in a nutshell, are the sources of structural transformation which were to reappear several decades later with technical change and sectoral shifts as key elements of the process. Kuznets' seminal analysis of structural change and retardation was rediscovered seventy years later by Metcalfe (2003), who considers it a pioneering precursor of the evolutionary approach.

Pasinetti on growth and change

For more than forty years Luigi Pasinetti persistently and with great perseverance has argued for a view of growth as a process of continuous change, not steady balanced growth and not a traverse between such states, but a never ceasing transformational process. His earlier work came at a time when growth theory was synonymous with *balanced growth* (the Acemoglu quote above in a Lampedusan moment illustrates how much things have changed but remain the same) and capital accumulation reigned supreme. Pasinetti's work is part of a Keynesian–Cambridge tradition, but no less so it can be seen as a revival of a classical (Smithian) tradition:

Pasinetti derives what are arguably the most characteristic concepts of his growth theory explicitly from Smith: the central role of technical innovation occurring unevenly in different sectors, and the method of analysis in terms of vertically integrated sectors, found in an embryonic form in the *Wealth of Nations*. (Walsh 2003, p. 372)

The structural dynamics approach to growth attempts to pick up where the classics, including Marx, left off. It does not see itself as *an* approach along with others and in that it resembles some of the neoclassical extremes it often targets. The approach, especially in its rich original Italian variant, can be read as part of the concerted attempt to demolish the edifice of neoclassical economics and establish a revitalized classical/Sraffian alternative in its stead. Spaventa (2004), in a revealing account of the objectives and the fervor in pursuing them of the then young members of a research group sponsored by the National Research Council (The Italian NRC), recounts among the aims:

The implacable pursuit of the *pars destruens*, in order to demonstrate the incoherence of the 'traditional' theory in its entirety . . . a return to the history of analysis, in order to specify and recover the premises and the research method of the classical economists, specially of Ricardo; the attempt to heal in Sraffian terms the incoherences of the Marxian theory of value. (p. 560, my translation)

This continuing preoccupation to distinguish and distance the approach from neoclassical economics has, I believe, reduced the attention to influences outside the tradition and limited its reach beyond it.

The natural economy: normative analysis without institutions

Structural dynamics, while portrayed as a general theory of growth in capitalist societies, was not designed as a tool to understand or reconstruct the process of Modern Economic Growth, nor is it a theory with verifiable empirical implications for advanced (capitalist) or for less developed countries. Of course, this does not imply that there are no predictions or implications that can be derived from the theory but only that for these one has to go beyond or outside the core 'natural system'. Instead it is a framework for normative analysis.

To avoid misrepresenting these most puzzling aspects of the Pasinettian approach I quote extensively from the summary presentation of Scazzieri (this volume), one of Pasinetti's closest collaborators:

> While taking inspiration from ... Adam Smith and David Ricardo, Pasinetti argues for a radical reformulation of their theories in order to disentangle their structural core from institutional and behavioural assumptions of a particular type. In this way, Pasinetti's theory of the natural economic system is an attempt to turn the classical theories of Smith and Ricardo into a fully-fledged pure (and general) theory of a production economy [437–8]. Pasinetti derives the natural system from the 'deep structure' of the real economic system [458]. At the same time, Pasinetti's natural system derives from a process of analytical simplification with respect to classical theories. This is a process by which the corpus of classical theory is, so to speak, 'stripped down' to its essentials, or to its minimal core ... stripped of inessential behavioural and institutional properties. Therefore, *the natural economic system is not a descriptive tool, nor is it a tool aimed at explaining in a direct way the actual workings of the real economic system. Natural dynamics ... leads to a normative theory precisely because it becomes a benchmark against which the actual workings of any given economic system may be assessed* [457] (italics added).

If one does not subscribe to the obviousness of the normative vision, or to the methodological starting point of searching for such a system as the desideratum for theoretical inquiry, then the relevance of the scheme is severely diminished without in any way detracting from its value as a contribution to classical economics or even moral philosophy.

It is ironic that one of the strong criticisms leveled against mainstream economics by radical economists in the 1960s was precisely that it ignored institutions. As it is often the case, mainstream economics has slowly begun to address some of those issues, the most recent example being the Nobel prize to Leonid Hurwicz for his work on mechanism design and institutions. In this light the call to study a 'natural economy' at a pre-institutional level seems anachronistic, as does the emphasis on a type of 'pure theory' at a time when the tide seems to have turned towards theory strongly linked with empirical and simulation-like analysis (see Colander (2000) and Deaton (2007)).

Structural dynamics: too little substitutability and missing agents

In this section I switch from the broad overview to the nuts and bolts of the approach to examine whether it can be considered an operationally useful approach for the tool kit of the economist interested in growth and development as an empirical phenomenon. After what was said above, this analysis could be likened to setting up a straw woman. Pasinetti could, rightly so, claim that most of the argument is not relevant for the avowed purpose of his approach. Still, it may be relevant for anyone interested in applying it to the study of development. I limit myself to a very sparing presentation of issues essential for the study of development, most of which appear in Kuznets, or are mentioned as deserving treatment by him.

Pasinetti sees his theory as hailing from and building on Adam Smith. But one will not find in his work a treatment of economies of scale or of the division of labor.

The key elements in the model are Engel coefficients and fixed rates of technical change. Both of these are given exogenously, without motivation or justification. Both are said to depend on 'learning', the prime mover of capitalist growth, portrayed as perhaps the most innovative concept. Learning and knowledge were indeed neglected categories in the early theories of growth, but they were always at center stage in the Kuznets study of Modern Economic Growth. After all, Modern Economic Growth was *defined* by Kuznets as the epoch characterized by the pervasive application of science-based technology to development. Moreover, when learning is invoked in structural dynamics it is left unexplained, without any hint as to its determinants.

In structural dynamics we find techniques of production, processes, exogenously given fixed coefficients or rates, but no agents with volition (households or firms) and therefore no price-responsiveness and no incentives. The absence of incentives and decision makers leads to excessive reliance on theoretical constructs with no life of their own. A prime example are the coefficients of the 'vertically integrated sectors' (VIS). This is a key innovative tool introduced by Pasinetti for the analysis of structural dynamics. Its coefficients are simply the Leontief total (direct and indirect) coefficients ('logically identical' as per Pasinetti) and yet they are claimed to 'have a deeper economic meaning and possess ... much more favourable characteristics for dynamic analysis' (Pasinetti, 1981, p. 114). Even if one were to grant this curious claim, it is still the case that only the direct coefficients would be of any relevance to economic actors, the VIS coefficients being *ex-post* constructs relevant only to the analyst. Steedman (2004), certainly a kindred spirit, asks whether vertically integrated sectors are useful in simplifying the analysis of a changing economy. Chagrined as he appears to be to do so, he still gives a negative answer:

> Such sectors are hypothetical constructions ... whilst actual investment decisions relate to investment in actual, individual industries and even in specific production processes. ... Similarly, technical change actually occurs at the level of quite particular production activities and, while the theorist can calculate the consequent changes at the vertically integrated level, the result is just that – a calculated accounting magnitude. (p. 361)

The supply of labor is assumed to grow at a fixed rate exogenously determined outside the model, in common with most of the growth models of the time. For Kuznets, however, the relationship between growth, demography, and distribution was of such importance that he devoted more than a decade of intensive work to it after receiving the Nobel award. His last and posthumous collection of studies was on *Economic Development, the Family, and Income Distribution* (Kuznets, 1989).

On theory, endogenizing, and convergence

Kuznets regarded a general theory of growth as a worthwhile goal but a very remote one for the present (Kuznets, 1955). For him the central problem was how to endogenize what economics mostly regards as givens: technology, population, tastes, and institutions – a view closer to the Austrians than to neoclassical economics (at the time he was writing, at least) or, for that matter, to the Keynesian–classical version in Pasinetti.

In a thorough review of Pasinetti's work on structural dynamics, Malinvaud (1995), after stressing the contribution of this and previous studies, chides Pasinetti for his reductionist view of theory which would exclude Kuznets and Leontief, among others. He also analyzes some of its limitations and suggests some additions. For Malinvaud, the exogeneity of the consumption coefficients is untenable:

> In order to explain the actual structural dynamics of final demand one must refer not only to new products and to income effects, but also to price effects ... So amended ... the physical quantity system is no longer clearly separated from the price system and determined only by structural evolution of consumption demand. (p. 62)

In discussing the 'natural economy' and Pasinetti's quest for 'fundamental relevance', Malinvaud suggests three additions, all quite subversive to the structural dynamics program but highly relevant to the study of economic development:

> Substitutability between goods for the satisfaction of real human needs, scarcity of resources, particularly of non-renewable ones, economies of scale in production. (p. 65)

Learning (technical change) in its various manifestations is the engine of growth for both Kuznets and Pasinetti. As Malinvaud points out (1995, p. 64), its diffusion is 'the best solution to the dilemma of development.' Both stress that this may not be easy or automatic. For Kuznets: 'Advancing technology is the permissive source of economic growth, but it is only a potential, a necessary condition, in itself not sufficient' (1973, p. 247). Its realization, as well as its transfer across nations, requires institutional and ideological adjustments. Kuznets illustrates this with some examples from modern economic growth: the modern large-scale plants needed to exploit inanimate power are not compatible with illiteracy or slavery, or with the rural mode of life or the veneration of undisturbed nature.

Pasinetti does not address the issue of realization of the potential for technical change or its sources. He does dwell, however, on the lack of diffusion and possible downside of what he takes to be the pattern of productivity growth across countries:

> The benefits deriving from productivity increases remain in the countries that have obtained them, and are not leaked by international trade to the remaining countries of the world. At the same time the poorest countries are compelled, by the very structural characteristics of their internal demand, to concentrate their production in sectors with very low, or even zero, rates of growth of productivity. The very same principles also help to explain phenomena to which development economists have paid so much attention, such as the declining trend in the terms of trade between the countries producing primary products and the countries producing manufactured commodities (see Prebisch, 1959). (Pasinetti and Scazzieri 1987, p. 528)

The experience of globalizing developing countries in the two decades since the above was published has not resembled the dire predictions there, nor have the facts confirmed the Prebisch thesis of a secular deterioration in the terms of trade of primary producing countries.

There is a great affinity between the structural dynamics approach and the structuralist approach to development of the 1950s.[10] Both share a view of lack of substitutability in production and demand, of low mobility of factors, and more generally of lack of flexibility. The resemblance extends to a general distrust of the market and advocacy of inward-oriented strategies and planning.

To conclude this section I want to present a different, more optimistic assessment of the possibility of bridging the gap between the approaches of Kuznets and Pasinetti. In a very thorough introduction to a volume of works by Kuznets translated into Italian, Onorato Castellino (1990) regards the 1981 study by Pasinetti (in its 1984 Italian translation) as an attempt 'to move from the abstractness of the models of development to the concreteness of the Kuznetsian visions' and, after describing the work and its influences, adds that even though Kuznets does not figure among the authors cited by Pasinetti 'one begins to discern between the two an ideal thread, a certain potentiality of a dialogue: the two halves of the world will be able perhaps, someday, to communicate and interact' (pp. 37–38, my translations). It would be nice . . .

[10] See Arndt (1985). Other prominent authors who contributed to this view include, besides Prebisch, Lewis, Myrdal, Nurkse, Rosenstein-Rodan, and Singer.

6 Where to now?

So far I have contrasted two main approaches to the study of growth and structural change and found one less relevant for the historical and current studies of the process of Modern Economic Growth. I argued for the relevance of the Kuznets approach even while aware that it is not much present in the current literatures of growth and development.

Twenty years ago various studies expanded the Kuznets approach to cover the developing countries over the first decades of the post-war period (see, for example, Syrquin, 1988, and Syrquin and Chenery, 1989). There has not been much systematic comparative work since then except for growth regressions which have ignored structure and are of limited relevance for country experience over time.

Structural change is ever so hesitantly making an appearance in studies of growth of less *and* more developed countries. Even references to Kuznets, other than in its 'Kuznets-curve' guise, are no longer black-swan events. It seems, therefore, a good point to ask what would be some of the issues to consider in a re-evaluation of the Kuznets approach today. The following is a brief list of such issues further discussed in Syrquin (2008), which also contains the references to the studies and approaches mentioned.

1. How robust have been the main trends analyzed and described by Kuznets and others against the momentous changes in the international economy since he wrote? Has the economic epoch characterized as Modern Economic Growth run its course and is it being superseded by a new one where ideas become more important than inanimate power and the nation state loses its distinctive character as the main unit of analysis?
2. Resource shifts are mostly ignored in old and new growth theories. Most empirical studies find the contribution of resource reallocation to productivity and growth to be lower than expected. The principal reasons are: insufficient disaggregation and ignoring quality changes, in particular, new goods and varieties. The growing availability of large micro data sets on firms and employment and the greatly enhanced computational capacity have now stimulated research on the dynamics of firms and the process of creative destruction. Studies for both developing and more advanced countries show the following:
   - Gross flows are large; namely, focusing on net changes in employment and unemployment ignores what is a most active process of job creation and job destruction and underestimates the costs associated with gross flows.

- Reallocation *within* sectors may be more important than reallocation *between* sectors.
- Reallocation from existing firms to more productive new entrants accounts for a significant share of total productivity growth.

As for new goods and varieties, well over 50 percent of the commodities we consume today did not appear at all in the typical consumption basket in 1900. What exactly is the meaning of models of unchanged sectors when the type or identity of the output is changing so drastically?

3. The last two decades have witnessed important advances in theoretical and empirical studies of growth, trade, and economic geography. In growth theory, structure continues to be almost absent, with only a few exceptions briefly mentioned above and at great length in Acemoglu (2008). More relevant have been the developments of 'new' trade theory and 'new' economic geography. Trade in differentiated products, transport costs, density, and specialization are among the topics in these literatures with important bearings on economic structure. The fall in transport costs could lead to a reversal of the process of urbanization, a central element of structural change, as the advantages of agglomeration in cities decline.
4. What are we trying to measure?

   Sectors: The division into components must have an analytical basis, 'sectors' must differ significantly from each other. With new technologies, much of what used to be 'services' is becoming part of what used to be 'manufacturing,' and much of employment growth in services reflects contracting out (outsourcing) of work previously done by manufacturing. Determining the national location of sectors is also becoming more difficult, if not impossible; whole industries no longer migrate, manufacturing is becoming a genuinely international affair.

   The denominator – GDP?: There is a need to re-evaluate the Kuznetsian themes of delimiting what enters into the economic calculation and where to draw the dividing line between final and intermediate outputs. Structure is still an essential ingredient in studying development. But 'structure of what'?[11]

[11] While revising what should and should not go into aggregate output we would still want to retain a concept of production for the total. Moving in the direction advocated by the Stiglitz Commission (see Stiglitz *et al.*, 2009) – created at the initiative of President Sarkozy – may improve the measurement of welfare but will lose all touch with structure.

REFERENCES

Acemoglu, D., 2008, *Introduction to Modern Economic Growth*, Princeton University Press.

Acemoglu, D., S. Johnson, and J.A. Robinson, 2002, 'Reversal of Fortune: Geography and Institutions in the Making of the Modern World Income Distribution,' *Quarterly Journal of Economics*, **117**(4): 1231–1294.

Arndt, H.W., 1985, 'The Origins of Structuralism,' *World Development*, **13**(2): 151–159.

Bauer, P. and B.S. Yamey, 1951, 'Economic Progress and Occupational Distribution,' *Economic Journal*, **61**: 741–755.

Baumol, W., 1967, 'Macroeconomics of Unbalanced Growth: The Anatomy of Urban Crisis,' *American Economic Review*, **57**(3): 415–426.

Castellino, O., 1990, 'Introduzione' in Simon Kuznets, *Popolazione, tecnologia sviluppo*, Ed. italiana a cura di Onorato Castellino, Bologna: Il Mulino.

Chenery, H. B., S. Robinson, and M. Syrquin, 1986, *Industrialization and Growth: A Comparative Study*, New York: Oxford University Press.

Colander, D., 2000, 'New Millennium Economics: How Did It Get This Way, and What Way Is It?,' *Journal of Economic Perspectives*, **14**(1): 121–132.

Deaton, A., 2007, 'Letters from America – Random Walks by Young Economists,' *Royal Economic Society Newsletter*, April.

Deutsch, J. and Syrquin M., 1989, 'Economic Development and the Structure of Production,' *Economic Systems Research*, **1**(4): 447–464.

Echevarria, C., 1997, 'Changing Sectoral Composition Associated with Economic Growth,' *International Economic Review*, **38**(2): 431–452.

Findlay, R., and Lundahl, M., 1994, 'Natural Resources, "Vent for Surplus" and the Staples Theory,' in G.M. Meier (ed.), *From Classical Economics to Development Economics. Essays in Honor of Hla Myint*, Houndmills, Basingstoke: Macmillan.

Fogel, R.W., 1989, 'Afterword: Some Notes on the Scientific Methods of Simon Kuznets,' in S. Kuznets, *Economic Development, the Family, and Income Distribution: Selected Essays*, Cambridge University Press.

Hagemann, H., Landesmann, M. and Scazzieri, R. (eds.), 2003, *The Economics of Structural Change*, 3 vols., Cheltenham: Elgar.

Hirschman, A.O., 1977, 'A Generalized Linkage Approach to Development, with Special Reference to Staples,' *Economic Development and Cultural Change*, **25**: 67–97.

Johansen, L., 1960, *A Multi-sectoral Study of Economic Growth*, Amsterdam: North-Holland.

Jorgenson, D.W., 1961, 'The Development of a Dual Economy,' *The Economic Journal*, **71**(282): 309–334.

Kelley, A.C. and J.G. Williamson, 1984, *What Drives Third World City Growth*, Princeton University Press.

Kongsamut, P., S. Rebelo, and D. Xie, 2001, 'Beyond Balanced Growth,' *Review of Economic Studies*, **68**(4): 869–882.

Kuznets, S., 1930, *Secular Movements in Production and Prices: Their Nature and their Bearing upon Cyclical Fluctuations*, Boston, MA and New York: Houghton Mifflin.

1940, 'Schumpeter's Business Cycles,' *American Economic Review*, **30**(2): 257–271.

1955, 'Toward a Theory of Economic Growth,' in R. Lekachman (ed.), *National Policy for Economic Welfare at Home and Abroad*, Garden City, NY: Doubleday.

1956–1967, Ten articles on 'Quantitative Aspects of the Economic Growth of Nations,' *Economic Development and Cultural Change*.

1966, *Modern Economic Growth*, New Haven, CT: Yale University Press.

1971, *Economic Growth of Nations: Total Output and Production Structure*, Cambridge, MA: Harvard University Press.

1973, 'Modern Economic Growth: Findings and Reflections,' *American Economic Review*, **63**(3): 247–258.

1989, *Economic Development, the Family, and Income Distribution: Selected Essays*, Cambridge University Press.

Lewis, W.A., 1954, 'Economic Development with Unlimited Supplies of Labor,' *The Manchester School*, **22**: 139–191.

Machlup, F., 1963, *Essays in Economic Semantics*, Englewood Cliffs, NJ: Prentice-Hall.

Malinvaud, E., 1995, 'Luigi Pasinetti's Structural Economic Dynamics: A Review Essay,' *Journal of Evolutionary Economics*, **5**(1): 59–69.

Metcalfe, J.S., 2003, 'Industrial Growth and the Theory of Retardation Precursors of an Adaptive Evolutionary Theory of Economic Change,' *Revue Économique*, **54**(2): 407–432.

Morris, C.T. and Adelman, I., 1988, *Comparative Patterns of Economic Development, 1850–1914*, Baltimore, MD: Johns Hopkins University Press.

Ngai, R., and Pissarides, C.A., 2006, 'Trends in Hours and Economic Growth,' *CEP Discussion Paper No 746*, Centre for Economic Performance, London School of Economics and Political Science.

North, D.C., 1981, *Structure and Change in Economic History*, New York: Norton.

Pasinetti, L.L., 1981, *Structural Change and Economic Growth*, Cambridge University Press.

1993, *Structural Economic Dynamics – A Theory of the Economic Consequences of Human Learning*, Cambridge University Press.

Pasinetti, L.L. and R. Scazzieri, 1987, 'Structural Economic Dynamics,' in J. Eatwell, M. Milgate, and P. Newman (eds.), *The New Palgrave Dictionary of Economics, vol. IV*, London: Macmillan Press Ltd.

Pasinetti, L.L. and R. Solow (eds.), 1994, *Economic Growth and the Structure of Long Term Development*, London: Macmillan.

Perlman, M., 2001, 'The Two Phases of Kuznets' Interest in Schumpeter,' in Biddle, J., Davis, J.B. and Medema, S.G. (eds.), *Economics Broadly Considered: Essays in Honour of Warren J. Samuels*, London and New York: Routledge, pp. 128–143.

Silva, E.G. and A.A.C. Teixeira, 2008, 'Surveying Structural Change: Seminal Contributions and a Bibliometric Account,' *Structural Change and Economic Dynamics*, **19**(4): 273–300.

Spaventa, L., 2004, 'Il Grupo CNR per lo Studio dei Problemi Economici della Distribuzione, del Progresso Tecnico e dello Sviluppo. Una Infrastructura di Formazione e di Ricerca,' in G. Garofalo and A. Graziani (eds.), *La Formazione degli Economisti in Italia* (1950–1975), Bologna: Il Mulino.

Steedman, I., 2004, 'Vertical Integration in the Changing Economy,' in R. Arena and N. Salvadori (eds.), *Money, Credit and the Role of the State: Essays in Honour of Augusto Graziani*, London: Ashgate.

Stiglitz, J.E., Sen, A. and Fitoussi, J.P., 2009, *Report by the Commission on the Measurement of Economic Performance and Social Progress*, www.stiglitz-sen-fitoussi.fr. See also: http://wikiprogress.org/w/index.php/The_Commission_on_the_Measurement_of_Economic_Performance_and_Social_Progress.

Stokey, N., 1988, 'Learning by Doing and the Introduction of New Goods,' *Journal of Political Economy*, **96**(4): 701–717.

Stone, R. and Brown, A., 1962, *A Computable Model of Economic Growth, No. 1 in A Programme for Growth*, London: Chapman and Hall.

Syrquin, M., 1988, 'Patterns of Structural Change,' in H.B. Chenery and T.N. Srinivasan (eds.), *Handbook of Development Economics*, Vol. 1, Amsterdam: North-Holland.

1993, 'Review of Taylor, L. ed., *Socially Relevant Policy Analysis: Structuralist Computable General Equilibrium Models for the Developing World*,' *Economic Development and Cultural Change*, **42**: 193–198.

2006, 'Simon Kuznets,' in D. Clark (ed.), *The Elgar Companion to Development Studies*, Cheltenham: Edward Elgar, pp. 315–322.

2008, 'Structural Change and Development,' in A.K. Dutt and J. Ros (eds.), *International Handbook of Development Economics*, Cheltenham: Edward Elgar.

2010, 'Kuznets and Pasinetti on the Study of Structural Transformation: Never the Twain Shall Meet?' *Structural Change and Economic Dynamics*, **21**(4): 248–257.

Syrquin, M. and H.B. Chenery, 1989, 'Three Decades of Industrialization,' *World Bank Economic Review*, **3**(2): 145–181.

Taylor, L., 1990, *Socially Relevant Policy Analysis: Structuralist Computable General Equilibrium Models for the Developing World*, Cambridge, MA: MIT Press.

Walsh, V., 2003, 'Sen after Putnam,' *Review of Political Economy*, **15**(1): 315–394.

4 Analyzing knowledge flows by means of vertical integration

Önder Nomaler and Bart Verspagen

1 Introduction

Luigi Pasinetti's (1973, 1981) notion of vertically integrated sectors has proven useful in the analysis of such widely varying phenomena as productivity growth (e.g. Dietzenbacher *et al.*, 2000) and pollution (Sánchez-Chóliz and Duarte, 2003). Of course, it also plays a central role in Pasinetti's own theoretical analysis of structural change and economic growth (e.g. Pasinetti, 1981, 1993). In this chapter, we propose a novel methodological framework for analyzing flows of knowledge between the 'science sector' (i.e. universities and public research organizations) and the 'technology sector' (i.e. the application of knowledge for economic purposes by commercial firms), and for analyzing knowledge flows between economic sectors (i.e. within the technology sector). The method draws to a very large extent on Pasinetti's notion of vertically integrated sectors.

The interaction between the (public) science sector and the (private) firm sector is seen as an important determinant of the technological competitiveness of firms and, at a higher aggregation level, regions and countries. For example, it is an often-held policy view that an important reason why Europe lags behind the United States in terms of technological performance is that the interaction between the science and technology spheres is less developed in Europe than in the United States (Dosi *et al.* (2006) summarize this argument and discuss it critically).

Knowledge flows, or interaction in a more general sense, between science and technology take many different forms, each associated with specific channels and types of knowledge (Cohen *et al.*, 2002). For example, knowledge may be transferred by means of personal contacts at conferences and workshops, or by mobility (change of jobs) of researchers, by (graduate) students, by joint research projects, or by publication channels such as scientific articles and patents. With regard to the relative importance of these channels or sources, Cohen *et al.* (2002, p. 14), reporting on the outcome of a survey among research and development (R&D) managers in US firms, conclude that 'publications/reports are the dominant channel, with 41 per cent of respondents rating them as at least moderately important'.

One way of quantifying the impact of the 'publication channel' on technology development is through the use of citations by patents to scientific publications (Narin *et al.*, 1997). This makes use of the need for patents to cite the 'state-of-the-art' with regard to the invention described in the patent. An important part of this state-of-the-art is provided by means of citations, either to other patents or to so-called non-patent literature. The latter often are citations to scientific articles or handbooks. Narin *et al.* (1997) count the frequency of such non-patent literature citations and trace the nature and geographical origin of the cited works. They conclude that the 'science intensity' of patents has increased over time, as evidenced by a rise in the average number of citations to science in a single patent, that the nature of the citation links is often geographically biased (patents tend to cite science from the same country), and that there are substantial differences between technology fields with regard to science intensity. The number of 'science references' per patent has now become a standard way of quantifying the impact of science on technology (e.g. Hicks *et al.*, 2001, Leydesdorff, 2004, Tamada *et al.*, 2006).

The use of citation analysis to measure the science–technology linkage is, to our knowledge, limited to the use of citations in patents to non-patent literature. Citations in patents to other patents are sometimes used as a frame of reference (e.g. benchmark the average number of citations to non-patent literature against the average number of citations to patents), but what is usually disregarded is the second- and higher-order effects that may occur when citations to non-patent literature propagate forward when the patent that makes the citation to science is cited by other patents. It is our aim in this chapter to provide a method of analyzing this citation process, taking account of 'direct' citations, as well as the 'indirect' effects that occur as a result of the forward propagation described above. In other words, our aim is to provide a method that provides a more complete impression of the science–technology linkages than is traditionally obtained by looking only at 'direct' citations. It is for this purpose that Pasinetti's notion of vertically integrated sectors proves very useful.

We start our discussion, in Section 2, with a general conceptual framework of how technology flows operate. This sets the general context of our theoretical approach, and links it to an observable database (i.e. patent citations). Section 3 discusses the general nature of our database, and the way in which patent citations can be interpreted as indicators of technology flows. In Section 4, we provide a formal theoretical framework for assessing the science–technology linkages at the sectoral level. Our approach is based on an aggregation of the citations data and an analytical abstraction that applies input–output methods, and in particular Pasinetti's vertically integrated sectors. Section 5 presents some empirical indicators that we derive from the methodology. In Section 6, we present empirical results based on these indicators. Finally, in Section 7, we summarize the argument and conclude.

2 A graph-theoretic view of technological change

The aim of our analysis is to build a theoretical model of the flows of ideas in the inventive process. Invention, or innovation more broadly, can be seen as a process that takes labour, capital and prior knowledge as inputs and produces new knowledge. We limit ourselves here to the part of this process in which prior knowledge contributes to the development of new knowledge, and hence do not consider the role of capital and labour in the inventive process. Our perspective is based on the idea of a network graph, in which new ideas (patents) are drawn from previous ideas (patents or pieces of scientific knowledge). We will use patent citations to indicate the relationships between ideas.

The view of patent citations as a network graph rests on five assumptions: (i) the complete knowledge domain can be divided into two broad categories: *science* and *technology*; (ii) within each of these two broad categories, knowledge can further be distinguished into different types or *fields* (e.g. electronics and mechanical engineering in technology, and physics and biology in science); (iii) we can usefully analyze the technology part of the system without considering its inputs back into the science part;[1] (iv) knowledge is cumulative: prior (accumulated) knowledge embedded in a set of patents, is propagated forward if this patent is cited; (v) on average, the magnitude of the knowledge transmitted forward by a single citation is constant across citations.

Our notion of a network of ideas is illustrated in a stylized example in Figure 4.1, which displays a network of knowledge flows (patent citations). The nodes in this network (the squares, circles and triangles) represent pieces of knowledge (ideas) and the arrows connecting them

[1] The latter assumption is perhaps the most controversial, as it seems to suggest a 'linear' view in which science impacts on technology but the reverse impact (from technology to science) is absent (see, e.g., Kline and Rosenberg (1986) for a critique of such a view). Although we are sympathetic to a more interactive view of the relationship between science and technology, we are willing to accept the assumption. The main reason is that our data, which are patent citations, allow us to observe the inputs of science (the scientific literature) into technology (patents), but not the reverse.

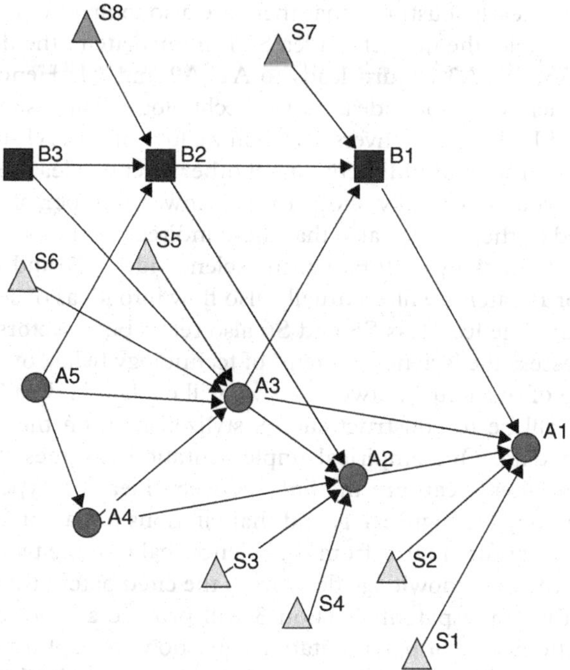

Figure 4.1 Stylized patent-citation network graph

illustrate the cumulative relations between the ideas. Thus, for example, idea A4 is an input into idea A2, which in turn is an input into idea A1. The different types of knowledge are represented by different symbols (Type A by a circle, Type B by a square and Type S by a triangle). Type S represents ideas that are in the realm of science and, according to assumption (iii), do not have any inputs from the other two types of ideas. These types, A and B, represent different fields in technology.

Relations between fields are selective and specific, i.e. some types of relations are more frequent than others. For example, in the diagram the composition of inputs into Type A ideas is different from those into type B ideas. Idea A1 takes as input two ideas of Type A (i.e. from its own field), one idea of Type B, and two ideas from science. Idea B1 takes as inputs one idea of Type A, one of Type B and one from science.

The issue that interests us is whether some types of technology have a higher dependence on, or input from, science than other types of technology. Traditionally (e.g. Narin *et al.*, 1997), this is measured by the number of citations to science, per patent. In terms of the network, this means that the number of incoming links from triangles is counted.

But the diagram clearly illustrates that there are also indirect inputs from science. For example, the impact of idea S5 is immediate in the development of idea A3, but A3 in turn leads to A1, A2 and B1. Hence S5 is 'embodied' somehow in four ideas in the technology realm, something that its shares with idea S6. Conversely, when we look at idea A1, it builds directly on S1 and S2 and indirectly on all other science ideas (S3–S8). The ideas of Type B generally show a much lower number of science ideas embodied in them. Note also that these indirect relations pan over the borders of technology sectors, i.e. the science ideas S7 and S8 that flow into sector B patents will eventually also flow into ideas of sector A, and similarly the science ideas S5 and S6 also reach both sectors.

In order to assess the 'science content' of technology fields, or sectors, we need a map of the actual network. As we will explain in detail below, our approach will be to construct such a stylized map on the basis of patent citation data. Our empirical implementation assumes that citations between patents capture the links between ideas of Type A and Type B (technology) in Figure 4.1, and that citations in patents to non-patent literature capture inputs from the science realm to the technology realm. We assume that knowledge flows from the cited patent (or science reference) to the citing patent. Section 3 will provide a more detailed discussion of the nature of patent citations and how we capture them.

Although patent databases are large (e.g. the main database that we will use has approximately 1.6 million patents), modern computers allow us to analyze the actual citation network graph that results from this and hence we would be able to make direct observations based on such a micro-account. However, this suffers from particular limitations in the available data, related to the fact that the actual databases that we have are truncated in various ways, and hence that we can observe only particular sub-parts of the whole knowledge flows network. Two types of truncation are relevant: in time and between patent systems.

With regard to time truncation, we have left and right truncation. With right truncation, the problem is that we can observe patent citations only up to the most recently published patent. For this patent, we know where its (direct) inputs came from (what it cited), but we do not know into which other patents (ideas) it will become an input. In Figure 4.1, ideas A1 and B1 are examples of right truncation. Left truncation in time results from the fact that patents and patent citations were not recorded from the beginning. For example, our patent data start in 1979 and no citations to patents prior to this year are available. In Figure 4.1, ideas B3, A4 and A5 are examples of this. We observe the patents that cite these patents, but we do not observe what they cite themselves and we cannot be sure that there are no other patents (published before the left truncation) that cite these patents.

An additional truncation problem occurs because patents can be filed under different national or international patent systems (associated with different patent offices, e.g. the European Patent Office (EPO), the US Patent and Trademark Office (USPTO) or other national patent offices). In the example of Figure 4.1, it may be the case that patents A1 and B2 are filed with the USPTO and the other patents are filed with the EPO. In reality, such citations between the different patent systems are frequent.[2] The truncation problem arises because we have only information on characteristics of patents of a single patent system (the EPO) and we lack complete information on patents in the other systems. Thus, in terms of Figure 4.1, if patents A1 and B2 are indeed outside the EPO system, we do not have specific information on them (e.g. we do not know their field of origin). Obviously, this distorts our picture since, for example, we cannot observe where one of the inputs into A2 comes from, or where A2 sends one of its outputs.

In order to avoid these truncation problems, we implement a more aggregate (sector-level) approach to mapping the knowledge flows network. This essentially consists of constructing for a single point in time a set of probabilities that a knowledge flow emerges between two sectors and assumes that these probabilities are constant in time, so that we can extrapolate them (we will test for the assumption of constant probabilities). This approach is based on the methods developed in input–output economics. In short, we avoid the truncation problems by sampling the data rather than summing it up. The sample is based on a particular generation of patents and their backward linkages (citations). We define such a generation of patents as all patents belonging to a particular year. The network representation that we build (described in Section 4) is based only on the direct citation inputs into this generation of patents, but it assumes that the indirect inputs (i.e. the citations made by the cited patents) can usefully be described by the same probabilities as observed in the single generation.

3 Patent citations: measurement and interpretation

We have already discussed briefly how we will use patent citations as a representation of the flows in our technology network (Figure 4.1). Although the use of patent citations has by now become quite widespread

[2] A further complication results from the fact that often one idea is filed under different patent systems, resulting in two 'varieties' (e.g. a USPTO and an EPO) of the same patent. The procedure we use to construct our patent citations dataset takes this into account and standardizes such cases to the single EPO variety of the patent. Details are given below.

in the literature (see, e.g., the overview of contributions in Jaffe and Trajtenberg, 2002), there are certain problems with this particular interpretation. Before we actually proceed to develop a theoretical framework and use it for empirical analysis, we briefly discuss these issues here.

Central in our approach is the notion of a patent citation. But, of course, patent citations were not introduced to facilitate the economic analysis of science and technology. Instead, the (legal) purpose of the patent citations is to indicate which parts of the described knowledge are claimed in the patent and which parts other patents have claimed earlier. From an economic point of view, however, the assumption is that a reference to a previous patent indicates that the knowledge in the latter patent was in some way related to the new knowledge described in the citing patent.

Authors such as Jaffe *et al.* (1993) and Maurseth and Verspagen (2002) have argued that the citation link can be interpreted as a knowledge spillover, i.e. an externality for the citing party. However, we are not specifically interested in the notion of knowledge spillovers but instead in the broader notion of technology flows (i.e. flows irrespective of whether they represent an externality in the economic sense), and hence accept patent citations as a broad indicator of knowledge relatedness and flows.

We will use only citations between European patents (including international patents under the PCT system filed through the EPO), i.e. we will consider only patent citations where both the citing and cited patent are applied for at the EPO. Besides a practical reason (we do not have information on patents in other systems than the US and EPO systems), there is a more fundamental reason to limit our citations information to the EPO patents. This is the fact that there are major differences between citation practices at the two patent offices. In the USPTO system, the applicant, when filing a patent application, is requested to supply a complete list of references to patents and non-patent documents that describes the state-of-the-art of knowledge in the field. In the EPO system, the applicant may optionally supply such a list. In other words, while in the US there is a legal requirement and non-compliance by the patent applicant can lead to subsequent revocation of the patent, in Europe it is not obligatory. As a result, applicants to the USPTO 'rather than running the risk of filing an incomplete list of references, tend to quote each and every reference even if it is only remotely related to what is to be patented. Since most US examiners apparently do not bother to limit the applicants' initial citations to those references which are really relevant in respect of patentability, this initial list tends to appear in unmodified form on the front page of most US patents.' (Michel and Bettels, 2001, p. 192).

This tendency is confirmed by the number of citations that on average appear on USPTO patents. Michel and Bettels report that US patents cite about three times as many patent references and three-and-a-half times as many non-patent references compared with European patents. Thus, our strategy of using only EPO citations implies that we take a more conservative view of knowledge flows.

In more specific terms, we use data from European patent applications[3] to analyze technology flows. Our data are extracted from the Bulletin CD-Rom issued by the EPO and from the REFI-dataset supplied to us on DVD by the EPO. The Bulletin dataset supplies us with the date of each individual patent, countries of residence of its inventors, and the technology class (International Patent Class, IPC) assigned to it by the patent examiner. We use the priority date of the patent (which is the date at which the knowledge in the patent was first patented, worldwide) to assign it to a year (when priority date is missing, we assume the patent was first applied at the EPO and hence use the EPO application date).

We also utilize a database supplied by the OECD covering the phenomenon of international patent families. In this context, the term patent family is used to describe a set of patents filed under different patent systems (e.g. EPO, USPTO) but covering the same invention. The Organization for Economic Co-operation and Development (OECD) database that we use (Webb *et al.*, 2004) provides a list of so-called equivalent patent numbers (e.g. EPO patent 1234567 is equivalent to USPTO patent 7654321). This database is updated using data from the Espacenet web server, which uses the same raw database as was used to construct the OECD database.

The REFI-dataset that is the source for our citations data also contains citations made in patent systems other than the EPO. The start of our citations database is a list of citing and cited patents (a so-called citation pair), covering a range of patent systems including the EPO. From this list, we identify the citation pairs in which the citing patent is an EPO patent or where the citing patent is found by our patent families database to be equivalent to an EPO patent. In the latter case, we substitute the original (non-EPO) citing patent with the equivalent EPO patent. Thus, we have, as an intermediate result, a list of citation pairs where all citing patents are EPO patents. We then select the subset of this list where also the cited patent is an EPO patent, or where the cited patent has an EPO equivalent. The final citation database, used in

[3] Below, we will use the term 'patents' to refer to patent applications and we consider these applications whether or not they are granted.

the analysis below, is then a list of approximately 1.64 million citation pairs, involving approximately the same number of EPO patents.

Obviously, related to the inter-industry point of view that we take, the assignment of a patent to an (economic) industry (sector) is crucial. We use the Merit IPC-Isic concordance table (Van Moergastel *et al.*, 1994) to make this assignment. This concordance table is based on a detailed comparison of the content of the IPC and Isic (rev. 2) classification schemes, and a matching of the activities described in both. The principle of the matching is that the patent is assigned to its most likely industry of origin (e.g. a textiles machine is assigned to the machinery sector, not the textiles sector). The concordance is done at the four-digit IPC level, and a mixture of two-, three- and four-digit Isic industries (these will be introduced below when we discuss the data). We use only the manufacturing sectors in the concordance and opt to aggregate the twenty-two sectors found in the concordance to nineteen. The concordance allows the assignment of a single IPC class to multiple Isic industries, based on a weighting scheme. This implies that patents are assigned fractionally, i.e. we do not necessarily have an integer number of patents in each industry.

4 Applying the idea of vertical integration: the knowledge flow network as an input–output system

Before we start, let us make a note on our matrix notation for consistency. A square matrix (of size $n \times n$, where n is the number of industries) will be indicated by a boldface and capitalized letter as in $\mathbf{X}$, while a column vector (of size n) by a boldface small letter as in $\mathbf{x}$ and a row vector as in $\mathbf{x}'$, where $'$ stands for transposition. We refer to individual elements of matrices by small letters with two subscripts (i.e. x_{ij} stands for the ith row j^{th} column element of matrix $\mathbf{X}$), while elements of vectors will be referred to by small letters with a single subscript (x_i stands for the ith element of the vector $\mathbf{x}$). The format $<\mathbf{x}>$ will be used to indicate a diagonal matrix (of size $n \times n$) constructed from the vector $\mathbf{x}$, which has x_i at its ith diagonal and zeros elsewhere. Finally, $\mathbf{i}$ ($\mathbf{i}'$) refers to the column (row) summation vector (i.e. $\mathbf{i}'=[1,1,1, \ldots 1]$).

In constructing a knowledge flow table in raw form, we start at the patent citation level. For each of our citation pairs, we have information on the industries of the citing and cited patents. Furthermore, patents are also classified according to the year of the priority date. We follow the usual approach in the literature by constructing a citation flow matrix **CPL** (we will omit time superscripts in our matrix notation, but all matrices refer to a specific year, unless otherwise indicated in the text) for year t, where t refers to the priority (invention) year of the citing patent (the patent that receives the knowledge flow). The rows and columns in the citation matrix represent industries of origin of the cited (row) and citing (column) patent. A column of this matrix will break down the citations made by industry j patents of year t (c_j^t) into $n+1$ (where n is the number of industries) categories such that

$$c_j^t = cnpl_j^t + cpl_{1j}^t + cpl_{2j}^t + \ldots + cpl_{nj}^t, \tag{1}$$

where $cnpl_j^t$ stands for the number of citations to non-patent literature made by year t, industry j patents[4] and cpl_{ij}^t for the number of citations to patents originating in industry i, made by year t, industry j patents. The number $cnpl_j^t$, usually scaled by the number of patents in industry j, year t, is what Narin *et al.* (1997) used as an indicator of the science intensity of industry j patents. However, from an input–output perspective, this is hardly a satisfactory measure, since it captures only the direct citations to science that industry j makes.

Let us define $v_j^t \equiv cnpl_j^t / c_j^t$ and $a_{ij}^t \equiv cpl_{ij}^t / c_j^t$ (note that by definition, $v_j^t + \sum_i a_{ij}^t = 1$). If the a's and v's are assumed to be constant over time, we can calculate the indirect science intensity of industry j patents by accumulating the $cnpl_i^t$ that are made in the patents that industry j cites (cpl_{ij}^t). But these patents in turn cite other patents, which cite non-patent literature as well as patents, and the process continues *ad infinitum*. To represent this process, which is akin to a Leontief multiplier process, we define the $n \times n$ matrix $\mathbf{A}$, whose elements are the a_{ij}^t values. In terms of its interpretation, this matrix is clearly analogous to the input-coefficient matrix of input–output economics, which decomposes the input requirements of a number of economic sectors over the sectors which supply these inputs. Let us also construct an $n \times n$ diagonal matrix $<\mathbf{v}>$ with elements v_j^t on the diagonal.

Now consider the following line of reasoning aimed at finding the total, i.e. directly and indirectly, accumulated science content (non-patent literature references) embedded in patents of industry j, year t. Clearly, $<\mathbf{v}>$ gives the fraction of 'direct science content' embedded in a single patent (per industry). But a 'second round' of science content flows from the patent literature citations and the non-patent literature that they (directly) cited in the past. This can be represented by the matrix

4 Note that we do not make any direct observation about the nature of the cited science knowledge. For example, if the chemistry sector cites a paper in electrical engineering, it will be recorded in the chemistry column, not in the electrical machinery or electronics column. Also note that we cannot observe whether a particular scientific paper (or other non-patent literature) is cited more than once. Hence we treat each non-patent literature reference as if it were unique.

product $<\mathbf{v}>\times\mathbf{A}$, which, for industry j, captures both science inputs that entered the system in industry j itself, and science inputs that entered the system in other industries (depending on **A**). Similarly, we can envisage a third round of embedded science, represented by $<\mathbf{v}>\times\mathbf{A}\times\mathbf{A}$, and a fourth round $<\mathbf{v}>\times\mathbf{A}\times\mathbf{A}\times\mathbf{A}$, etc. The complete citation chain, for a single patent, is described by the following matrix product:

$$\mathbf{D} = <\mathbf{v}>\times\,[\mathbf{I}+\mathbf{A}+\mathbf{A}^2+\ldots+\mathbf{A}^\infty], \qquad (2)$$

where **I** is the $(n\times n)$ identity matrix.

The term in the brackets is quite familiar from input–output economics. It is the power series expansion of the Leontief inverse $(\mathbf{I}-\mathbf{A})^{-1}$, which is convergent if all column sums of the elements of matrix **A** are strictly less than one, and all coefficients are non-negative (both of which are naturally satisfied in our matrix **A**). Thus, Equation (2) can also be written as

$$\mathbf{D} = <\mathbf{v}>\times\,(\mathbf{I}-\mathbf{A})^{-1}. \qquad (3)$$

Let us now define the vector $\mathbf{s}' \equiv (\mathbf{D}\times\mathbf{c})'$, where **c** is the column vector of the c_j^t values, i.e. **c** is simply the total citations (to patents and non-patent literature) made by the industries. $\mathbf{s}'$ represents the total (direct and indirect) science input in citations that has flowed into the system through the various industries, either in year t or prior to that, and transmitted forward in time through (a long chain of) patent citations. The jth element of $\mathbf{s}'$ represents total science inputs that were introduced into the system by patents of industry j.

In other words, $\mathbf{s}'$ represents the total set of science inputs that was necessary, over the history of the system, in order to sustain the science inputs that were used in the current period (i.e. the citations made to science literature in the current period). The way in which $\mathbf{s}'$ is constructed, i.e. the matrix **D**, incorporates Pasinetti's notion of vertically integrated sectors. To see this, imagine that we would produce the vector $\mathbf{s_k}' = (\mathbf{D}\times\mathbf{c_k})'$, where $\mathbf{c_k}$ is a column vector with all zeros except a 1 at row k. Hence $\mathbf{s_k}'$ is a vector that reflects the total set of science inputs, decomposed by sector of origin, that is necessary to sustain a single citation made in sector k. The vector $\mathbf{s_k}'$ decomposes the citation in sector k into its constituent parts, which are inputs of a variegated nature. In other words, the vector $\mathbf{s_k}'$ shows how sector k can be seen as a vertically integrated system.[5]

[5] One may also note the similarity between the formal definition of **D** and the formal definition of, e.g., vertically integrated labour coefficients in an input–output system. The latter is equal to $\mathbf{1}\times(\mathbf{I}-\mathbf{A})^{-1}$, where **1** represents direct labour coefficients.

The columns of the matrix **D** all sum to 1.[6] This implies that the sum of the elements of **c** is equal to the sum of the elements of **s**′. Because **s**′ represents the distribution of the 'production' of science inputs (non-patent citations), we can conclude that in the formal system described so far, the total number of citations made by patents in year t is equal to the total number of science references embodied in these citations. In other words, if we define an average 'composite' citation by the fractions a_{ij} and v_j (i.e. a composite citation made by industry j cites v science references and a_{ij} patents of industry i), this embodies exactly a single unit of science input.[7] Thus, a unit of 'pure' science references is a natural measurement of knowledge in our system.

Figure 4.2 represents a stylized example of a chain of citations that is described by the system as introduced so far. The circles represent two industries, distinguished by the colours dark grey and light grey. The squares represent the science sector. We also define two types of science inputs, dark grey and light grey, based on the sector that they feed into. The arrows represent citations between the different units (industries and the science sector) and the numbers indicate the number of citations made on a particular link. Thus, we see that for generation $t = 0$, the light grey sector makes a total of six citations, of which three are to patents of the dark grey sector, one is to patents of the light grey sector itself and two are to science references. The dark grey sector makes a total of nine citations, of which six are to the dark grey sector itself, two are to patents of the light grey sector and one is to the science sector. These numbers can be used to set up the following specific realizations of **A** and **v**′:

		Light grey	Dark grey
A	Light grey	1/6	2/9
	Dark grey	3/6 = 1/2	6/9 = 2/3
v′	Science	2/6 = 1/3	1/9

6 The vector of the column sums of matrix **D** is $\mathbf{i}' \times < \mathbf{v} > \times (\mathbf{I}-\mathbf{A})^{-1}$. Let us call this vector of column sums $\boldsymbol{\varepsilon}$. Then $\mathbf{i}' \times < \mathbf{v} > = \boldsymbol{\varepsilon} - \boldsymbol{\varepsilon} \times \mathbf{A}$, which, due to the identity $v_j^t + \sum_i a_{ij}^t = 1$ implies the equation system

$$\varepsilon_j - \sum_{i=1}^{n} \varepsilon_j a_{ij} = v_j = 1 - \sum_{i=1}^{n} a_{ij} \text{ for all } j = 1, 2, \ldots n.$$

If we define the instrumental vector $\boldsymbol{\delta}$, where $\boldsymbol{\delta}_j = 1 - \boldsymbol{\varepsilon}_j$, this equation system is equivalent to $\boldsymbol{\delta} = \boldsymbol{\delta} \times \mathbf{A}$. Clearly, unless each column sum of matrix **A** adds up to 1 (which is never the case for any A matrix in IO systems), $\boldsymbol{\delta} = \boldsymbol{\delta} \times \mathbf{A}$ solves for $\boldsymbol{\delta} = \mathbf{0}'$, which implies $\boldsymbol{\varepsilon} = \mathbf{i}'$.

7 This characteristic of the system is partly the result of the implicit assumption that in the citation system total inputs in a sector are equal to total outputs. We will relax this assumption below.

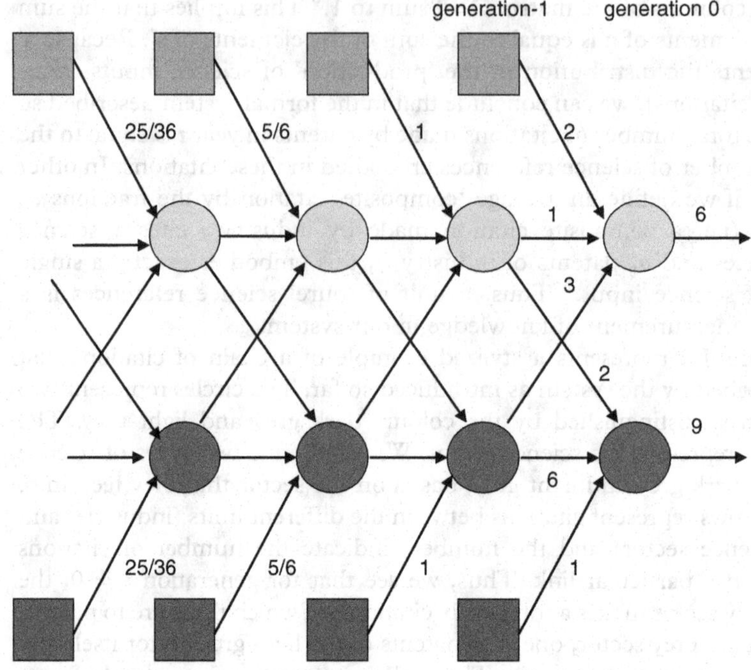

Figure 4.2 Stylized citation network graph used to illustrate formal approach

Under the assumption of a fixed **A** and **v** prior to generation 0 (this is the rightmost set of patents), we can derive the number of citations that must be present on every one of the arrows that points to generations of patents prior to generation 0. For example, at generation 1, a total of three citations leave the light grey sector (output) and this must be matched by an equal input. $v_{\text{light grey}} = 1/3$ of this (i.e. a total of 1) comes from the science sector, $a_{\textit{dark grey,light grey}} = 1/2$ of this (a total of 3/2) comes from the dark grey sector and $a_{\textit{light grey,light grey}} = 1/6$ of this (a total of 1/2) comes from the light grey sector itself $(1 + 3/2 + 1/2 = 3)$.

In this way, all the links originating directly from science have been filled in in the figure. Obviously, in order to obtain a complete picture, we would have to extend the diagram infinitely to the left. In that (imaginary) case, the sum of all values on the arrows originating from the dark grey and light grey squares (science sector) would be equal to 15 (6 + 9), which is the total number of citations made by patents of generation 0 (i.e. the sum of elements of vector **c**). **c** is represented in the diagram by the two horizontal arrows on the right-hand side.

The vector $\mathbf{s}'$ may be obtained by summing the top (light grey) and bottom (dark grey) rows of science inputs. Making the actual calculation $\mathbf{s}' = (\mathbf{D} \times \mathbf{c})'$, we obtain $\mathbf{s}' = [8,7]$. Hence, a total of 8 units of pure (light grey) science have been introduced into the system by the light grey sector, and 7 units of pure (dark grey) science by the dark grey sector. In a version of a diagram that would extend infinitely to the left, the sum of flows originating from the bottom (dark grey) science row would be 7, that from the top (light grey) 8. Note that, indeed, the sum of elements of $\mathbf{s}$ is equal to the sum of elements of $\mathbf{c}$ ($8 + 7 = 15 = 6 + 9$).

So far, our perspective has been backward, i.e. we have asked how many pure science units are embodied in the citations made by patents published in year t. We may also take a forward perspective, which asks how much knowledge (in pure science units) is passed on to future generations. Let us introduce the column vector $\mathbf{g}$ to denote this forward flow of knowledge, where the convention is that the jth element of $\mathbf{g}$ denotes the amount of knowledge passed on by patents of industry j to future generations.

Obviously, we do not observe the citation behaviour of future patents (yet) and hence there is no way in which we can observe $\mathbf{g}$. However, if we apply our assumption that at each generation incoming knowledge flows are equal to outgoing knowledge flows also to forward streams, we deduce that $\mathbf{c}$ will be equal to $\mathbf{g}$, or, in words, that the total number of citations that a generation of patents makes (by sector) is also equal to the amount of knowledge it passes on to future generations of patents. The intuition behind this is that each generation of patents simply passes on the knowledge it received from previous generations of patents (by means of patent-to-patent citations), plus the knowledge it took directly from the science sector.

The system as described so far can also be summarized in tabular form, as in Figure 4.3. A narrative of constructing this patent flow table starts with the calculation of the (row) vector $\mathbf{s}'$. This vector results from the empirically observed citation flow matrix **CPL** (Equation 1 above) and the matrices **A** and $<\mathbf{v}>$ and vector **c** that are all calculated from **CPL**. Given $<\mathbf{v}>$, we calculate the total number of citations necessary to bring the amount of knowledge represented by $\mathbf{s}'$ to generation t patents. This is represented by the row vector $\mathbf{tcm}'$. In terms of Figure 4.2, this is the sum of all arrows in the diagram, except the two right-most arrows leaving generation 0 patents.

In a similar way, and using the elements of **A**, we may fill in the top-left block of the table, which represents the patent-to-patent citations part of **tcm**. Row-wise, the elements in this block of the table represent the patent-to-patent citations that leave patents of a specific sector, or, in other words, knowledge that is transmitted from this sector to other

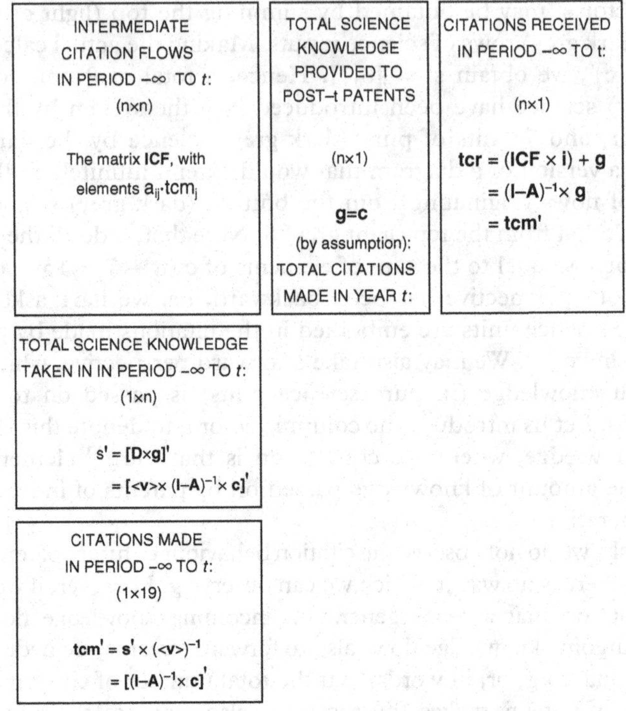

Figure 4.3 The construction of the patent citation flow table

sectors. The column vector **g** is put to the right of this, so that we capture in every row also the knowledge that is transmitted to future generations of patents. As we have already explained above, the assumption $\mathbf{g} = \mathbf{c}$ is a reflection of our assumption that each generation of patents simply passes on the knowledge it received from previous generations of patents plus the knowledge it took directly from the science sector. Finally, the rows will sum to the same total as the columns sum to, and hence we put $\mathbf{tcm}'$ as the row totals on the far right of the table.

Readers who are familiar with the Leontief economic input–output system may recognize that our constructed patent-flow table is in many regards similar to this.[8] The matrix **ICF** is reminiscent of the matrix of intermediate flows of goods between sectors. A crucial difference,

[8] Note that in our own view, an analogy between the economic input–output table and our patent citation flow table is natural, but there is no need to subscribe to this analogy in order to appreciate the calculations that we will provide in the remainder of this chapter.

Table 4.1. *Factor analysis on the indicators*

Indicator	Factor 1 loadings (science intensity)	Factor 2 loadings (pervasiveness)
Backward multiplier	−0.953	0.195
Forward multiplier	−0.917	0.263
Net multiplier	0.942	0.003
Science citations per patent	0.846	−0.400
Self-use	0.929	−0.262
Self-supply	0.605	−0.296
Use pervasiveness	−0.528	0.723
Supply pervasiveness	−0.036	0.953
per cent variance explained (cumulative)	**70.1**	**14.7 (84.1)**

Factors rotated using varimax algorithm

however, between our matrix **ICF** and a matrix of intermediate deliveries lies in the time horizon applied to construct these matrices. In national accounts, the complete chain of intermediate goods flows that leads to a final product is typically observed within a year. Meanwhile, the average lag between a cited and citing patent is typically several years, implying that a chain of several patent citations can quickly run over a period of decades. This is why we have to resort to indirect observations based on the assumption of constant <**v**> and **A** to construct our matrix **ICF** for the period $-\infty$ to t, instead of directly observing it in its entirety for a fixed period of time. The main vehicle that we use to map the assumed constant <**v**> and **A** into a complete input–output-like system, as in Table 4.1, is the vertical integration matrix **D**.

Continuing the analogy to input–output economics, science inputs play the role of primary inputs, and **s**′ is similar to a value added vector. Finally, **g** is similar to the investment part of final demand. Because we have no equivalent of final consumers in our system, all 'final demand' is necessarily carried on to the future (investment).

Scientific knowledge is brought into the system in a cumulative manner by the non-patent literature citations, given by the vector **s**′, is transmitted forward (up to year *t*) by the patent citations given by the intermediate flow matrix **ICF**, and is finally transmitted to the future, (i.e. post year-*t* patents) by the final set of **g** patent citations. Throughout this process the total number of (patent-to-patent and patent-to-non-patent literature) citations made by the sectors is given by the row vector **tcm**′, and similarly the total number of citations received by the sectors is given by the column vector **tcr**. Just similar to the equality of total expenditures to total output in an economic input–output system, in our system **tcm** = **tcr**, and similar to the equality of total final demand to total value added, in our system $\mathbf{s}' \times \mathbf{i} = \mathbf{i}' \times \mathbf{g}$.

5 The empirical implementation and proposed indicators

In actually constructing the knowledge flow table in its raw form (as represented in Equation 1), we start at the patent citation level. We represent patent citations as pairs of citing and cited patents. For each of those pairs, we have information on the sectors of the citing and cited patents. Denoting the sector of the cited patent by i, and the sector of the citing patent by j, we record this particular citation as a knowledge flow of value 1, in the cell (i,j) of the matrix called **CPL**.[9] We have yearly versions of the **CPL** matrix for 1979–2005, where the year refers to the priority date of the citing patent. Citations to non-patent literature are entered into the row-vector **cnpl**′, in the column i, where i is the sector of the citing patent. Because we look at direct citations only, the problem of right time-truncation is solved: we always observe all incoming citation links in a matrix for a particular year.

But this is obviously not the case for left-truncation: any citation to a patent that falls before the first date for which we have patent information (e.g. sector/IPC class) is not recorded. Hall *et al.* (2002, pp. 421–424) show that, in the USPTO database, about half of all citations to a particular (average) patent are made within a period of ten years. For the most recent year for which we can construct a reliable matrix (1999 or 2000), we can broadly cover cited patents over a 15–20-year time lag. Hence, we can be confident that the large majority of incoming citations are covered.

The problem of truncation between patent systems is somewhat harder to deal with in a completely adequate way, although we did correct partially for this by using the (updated) OECD database of patents equivalents (see above). But we still have the problem that we do not capture all patent-to-patent citations, while we capture all (direct) citations to the non-patent literature. This will bias the value of elements of matrix <**v**> upward. We discuss this problem in more detail in the working paper version of this chapter, where we conclude that an

[9] As explained above, our IPC-Isic concordance sometimes assigns a patent to multiple Isic sectors, with particular weights assigned to each of the sectors. We apply a fractional counting method for these cases. The value assigned to cell (i,j) of the matrix is equal to the product of the weights of the sectors i and j. Because the set of weights sums to one for both the citing and cited patent, each citation will count for one after it has been divided over all possible combinations of citing and cited sectors.

imperfect correction for this truncation problem is feasible.[10] We have used this correction method on our data, but choose to report results based on uncorrected data. The impact of the correction is not large and corrected results are available on request.

Indicators

Based on the input–output tables discussed so far, we construct a number of indicators aimed at scoring the sectors in terms of their role in the knowledge transfer system. We discuss these indicators one by one. As will become clear, the vertical integration matrix $\mathbf{D} = <\mathbf{v}> \times (\mathbf{I} - \mathbf{A})^{-1}$ will play an important role in these indicators and hence it is central in both the construction of the patent citation flow table and the indicators we build on it.

Backward multipliers

In input–output economics, backward multipliers capture the general idea that due to the derived demand for intermediate goods, an increase in demand for one sector will increase the total gross production of the economy by more than the original increase in demand. Furthermore, the resulting output increase is not confined to the sector where the original increase in demand takes place. Backward multipliers are generally calculated as the column j sum of the so-called Leontief inverse, i.e. $\mathbf{i}' \times (\mathbf{I} - \mathbf{A})^{-1}$. Similarly, defined backward multipliers are useful indicators in our patent citation flows table, although their interpretation is not completely analogous to input–output economics.

Let the vector $\boldsymbol{\lambda}_t$ denote the counterpart of the backward multiplier vector as applied to the constructed cumulative citation-flows table year t. That is, let

$$\boldsymbol{\lambda}_t' = \mathbf{i}' \times (\mathbf{I} - \mathbf{A}_t)^{-1} \tag{4}$$

Given this specification, for each industry j, the backward multiplier λ_{tj} indicates the total number of patent-to-patent citations that is necessary to make one (extra) unit of composite scientific knowledge available in year t patents of industry j, which can, in turn, be transmitted forward to post year t patents (of various industries). In terms of Figure 4.2, the backward multiplier measures what happens, under constant input-coefficients, if the right-most arrow in one of the sectors is increased

[10] The working paper version is available, among others, at www.merit.unu.edu as Working Paper 2007–22.

by one. For this to happen, the value of science inputs (arrows originating from squares) in the diagram will also have to increase by one. The backward multiplier measures by how much the value of the arrows between patents (circles) will have to increase to accommodate this increase.

Because there is a strict generational separation between the citations in the diagram, and the input coefficients are fixed, an increase of the value on the patent-to-patent arrows in the figure corresponds to a citation chain that stretches further and deeper to the left (i.e. backwards in time). Hence the backward multiplier is also an indicator of the average time-lag for scientific knowledge to become embodied in the present generation of patents (and available for future citation) and hence an indicator for the relative age of knowledge accumulated in the patents of the industry.

Let us give a single-sector example to clarify the interpretation of these backward multipliers. Assume that out of all citations, $100x$ $(0 < x < 1)$ per cent goes to NPL and $100(1-x)$ per cent goes to other patents. Note that with smaller x, less science knowledge flows in at the present generation of patents, or, in other words, more science knowledge flows in at earlier generations. With constant x, this naturally holds at all generations, which implies that with smaller x, the average age of the knowledge embodied in current generations is higher.

Our notation implies that the 1×1 input-coefficient matrix $\mathbf{A}=1-x$ and $\mathbf{v}=x$. Thus, x of a one-unit increase of knowledge accumulated in year t patents comes from the x immediate NPL citations. The rest of the knowledge comes from the $1-x$ citations that are directed to older patents, which pass on 'second-hand' scientific knowledge to generation t. The second-hand knowledge transmitted by these $1-x$ citations had been supplied by the $x(1-x)$ NPL citations of the previous generation patents, plus $(1-x)^2$ patent citations directed to the earlier generation of patents. Similarly, the knowledge transmitted by these $(1-x)^2$ patent citations had been supplied by the $x(1-x)^2$ NPL citations of the previous generation patents, plus $(1-x)^3$ patent citations directed to the (even) earlier generation of patents. Keeping on compounding backwards through the history of citations, it is confirmed that each unit of knowledge accumulated in patents of t was introduced into the system by a total of $x + x(1-x) + x(1-x)^2 + \ldots + x(1-x)^\infty = 1$ NPL citations, and this was transmitted to patents of t through a total of $(1-x) + (1-x)^2 + \ldots + (1-x)^\infty$ patent-to-patent citations. Adding up these two numbers, we arrive at the total number of citations (to patent and non-patent literature) that is responsible for the extra unit of knowledge accumulated in patents of year t, which is equal to $1+(1-x)+(1-x)^2+ \ldots + (1-x)^\infty = 1/x$. Thus, the backward multiplier λ is equal to

$1/x$, and since x is related to average age of embodied knowledge, the multiplier serves as an indicator of age. More precisely, since x is inversely related to average age of embodied knowledge, the multiplier is positively related to this.

Note that since $\mathbf{D} = <\mathbf{v}> \times (\mathbf{I} - \mathbf{A})^{-1}$ as described in Equation (3), one can also express the backward multipliers as $\boldsymbol{\lambda}_t' = \mathbf{i}' \times <\mathbf{v}>^{-1} \times \mathbf{D}$, or equivalently as $\lambda_j = \sum_{i=1}^{N} \left(\frac{1}{v_i} \cdot D_{ij} \right)$. This implies that the backward multipliers are actually the weighted average of the (inverse of the) share of non-patent literature citations of all sectors, where the set of weights for each sector j is given by the shares of each sector-specific type of scientific knowledge embedded in the total knowledge stock of sector j patents.

This underlines again the crucial role of the notion of vertical integration in our analysis: our backward multipliers are structural indicators that reflect the idea of vertically integrated sectors. The citation network structure captured by our patent citations flow table indicates that, at the industrial aggregate level, only a part of the scientific knowledge that is eventually transmitted to industry j patents of year t comes from the immediate NPL citations of this industry itself. Another good deal comes from citations to older patents, including some of other industries, and this goes back in time *ad infinitum*. Thus, the total knowledge embodied in current-generation patents is generally a mixture of bits and pieces of various types of industry-specific knowledge, and the backward multipliers capture this.

Forward multipliers

These multipliers are technically similar to the backward multipliers but they are based on output coefficients, not on input coefficients. Accordingly, in economics, these multipliers capture supply-push effects rather than demand-pull effects. The forward multiplier of industry j indicates the increase in total expenditures of the economy that would be caused by a unit increase in sector j value added. Since the idea of a supply-driven model was originally introduced by Ghosh (1958), these multipliers are also referred to as the Ghosh multipliers.

Although the direct citation matrix $\mathbf{A}$ that we collect from the data does not allow the calculation of output coefficients, once the cumulative patents citations flow table (Figure 4.3) is constructed, one can calculate an output coefficient matrix $\mathbf{B_t}$, where $b_{t,ij} = icf_{t,ij}/tcr_{t,j}$. Given this matrix, the vector of forward multipliers is calculated as

$$\gamma_\mathbf{t} = (\mathbf{I} - \mathbf{B_t})^{-1} \times \mathbf{i}. \tag{5}$$

In the context of the patent citation network, these forward multipliers have the following interpretation. For each industry *j*, the forward multiplier $\gamma_{t,j}$ indicates the total number of citations necessary to transmit one (extra) unit of industry *j*-specific scientific knowledge, through the citation network, to patents of year *t* (of potentially a number of different industries). In line with the interpretation of the backward multiplier, the forward multiplier of industry *j* is a relative indicator of the average age of industry *j*-specific scientific knowledge (i.e. knowledge introduced by industry *j* patents), as embodied in the current generation of patent citations. The intuition in terms of age of knowledge behind these forward multipliers is quite similar to that of the backward multipliers (in a single-sector world, e.g. forward and backward multipliers are equal).

Still, forward and backward multipliers are quite different in terms of their interpretation. While backward multipliers are about the process of accumulation of the pool of different types of knowledge embodied in patents of a given industry, the forward multipliers are about the process through which a given type of knowledge is transmitted forward and distributed over the patents of all industries. This highlights the importance of a conceptual distinction between the two alternative temporal directions in which one can look at our cumulative citation flows system (cf. Figure 4.2). A backward-looking approach perceives the patents of different industries as different sinks. A different composition of a variety of types of industry-specific scientific knowledge of different industries eventually accumulates in each sink, and the backward-looking approach considers the composition of knowledge found in each sink. The forward-looking approach, meanwhile, looks at sources, each of which introduces a different type of industry-specific scientific knowledge and distributes these forward over the patents of a variety of industries.

The next indicator that we will discuss below aims at analyzing the relative strength of the patents of different industries in terms of their double role in performing as sources and sinks at the same time. As we will argue, some industries are relatively more active in their role to perform as sources than they are in performing as sinks and vice versa.

Net science multipliers

The magnitude g_i ($= c_i$) reflects the vertically integrated nature of the sectors in the knowledge flow table; it is the amount of *composite* scientific knowledge that is accumulated in industry *i* patents of year *t*, which is made available to future (i.e. post year *t*) patents. s_i is the amount of *pure* industry *i*-specific scientific knowledge which is introduced into the patent system by industry i patents during the time interval $[-\infty, t]$ and distributed over patents of various industries. $g_i > s_i$ would indicate that industry i patents are more important as sinks of knowledge than as sources, and vice versa for $s_i > g_i$. Therefore, we define a ratio μ_{ti}, which is the ratio of scientific knowledge introduced by *all* industries, which eventually ends up in industry i patents of year t, and the scientific knowledge introduced by industry i that ends up in all patents of year t. Thus $\mu_{ti} > 1$ (<1) would indicate that industry i is a net knowledge supplier (user).

We note that this idea is quite similar to what Oosterhaven and Stelder (2002) call net multipliers in an economic input–output context. Dietzenbacher (2005) shows that such net (value added) multipliers give the ratio of value added to final demand. This is obviously very similar to our source/sink interpretation of knowledge flows. This is why we call this indicator the net science multiplier indicator. Following Oosterhaven and Stelder (2002) and Dietzenbacher (2005), we calculate the row vector $\boldsymbol{\mu}_t$, which is a vector whose i^{th} element is equal to $\mu_j = g_i/s_i$, as follows:

$$\mu_t' = \mathbf{s}' \times <\mathbf{tcm}>^{-1} \times (\mathbf{I} - \mathbf{A})^{-1} \times <\mathbf{g}> \times <\mathbf{s}>^{-1}. \tag{6}$$

On the basis of Table 4.1 (i.e. $\mathbf{tcm} = (\mathbf{I}-\mathbf{A})^{-1} \times \mathbf{c}$ and $\mathbf{s}' = [<\mathbf{v}> \times (\mathbf{I}-\mathbf{A})^{-1} \times \mathbf{c}]'$), and also letting $\mathbf{L}$ denote the Leontief inverse $(\mathbf{I}-\mathbf{A})^{-1}$, it is clear that the element in the jth diagonal of the inverse matrix $<\mathbf{tcm}>^{-1}$ is $1/\sum_{j=1}^{N} L_{ij}C_j$, whereas the ith element of the row vector $\mathbf{s}'$ is $v_i \sum_{j=1}^{N} L_{ij}C_j$, which implies that the term $\mathbf{s}' \times <\mathbf{tcm}>^{-1} = \mathbf{i}' \times <\mathbf{v}>$. Consequently, given $\mathbf{i}' \times <\mathbf{v}> \times (\mathbf{I}-\mathbf{A})^{-1} = \mathbf{i}'$, the calculation of $\boldsymbol{\mu}_t$ reduces to

$$\mu_t' = \mathbf{i}' \times <\mathbf{g}> \times <\mathbf{s}>^{-1}. \tag{7}$$

Self-reliance of sectors

The matrix $\mathbf{D} = <\mathbf{v}> \times (\mathbf{I} - \mathbf{A})^{-1}$ breaks the embedded knowledge in the patents of each sector down to its sector-specific components. The extent to which a sector relies on scientific knowledge introduced by itself, i.e. the extent to which the vertically integrated sector and the actual sector 'overlap', can be assessed by looking at the weight on the diagonal of this matrix. The most straightforward way of measuring this is simply

$$\delta_j = D_{jj},$$

which we refer to as the self-use of knowledge indicator. It is the share of sector j-specific knowledge in the composite knowledge mix of sector j patents.

Similar to **D**, we construct a matrix **K** that decomposes the knowledge supplied by an industry i in terms of the industries that use its knowledge. This uses the output coefficient matrix $\mathbf{B_t}$ as well as the diagonal matrix $<\mathbf{f}>$, which has the ratio g_j/tcr_j (i.e. the share of citations received by industry j patents of year t in all citations received by industry j patents of $[-\infty, t]$) on its jth diagonal. The matrix

$$\mathbf{K} = (\mathbf{I} - \mathbf{B})^{-1} \times <\mathbf{f}> \tag{8}$$

is then quite similar to **D**: k_{ij} gives the share of the industry i-specific knowledge (introduced and transmitted by industry i patents in $[-\infty, t]$) which is eventually transmitted to industry j patents of year t. Since these are shares, all row sums of **K** are equal to 1 ($\mathbf{K}\times\mathbf{i}=(\mathbf{I}-\mathbf{B})^{-1}\times<\mathbf{f}>\times\mathbf{i}=\mathbf{i}$). Using **K**, we introduce a similar measure to δ, but which focuses on the knowledge supply of the sectors. This is

$$\kappa_j = K_{jj},$$

which is the share of sector i-specific scientific knowledge transferred by sector i to itself, or the self-supply indicator. It is an indicator of how much a sector generates internal knowledge versus knowledge that is used by other sectors.

Pervasiveness of knowledge suppliers and users

Independently of the amount of knowledge that an industry supplies to the aggregate system, or the amount that it uses, the distribution of its knowledge supply or demand over the range of industries is an important indicator. For example, the distribution of knowledge inputs of a certain industry over all industries in the system indicates to which extent that industry is dependent on a small range of industries for its (ultimate) knowledge inputs. Similarly, the distribution of knowledge supply of an industry over all industries is an indication of how pervasive knowledge of a particular industry is.

We may again use the idea of vertical integration or the matrix $\mathbf{D} = <\mathbf{v}> \times (\mathbf{I} - \mathbf{A})^{-1}$ to construct an indicator for this. We start by looking at the off-diagonal elements of this matrix (the diagonal elements are captured in the previous indicator) and consider the column for every sector. For this column, we calculate an inverse Herfindahl index for industry j as

$$h_j^{src} = \frac{1}{\sum_{i=1}^{N,i\neq j} \left(\frac{d_{ij}}{1-d_{jj}}\right)^2}. \tag{9}$$

This gives the Herfindahl equivalent number of industries that supply industry j with various types of industry-specific scientific knowledge, and is an inverse index of concentration of the knowledge sources of industry j. Clearly h_j^{src}, which is our indicator of knowledge-use pervasiveness, indicates the variety in inter-industrial backward citation linkages between industry j and all other industries.

Similarly, we construct an inverse Herfindahl indicator for knowledge supply, using the row-wise, off-diagonal elements of **K** as follows:

$$h_j^{snk} = \frac{1}{\sum_{i=1}^{N, i \neq j} \left(\frac{k_{ij}}{1 - k_{jj}} \right)^2}. \tag{10}$$

h_i^{snk} gives the Herfindahl equivalent number of industries that eventually embed the industry i-specific knowledge that is introduced and transmitted by industry i patents. It indicates the variety in inter-industrial forwards citation linkages between industry i and all other industries, and is a measure of how pervasively industry i influences the other industries in the system.

6 Empirical results

Our research question is about the impact of science on technology and about the insights that can be gained by our proposed inter-sectoral approach in comparison to an approach based on the single indicator of the number of patent-to-science citations per patent. The patent citation flow table that we constructed depends crucially on the citation structure between sectors being stable over time, because we use citation data on patents of a single year and assume fixed coefficients in backcasting the flow of citations that feeds into these patents. The working paper version of this chapter (see note 10) includes a section that extensively documents this time-invariance empirically, which is why we can be confident that the assumption of time-invariance of the **A** matrix is reasonable, and this justifies the power series expansion interpretation of the Leontief inverse, which lies at the very core of our vertically integrated sectors-based approach. Thus we present here the results for 1992, which is representative of the other years between 1985 and 2004.

Given our interest in the value added of the inter-sectoral approach, we start our empirical analysis by a factor analysis of the various indicators. This enables us to reduce the number of dimensions in which we score the sectors and to assess the role of the traditional indicator (patent-to-science citations) in comparison with the other indicators. In addition to this indicator, we include the forward and backward multipliers, the net multipliers, the two diagonal share indicators and the two pervasiveness indicators. All of these indicators have been introduced above; their numerical values are documented in Appendix 4.2. The results of the factor analysis (principal components) are documented in Table 4.1.

The results show very clearly that the science citations per patent indicator capture only one dimension in the data. This is the first factor and hence the one that explains the largest proportion of the variance (almost 70 per cent). This factor loads high on the number of science citations per patent, on the net multiplier, on self-use and, to a lower extent, self-supply. It loads strongly negative on backward and forward multipliers and, to a lesser extent, on use pervasiveness. We label this factor 'science intensity', although this does not cover the complete content of the factor. In particular, the loadings suggest that science intensity implies low backward and forward multipliers, and high self-dependence of the sector.

The results for the backward and forward multipliers are in line with our expectations, based on the interpretation of the multipliers as the average age of the scientific knowledge embodied in patents. Sectors that are highly science intensive have a rapid turnaround time of scientific knowledge and hence score low on both types of multipliers. Interestingly, the normative interpretation of these multipliers (interpreted in terms of age of knowledge) runs against the interpretation in economic input–output accounts, where high multipliers usually have a positive normative interpretation.

Note that the result is quite opposite for the net multiplier, which captures to what extent a sector is a net supplier or user of knowledge. Here we observe a positive correlation between the science intensity and the net multiplier, i.e. highly science-intensive sectors are generally responsible for a larger fraction of the knowledge introduced into the system than the fraction of knowledge used.

The first factor also shows that high science intensity comes with high self-dependence, especially so in terms of using knowledge. Note that this is, contrary to the result for the backward and forward multipliers, not related to any specific mechanism embedded in the definition of these indicators. However, it is intuitively plausible if we accept that scientific knowledge is specific to the sectors in our analysis: if a sector depends highly on input of scientific knowledge, and if this knowledge is specific, it will have to rely to an important extent on sourcing this knowledge itself.

More interesting from the point of view of our intersectoral perspective is the second factor, which explains around 15 per cent of the variance. This is the factor that has a factor loading for the number of science citations per patent that is relatively low, even in terms of its absolute value (e.g. the absolute value of 0.4 is below a threshold of ½ that is often used to indicate important factor loadings). This means that the second factor captures an element in the data that is not strongly related to the direct science intensity of a sector. Hence this aspect is specific to the inter-sectoral approach that we used and would not be apparent in the usual approach of looking only at the number of science citations per patent.

The second factor loads high only on the two pervasiveness indicators. High values of these indicators (inverse Herfindahl) indicate that a sector caters its knowledge to a broad range of other sectors (supply), or sources its knowledge from a broad range of other sectors (use). The factor loadings indicate that these two processes (pervasive use and supply) tend to go together, but they are largely uncorrelated to the first dimension of science intensity.

Hence we conclude that science intensity and pervasiveness of sectors in terms of knowledge flows are two separate dimensions. The first of these, science intensity, may well be captured by the normal approach of measuring science citations per patent, but it says very little about pervasiveness of knowledge flows from a sector. This suggests that the value added of a multisectoral approach lies mainly in being able to provide a better picture of the pervasiveness of knowledge flows.

We have already seen that science intensity, as measured by the number of science citations per patent, tends to be related to the net multiplier, i.e. whether sectors are net suppliers or users of knowledge. Figure 4.4 plots these two indicators against each other. The relationship occurs as somewhat non-linear, with the net multiplier flattening off for high values of science intensity. The figure also shows that the observations (roughly) fall into two quadrants: sectors with more than half a science citation per patent are the ones that have a net multiplier of one or higher.

Figure 4.5 plots the two indicators that provide additional information relative to the dimension of science intensity, i.e. the two pervasiveness indicators. There is a broad positive relation between them, but it is far from perfect. The figure allows us to broadly classify the sectors in two ways. First, we can observe that there is a dichotomy between the sectors in terms of their general level of pervasiveness (both use and supply): we have a group of sectors on the bottom left of the figure and one on the top right, with only a very limited number of observations in between

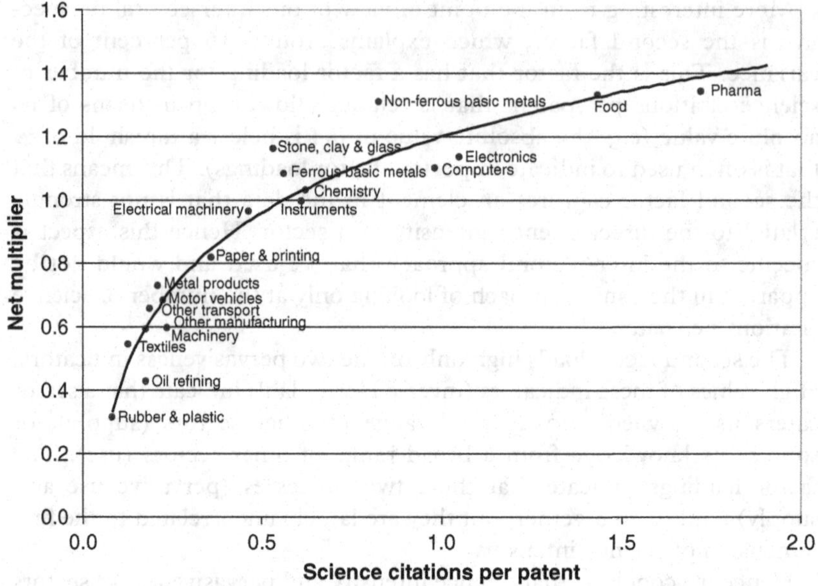

Figure 4.4 Science intensity and net science multipliers (λ and γ)

(motor vehicles and electrical machinery). Interestingly, among the sectors in the low-pervasiveness part of the graph, we predominantly find sectors that also have high science intensity and a high net multiplier (cf. Figure 4.4). Oil refining is the only sector that is clearly in the low-pervasiveness group *and* it has a low science intensity and net multiplier. All the other sectors with low pervasiveness have net multipliers very close to or larger than one (and correspondingly, high science intensities, >½ science citation per patent). Some of the highly science-intensive sectors, those related to materials (basic metals, stone, clay and glass, rubber and plastic), are among the highly pervasive ones, together with paper and printing, and machinery.

Thus, there are a few sectors that are exceptions to the general tendency for science-intensive sectors to have low pervasiveness. Instruments is the strongest exception, but also the two basic metals sectors and stone, clay and glass. These are all sectors that have high science intensity and corresponding high multipliers, but also high pervasiveness. Note that instruments is the only sector in this list of exceptions that is generally considered as high-tech.

The second way in which we can classify the sectors in Figure 4.5 is by whether they are particularly pervasive in terms of supply or use of

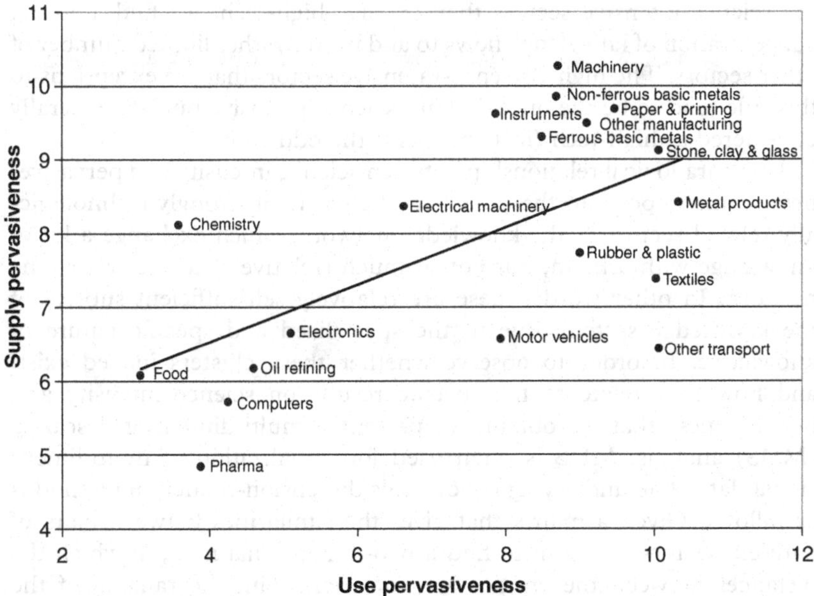

Figure 4.5 Use pervasiveness versus supply pervasiveness

knowledge. This can be evaluated on the basis of whether sectors are above or below the regression line. Sectors that are above (below) the line are particularly pervasive with regard to their knowledge supply (use). In the group of sectors with low pervasiveness, most are relatively more pervasive in terms of their use than in terms of their supply. Chemistry is the only exception – it is relatively much more pervasive with regard to its supply than with regard to its use. In the group of highly pervasive sectors, the sectors are more evenly distributed above or below the regression line. Interestingly, the sectors with high science intensity (science citations per patent) tend to be above the line, the low science intensity sectors below the line.[11]

We are thus left with a somewhat paradoxical situation. The science-intensive (and often high-tech) sectors appear to be the largest net suppliers of knowledge (according to our net science multiplier measure, $\mu_j>1$), but only in a limited number of cases does this come together with a pervasive influence on a large range of other sectors. Especially in

[11] The positive correlation between science intensity and supply/use pervasiveness is confirmed by a plot of science citations per patent versus supply/use pervasiveness (not documented but available on request).

the science-intensive sectors that are also high-tech, we find a strong concentration of knowledge flows to and from a rather limited number of other sectors. The highly science-intensive sectors that are exceptions to this rule tend to be the ones that are science intensive but not generally considered as high-tech (instruments is the odd case).

This paradoxical relationship between science intensity and pervasiveness seems to point to the existence of clusters of strongly technologically related sectors in the knowledge network, which exchange a lot of knowledge within them, but not so much (relatively) to the rest of the network. In other words, these are relatively self-sufficient subsets of the knowledge system, due to the specialized and specific nature of knowledge. In order to observe whether these clusters indeed exist, and how they relate to the specific results on science intensity and pervasiveness that we obtain, we present a multi-dimensional scaling (MDS) analysis. MDS is often used for visualization of multidimensional data. The underlying logic of this dimension-reduction method is as follows. Given a matrix that gives the similarities between pairs of entities (sectors), we aim to find a two-dimensional map, in which the distances between the entities are consistent with the ranking of the inverse similarities in the original matrix. A heuristic algorithm is used to find such a map in an iterative way. Note that the (horizontal and vertical) dimensions on this map have no other function than to provide a number of degrees of freedom for the mapping (a 3D mapping would provide better results, but the 2D map we use is easier to interpret) and they have no particular *a priori* interpretation. The MDS analysis is based on an indicator of mutual dependency between the sectors, which we explain in detail in Appendix 4.1. This indicator is based on our matrices **D** and **K**.

The MDS results are in Figure 4.6, where we observe three distinct clusters, plus a large group of sectors in the centre of the graph. Note that the fact that two sectors are near to each other in this map is an indication of the fact that they have intensive knowledge-exchange relationships. The three (peripheral) clusters indeed correspond closely to the general intuition about technological relatedness. The first cluster, on the left of the figure, includes sectors that are strongly related to ICTs (electronics, electrical machinery, computers and office equipment, and finally instruments somewhat closer to the centre). The sectors of the second cluster (pharmaceuticals, chemistry and food products) share an agri-bio focus. The third cluster (ferrous and non-ferrous basic metals) is metallurgy-based. As the pervasiveness indicators suggested, the large group of sectors in the middle show a much weaker mutual interdependence structure, and the dependence of each sector in the centre is rather

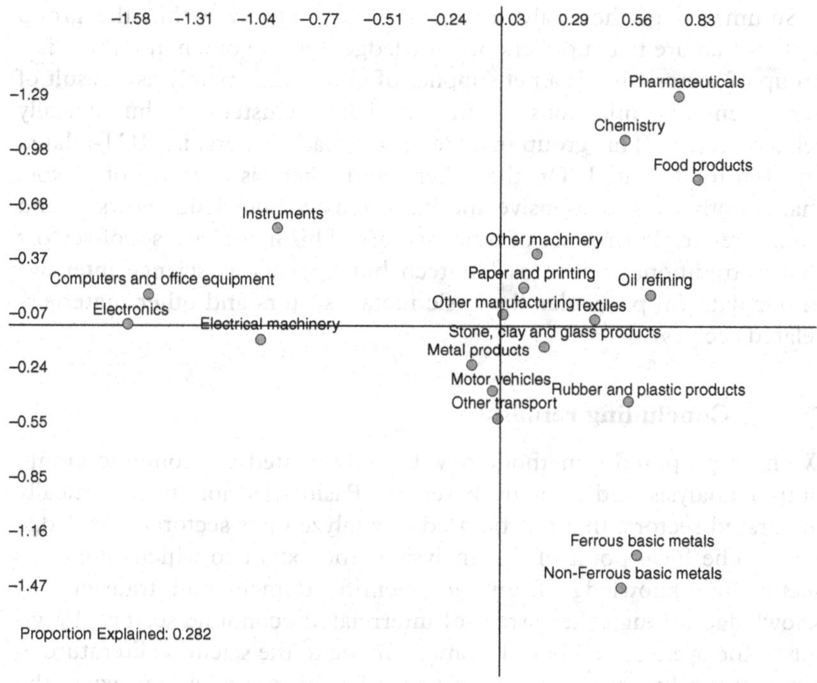

Figure 4.6 MDS map of mutual knowledge dependencies among the sectors

distributed. These sectors also have relations with each of the three other clusters.

This map of technological relatedness suggests that the dual structure of the relationship between science intensity and pervasiveness of knowledge flows is rooted in the existence of the three clusters. Both the agri-bio and ICT clusters have strong internal knowledge flows and this leads to the emergence of their central sectors (e.g. pharmaceuticals in the agri-bio cluster, electronics and computers in the ICT cluster) as net knowledge suppliers. However, the influence of these central sectors is much stronger within the cluster than in the total system, leading to their limited pervasiveness.

This is much different for the metallurgy cluster. This is made up of only two sectors, which are strongly related, but are also small and have a more pervasive linkage to the rest of the system. In other words, they lack the relatively strong internal dynamics found in the other clusters and hence appear as much more pervasive.

Summarizing, the analysis suggests a dichotomy within the group sectors that are net suppliers of knowledge. On the one hand, there is a group of sectors that is a net supplier of knowledge mainly as a result of very intensive connections within a specialized cluster of technologically related sectors. This group includes two broad clusters, i.e. ICT-related and bio-food-related. On the other hand, there is a group of sectors that is both science intensive and has intensive knowledge flows to and from a relatively large set of other sectors. This includes a set of sectors that is traditionally seen as low-tech but appears as science intensive in our data (in particular the basic metals sectors and other materials-related sectors).

7 Concluding remarks

We have proposed a methodology, broadly related to economic input–output analysis and strongly based on Pasinetti's notion of vertically integrated sectors, that can be used to analyze inter-sectoral knowledge flows. The focal point of the analysis is the extent to which economic sectors use knowledge from the scientific domain and transfer this knowledge through the system of interrelated economic sectors. Previously, the average number of citations made to the scientific literature in a patent produced in a particular sector has been used as a proxy of the science intensity of R&D activities in the sector. Our analysis provides an inter-sectoral insight into this indicator.

We propose measures that assess the net supply of knowledge to other sectors (i.e. the amount of scientific knowledge supplied to other sectors minus the amount used from other sectors, the so-called net multiplier), the knowledge self-reliance of the sectors (i.e. the relative amount of knowledge that the sector uses from or supplies to itself) and the pervasiveness of knowledge use and supply (i.e. the extent to which a broad range of other sectors is served by knowledge flows from a sector, or the extent to which knowledge is sourced from a broad range of other sectors).

We arrive at the following empirical results. First, we show that high science intensity generally also implies net supply of knowledge to other sectors. Thus, it seems to be the case that high science intensity (a high number of science citations per patent) is indeed an indication of the potential of a sector to diffuse scientific knowledge into the economic system. Second, we show that science-intensive sectors also rely to an important extent on their own knowledge imports. The diagonal elements of our sector-by-sector knowledge flow matrix carry relatively much weight in the science-intensive sectors. This is a first indication of the fact that scientific knowledge is highly specialized and specific. Finally, we show that the number of science citations per patent is not a good indicator for the knowledge pervasiveness of sectors. Such pervasiveness, in terms of both knowledge use and supply, appears in our analysis as a dimension that is quite separate from science intensity as measured in the traditional way. In particular, the traditional high-tech sectors, which are only a subset of the science-intensive sectors, are particularly non-pervasive, especially so in terms of their knowledge supply to other sectors. They tend to supply knowledge to and from a subset of sectors, including themselves. We show that these subsets of sectors form closely interacting knowledge clusters (in particular, ICT and bio-food). Other highly science-intensive sectors (materials and machinery) are more pervasive than these high-tech sectors.

In general terms, our results thus stress two broad conclusions with regard to the economic nature of scientific knowledge. First, sectors differ to an important extent with regard to the degree to which they are capable of transferring knowledge from the scientific to the economic domain. The economy relies on a relatively small range of sectors to achieve this transfer. At the same time, our second conclusion argues that often, scientific knowledge is highly specialized and specific to the sectoral context in which it is introduced in the economy. When this is the case, once knowledge is introduced by the science-intensive sectors, it tends to stay within a limited cluster of technologically related sectors.

We can speculate that the latter phenomenon is related to the specific nature of knowledge and production relations in which knowledge is applied. How it comes about is something that our analysis cannot explain. But it is clear from our results that the specific and specialized nature of knowledge provides a limit to the inter-sectoral diffusion of it, and this constitutes a potential source of unbalanced growth and development between economic sectors, much in line with what is observed and analyzed in inter-sectoral economic analysis.

Appendix 4.1: Indicators used for graphing technological clusters

The first indicator is based on the matrix **D**, of which each element d_{ij} indicates the share of industry i-specific scientific knowledge in the total stock of scientific knowledge that is accumulated and eventually transmitted to industry j patents of year t (based on direct and indirect knowledge flows). Thus, each column j of this matrix (which adds up to 1) decomposes each unit of the accumulated knowledge in sector j patents into its sector-specific knowledge components.

Based on matrix **D** we define a proximity matrix which captures the pair-wise dependency of the sectors. We call this symmetrical square matrix **SimD** and the elements of this are defined as

$$SimD_{ij} = \left(\frac{D_{ij}}{1 - D_{ii}} \cdot \frac{D_{ji}}{1 - D_{jj}}\right)^{\frac{1}{2}} \text{ for } i \neq j,$$

$$SimD_{jj} = 1 \text{ for each sector } j.$$

Since $\sum_{i=1}^{19} D_{ij} = 1$ for each sector j, $1-D_{jj}$ is the share of all non-sector j-specific types of knowledge embedded in sector j patents and therefore $D_{ij}/1-D_{ii}$ is the share of sector i-specific knowledge in all non-sector j-specific knowledge embedded in sector j patents of year t. The presence of $1-D_{jj}$ and $1-D_{ii}$ in the denominator (instead of 1) filters the effects of the heterogeneity in self-citation rates from these pair-wise mutual dependence indicators, and the multiplicative nature of the indicator emphasizes the mutuality by the simultaneous consideration of the importance of sector i-specific knowledge in sector j patents and the importance of sector j-specific knowledge in sector i patents. Thus, $SimD_{ij}$ measures the extent to which sectors i and j are mutually dependent in terms of the sector-specific knowledge they *use* from each other.

We can also build an alternative matrix **SimK** of the mutual knowledge dependencies among the sectors on the basis of the matrix **K**:

$$SimK_{ij} = \left(\frac{K_{ij}}{1 - K_{ii}} \cdot \frac{K_{ji}}{1 - K_{jj}} \right)^{\frac{1}{2}} \text{ for } i \neq j,$$

$$SimK_{jj} = 1 \text{ for each sector } j.$$

Since **K** is based on the output coefficient matrix **B**, $SimK_{ij}$ measures the extent to which sectors i and j are mutually dependent in terms of the sector-specific knowledge they *supply* to each other.

Finally, we combine the supply and use similarity measures into a single metric, so that we cover **SimK** and **SimD** simultaneously. This is the matrix **SimDK** that is defined by $SimDK_{ij} = SimD_{ij} \cdot SimK_{ij}$. This is the matrix that is used as an input into the MDS analysis.

Appendix 4.2: Indicator scores of the sectors

Definitions are given in the text; all data refer to calculations made with 1992 data.

Sector	Backward multiplier	Forward multiplier	Net science multiplier	Science citations per patent	Self-use	Self-supply	Use pervasiveness	Supply pervasiveness
Electrical machinery	4.91	5.05	0.97	0.48	0.55	0.56	6.64	8.30
Electronics	3.39	3.90	1.14	1.05	0.78	0.69	5.11	6.65
Chemistry	4.67	5.17	1.03	0.62	0.52	0.50	3.60	8.10
Pharmaceuticals	2.84	3.98	1.34	1.91	0.81	0.61	3.89	4.92
Oil refining	6.76	6.01	0.43	0.18	0.18	0.43	4.62	6.17
Motor vehicles	9.11	7.38	0.54	0.13	0.29	0.53	10.04	7.44
Other transport	7.71	6.60	0.66	0.19	0.29	0.44	10.07	6.47
Ferrous basic metals	5.00	5.21	1.08	0.56	0.47	0.44	8.64	9.24
Non-ferrous basic metals	4.41	5.11	1.31	0.83	0.55	0.42	8.70	9.71
Metal products	6.76	6.08	0.72	0.21	0.29	0.40	10.39	8.32
Instruments	4.74	4.87	1.00	0.61	0.63	0.63	8.05	9.55
Computers and office equipment	3.61	4.00	1.10	0.98	0.74	0.68	4.26	5.71
Other machinery	6.95	6.14	0.59	0.18	0.28	0.47	8.71	10.26
Food products	3.25	4.34	1.33	1.43	0.59	0.44	3.07	6.10
Textiles	6.75	6.09	0.68	0.22	0.21	0.30	7.94	6.57
Rubber and plastic products	7.80	6.39	0.31	0.08	0.09	0.29	9.04	7.65
Stone, clay and glass products	5.42	5.65	1.16	0.53	0.40	0.35	10.03	9.21
Paper and printing	5.79	5.51	0.82	0.36	0.30	0.37	9.18	9.59
Other manufacturing	6.30	5.62	0.60	0.24	0.21	0.35	9.15	9.33

REFERENCES

Cohen, W.M., Nelson R.R. and J.M. Walsh (2002). 'Links and impacts: the influence of public research on industrial R&D', *Management Science*, **48**(1), 1–23.

Dietzenbacher, E. (2005). 'More on multipliers', *Journal of Regional Science*, **45**, 421–426.

Dietzenbacher, E., Hoen, A. and Los, B. (2000). 'Labor productivity in Western Europe 1975–1985: an intercountry interindustry analysis', *Journal of Regional Science*, **40**, 425–452.

Dosi, G., Llerena P. and Sylos Labini, M. (2006). 'The relationships between science, technologies and their industrial exploitation: An illustration through the myths and realities of the so-called "European Paradox"', *Research Policy*, **35**, 1450–1464.

Fleming, L. and Sorenson, O. (2004). 'Science and diffusion of knowledge', *Research Policy*, **33**, 1615–1634.

Ghosh, A. (1958). 'Input-output approach in an allocation system', *Economica*, **25**, 58–64.

Hall, B.H., Jaffe, A.B. and Trajtenberg, M. (2002). 'The NBER Patent-citations data file: lessons, insights and methodological tools', in Jaffe and Trajtenberg (2002), pp. 403–460.

Hicks, D., Breitzman, T., *et al.* (2001). 'The changing composition of innovative activity in the US – a portrait based on patent analysis', *Research Policy*, **31**, 681–703.

Jaffe, A.B. and Trajtenberg, M. (2002). *Patents, Citations & Innovations. A Window on the Knowledge Economy*, Cambridge, MA: MIT Press.

Jaffe, A.B., Trajtenberg, M. and Henderson, R. (1993). 'Geographic localization of knowledge spillovers as evidenced by patent citations', *Quarterly Journal of Economics*, **108**, 577–598.

Kline, S.J. and Rosenberg, N. (1986). 'An overview of innovation', in: *The Positive Sum Strategy: Harnessing technology for economic growth*, Landau, R. and Rosenberg, N. (eds) Washington, DC: National Academic Press, pp. 275–306.

Leydesdorff, L. (2004). 'The university–industry knowledge relationship: analyzing patents and the science base of technologies', *Journal of the American Society for Information Science and Technology*, **55**, 991–1001.

Maurseth, P.-B. and Verspagen, B. (2002). 'Knowledge spillovers in Europe. A patent citation analysis', *Scandinavian Journal of Economics*, **104**, 531–545.

Michel, J. and Bettels, B. (2001). 'Patent citation analysis. A closer look at the basic input data from patent search reports', *Scientometrics*, **51**, 185–201.

Miller, R.E. and Blair, P.D. (1985). *Input-output Analysis. Foundations and Extensions*, Englewood Cliffs, NJ: Prentice Hall.

Narin, F., Hamilton, K.S. and Olivastro, D. (1997). 'The increasing linkage between U.S. technology and public science', *Research Policy*, **26**, 3, 317–330.

Oosterhaven, J. and Stelder, D. (2002). 'Net multipliers avoid exaggerating impacts: with a bi-regional illustration for the Dutch transportation sector', *Journal of Regional Science*, **42**, 3, 533–543.

Pasinetti, L.L. (1973). 'The notion of vertical integration in economic analysis', *Metroeconomica*, **25**, 1–29.

(1981). *Structural Change and Economic Growth. A Theoretical Essay on the Dynamics of the Wealth of Nations*, Cambridge University Press.

(1993). *Structural Economic Dynamics: A theory of the economic consequences of human learning*, Cambridge University Press.

Sánchez-Chóliz, J. and R. Duarte, (2003). 'Analysing pollution by way of vertically integrated coefficients, with an application to the water sector in Aragon', *Cambridge Journal of Economics*, **27**, 433–448.

Tamada, S., Naito, Y., Kodama, F., Gemba, K. and Suzuki, J. (2006). 'Significant difference of dependence upon scientific knowledge among different technologies', *Scientometrics*, **68**, 289–302.

Van Moergastel, T., Slabbers, M. and Verspagen, B. (1994). *MERIT concordance table: IPC – ISIC (rev. 2)*, MERIT Research Memorandum 2/94–004, University of Maastricht.

Webb, C., Dernis, H., Harhoff, D. and Hoisl, K. (2004). 'A first set of EPO patent database building blocks for analysing European and international patent citations'. *OECD mimeo.*

5 Growth: towards a structural endogenous macro-model

William J. Baumol

1 Introduction

Technical progress, productivity, consumption, investment, are no longer sufficient to define the economic system in a dynamic research. We must go beyond this, and find out what lies behind the façade of these aggregate expressions. In short, the research must be formulated in disaggregate terms. (Pasinetti and Spaventa 1960, p. 1770)

The valuable approach that is referred to as 'structural dynamics' is clearly a major contribution of Luigi Pasinetti and Luigi Spaventa, one that has been much further utilized and explored by the former. I have encountered no formal definition of the analysis, but I take it to mean that it is one whose approach brings out the pertinent relationships explicitly and in a way that makes it possible to discern clearly the implications for policy and for the prospects for development. It is indeed a very fruitful development, one that has usefully been taken in Keynesian directions, but whose spirit can also take us far along other significant avenues. The purpose of this chapter is to illustrate one way in which this can be done.

2 'Realism' in theory as a cost–benefit tradeoff

Structural analysis offers many benefits. To me, however, the primary virtue of this approach does not lie in its pursuit of added realism. As a matter of fact, all economic models can be characterized as deliberate falsifications. For it is in these misrepresentations that much of their value is to be found. If such a model is to be usable for analytic purposes, oversimplification of reality, often drastic oversimplification, is unavoidable. The construct must systematically abstract from minor influences and relationships, even though there is hardly a situation in reality where

I am deeply grateful to the Ewing Marion Kauffman Foundation for its generous support of this work and the collegial and helpful exchanges with members of its staff.

they are not present in profusion. Such pruning of the many minor complications is essential for the construction of models that serve their main purpose: insight into the explanation of real phenomena and real relationships. Each complication that is incorporated into a model constructed for analytic purposes has a tradeoff in reduced analytic tractability of the construct.

Of course, one should not denigrate material that is purely descriptive, that characterizes some phenomenon as fully as it can and proceeds with an attempt to point out its every complication and the multitude of influences, however minor, by which it is driven.

But neither the human mind nor any of the investigative tools it has created is generally capable of embracing such an extensive catalogue and of studying its workings in their entirety. Consequently, one of the critical skills of the theorist is the ability to carry out a pruning process that does not throw out the baby with the bathwater. Any models that result, evidently, are unrealistic and deliberately so. So a deliberate move to enhance the realism of such a model may turn out to be more vice than virtue. At the very least, the creator of such an improvement bears the responsibility of showing that it has not undermined the capability of subjecting the model to systematic analysis.

I conclude that an increase in the realism of a model is not a costless exercise and that, ideally, we may well wish to aim for something like an optimal compromise between realism and analytic tractability. Structural analysis does not need to suffer from this handicap and, indeed, it has benefited from the aggregative simplification that is inherent in its macroeconomic character.

3 On structural growth analysis and endogeneity of models

In a 2009 paper I argued that for a growth model to be truly endogenous, in the sense of providing added illumination on the nature of the growth process, it is apt to require some microeconomic elements. For much of what goes on in the growth process entails the response of individual performers to the incentives that current institutions provide. But here I will attempt to show that in taking this position I have overstated my case, and that one can make progress towards construction of an operational macromodel in which the nature of the process is laid out for intuitive inspection, at least to a point. In other words, I will try to offer a model that is *structural* in the sense that it displays the operational components and shows their interactions explicitly, rather than presenting us with an aggregation of black boxes. Moreover, I will seek to show that this can be done despite a considerable level of aggregation of the components, as a macro approach requires.

The essence of the difference from at least some of the models that bear the label 'endogenous' is that here the focus will be on an important class of actors and their activities, rather than upon the product of some more commonly cited variable, such as produced capital stock or accumulated human capital. Moreover, there is a script that the actors in question follow, though different performers follow it in different ways – a script which will be described in broad outline. With this account, the implied model that encompasses the story becomes structural, shedding any reduced form attribute.

4 Invention, entrepreneurship and growth: the scenario

The story, in short, is the following. Two members of the cast of characters whose activity is critical for the growth achievement of the economy are the inventor and the entrepreneur. It is evidently the former who makes possible a very substantial growth performance by the economy. Indeed, it can be argued that very little else is a critical source of historically unprecedented growth. True, few will deny that expanded education and the resulting acquisition of human capital have made a substantial difference, while accumulation of physical capital was indispensable for the explosion of output of recent centuries. But this can be countered by the observation that in the diminutive growth pattern that prevailed before the eighteenth century, illiteracy and the absence of large-scale production venues containing powerful productive equipment (i.e. large mechanized factories) were attributable not only to custom, culture and absence of the requisite technical information but also to lack of the necessary resources. In the impoverished communities that preceded the industrial revolution, output barely sufficed for survival of the bulk of the population, and in the frequent periods of famine even the bare subsistence level of output was beyond reach. Evidently, the resources required to provide anything like universal elementary education and facilities that would today be accepted as genuine factories were totally unattainable. It would appear, then, that the inventions that followed the end of the eighteenth century were indispensable for subsequent growth not only in the most obvious way, via their own inherent power, but also indirectly by their contribution of the resources without which widespread education and substantial expansion of the capital stock would have been unattainable.

The entrepreneur: the other key performer

So we must surely acknowledge the crucial part played by invention in any growth process and, most notably, in the era of totally unprecedented explosion of output in recent centuries. So far, this is all entirely obvious. But what is not obvious is that even a remarkable inventive performance is, by itself, likely to prove insufficient to carry out the task of substantial growth enhancement. A little consideration of the matter should render this plausible, albeit nevertheless a bit surprising. For example, there is evidence that the economy of the Soviet Union achieved a very respectable record of technical invention. After all, its scientists and engineers were well educated and performed very effectively in generating inventions of military significance and contributions to the space race. Yet those inventions that could have contributed materially to the wellbeing of Soviet consumers generally languished. The same was true of many of the remarkable technological contributions that punctuate the history of Tang and Sung China. Moreover, Heron of Alexandria offered the economy of Ancient Rome a working steam engine that, as Abraham Lincoln emphasized, never was put to use as more than what he described as 'a toy'.

In all of these cases, a simple and identical explanation is persuasive. In each, the institutional arrangements were such as to lead enterprising individuals in directions other than marketing of useful inventions or their products. Unlike what faces a modern innovative entrepreneur, there was little incentive to lead such inhabitants of the Soviet Union and the earlier societies mentioned to seek out promising inventions, or to supervise their improvement in order to enhance their saleability via increased reliability, capacity and user friendliness. In the Soviet Union the opportunities for advancement lay in membership of the bureaucracy or the military or in promotion of inventions useful for military purposes. In Tang and Sung China the attractive goal for the enterprising was a post in the judiciary that could devolve upon a mandarin who had achieved his exalted position via success in the Imperial examinations, and who could then proceed to improve his economic status through the bribes that he could expect from litigants who came before him. In Rome, the market for inventions had two primary sources of customers for invention: the armies and the religious sects whose priesthood used the inventions to astonish worshippers and impress them with the magical powers of the priests. The last of these outlets, indeed, was the user of Heron's steam engine that, rather than serving as a mere toy was, instead, an advertising instrument of the religious sects used to draw in worshippers.

From this discussion two conclusions emerge. First, effectiveness of invention in materially contributing to economic growth requires the presence of enterprising individuals who are skilful in discerning profitable uses for those inventions and who are prepared to devote themselves to ensuring that those inventions are indeed put to profitable use. Those profits, incidentally, need not only take the form of financial revenue; social standing can also be an effective reward, as can the acquisition of power such as that accruing to a prosperous industrialist who has built his position on innovation.

The second conclusion to which this discussion leads is that enterprising individuals, who consider whether to devote themselves to productive activities or to activities that contribute little to economic growth or even impede it, will choose among these directions for their efforts on the basis of current institutions – the directions for which the institutions offer the most promising rewards.

This gives us two parts of three required foundations for our growth story. The first pillar of the scenario is the contribution to rapid growth of the implicit partnership of inventors and entrepreneurs, with the latter working to ensure that the products of the inventors will be put to effective use. The second pillar is the institutional set-up that provides the incentive for enterprising individuals to turn their efforts to productive innovation, rather than innovative rent seeking or corruption, crime or other forms of profitable violence (as in aggressive and innovative military activity).

But there is still need for a third element to make the tale truly endogenous – a tale in which there is a complete and internally compatible driving mechanism. If the institutions were to evolve entirely in response to influences that lie outside the scenario, as described to this point, then the mechanism is evidently not basically endogenous. If the developments are a response primarily to influences such as culture and religion, the scenario is unavoidably governed to a substantial degree by influences that must be considered exogenous, meaning that, so far as the workings of the model are concerned, those influences must be treated as fortuitous and not explainable as yet another set of consequences of the economic arrangements. But if the growth performance of the economy itself plays a substantial role in determining the character of the pertinent institutions and their evolution, then the components of the machine become mutually interdependent and the entire working of the mechanism becomes amenable to representation and analysis in a comprehensible (and, possibly, intuitively comprehensible) endogenous model that is clearly structural.

5 The remaining pillar: the influence of growth on institutions

Next, in search of the missing prime component of the story, I am driven to unexplored territory. Accordingly, I cannot pretend to offer more than hypothesis, with little or no evidence. Yet much of what will be proposed here surely has a degree of plausibility and I hope it will invite testing by others. But first let me make clear that the proposition I will offer is considerably more modest than it may appear to be from what has been said so far. It does not suggest that the pertinent institutions are determined entirely by the economy's growth performance and that there are no other significant influences. This would all too evidently be nonsense. Rather, what is suggested is that the selection of the institutions adopted by a society and their evolution entail multivariate functions, with economic growth being only one of the variables, albeit one that is hardly unimportant. Thus, a *ceteris paribus* change in the growth rate, if not of negligible magnitude or highly transitory, can be expected to exercise a profound influence upon the institutions and the structure of the payoffs they offer to different types of entrepreneurial activity.

But even this more circumscribed form of the hypothesis, albeit rather more modest, has a good deal to be modest about. In the discussion that follows, some conjectures about the nature of the influence of growth performance will be laid out and some intuitive support of the hypothesis will be attempted, in the hope of providing it with a degree of plausibility. After that, the section that follows will provide a very elementary but formal model encompassing all the three elements on which the story rests, showing how the parts of the model fit together and how the behaviour of the model can be analyzed formally to yield a depiction of the growth behaviour of the economy.

Growth rate and redistributive versus productive wealth seeking

For the purpose of our argument, we can distinguish two broad-brush approaches to the enterprising pursuit of wealth. The entrepreneurs can take steps whose expectable outcome is an increase in the product created by the economy, seeking to ensure that a not insignificant share of the incremental output accrues to its contributors. Or, instead, the entrepreneurs can seek to enhance their *share* of the economy's output, while doing nothing to enhance the magnitude of the total. That is, they can either work to enlarge the pie or simply seek to expand the size of the slice that they obtain. It is convenient to distinguish these approaches by labelling them 'productive entrepreneurship' and 'redistributive (unproductive) entrepreneurship', respectively, with an important sub-group of the productive entrepreneurs being the innovative entrepreneurs who specialize in ensuring that promising inventions are put to effective use in production. Now, it is arguable that until relatively recent times enterprising individuals focused their efforts predominantly, indeed almost exclusively, on redistributive activity. The promise of this approach is much more straightforward and can seem far less uncertain than the other. If you are stronger than your neighbour, you can confidently undertake to expropriate his oxen. That, in essence, was the occupation of enterprising monarchs and, often, of their nobility as well. Innovative ways to gather the fruits of corruption are another form of redistributive entrepreneurial activity that is still widespread. The forms taken by this general approach to wealth gathering are many and they often entail little sophisticated foresight on the part of the actors.

Productive entrepreneurship, in contrast, typically requires coordination of matters that are far less obvious and straightforward. It is much more difficult to foresee what market will emerge for an innovative product, how that product can be tailored to the prospective users' needs and preferences, who will receive the benefits, if any, and when, if ever, they will accrue. Even if I succeed in my effort to enlarge the pie, how can I ensure that any substantial part of the increment will come to me?

Patents are a clear example of an institution that reduced the uncertainties of innovative entrepreneurial activity. They made their appearance only in the early renaissance. But even once they became available, they had many features that limited severely their contribution to the certainty and expectable reward of the innovative entrepreneur. Initially, indeed, their purpose was characteristically redistributive rather than innovative. They were offered in England as a reward to foreign (notably, French) skilled workers, who were willing to smuggle out trade secrets (as in the production of silk) and who put the secret processes to work in starting up a rival British industry. Even when, in the eighteenth century, they came to be used to encourage the creation of new products and new productive techniques, in England and France they were set up to be extremely costly to the applicant for a patent, and they were beset by substantial legal uncertainties. This enabled the US to forge ahead in the innovation race when patenting was explicitly enshrined in the American Constitution and the patenting fee set very low.

But the incentives for adoption of this institution surely included the successful innovation and economic growth that were already under way in both the former colonies and the mother country. Success in the arena of innovation had a number of consequences. Most immediately, it contributed to growth and added respectability to careers in invention and entrepreneurship, as any biography of Benjamin Franklin illustrates dramatically. But the resulting economic growth, in turn, contributed the resources that could finance expansion of educational activity and increased investment in physical capital, both serving to enhance the attractiveness and opportunities for success in productive entrepreneurial activities.

This, then, is our third relationship: the influence of economic growth as a stimulant of productive entrepreneurship and an enhancement of its prospective rewards.

6 Towards a formal model

To recapitulate, we now have three component relationships: first, growth rate of output per capita as a function of the quantity and variety of innovative and entrepreneurial activity; second, the total number of active entrepreneurs, as a function of the growth rate; and finally, the allocation of the set of entrepreneurs between redistributive and productive (innovative) activities as a function of their relative payoffs. To illustrate the workings of the kindergarten formal model without injection of unnecessary complications, all the following relationships are assumed to be linear, though that is surely an unrealistic premise. The discussion employs the following notation:

r_t = the growth rate of per capita output of the economy in period t
E_t = the total number of active entrepreneurs in that period
E_{pt} = the number of productive (innovative) entrepreneurs
E_{ut} = the number of unproductive entrepreneurs
W_{pt} and W_{ut} = respectively, the current rates of remuneration of the two groups.

We can immediately form our first relationship, that between entrepreneurial activity and growth:

$$r_{t+1} = r_t + a_p(E_{pt}) - a_u(E_{ut}),\ a_p, a_u \quad \text{constants} \tag{1}$$

Second, we have the tautology

$$E_t = E_{pt} + E_{ut}. \tag{2}$$

Then we have the expression describing the stimulating effect of growth upon total supply of entrepreneurs:

$$E_t = h^* + h(r_t). \tag{3}$$

Finally, we come to the allocation of entrepreneurs between productive and unproductive activity, depending on the relative wages offered by the two occupations:

$$E_{pt}/E_{ut} = W_p/W_u. \tag{4}$$

We next use straightforward substitution to transform these relationships into a first-order difference equation in r_t. First we use (2) and (4) to express E_{pt} and E_{ut} in terms of E_t. We obtain at once

$$E_{pt} = E_t - E_{ut} = E_t - E_{pt}W_u/W_p$$

so that

$$E_{pt} = E_t/(1 + W_u/W_p) \text{ and } E_{ut} = E_t[1 - 1/(1 + W_u/W_p)].$$

Writing K for $1/(1+W_u/W_p)$ and substituting the last two expressions into (1) we get

$$r_{t+1} = r_t + a_pE_tK - a_uE_t(1 - K) = r_t + (h^* + hr_t)[a_pK - a_u(1 - K)]. \tag{5}$$

Simplifying once more by writing Z for the expression in the square brackets, (5) becomes

$$r_{t+1} = h^*Z + (1 + hZ)r_t \tag{6}$$

which is evidently a first-order linear difference equation in r_t with constant coefficients, a difference equation of the simplest form, with the well-known explicit solution

$$r_t = r_0(1 + hZ)^t + h^*/ - hZ \text{ where} \tag{7}$$

$$Z = [a_pK - a_u(1 - K)] \text{ and } K = 1/(1 + W_u/W_p). \tag{8}$$

Thus, (7) and (8) take the simplest form we encounter in dealing with a difference equation model:

$$r_t = u + vx^t, \text{u and v constants.} \tag{9}$$

As is obvious, the intertemporal trajectory of r evidently depends on the magnitude and sign of

$$\begin{aligned} x &= 1 + hZ = 1 + h[a_pK - a_u(1 - K)] \\ &= 1 - ha_u + h(a_p + a_u)/(1 + W_u/W_p). \end{aligned} \tag{10}$$

This clearly presents us with four possible types of time path: stable monotonic, unstable monotonic, stable oscillatory and unstable oscillatory.

There is no point in going further along these lines because, as can hardly be denied, the model is markedly oversimple and patently unrealistic. At the very least it requires sufficient complication to bring in other critical variables, their position in the structure of the model and the nature and magnitude of their influence. But that is all a task for future research. My purpose here has not been to provide a model that is rendered defensible by the range of considerations it encompasses or empirical evidence that supports its realism and accuracy. Rather, my more limited goal has been to show only that it is indeed possible to construct a *structural* macromodel that includes the role of the entrepreneur as an indispensable contributor to rapid economic growth. Its aim is to point out a promising direction for such work, in the hope that others will find themselves able to follow this lead and consider it profitable to do so.

REFERENCES

Baumol, W.J. (2009), Endogenous Growth: Valuable Advance, Substantive Misnomer, in Boianovsky, M. and Hoover, K.D. (eds.), *Robert Solow and the Development of Growth Economics*, Durham and London: Duke University Press, pp. 304–314.

Pasinetti, L. and Spaventa, L. (1960), Verso il superamento della modellistica aggregata nella teoria dello sviluppo economico, *Rivista di Politica Economica*, vol. XXV, 1751–1781.

Part II

Structural dynamics: the Cambridge Keynesian perspective

6 Luigi Pasinetti: the senior living heir of the Cambridge School of Economics and the last of the great system-builders

Geoffrey Harcourt

1 Introduction

Luigi Pasinetti and I were PhD students together in Cambridge in the 1950s. We met informally to discuss Joan Robinson's *magnum opus, The Accumulation of Capital* (1956), which she called 'my big book'. Luigi was way ahead of me in his understanding of the intricacies of her analysis of, for example, Wicksell effects, the Ruth Cohen curiosum, and so on, but we were at one in our admiration of her overall performance in the book. (It was published when she was the same age as Keynes was when he published *The General Theory*.) Subsequently we were colleagues in the Cambridge Faculty in the 1960s. I read some of Luigi's papers then in draft and I have continued to do so in subsequent years when I was in Australia and then back in Cambridge while he returned full time to Italy. He, in turn, was very kind to me, especially with his detailed, useful comments on certain key sections of my 1972 book on capital theory. Mauro Baranzini and I much enjoyed preparing the *Festschrift* volume for Luigi's sixtieth birthday (Baranzini and Harcourt, 1993). (We started five years before his birthday and presented it to him three years after, vaguely right even if precisely wrong.)

Luigi's 1993 guide to his 1981 *magnum opus* contains the brilliant concept of human learning and its consequences set in the context of a 'pure labour' economy and examining theoretically its development through time, 'an abstraction [which is nevertheless] aimed at grasping the basic features of the industrial economies of our time' Pasinetti, (1993, p. xiii). I also read his outstanding plenary lecture, 'The Cambridge School of Keynesian Economics,' Pasinetti (2005a), to the 2003 'Economics for the Future' conference which was organized by the Cambridge Political Economy Society to celebrate 100 years of the Economics Tripos at Cambridge[1];

[1] It was sad that Luigi could not give the lecture in person, due to illness in his family. I was an inferior substitute, though I hope my presentation of the lecture did justice to its central messages.

the introduction by Mauro and myself to Luigi's *Festschrift* volume; and, of course, others of his books and essays. I have also had the privilege of reading for the Cambridge University Press his book, *Keynes and the Cambridge Keynesians* (2007).

2 Pasinetti, Malthus and historical induction

All through his career Pasinetti has stressed the natural links of Keynesian developments, on the one hand, to our classical forebears, on the other. He early on realized that the intervening developments of neoclassical economics, a misnomer if ever there was one, could not be ignored because its conceptual foundations had to be criticized, but could be reached over when the positive developments of Keynesian and post-Keynesian theory were being written. Here is a typical statement:

> Keynes' theory of effective demand, which has remained so impervious to reconciliation with marginal economic theory, raises almost no problem when directly inserted into the earlier discussions of the Classical economists. Similarly, ... the post-Keynesian theories of economic growth and income distribution, which have required so many artificial assumptions in the efforts to reconcile them with marginal productivity theory, encounter almost no difficulty when directly grafted on to Classical economic dynamics. (Pasinetti, 1974, p. ix)

In his Cambridge lecture, Pasinetti lists 'eight "constructive" features [of] the Cambridge School of Keynesian economics' (Pasinetti, (2005a, p. 841). The third is listed as '*Malthus and the Classical economists (not Walras and the Marginalists) as the inspiring School from the History of Economic Thought*' (p. 842, emphasis in the original). In thinking about Pasinetti's role here I was struck by how close his approach is to that of Malthus, whose own approach was set out superbly by Maynard Keynes in his essays on Malthus, 'the first of the Cambridge economists' (Keynes, 1935). In his 'Centenary Allocution' (originally published in the June 1935 issue of the *Economic Journal*), Keynes wrote:

> Let us ... think of Malthus today as the first of the Cambridge economists – as ... a great pioneer of the application of a frame of formal thinking to the complex confusion of the world of daily events. Malthus approached the central problems of economic theory by the best of all routes. He began to be interested as a philosopher and moral scientist ... applying the *a priori* method of the political philosopher. He then immersed himself ... in the facts of economic history and of the contemporary world, applying the methods of historical induction and filling his mind with a mass of the material of experience. And then finally he returned to *a priori* thought, ... this time to the pure theory of the economist proper, and sought ... to impose the methods of formal thought on the material presented by events, so as to penetrate these with understanding by a mixture of

intuitive selection and formal principle and thus to interpret the problem and propose the remedy. In short, from being a caterpillar of a moral scientist and a chrysalis of an historian, he could at last spread the wings of his thought and survey the world as an economist! (Keynes, 1935, p. 233)[2]

In several places, Pasinetti describes how his personal experiences as a young person made him aware of the deep problems of the post-war economy in which he grew up: 'The work which is here presented is a theoretical investigation into the long-term evolution of industrial economic systems. A combination of three factors – one factual ... – originally prompted this investigation. The factual element was provided by the extremely uneven development – from sector to sector, from region to region – of the environment in which I lived (post-war Europe) at the time I began my training in economics' (Pasinetti, 1981, p. xi). So, like Malthus, he built his approach to economic theory on observations and experiences.

3 Pasinetti, Classical and Keynesian pioneers

There are few economists writing today with Pasinetti's clarity of vision and expression. He is able to absorb large literatures and impose on them crystal-clear précis of their essential characteristics. In this way contrasts in approaches and methods, often inevitably obscured in the originals, emerge beautifully and succinctly. A typical example is in the essays Pasinetti has written on the essential difference between neoclassical economics, which concentrates on the nature of exchange, especially in static situations, in order to draw out its theories of value, pricing and distribution, even accumulation and growth, and the classicals, where production is the organizing concept for their parallel developments usually set in dynamic, changing situations. This links well not only with classical writings, especially by Marx where the sphere of production is a dominant entity, but also to Keynes's own revolutionary theory of a monetary production economy. I would add that it is also the principal emphasis in John Kenneth Galbraith's most important book, *The New Industrial State* (1967), where the owners and managers of large companies are concerned with production and related accumulation plans, and with bending consumers' and purchasers' demands to match these former plans, often aided and abetted by government, not least Bush the younger in the US. The Keynesian input is that their efforts in these

[2] I rediscovered this wonderful passage when preparing a paper on 'The Cambridge approach to economics' for a conference in Berlin in October 2005 (Harcourt, 2006).

dimensions are all directed at attempting to minimize the impact of inescapable uncertainty on decisions and outcomes.

No one has been more aware than Pasinetti of the concern of our classical pioneers with what William Baumol (1951) called their 'magnificent dynamics' – the progress through time of industrialized economies in which changes in methods of production and patterns of spending overall and in composition, all endogenous processes (though their explanations are still rudimentary), interrelate both to raise productivity and potentially to increase standards of living, but also to produce deep malfunctionings on the way. These malfunctionings require, first, understanding and then the formation of sensibly based humane policies to offset their harmful effects.[3]

4 Pasinetti's Cambridge inspirations

As Pasinetti has pointed out in a number of places, he became associated early on with the first generation of Keynes's pupils – Richard Kahn, Joan Robinson, Nicky Kaldor (by osmosis) – those who were principally concerned with 'generalizing *The General Theory* to the long period', as Joan Robinson put it (see, for example, Robinson, 1979). He was also influenced by Richard Goodwin and Piero Sraffa.[4] Goodwin developed two parallel approaches over his working life and achieved a splendid synthesis of them in his later Italian years in Goodwin and Punzo (1987). One came out of the approaches of his 'American' mentors, Wassily Leontief and Joseph Schumpeter; it was concerned with production interdependence in advanced societies. The other was concerned with cycle and growth interrelationships (so Schumpeter played a dual role) and with Keynes's employment theory and Roy Harrod's work on cycles and then on growth dynamics. (Harrod was Goodwin's tutor at Oxford in the 1930s.) To these influences must be added Sraffa's rehabilitation

[3] In Pasinetti's fine essay (2005b) on Franco Modigliani, he singles out, as do other contributors to the volume, how these twin perspectives always drove Modigliani's life-long endeavours. Pasinetti makes crystal clear as ever, though, that Modigliani's (and Paul Samuelson's and Bob Solow's) version(s) of Keynes, especially the centrality of a rigidly downward money wage, is (are) not either Keynes's or Pasinetti's version, that *The General Theory* can grow out of Marshall but not Walras. See Samuelson (2005) and Solow (2005).

[4] In the Preface to Pasinetti (1974, p. x) he wrote: 'I am glad to take this opportunity to express my deep gratitude to that remarkable group of thinkers – Richard Kahn, Nicholas Kaldor, Joan Robinson and Piero Sraffa – whom I had the rare fortune of meeting, discussing with so often and then being associated with, in Cambridge, ... the most stimulating place ... for progressive thought in economic theory. [His] thanks also [went to] Richard Goodwin, James Duesenberry, Franco Modigliani, James Meade and Robin Marris.' Not a bad roll call.

of classical political economy (and his prelude to a critique of economic theory), the nature of production interdependence thrown up by the organizing concept of the surplus, its creation, extraction, distribution and use, in Sraffa's view at an instance in time. Associated with both these strands was the influence of Marx on Sraffa and Goodwin. (Goodwin also regarded Knut Wicksell as his favourite economist.) It was not for nothing I once dubbed Dick 'a Twentieth Century eclectic' (Harcourt, 1985; Sardoni, 1992, Chapter 21).

Pasinetti also absorbed, as we all did then (would that I could say 'now' as well), Keynes's theory of the determination of overall employment in the short period. Some of Pasinetti's most profound contributions are concerned with either developing Keynes's theory or defending specific strands of it. I think here especially of Keynes's theory of investment in Chapter 11 of *The General Theory* whereby Keynes and Pasinetti (see, for example, Pasinetti, 1997a), argue for a negative association between the rate of interest and planned rates of investment in given situations. Pasinetti points out that this does not need an assumption of, or even an argument for, a negative association between the rate of interest and the investment intensity of the techniques chosen. All that is required is that at any moment in time there is a known stock of potential investment projects, more of which will appear to be profitable, the lower is the level of the rate of interest we consider. They cannot, however, be ordered by investment intensities, in the sense that the latter could take on any values *vis à vis* one another. We need to suppose further that it *is* possible to take a given situation and ask what would be different at different values of the rate of interest. Pasinetti considers this to be a legitimate procedure *in the short period*, that the only differences will be different rates of planned investment expenditures, that the feedback through the whole economy on prices etc. of Sraffa's and, for example, Pierangelo Garegnani's analysis, explicitly long period, may be ignored in the short period because it does not occur. Of course, as a consequence of different rates of investment there will be different levels of outputs, employment, prices and so on, but these arise as the consequences of the usual short-period analysis.

5 'Natural' and institutional economic mechanisms in Pasinetti's contribution

Perhaps the most strikingly original aspect of Pasinetti's many contributions, to my mind, is his distinction between institution-free propositions of economic theory, the 'natural' relations of a system, and propositions constrained by time and place because of existing and/or evolving institutions.[5] In Pasinetti (1997b), he argues that the distinction is only cloudily implicit in Keynes's revolutionary contributions, that it needs to be made explicit if we are to produce bodies of theory and approaches to theorizing that can rival, and ultimately dominate and hopefully displace, those of the mainstream. Thus, Pasinetti stresses that Keynes wrote of 'the *principle* of effective demand' (the title of Chapter 3 of *The General Theory)*, not the *theory.* Nevertheless, in Pasinetti's view, Keynes never made completely explicit the first, institution-free account of the principle, though he gave many hints and clues and he adapted Marshall's tools to take in the concepts of aggregate demand and supply to explicitly determine the *point* of effective demand.

To get to the most fundamental level of analysis Pasinetti explains how the 45° line (which, he argues, has done so much damage to the development and understanding of Keynes) nevertheless is the appropriate tool for this particular task. Pasinetti banishes the usual interpretation of the aggregate demand function as the level of planned expenditures on consumption and investment goods in a given short period (as seen by the onlooking macroeconomist) plotted against either total income or total employment levels and makes the causal relationship run from expected levels of aggregate demand (the summation of the individual levels expected by business people) to corresponding levels of production. The 45° line ceases to be a construction line devoid of economic meaning and becomes instead a simple way of expressing the relationship between *expected* sales in the economy at a moment in time (whether they be sales of consumption goods or investment goods *including* own sales to inventory) and the production of commodities generated by and corresponding to them. Provided we assume that business people never produce unless expected sales fit into one of these categories (and we measure in the same units on both the horizontal and vertical axis), we must end up with a 45° line. Pasinetti's construction is the reverse of Say's Law. He extends these ideas to the long-period development of the economy, pointing out that any institutional mechanism that may be invented for the matching of production to demand must have to rely on the same basic principle of effective demand.

[5] Another candidate among several is his solution of Ricardo's search for an invariable standard of value which is independent of different distributions of income, levels and compositions of activity and methods of production with his concept of vertically integrated sectors – 'vertical integration with regard to final goods as soon as our inquiry begins to consider movements through time' (Pasinetti, 1993, p. 13). All of these are specific issues in his overall development of the analysis of structural dynamic systems. I am grateful to Prue Kerr for urging that I stress this.

Both of Pasinetti's great books are built on the foundations of this distinction, starting with the first which has a dimension of universality necessarily lacking from the second set of developments. This procedure parallels but is not exactly the same as Joan Robinson's and Kahn's concern with Golden Age analysis in logical time as the necessary preliminary to the analysis of processes occurring in historical time. In Harcourt (2007) I argued that neither Joan Robinson nor Kahn was able to get very far with the second task but that Kalecki and Goodwin in their separate, independent but also parallel ways had. To this conclusion I couple the extraordinary, independent contributions of Luigi Pasinetti, the publication of whose *magnum opus* we are celebrating.

REFERENCES

Baranzini, M. and Harcourt, G.C. (eds) (1993), *The Dynamics of the Wealth of the Nations. Growth, Distribution and Structural Change. Essays in Honour of Luigi Pasinetti*, Basingstoke, Hants: Macmillan.

Baumol, W.J. (1951), *Economic Dynamics. An Introduction*, London: Macmillan.

Galbraith, J.K. (1967), *The New Industrial State*, Boston, MA: Houghton Mifflin.

Goodwin, R.M. and Punzo, L.F. (1987), *The Dynamics of a Capitalist Economy*, Oxford: Polity Press.

Harcourt, G.C. (1972), *Some Cambridge Controversies in the Theory of Capital*, Cambridge University Press.

(1985), 'A twentieth-century eclectic: Richard Goodwin', *Journal of Post Keynesian economics*, **7**, 410–21, reprinted in Sardoni (ed.) (1992), 379–87.

(2007), 'What is the Cambridge approach to economics?' in Hein, E. and Truger, A. (eds) *Money, Distribution and Economic Policy. Alternatives to Orthodox Macroeconomics*. Cheltenham, Northampton, MA: Edward Elgar.

Harcourt, G.C. and Riach, P.A. (eds) (1997), *A 'Second Edition' of The General Theory*, 2 vols, London: Routledge.

Keynes, J.M. (1935), 'The Commemoration of Thomas Robert Malthus: Three allocutions: III Mr Keynes,' *Economic Journal*, **XLV**, 230–4.

(1936), *The General Theory of Employment, Interest and Money*, London: Macmillan.

Pasinetti, L.L. (1974), *Growth and Income Distribution. Essays in Economic Theory*, Cambridge University Press.

(1981), *Structural Change and Economic Growth. A Theoretical Essay on the Dynamics of the Wealth of the Nations*, Cambridge University Press.

(1993), *Structural Economic Dynamics. A Theory of the Economic Consequences of Human Learning*, Cambridge University Press.

(1997a), 'The marginal efficiency of investment' in Harcourt and Riach (eds.), vol. 1, 198–218.

(1997b), 'The principle of effective demand' in Harcourt and Riach (eds.), vol. 1, 93–104.

(2005a), 'The Cambridge School of Keynesian Economics,' *Cambridge Journal of Economics*, **29**, 837–48.

(2005b), 'How much of John Maynard Keynes do we find in Franco Modigliani?', *Banca Nazionale del Lavoro Quarterly Review*, LVIII, 21–39.

(2007), *Keynes and the Cambridge Keynesians. A 'Revolution in Economics' to be Accomplished*, Cambridge University Press.

Robinson, J. (1956), *The Accumulation of Capital*, London: Macmillan.

(1979), *The Generalization of the General Theory and Other Essays*, London: Macmillan.

Samuelson, P.A. (2005), 'Franco: a mind never at rest', *Banca Nazionale del Lavoro Quarterly Review*, LVIII, 5–9.

Sardoni, C. (ed.) (1992), *On Political Economists and Modern Political Economy. Selected Essays of G.C. Harcourt*, London: Routledge.

Solow, R.M. (2005), 'Modigliani and Keynes', *Banca Nazionale del Lavoro Quarterly Review*, LVIII, 11–19.

7 Towards a synthesis in Post-Keynesian economics in Luigi Pasinetti's contribution

Heinrich Bortis

1 Introduction: a hopeless situation

The work of Maynard Keynes and of Piero Sraffa lies at the core of a revolution in economic theorising during Shackle's *Years of High Theory – 1926–1939*. Indeed, '[our] period opens with the Sraffian Manifesto of 1926 [*The Laws of Returns under Competitive Conditions*], demanding the revision of [Marshallian] value theory [which, finally, in 1960, resulted in a classical theory of production, value and distribution]. The other great traditional branch of economics is monetary theory, and our period sees it transformed by [Keynes into a general theory of output and employment, interest and money, which, for the first time, convincingly challenged Say's Law]' (Shackle 1967, p. 12). Undeniably, 'Keynes and Sraffa laid the foundations for a monetary theory of production, capable of carrying a solid theoretical structure, and initiated a tremendous discussion, critical and constructive, on this subject' (Bortis 2003b, p. 96). However, no coherent – post-Keynesian – theoretical system capable of competing with neoclassical Walrasian–Marshallian economics has come into being so far.

Indeed, Joan Robinson later remarked on this twin revolution that 'Keynes evidently did not make much of [Sraffa's 1928 draft of *Production of Commodities by Means of Commodities*] and Sraffa, in turn, never made much of the *General Theory.* It is the task of post-Keynesians to reconcile the two' (Robinson 1978, p. 14). But how to reconcile Keynes's short-period model set in historical time, where uncertainty and expectations prevail, with Sraffa's timeless and deterministic long-period equilibrium model? There was, in fact, a deep gap between Keynes and Sraffa.

Later, this cleavage showed up within post-Keynesian economics which emerged in the 1950s and 1960s, comprising, according to Harcourt and Hamouda (1992, pp. 213–222), three broad, partly overlapping

This chapter is based on *Keynes and the Classics: Notes on the Monetary Theory of Production* (Bortis 2003a).

strands: the Keynesian Fundamentalists, the Robinsonian–Kaleckians, and the neo-Ricardians. In the main, the Keynesian Fundamentalists and the neo-Ricardians have largely ignored each other from the 1950s until the present.

This chapter starts from this seemingly hopeless situation. It is made up of two parts. In the first, it is argued that Luigi Pasinetti has made decisive steps to close the gap between Keynes and Sraffa at the level of fundamental pure theory, i.e. on the level of principles, which are independent of any historical realisations and specific institutions, but *imply* a certain form of the institutional set-up (Bortis 1997, 2003a). In fact, Pasinetti's work is in the classical tradition, to which Sraffa belongs, but open in the direction of Keynesian and post-Keynesian work. In the second part, it is argued, in the first place, that through his crucial contribution to close the gap between Keynes and Sraffa, Pasinetti has laid the conceptual foundations of classical–Keynesian political economy which may be considered a synthesis and an elaboration of post-Keynesian political economy. Subsequently, we sketch the basic features of the classical-Keynesian system. The chapter ends with a tribute to Luigi Pasinetti.

2 Closing the gap between Keynes and Sraffa

Keynes and Sraffa: uncertainty versus determinism

Most, if not all, Keynesian fundamentalists and most neo-Ricardians would argue that it is impossible to close the gap between Keynes and Sraffa. This is one of the main conclusions of John King's excellent *History of Post Keynesian Economics since 1936* (King 2003). Broadly speaking, Keynes's *General Theory* is dominated by investors who act under uncertainty about the future and whose actions are coordinated by the functioning of the socio-economic system regarding employment determination through the principle of effective demand. This principle is embodied in the multiplier relation, which, given autonomous demand, governs output and employment in a monetary production economy. In sharp contrast, Sraffa's *Production of Commodities* pictures how value and distribution are governed, in principle, within the social process of production by technological and institutional structures. Here, determinism prevails. Given this sharp contrast between Keynes and Sraffa, Alessandro Roncaglia, for example, thinks that, at best, a loose bridge may be built 'between Sraffa's analysis of prices and Keynes' analysis of production levels. [Sraffa] looks to conditions for reproduction of the economic system. . . . When the technology changes, the relative prices will [as a rule] also change' (Roncaglia 2000, p. 64). These price changes cannot be known *ex ante* because 'of that all-pervasive uncertainty constituting a key feature of Keynes' vision, leading him to grant expectations a central role in his theory. For this reason the two problems – Sraffa's and Keynes' – must be kept apart. Nevertheless, given Sraffa's approach to his problem – isolating it from the determination of quantities produced while avoiding any opening in the direction of "Say's law" – we may consider his analysis of the prices–distribution link conceptually compatible with Keynes' analysis of employment, once the latter has been cleared of marginalist encrustations' (Roncaglia 2000, p. 65). Since the future course of prices and quantities is unknown, it is not possible to go beyond the short term. All that can be done is to replace the Marshallian marginalist price remnants in Keynes' *General Theory*, which vary with changes in output levels, with some kind of fixed prices based upon the mark-up principle. This would, incidentally, require that Sraffa's prices of production are no longer seen as *conditions* for reproduction (Roncaglia) but as a pure theory of prices of production, with applied prices of production being set on the basis of normal cost calculation. Sraffa must be anchored in the real world and should not stay at the level of (Kantian) ideas produced by the human mind. Conceiving of Sraffa prices only as conditions for reproduction leads, as far as we can see, inevitably to setting prices through some planning mechanism: these conditions would have to be imposed on the real world. Considering, however, the prices of production as picturing how the pricing process goes on *in principle* within the social process of production provides the possibility of linking distributional states – an institutionally determined rate of profits – not only to Sraffa prices but also to the determination of the level of employment through the propensity to consume. A rising profit share would reduce the propensity to consume and the level of employment, and vice versa. This way of looking at things can be elaborated; for example, the capacity effect of investment can be taken account of and combined with the income effect. This is, broadly speaking, the way taken by Kalecki in his theory of cyclical growth (Kalecki 1971, pp. 165 ff.).

If post-Keynesian political economists want to erect a theoretical structure constituting an alternative to the neoclassical Walrasian–Marshallian system and its modern elaborations, then 'broad consistency' between Keynes and Sraffa, leading up to building loose bridges between the two theories, is clearly not sufficient. Even less satisfactory is to leave the gap as it is. Keynesian Fundamentalists and Kaleckians–Robinsonians would argue that Sraffa's theoretical system represents a long-period equilibrium model and that economies cannot get into long-period equilibria in a Keynesian world of uncertainty about the future, requiring a continuous revision of long-period expectations. The neo-Ricardians would reply that institutional–technological structures are the constant or slowly changing elements of the real world of the classical political economists which govern prices and quantities, and distributional outcomes, on a fundamental level. One cannot build economic theory upon psychological foundations, which echoes Sraffa's criticism of the *General Theory.*

The gap between Sraffa and Keynes is, probably, the fundamental reason why neoclassical economists do not take the post-Keynesian system of political economy seriously. Indeed, in an excellent textbook on old and new macroeconomics, it is argued that 'post Keynesianism does not represent a coherent theory and can, therefore, not be dealt with in an introductory textbook' (Felderer-Homburg 2003, p. 101). The gap between Keynes and Sraffa is certainly the main reason why post-Keynesian textbooks, by Joan Robinson/John Eatwell and Francis Cripps/Wynne Godley, for example, were not successful. The descriptions of steady states and golden ages contained in both books were simply not taken seriously by the neoclassicals and most post-Keynesians, the most important – implicit – reason being the presence of time. It should be remembered that principles in general and pure theories in particular should be *independent* of space and time, hence of concrete institutional set-ups; principles, however, *imply* certain types of institutions.

The problem

In all likelihood, the only way to bridge the gap between Keynes and Sraffa is to set up a coherent set of principles bringing together the classical view of value and distribution, based upon the labour value principle and the surplus principle of distribution, respectively, and the Keynesian vision of employment and output determination through the principle of effective demand. Based upon Pasinetti (1986a), this has been attempted in Bortis (2003a). This means reasoning, not literally but, in a broad-ranging way, in the spirit of Keynes and Sraffa. Based upon the set of classical–Keynesian principles, a broadly structured system of long-period, medium- and short-term theories along post-cum-classical–Keynesian lines may be erected (for a very sketchy outline see Bortis 1997). This would enable us to put the *original* works of Keynes and Sraffa – *The General Theory of Employment, Interest and Money* and *Production of Commodities by Means of Commodities* – in their respective places within a system of classical–Keynesian political economy, i.e. within a system of *theories* dealing with real-world phenomena.

The classical system, taken in a wider sense, embodies two aspects of the social process of production, i.e. the nature (inter-industry) approach and the (vertically integrated) labour approach, reflecting the famous Marxian statement that social production is an interaction between man (labour) and nature (land). The nature approach is pictured in François Quesnay's *Tableau économique*, the labour approach in Ricardo's *Principles*. Modern classical theory builds on these foundations: Leontief and Sraffa start from Quesnay's *Tableau* (Sraffa is explicit on this); Pasinetti, evidently, builds on Ricardo's *Principles*. As will be seen below, the Pasinetti transformation links the inter-industry and the labour approach such that the labour model embodies the inter-industry model at the basis of principles. The crucial point to be developed is that Luigi Pasinetti's *labour model*, set forth in five pages of his splendid article on the *Theory of Value – a Source of Alternative Paradigms in Economic Analysis* (Pasinetti 1986a, pp. 421–427), provides the analytical vehicle for bringing together Keynes and Sraffa at the level of first principles (see on this Bortis 2003a). Based upon these principles it should be possible to erect a broadly coherent, and *open*, system of classical–Keynesian political economy which would appear as a synthesis, an elaboration and an extension of post-Keynesian political economy. Thus, at the level of theories, very little would be new. The great number of fine pieces of existing post-Keynesian theory would have to be adapted, elaborated, completed, synthesised and put at the right place.

At this stage it may be asked why the starting point to bring Sraffa and Keynes together should be Pasinetti's *Theory of Value* (1986a) and not *Structural Change and Economic Growth* (Pasinetti 1981), or 'Sraffa's circular process and the concept of vertical integration' (Pasinetti 1986b), which contains a final section entitled 'Sraffa and Keynes – a meeting point' (pp. 14–16).

In Pasinetti (1981), the Leontief–inter-industry model is integrated into the labour model to study structural changes in a growing economy. In addition, we gain, in a classical environment, 'profound insights into the nature of technical change (pp. 61 ff. and 206 ff.), the basic functions of the price system (pp. 133 ff.), the significance of the rate of interest (Ch. 8), the meaning and the implications of the choice of techniques (pp. 188 ff.), and one could go on' (Bortis 2003a, pp. 428–429). The natural system set up by Pasinetti to deal with structural change and economic growth is a normative model which possesses highly desirable properties – for example, the full employment condition ought to be fulfilled. Moreover, 'when there is both population growth and technical progress, there are as many natural rates of profit as there are rates of expansion of demand (and production) of the various consumption goods' (Pasinetti 1981, p. 130). These are very specific requirements to ensure that structural change may go on smoothly. Deviations from the norm, brought about by structural unemployment, for example, can then be assessed and remedies proposed.

The aim pursued in Bortis (1997, 2003a), however, is entirely different. Here, the problem is to distil invariable principles regulating value, distribution and employment out of a – humanist, social liberal – vision of man and of society. The questions are, for example: What is a price? How is distribution fundamentally regulated? Pasinetti (1986a) precisely deals with essentials or fundamentals regarding value. Moreover, contrary to Pasinetti (1981), we need an explicit *macroeconomic* theory of the Keynesian type to be able to deal with the problem of determining the level, the scale, of employment and output *as a whole*. Employment determination through effective demand *must* be macroeconomic since monetary effective demand affects, in principle, *all* the sectors of an economy in the *same* way. However, a theory of employment is only implicit in Pasinetti (1981) through the necessary condition for full employment, for example relation II.2.8, p. 32.

Pasinetti (1986b) starts from Sraffa's (1960) model of circular and social production, on which basis the problems of value and distribution are dealt with in a classical vein. Pasinetti's aim is to overcome Sraffa's limitation of given quantities in order to render possible dynamic analysis. To do so 'Keynesian analysis must be developed beyond its macro economic original conception [which has to be] broken down into as many vertically integrated sectors as there are final commodities. The analytical device of the sub-systems' (pp. 15–16) '"shows at a glance" [Sraffa] the amount of labour which directly and indirectly goes into producing each commodity' (pp. 7–8). This opens the way to dynamic analysis: changing structures are incorporated in sectorial output and employment levels which may change, grow or decline over the course of time. Pasinetti (1986b) provides exciting perspectives for theoretical and empirical work regarding the interaction between structural changes-cum-technical progress, prices of production, distribution and output and employment levels. Once again the link between the classics and Keynes is established, but at the level of theories (structural change, value, distribution and growth), not of principles. For example, Pasinetti (1986b) implies prices of production, a specific type of price. The question as to the *nature* of the price is not, and need not be, asked.

However, the question as to the *nature* of price is asked in Pasinetti (1986a). Indeed, the meaning of prices in a pure exchange or preference economy is compared with a pure labour model and the meaning of prices therein (pp. 416–424). In a few pages Luigi Pasinetti brings to the open 'the fundamental differences between exchange-based neoclassical pure theory and production or labour-based classical theory [which are] set forth on the level of *principles*, illuminating thus the basic options in economic theory open at present' (Bortis 2003a, p. 415). Now, the problem of value is, in a way, the *key* problem in economic theory. Starting from a subjective or preference, exchange-based theory of value or from an objective, production or labour-based theory of value leads on to entirely different theories of distribution, employment, money, international trade and so on. Neoclassical theory builds upon the subjective theory of value. Hence the starting point for an alternative to the neoclassical theoretical system must be the pure labour model (Pasinetti 1986a, pp. 421–427), which contains the pure nature (inter-industry) model. Pasinetti's labour model may quite easily be elaborated to yield a complete classical model at the level of *principles* (Bortis 2003a, pp. 445–460).

Subsequently, bringing together Keynes and Sraffa boils down to linking classical and Keynesian political economy on the basis of the principles underlying these theories (Bortis 2003a). Upon the system of *principles* a system of classical–Keynesian *theories* can be set up. It is within this latter system that the *original* works of Keynes and Sraffa have to be put at the appropriate place. However, this is, of course, only part of the project. The classical–Keynesian system of theories must comprise *all* the post-Keynesian strands, the Keynesian Fundamentalists, the Robinsonian–Kaleckians and the neo-Ricardians. But even more, the classical–Keynesian system must be open to allow all types of heterodox economics and (humanist) Marxist political economy as well as large parts of neoclassical economics – dealing with the behaviour of individuals and collectives – to come into the picture. In this way most differing aspects of an evolving real world may be tackled. And, to avoid misunderstandings, it should be mentioned that Walras and Marshall will, for ever, remain monuments in the history of economic theory because without knowing about their theories, one cannot understand the meaning and the significance of the twin Keynes–Sraffa revolution. Hence the purpose of the classical–Keynesian synthesis is essentially positive and constructive, nobody is to be excluded; rather, the aim is to gather all the forces required to meet the formidable challenges facing us on a world scale: social problems (poverty and misery), economic issues (employment and distribution), environmental problems and the issue of sustainable development on a world level, and last, but not least, the rebuilding of states.

Before being able to deal in somewhat greater detail with the issue at stake, closing the gap between Keynes and Sraffa, two methodological issues have to be dealt with: first, as already alluded to, the difference between principles and theories, and second, the notion of equilibrium implied in the subsequent analysis.

Principles and theories

Principles and theories imply two entirely different methods to get hold, probably and sketchily, of aspects of socio-economic reality and are associated, broadly and tentatively, with two different but complementary concepts of social science.

> The first, conventional, notion of science sees the theoretical economist as a model builder, possibly in view of establishing testable propositions. He endeavours to *explain* economic phenomena starting from *given* premisses and engages in the search for empirical regularities within economic phenomena. Even on the macroeconomic level, theoretical explanation is frequently complemented by empirical means, with the Phillips curve, the work done on the Keynesian consumption function, and the close association between price levels and quantities of money perhaps being most prominent. On the sectoral and on the microlevel, explanatory models and empirical investigations abound.
>
> However, scientific work always rests upon fundamental principles, which, as a rule, are taken for granted. Neoclassical scientific work is based upon the marginal principle, Keynesians rely upon the principle of effective demand. This leads to a second notion of science. Here the theorist attempts to distil principles or fundamentals in view of *understanding* how socio-economic systems essentially function. For example, the question is about the fundamental forces governing prices, distributional outcomes or employment levels. In this sense, Ricardo wrote on the principles of political economy, Marshall on the principles of economics. Based upon the principle of effective demand, Keynes aimed at establishing a general theory of employment, interest and money. In a way principles – the marginal principle, the surplus principle, the principle of effective demand – form the basis upon which theoretical work dealing with phenomena takes place. (Bortis 2003a, pp. 411–412)

In a way, theories are *reflections* of real-world phenomena; for example, the price of production is a theoretical concept which reflects essential elements of prices calculated within enterprises in the framework of normal cost calculation; as such, the price of production reflects technical conditions of production and the institutional determination of distributional variables such as money wage rates and target rates of profits. Principles, however, represent *recreations* or *reconstitutions* of essential elements of phenomena, for example prices, distributional outcomes and employment levels. The questions are: what, fundamentally, determines a price; is it labour or utility? Are the fundamental forces governing distribution social forces, associated with social power, or market forces, i.e. supply and demand? Is employment determined on the labour market or governed by effective demand? Alternatively, regarding value, the question is: what, fundamentally, *is* a price? What is its nature? And so for all other economic phenomena, distribution, employment and so on. Hence, 'principles represent the essential elements underlying a certain phenomenon, or the constitutive elements of an object. [Distilling principles requires considering the whole of society and of man], and all information available must be examined, scientific and non-scientific, theoretical and empirical and historical, whereby the objectively given material is dealt with by reason based on a metaphysical vision that, in turn, is associated with intuition' (Bortis 2003a, p. 412). In distilling principles, it is crucial to leave aside all accidental elements to put to the fore the constitutive, the essential or the fundamental. Since principles or sets of principles are reconstructions or recreations of essential elements of phenomena, these have *not* to be realistic in the scientific sense, 'since they are not reflections or copies (*Abbilder*) of certain spheres of the real world that can eventually be associated with testable propositions. In their being reconstructions of essential aspects of real world phenomena, principles illuminate these phenomena from inside and initiate the formation of empirically testable theories. In this sense Walras's *General Equilibrium Model* contributes to understanding how Adam Smith's *invisible hand* might work in principle. With the Walrasian model in the background the neoclassical economists have built simplified textbook theories of value, distribution and employment upon the marginal principle which is behind all demand and supply curves; in many instances, the Cobb–Douglas production function or Samuelson's surrogate production function are used to elucidate the implications of the marginal principle – the Walrasian model is too complex for an easily understandable exposition of the neoclassical principles and their implications' (Bortis 2003a, p. 413). Finally, in Pasinetti's *Theory of Value* (Pasinetti 1986a), 'the fundamental differences between exchange-based neoclassical pure theory and production or labour-based classical theory are set forth on the level of *principles*, illuminating thus the basic options in economic theory open at present. In the following it is suggested that the classical principles ought to be elaborated and to be brought together with Keynes's, adapted to the classical long-period method' (Bortis 2003a, p. 415). This, as will be seen, implies bringing together Keynes and Sraffa at the level of principles.

The equilibrium notion

The clue for bringing together Keynes and Sraffa at the level of principles, in a way, to synthesise proportions-based classical theory of value and distribution with Keynes's theory of employment dealing with the scale of economic activity, lies in the notion of long-period equilibrium (Bortis 1997, pp. 75–103). The conventional view starts from a disequilibrium situation in the present, which, in a stationary state, would work out and produce an eventual tendency towards a future equilibrium situation. This equilibrium concept is untenable once historical time is introduced as Joan Robinson emphasised time and again (Robinson 1956 [for example, pp. 57–60, 114–23 and 173–6]): an economy cannot get into an equilibrium if there is uncertainty about the future and if, as a consequence, expectations are liable to disappointment. The equilibrium position must, therefore, be sought in the present. The first step is to abstract from temporary and rapidly changing short- and medium-term elements of reality, i.e. *behavioural* elements related to markets and to business cycles (Bortis 1997, p. 106, scheme 3). This is to dig deeper to bring into the open the permanent or slowly evolving elements of the real world made up of the technological and economic *structure*, i.e. the material basis of a society, and the social, political, legal and cultural superstructure erected thereupon. Technology and institutions represent the stable features of social reality which the classical economists (Ricardo in the main) had in mind when they conceived of labour values (and prices of production) as the natural and fundamental prices from which actual or market prices temporarily deviate (Ricardo 1951, p. 88). [The *classical* equilibrium prices and quantities, as [are] implied in the price and quantity systems (12) and (21) below, complemented by the supermultiplier relation (37) below represent, therefore, a *system equilibrium*, not a market equilibrium.] The latter conceives of the market as an autonomous subsystem surrounded by a social, political and legal framework. The former, however, implies that prices and quantities are directly or indirectly governed by the entire socio-economic system, i.e. by technology and institutions, which form a structured entity. This is the main tenet of Bortis (1997).

To conceive of the long run as being situated in the present has already been envisaged by Marshall. In fact, Robertson, relying on Guillebaud, mentions that 'Marshall used the term "the long period" in two quite distinct senses, one which stands realistically for any period in which there is time for *substantial* alterations to be made in the size of plant, and one in which it stands conceptually for the Never-never land of unrealized tendency' (Robertson 1956, p. 16). In Bortis (1997, pp. 81–89), it is suggested that, appearances notwithstanding, Marshall's second definition of 'the long period', not the first one, is relevant for long-period analysis. Indeed, with the usual first meaning of this notion, the long-period equilibrium is located in the future and would come about if the persistent economic forces could work out undisturbed, i.e. if there was a stationary state or a steadily growing one. This first of the Marshallian definitions is largely irrelevant because 'in the long run we are all dead'; moreover, there are no 'stationary conditions and steady states'; and, finally, there are the results of the capital theoretic discussion: lower factor prices cannot, in principle, be associated with larger factor quantities. The second meaning of 'the long period', however, allows us to locate the long-period equilibrium in the *present* and to associate it with an institutionally governed system equilibrium (Bortis 1997, Chapters 3 and 4).

This takes us back to the classicals and Marx, whose [surplus] approach to economic problems has proved so immensely fruitful. (Bortis 2003a, pp. 419–420)

Throughout his entire work, Luigi Pasinetti works with the classical method. Principles or fundamental pure theory (Pasinetti 1981) and pure theories (Pasinetti 1977) tell us how the relevant causal forces work in principle, independently of space and time, that is independent of specific institutions and of specific technological structures. However, principles and theories of the classical type *imply* a corresponding type of institutional set-up, the classical institutional and technological material basis and the institutional superstructure. To complete the picture we may add that neoclassical/Walrasian pure theory, fundamental and secondary, *implies* another type of the institutional set-up: the potentially self-regulating market stands in the centre, surrounded by a political, judicial, social and cultural framework.

Nature and man (land and labour), and the social process of production

The starting point is the social process of production, which, basically, may be seen as an interaction between man (labour) and nature (land) by means of real capital, i.e. tools and machines (Bortis 2003a, pp. 433–436). The *nature or land* aspect of social production is set out in Pasinetti (1977). Here the (Leontief) inter-industry flows are pictured: primary goods taken from nature and intermediate goods are transformed into final products in a social and, in part, circular process involving production of commodities by means of commodities – and labour (Sraffa). The *labour* aspect of production is set forth in Pasinetti (1981 and 1986a): direct and indirect labour, in association with past labour embodied in fixed capital, produce the primary, intermediate and final products (Bortis 2003a, pp. 433–436).

Analytically, the land and labour aspects of the social process of production are linked by the *Pasinetti transformation*: the vector of direct labour is multiplied by the transposed Leontief-inverse to yield the total (direct and indirect) labour required to produce the various commodities (Bortis 2003a, p. 438).

Since the i-th row of the Leontief-inverse contains the quantities of each good required directly and indirectly to produce one unit of good i, the i-th element of the n-vector stands for all the labour used directly and indirectly in the whole production system to produce one unit of commodity i. Since production runs from primary through intermediate goods to final goods, there is, evidently, vertical integration, with the final goods summarising all the 'lower-level' efforts made to produce them.

Linking the classics with Keynes

The classical (Ricardian) labour model obtained by the Pasinetti transformation determines relative prices and quantities only (Pasinetti 1981, p. 23, note 30). To obtain absolute prices, the money wage rate (w) must be fixed; to determine absolute quantities requires fixing the level of employment (N) (Pasinetti 1981, pp. 32/33, Pasinetti 1986a, pp. 422/423). Now, in Chapter 4 of the *General Theory* – 'The choice of units' – Keynes states: 'In dealing with the theory of employment I propose . . . to make use of only two fundamental units of quantity, namely, quantities of money-value and quantities of employment. . . . We shall call the unit in which the quantity of employment is measured the labour-unit; and the money-wage of a labour-unit we shall call the wage-unit' (Keynes 1973/1936, p. 41). Thus, the labour model emerging from the Pasinetti transformation links the whole body of classical theory to Keynes's employment theory and, as such, closes the gap between Keynes and Sraffa on the level of fundamental pure theory, i.e. on the level of principles. In doing so, Luigi Pasinetti has laid the long-period foundations for classical–Keynesian political economy, which may be considered a synthesis and an elaboration of the post-Keynesian strands of thought. To broadly sketch the classical–Keynesian system is the object of the next section. A central problem is to adapt Keynes's short-period theory of employment to the long run to make it compatible with the classical (Ricardian) theory of value and distribution which focuses on stable or slowly changing magnitudes (institutions and technology) and is, as such, of a long-period nature (Bortis 1997, pp. 142–204, and Bortis 2003a, pp. 415–423 and 460–467).

3 An outline of the classical–Keynesian system

In a second step, we attempt to broadly picture the principles underlying the classical–Keynesian system and suggest how these may be linked with the very rich Keynesian, post-Keynesian but also Marxist approaches – remembering here that Keynes was much more than just a political economist, he was in fact a social and political scientist in the widest sense of the word, and that Marx was a humanist, deeply concerned about the immense social problems of his time, not a precursor of Stalin. Moreover, it is Marx's historical and sociological method that is crucial, not some aspects of the material content of his work (Bortis 1997, pp. 125–130). For example, the property issue is certainly important, but not decisive; in fact, private property may co-exist with social and state property, with the dominating form of property depending upon prevailing values having developed historically in some country or region. What really matters is the Keynesian question as to the nature of unemployment: is it, in the main, system-caused and involuntary or behavioural and voluntary?

Some problems of method

The present remarks on method are linked up with the subsections on *principles and theories* and on *the notion of equilibrium* in section 2 above. These issues are now taken up in the context of the classical–Keynesian approach to economic problems.

The preceding remarks suggest that Keynes should not be associated with neoclassical economics (mainly Marshall) as Paul Samuelson has advocated. Indeed, his celebrated Neoclassical Synthesis is based upon Hicks's IS–LM diagram, which reduces Keynes to equilibrium economics. Following Luigi Pasinetti, we want to suggest that Keynes should be linked with classical political economy in a wider sense. Methodologically, this means setting up *causal* models and combining them subsequently. According to classical political economy, value and distribution are determined within the social and circular process of production. With values and prices of production fixed, Keynes's principle of effective demand would come in to determine quantities. It has been stated time and again that Keynes's theoretical model naturally implies a fix-price theory.

On a fundamental level the labour value principle plays an essential role. After all, in social production, conceived of as an interaction between man (labour) and land (nature), it is man (labour) who plays the crucial (active) role. The basic model must, therefore, be a vertically integrated (Ricardo–Pasinetti) labour model into which a simplified version of the horizontal (inter-industry) Leontief model may be integrated (Bortis 2003a, pp. 433–445). More sophisticated models picturing the Quesnay–Sraffa–Leontief nature aspect of production may then be grafted upon the basic labour model. Subsequently, classical models may conveniently be combined with Keynesian models. However, there is no need to construct a classical–Keynesian supermodel, since such a model would be completely unmanageable. An all-embracing model is required only at the level of principles, and it is this basic model we are mainly dealing with in the following.

In the spirit of classical political economy of the Ricardian type, we shall consider only the influence of permanent or slowly evolving factors – institutions and technology – upon economic phenomena, mainly prices, the distribution of incomes, employment and involuntary unemployment.

Hence the long-period prices and quantities set forth below all depend upon technology and institutions and form, as such, a *system equilibrium*. Here, the entire socio-economic system enters the picture. This contrasts with the neoclassical market equilibrium, where the legal, social and political institutions are relegated to the framework surrounding the market.

The classical political economists have indeed conceived of society as a system of institutions. There is a material basis with the social process of production at the centre. The surplus emerging from this sector allows a society to build up and maintain an institutional superstructure, political, legal, social and cultural. Classical–Keynesian political economy is about the way in which the institutional and technological system governs the persistent economic phenomena: the fundamental prices rooted in production, the distribution of incomes and the level of employment, and, as a rule, persistent involuntary unemployment.

Now, institutions and technology are precisely facts of the existing situation on which we have little reason for expecting a change or on which the direction of change is broadly known, as is the case with technology where, moreover, changes occur, as a rule, at the margin. Regarding investment, the difference between the normal (satisfactory) rate of profits and the realised rate of profits precisely constitutes a *given* fact which is very important for investment decisions, and the importance of this fact increases if the difference is larger and more durable (Bortis 1997, pp. 207–214). In a way, then, Keynesian long-period analysis could be called Keynesian Institutionalism, which differs from the traditional system-based, institutionalism of the German Historical School, in the main, by its explicit theoretical foundations.

The output and employment trend may be conceived of as a – hidden – fully adjusted situation characterised by normal prices and quantities and normal degrees of capacity utilisation (Bortis 1997, pp. 75–89, 142–204). Normal or long-period prices and quantities, including investment volumes, depend upon the entire institutional system, i.e. on the material basis and upon the institutional superstructure. This is a crucial point. In the long run, the investment volume represents, like consumption, *derived* demand, depending upon the evolution of long-period output, with economic activity being set into motion by the autonomous demand components, exports and/or government expenditure.

Hence normal prices and quantities constitute a system equilibrium. Since normal output does not, as a rule, correspond to full employment output, permanent involuntary unemployment obtains. Normal prices are, in turn, governed by the conditions of production and distributional arrangements. The latter implies that normal prices are, in principle, associated with an equal (target) profit rate (r*) which entrepreneurs consider satisfactory and which, therefore, enters their (normal) price calculation.

In the following it is to be suggested how this determination goes on in principle. Dealing with principles means that a model need not reflect reality and, as such, need not lead to testable propositions. As suggested above, a model of principles represents a reconstruction or recreation of what is probably essential to specific real-world phenomena, leaving aside everything which is accidental (Bortis 2003a, pp. 411 ff.). Principles also contain a *normative* dimension that, again, points to the fact that models of principles are reconstructions of essential elements of specific real-world phenomena and not reflections. A striking historical example is Walras's *General Equilibrium Model*, which on the normative side is associated with a Pareto Optimum. This model was elaborated in time of economic crisis – the last quarter of the 19th century. Its purpose is to represent the ideal liberal economy and not the distorted capitalist reality.

In a wider view, the present set of principles is intended to constitute a theoretical alternative to Léon Walras's *General Equilibrium Model*, i.e. to the neoclassical principles, based upon an elaboration and extension of the (classical) labour model set forth in Pasinetti's (1986a) *Theory of Value: A source of alternative paradigms in economic analysis*. This choice has been justified above.

The social process of production as the starting point

The manner

'in which classical and Keynesian elements of political economy must be combined emerges from the very nature of the social process of production. Indeed, Marx suggested conceiving of this process as an interaction between man (labour) and nature (land). In this interaction labour is evidently the active element while land is passive. In the 17th century already William Petty suggested that ['labour is the Father and active principle of Wealth, as Lands are the Mother' (Petty 1662, p. 68)]. The land and labour features of production give rise to distinguishing three kinds of basic goods, absolutely necessary for production: land basics, labour basics and labour–land basics. *Land basics* are primary products taken from nature, for example iron ore or crude oil, which are made ready for productive use in the form of steel or petrol, respectively. Subsequently, land basics or primaries are used to produce intermediate products: wheat, flour, leather, bricks, for instance. Primary products and intermediate products represent part of the means of production that are converted into final products, specifically: bread, shoes, houses, various machines and equipment; generally: private consumption goods; private and public capital goods; and goods making up for state or public consumption. *Labour basics* are final products and correspond to the socially necessary consumption goods required to maintain the persons who are active in the 'profit sector' and who, through the social surplus, enable a 'non-profit sector', including the state, i.e. the political institutions. Finally, *labour–land basics* are machine tools, i.e. machines to make machines, representing past labour and enable the labour force operating in the 'profit sector' to enter into contact and to interact with nature through the social process of production, i.e. to extract primary goods, nature or land basics, with the aim of transforming them, passing through intermediate products, into final products, including labour basics. The primary land basics move between industries in horizontal inter-industry models to produce, in a first stage, primary goods entering the production of all goods, as pictured by Sraffa's model in which inputs and outputs coincide. Since the output of land basics enters the production of all intermediate and final goods, necessary technical relations exist between land basics and the final output. The prices of nature basics are thus determining the prices of final products. Hence the fundamental relations between value and distribution may be studied within the social process of production of primaries or land basics as Sraffa, with [great] intuitive insight and analytical ability, did indeed on the basis of a model implying non-uniform compositions of capital (Sraffa 1960). In fact, land basics contain, potentially, all final outputs, including labour basics, i.e. necessary consumption goods. (This was also the view of François Quesnay from whose *Tableau économique* Sraffa's *Production of Commodities by Means of Commodities* directly derives (Sraffa 1960, p. 93).)

The output of land basics is, in a second stage, taken up to produce all intermediate goods. In a third stage, primary and intermediate goods are transformed into final goods consisting of labour basics, of labour–land basics and of non-basics. Part of the output, necessary consumption, is used up by the persons active in the 'profit sector'; the remaining output represents the social surplus: gross investment, consumption exceeding the necessary consumption of the workers and employees in the 'profit sector', the necessary consumption of the 'non-profit sector' population and the non-necessary consumption of the entire population, as well as social and state consumption, for example, for cultural purposes in the broadest sense and for running the judiciary system, the education system and government administration.

This view of production – primary products are passing through intermediate products, transformed into final goods – explains the triangular structure of the Leontief matrix in which Sraffa's land basics are located in the upper left corner. Land basics are produced with land basics and hence the corresponding transaction table and the coefficient matrix form a square matrix. The output of primary goods is distributed to the industries producing intermediate and final goods. Intermediate goods require as inputs land basics and other intermediate goods. The corresponding coefficients form another square matrix beginning at the lower right-hand corner of the Sraffa land basics matrix. Final goods are produced with land basics and intermediate goods. Consequently, primary products enter the production of all goods; intermediate products enter the production of other intermediates and of final goods. The latter are only outputs. Hence for intermediates some positions to the left of the main Leontief diagonal are positive. By definition, for final goods only the net output vector contains positive elements. The broadly triangular structure of the Leontief matrix thus emerges, with zero positions dominating to the left of the main diagonal.

The vector of net outputs has zero positions for primary and intermediate products. The lower part of this vector is occupied by the final outputs. These are made up of private and public investment (capital) and consumption goods. For each product, primary, intermediate and final goods, there is a specific capital good. Moreover, among the capital goods there is a particular type, i.e. machine tools or machines to make machines, a point emphasised in Lowe (1976). Machine tools are, in association with labour, capable of reproducing themselves and of producing the corresponding investment goods for each industry, that is for all primary, intermediate and final goods industries. Obviously, the machine tool sector is of basic importance for the social process of production. As has been suggested, this sector enables man (labour) to enter into contact and to interact with nature. (Incidentally, in traditional societies, this role was held by the blacksmith, who always occupied a privileged position in pre-modern societies because he produced the tools and the weapons.) Because of their fundamental importance in the social process of production, machine tools may, therefore, conveniently be called labour–land basics. The presence of the machine-tool sector also implies Sraffian 'production by means of commodities', not only among the processes linking primary and intermediate goods to final goods but also on the *final* product side. The basic two-sector model put to use in the capital theory debate – a capital good (machine tool) sector producing a capital good for itself and for the consumption goods sector is a striking example (Garegnani 1970 and Harcourt 1972).

The second type of final goods are the consumption goods. These are of three broad types: necessary consumption goods, non-necessary consumption goods and goods for social and state consumption. (Bortis 2003a, pp. 433–435)

Perhaps we may mention that Sraffa (1960) is treated here as a pure nature (inter-industry) model containing nature basics only, i.e. primary goods taken from nature, and as such has been included in the left top corner of our Leontief matrix. The two other types of basic goods, labour basics (necessary consumption goods) and land–labour basics (machine tools producing all capital goods), are included among the final goods. In fact, in Sraffa (1960), all three types of basic goods appear which, as will be suggested at the end of the next section, renders the treatment of value and distribution and the link with Keynesian employment models rather difficult.

Production, value and distribution

To deal with the principles (or fundamentals or essentials) of value and distribution within the immensely complex social and circular process of production sketched in the previous section, all accidental elements have to be left aside. In this vein, two simplifying assumptions are made, which, when given up, leave all the conclusions following from the principles qualitatively intact when the analysis moves to the level of theories reflecting aspects of the real world. First, a vertically integrated economy is considered, and second, the conditions of production are similar in all the sectors of production in the sense that the relationship between total labour – direct and indirect – contained in some capital good used to produce some commodity i and the total labour embodied in this commodity – n_{iK}/n_i – is the same in all the sectors of production (consumption goods, capital goods, intermediate and primary goods). The heterogeneity of the goods is ensured by two factors: in the first place, the absolute values of n_{iK} and n_i diverge between the various sectors; and second, the same quantity of abstract labour is contained in qualitatively very different goods.

From these assumptions the labour principle of value emerges together with the surplus principle of distribution involving a uniform rate of profits. Both principles are put to practical use here in a broad humanist–ethical sense, not in the sense of class struggle (which, however, may arise if there is large-scale alienation, brought about by mass unemployment, for example).

In the sense of the classical political economists, but also of Aristotle and of Thomas Aquinas, the value of goods and services is, in principle, determined by the 'quantity of direct and indirect labour' contained in them. This quantity is, in turn, determined by three factors: first, by labour time; second, by the reduction coefficients, which reduce complex labour to simple labour – the reduction coefficients are expressed in the wages structure, the determination of which is a complex problem of social ethics and should be essentially based on an evaluation of work places; third, on the social appreciation of a product.

Distribution on the basis of the *surplus principle* is a complex social process. First, the great shares in income must be determined, i.e. the shares of (normal or ordinary) wages, made up of necessary and of surplus wages, and the surplus proper, made up of profits and rents. Profits are socially necessary to run the production system, i.e. the enterprises; they represent, very broadly speaking, an award for good management, investible funds, and render possible the setting up of sinking funds in view of an uncertain future (*see* Bortis 1997, pp. 158–175). Rents, in turn, are made up of land *and* labour rents. The latter are equivalent to surplus wages due to special abilities or privileges, e.g. of managers, engineers, surgeons, artisans, artists, sportsmen and so on. Second, the structure of necessary and surplus wages (normal or ordinary wages), surplus wages due to special abilities and privileges, and of profits and rents has to be broadly determined. Most important is the determination of the structure of ordinary and surplus wages, a task to be performed, possibly in an indicative way, through work evaluation inside the enterprises and through trade unions between industries and sectors. In a classical vein, the market would have to bring into line market wage and profit rates, and land rents into line with the socially determined magnitudes through changing output levels. All in all, distribution emerges thus as the core issue of social ethics.

The surplus produced in the 'profit sector' (the 'productive' sector of the classics) of an economy should be used to build up a socially appropriate, 'non-profit' sector (the 'unproductive' sector in classical terminology) in the widest sense of the word, comprising political, legal, social and cultural institutions. As such, the surplus is obviously socially necessary since it is required to build up an institutional superstructure upon the material basis. Hence, the surplus, if used in an appropriate way, leads to a good and proper functioning of society at large, including the material basis that produces the social surplus.

Inappropriate uses of the surplus lead to social and individual *alienation:* the distribution of incomes and wealth may become very unequal and involuntary (system-determined) mass unemployment may develop as a consequence; both lead, as a rule, to social exclusion, misery and an increasing number of crimes; terrorism, too, has deep roots in misery and despair. Hence, the production, extraction, distribution and use of the surplus is the most important problem of social and political ethics (Harcourt 1986, p.5).

Value and distribution are regulated within or in direct association with the social process of production.

The *price equations* in a vertically integrated production system are as follows:

$$\mathbf{pA} + w_n \mathbf{n_d} k = \mathbf{p} \tag{1}$$

A is the broadly triangular Leontief–Sraffa matrix sketched above (*see also* Bortis 2003a, pp. 433–36). The coefficients of the matrix **A**

$$a_{ij} = x_{ij}/X_j \tag{2}$$

indicate the quantity of good i required to produce a unit of good j. **p** is the (row) vector of prices. At first, there are the prices of primary goods (land basics), subsequently the prices of intermediate goods and, finally, the prices of final goods.

Hence **pA** represents the monetary value of the basic and intermediate goods (the monetary value of inputs) utilised in the social process of production for each good (primary, intermediate and final). The expression

$$w_n \mathbf{n_d} k \tag{3}$$

represents value added and its distribution between wages and profits (and rents). $\mathbf{n_d}$ is the (row) vector of direct labour per unit of each product (primary, intermediate and final goods). w_n (a scalar) represents the money wage rate per unit of simple, unqualified labour (with complex types of labour, qualified in most varying degrees, being multiples of simple labour). The scalar k is the 'mark-up' on average costs at normal capacity utilisation. In a microeconomic view, k governs gross profits such that invested fixed capital gets a normal rate of profits r^* including the rate of depreciation. In a wider, macroeconomic, view, k may be reinterpreted to contain, in addition to gross profits, surplus wages, labour rents, due to specific abilities or privileges, for example, and land rents. Hence the microeconomic 'mark-up' is, on the macroeconomic level, transformed into the 'surplus coefficient', governing, in principle, the size of the social surplus over socially necessary wages.

Methodologically speaking, the present analysis is situated at the level of principles. Consequently, the relevant causal forces are presented in their pure form, independently of their historical realisations (Keynes' pure and applied theory). Moreover, we consider only what is essential to our analysis. In this sense, labour values constitute the essence of prices. This implies abstracting from specific conditions of production and from market conditions, and supposes a vertically integrated economy. Past labour is embodied in fixed capital.

The fundamental prices (Equations 4–7 below) emerge from the social process of production and represent, in principle, the social effort that has been made to produce the various goods; hence, in a classical–Keynesian view, prices of produced goods are not scarcity indicators. In fact, at the level of principles, direct and indirect labour is basic to the value of goods and services.

As has already been suggested, distribution is, essentially and ideally, a social process with trade unions, entrepreneurial associations and the state intervening to bring about as much distributional justice as is humanly possible (in present economic reality, however, the single worker or employee is frequently directly faced with the entrepreneur). The links existing between value and distribution at the level of principles emerge formally from isolating the price vector in Equation (1) on the left-hand side (*see* Bortis 2003a, pp. 436–445):

$$\mathbf{p} = w_n[(\mathbf{I} - \mathbf{A})^{-1}]' \mathbf{n_d} k \tag{4}$$

This operation, which links the nature (land or inter-industry) model to the vertically integrated labour model, might be called the Pasinetti transformation (Pasinetti 1981, pp. 109–112). Multiplying the (column) vector of direct labour, $\mathbf{n_d}$, with the rows of the transposed Leontief inverse yields the vector of total – direct and indirect – labour ($\mathbf{n}$) required to produce some good i:

$$\mathbf{n} = [(\mathbf{I} - \mathbf{A})^{-1}]'\mathbf{n_d} \tag{5}$$

Inserting relation (5) into Equation (4) and multiplying the capital good row for each good by a coefficient so as to make the ratio n_{iK}/n_i equal to unity for all goods (Bortis 2003a, p. 438) yields the classical – Ricardo–Pasinetti – price equations:

$$\mathbf{p} = w_n \mathbf{n}\, k \tag{6}$$

which can be interpreted sectorially (p and n as vectors) or macroeconomically (p and n as scalars).

Specifying the mark-up, k yields a simplified price equation for all goods:

$$p_i = w_n n_i [1 + (r\, n_{iK} k)/n_i] = w_n n_i k \tag{7}$$

The macroeconomic equivalent of these equations is the Kalecki–Weintraub price equation:

$$p = w_n n\, k \tag{8}$$

Since the mark-up k must equal the expression within square brackets in (7) for equal conditions of production in all sectors (n_{iK}/n_i is the same everywhere, to simplify equal to unity as is argued in Bortis 2003a, p. 443, rel. 19.16), we get – on the macroeconomic level – the following relations for the mark-up k and the wage share 1/k if the surplus consists of profit only:

$$k = n/(n - r\, n_K) \tag{9}$$

and

$$1/k = 1 - r(n_K/n) \tag{10}$$

Both relations imply that all economic values are created by the workers and employees in the profit sector (the classical productive sector).

From a distributional perspective, the social surplus may, as already suggested, be interpreted in a wider, macroeconomic sense, to include gross profits, surplus wages over socially necessary wages, labour rents as are due to exceptional abilities or privileges, land rents and profits. The use of the social surplus, ideally, provides the material basis for all the persons active in the non-profit sector in the widest sense, including the state, to create political, social, legal and cultural values through the actions of individuals and collectives within the institutions established in the institutional superstructure. These values cannot, in principle, be measured in money terms. Highly unequal distributions of the surplus and the ensuing inappropriate use of the social surplus are, as a rule, associated with alienated social states of affairs.

The Equations (6–8) capture the essentials of classical (Ricardian–Pasinettian) price theory: the prices of *produced* goods reflect the social effort undertaken to produce them in terms of direct and indirect labour; distribution, based upon the surplus principle, is a complex social process.

The treatment of value and distribution within the social and circular and vertically integrated process of production suggested in this and in the preceding section enables us to deal with three problems associated, in our opinion, with Sraffa's model of circular production, value and distribution. *First*, the notion of land basics or primary products enables us to deal with the problem that, with Sraffa, inputs equal output. Indeed, in the upper left hand corner of the Leontief matrix iron ore is transformed into steel, crude oil into petrol, and so on; the outputs of land basics are subsequently transferred to all intermediate and final goods sectors. *Second*, treating fixed capital goods as final products, all produced by machine tools and labour, rather than to treat fixed capital as joint products renders the whole analysis of value and distribution within social and circular production much easier; specifically, profits may now be calculated on fixed capital by way of a mark-up on circulating capital which includes direct wage costs and the costs of intermediate and primary goods, which also become wage costs if there is vertical integration. [Even more appropriately, the mark-up may be calculated on average total costs at *normal capacity utilisation* – normal prices imply normal quantities!] *Third*, the social and circular process of production implies, in fact, production of commodities by means of commodities *and labour*. This means that the feature of *circularity* appears in three instances in the social process of production: In the first place, there is production of primary commodities by primary commodities and labour in the upper left Sraffa corner of the Leontief system. Secondly, in the realm of final products, there is production of commodities by means of commodities in the capital goods sector where all specific capital goods are produced by machine tools, which also produce and reproduce themselves. Thirdly, and perhaps most importantly, necessary consumption goods which are final goods have to move to all, even to the most remote corners, of the social and circular production system, because of the fact that there is production of commodities by means of commodities *and labour*, a fact pictured by relation (5) above which indicates the Pasinetti operation of calculating vertically integrated labour by multiplying the transposed Leontief inverse by the vector of direct labour. (Bortis 2003a, pp. 444–445)

Proportions and scale: classical and Keynesian macroeconomics – monetary theory of production

In a classical–Keynesian view, the social process of production is at the centre of a monetary production economy. Distribution – the shares of wages, profits and rents in domestic income and the structure of wages, profits and rents – gives rise to specific proportions, that is part–whole relationships. Relative prices and quantities, and the distribution of labour between sectors and industries, are also proportions. These proportions and their explanation are at the heart of classical political economy, which deals also with the circulation of goods and money. The breadth of the circuit, or the scale of economic activity, is the object of Keynesian political economy. The next two sections deal with the proportions and the scale aspect respectively.

The synthesis of the proportions aspect and of the scale aspect yields a classical–Keynesian political economy, i.e. a monetary theory of production, where money is all-important to run the economy, since money always buys goods and never goods buy other goods, and where, as a consequence, the real and the financial sector are inextricably linked:

$$M - C \ldots P \ldots C' - M' \qquad (11)$$

Entrepreneurs have money and finance (M) at their disposal to buy means of production (raw materials and intermediate goods, machinery) and to hire labour (C). Within the social process of production P, labour, using machines, transforms the primary and intermediate goods into final goods C'. These are sold on the final goods markets for money M', which represents effective (monetary) demand for goods and services.

The proportions aspect of classical–Keynesian political economy

In this section, all equations are based upon Pasinetti's seminal *Theory of Value* (1986a) and slightly elaborated.

The price system (12) depicts monetary flows and has several aspects which are considered in turn: first, there is the formation of prices; second, the formation of incomes and their distribution is suggested; and third, there is the spending of income by private households, enterprises and the state:

$$\begin{bmatrix} 1 & 0 & \cdots & 0 & -n_1 \\ 0 & 1 & \cdots & 0 & -n_2 \\ \vdots & \vdots & \ddots & \vdots & \vdots \\ 0 & 0 & \cdots & 1 & -n_m \\ -c_1 & -c_2 & \cdots & -c_m & 1 \end{bmatrix} \begin{bmatrix} p_1 \\ p_2 \\ \vdots \\ p_m \\ w_n k \end{bmatrix} = 0 \qquad (12)$$

In this equation system the c_i are fractions of real income – in terms of (full employment) labour embodied N_f – spent on good i (13), or demand coefficients per labour unit (13a):

$$Q_{if} = c_i N_f \tag{13}$$

$$c_i = Q_{if}/N_f \tag{13a}$$

The formation of absolute prices within the social process of production can take place only once the distributional variables are determined, i.e. the money wage rate w_n of some labour unit, and the mark-up k, including the uniform target profit rate (r); as mentioned above, the labour unit could, for example, consist of simple, unqualified labour with qualified labour as multiples – reduction coefficients – of unqualified labour; obviously, the reduction coefficients have a wide normative dimension, associated with distributive justice. One must sharply distinguish between actually existing, *normal*, and *natural*, normative or socially desirable reduction coefficients. On the level of principles, the natural is, in fact, the normative form of the normal.

The (absolute) prices (Equation 14) represent the money value of the social effort to produce the individual goods within the social process of production. These prices result from multiplying the first m–1 rows in the above matrix with the price and income vector.

$$p_i = w_n n_i k = w_n (1/A_i) k \, (i = 1, 2, m) \tag{14}$$

The A_i represents sectorial labour productivities.

The formation of absolute prices is intimately linked to the formation of incomes and its distribution. The price Equation (14), in fact, implies that the money value of sectoral outputs equals the sectoral incomes in money terms. However, this second aspect of the system (12) also implies, as will be seen below, that this system determines *relative* prices only. This means that distribution is a problem of proportions. In fact, proportions associated with the social effort to produce goods are intimately related to *distributive* justice, first, through the reduction coefficients governing the wages structure, as emerges most clearly through relative prices:

$$p_i/p_j = n_i/n_j \tag{15}$$

and second, through the distributional relationships governing the wages share and the 'property share', or, in a wider social view, the 'surplus share', which would also include surplus wages:

$$W/Y = 1/k \text{ and } (P + R)/Y = 1 - (1/k) \tag{16}$$

Third, the spending of incomes by households, enterprises, non-profit organisations and the state is pictured by the last equation in the equation system (12):

$$c_1p_1 + c_2p_2 + \ldots + c_mp_m = w_nk \tag{17}$$

The economic meaning of this relation emerges more clearly if account is taken of the spending coefficients defined as demand per profit-sector labour unit (relation 13a above):

$$\sum c_ip_i = \sum (Q_{if}/N_f)\, p_i = w_nk \tag{18}$$

Taking account of the price Equation (14) in relation (18), we get the definitions

$$\sum (N_i/N_f)\, w_nk = w_nk \tag{19}$$

$$\sum (N_i/N_f)\, w_nk\, N_f = w_nk\, N_f = Y \tag{19a}$$

From these relations immediately follows

$$\sum (N_i/N_f) = 1 \tag{20}$$

To recall, N_i is total – direct and indirect – labour used to produce good i, N_f is the full employment labour force in the productive sector of an economy.

Definition (20) indicates the distribution of the profit-sector labour force within an economy, which represents a most important proportion in a monetary production economy. Indeed, the distribution of economically productive labour depends upon the way in which incomes are spent, if labour productivity is given; in fact, definition (20) has been derived from relation (17). In turn, the way of spending incomes depends heavily upon income distribution.

The quantity system

$$\begin{bmatrix} 1 & 0 & \cdots & 0 & -c_1 \\ 0 & 1 & \cdots & 0 & -c_2 \\ \vdots & \vdots & \ddots & \vdots & \vdots \\ 0 & 0 & \cdots & 1 & -c_m \\ -n_1 & -n_2 & \cdots & -n_m & 1 \end{bmatrix} \begin{bmatrix} Q_{1f} \\ Q_{2f} \\ \vdots \\ Q_{mf} \\ N_f \end{bmatrix} = 0 \tag{21}$$

informs us, first, about the demand for and the circulation of goods (the first m lines of the matrix are multiplied by the quantity vector):

$$Q_{if} = c_iN_f(13),$$

second, about the production and the supply of goods:

$$n_i = N_i/Q_{if} \tag{22}$$

and third, about the 'macroeconomic equilibrium of demand and supply':

$$n_1Q_{1f} + n_2Q_2f + \ldots . + n_mQ_{im} = \sum N_i = N_f \tag{23}$$

Relations (22) and (23) obtain from multiplying the last line in the above matrix by the quantity vector. In relation (23) supply is on the left-hand side; demand appears in the form of 'real' income (labour time) on the right-hand side of this equation.

Relation (22) implies that in a social production (or labour) economy, technical progress is always labour saving: less direct and indirect labour is required to produce a certain good. This renders possible an increase in money wages, with prices and mark-ups given, or enables the cheapening of production, given money wages and mark-ups, or the realisation of higher profit rates (an increase in the mark-up).

The determinant of the price system (12) and of quantity system (21) is given by the following expression (Pasinetti 1986a, p. 422, relation 16):

$$c_1n_1 + c_2n_2 + \ldots . + c_mn_m - 1 = 0 \tag{24}$$

Taking account of the definition of the demand coefficients c_i (relation 13a) and of the labour (production) coefficients n_i (relation 22) yields, again, an expression picturing the sectorial distribution of profit-sector labour:

$$N_1/N_f + N_2/N_f + \ldots . + N_m/N_f = 1 \tag{25}$$

These relations tell us that the distribution of direct and indirect labour among the various sectors of an economy, as indicated by definition (25), is governed by two elements (relation 24): first, the size of the demand for the different goods (c_i), and second, the quantity of labour required to produce a unit of some good (n_i). Both relations, (24) and (25), thus express fundamental proportions prevailing in any monetary production economy.

The fact that the determinant of the coefficients matrix of the systems (12) and (21) is zero (relation 24) has important economic implications. This condition guarantees economically meaningful solutions for the equation systems (12) and (21), that is, *positive* prices and quantities. In fact, in both equation systems the last equation is not independent of the other equations. This implies that only *relative* prices and quantities, p_i/p_j and Q_{if}/Q_{jf}, are determined.

As has already been suggested, absolute prices are determined once distribution is regulated: the level of money wages w_n and the normal rate of profits implied in the mark-up k must be fixed in advance. This goes on through complex social processes. Hence, in principle, distribution ought to be determined *before* production can start. In a way, distribution is the primary and fundamental problem in political economy (Ricardo 1951, p. v).

Absolute quantities are determined once the level of employment (N) is given. Until now we have postulated the ideal case, i.e. full employment (N_f). In the next section, the determination of the long-period level of employment, governed by persistent factors, i.e. technology and institutions, will be considered. This amounts to looking for the factors governing the breadth of the economic circuit or the scale of economic activity in the long term.

The scale aspect of classical–Keynesian political economy

The scale of long-period economic activity is governed by long-period effective demand, which depends, in turn, upon the institutional and technological system, made up of the material basis and of the institutional superstructure, i.e. upon the socio-economic structure. Institutions partly determine behaviour through formal and material restrictions, as is the case with social institutions such as enterprises, associations, state administration, the legal system or 'individualistic' institutions, consumption habits, for example (on this *see* Bortis 1997, Chapters 2, 3 and 4). The long-period or trend level of domestic output may get established well below full employment, thus giving rise to permanent long-term involuntary unemployment. The existence of persistent involuntary unemployment is empirically well founded. For example, from the early 1980s onwards the trend unemployment rate was about 12 per cent in France and 10 per cent in Germany.

Formally, involuntary unemployment as determined by the socio-economic system is represented by the definitions (26–29) below – u is the rate of unemployment (26) and 1 – u is the rate of employment (27). Now, the quantity vector in system (21) must be multiplied by the coefficient 1 – u to obtain a new quantity vector (28) with the level of employment N lower than the full employment level N_f (29). Hence the coefficient *1 – u* could be termed the *employment scalar.*

$$u = (N_f - N)/N_f \tag{26}$$

$$1 - u = N/N_f \tag{27}$$

$$[Q_1, Q_2, \ldots, Q_m, N] \tag{28}$$

$$N < N_f \tag{29}$$

Definitions (28) and (29) imply that the structure of final output does not change as the level of employment varies. This, of course, is valid only as long as principles – independent of space and time – are considered. Considering principles enables us to separate the analysis of the pure (classical) proportions model (previous section) and the pure (Keynesian) scale model. In the real world (of phenomena) structures (proportions) will, of course, change as the level of employment or the scale of economic activity varies.

In definition (30) total supply equals total demand, whereby demand *governs* supply. Supply is given by the gross domestic product Q, which equals labour productivity A times employment in the profit sector N. The real wage rate is $w = w_n/p$, that is, the money wage rate w_n divided by the money price of a bundle of necessary consumption goods p. Normal wages wN are supposed to be entirely consumed. The surplus is made up of profits P and of land and labour rents R, with labour rents accruing on account of special abilities and dispositions; c_s is the fraction of the surplus (privately) consumed. I is gross investment, G state expenditures, π stands for the terms of trade [$X/M = (ep_M)/p_X$], p_X represents export prices in domestic currency, p_M import prices in foreign currency, e is the exchange rate, and X and M are export and import quantities respectively.

$$AN = Q = wN + c_s(P + R) + I + G + X - \pi M \qquad (30)$$

Imports M as a fraction b of GDP or domestic income Q = Y are of two kinds. Necessary imports $M_1 = b_1Q$ (raw materials, necessary consumption goods, machines to produce necessaries) are related to production, while non-necessary imports $M_2 = b_2Q$ are related to consumption out of the surplus.

$$M = bQ = M_1 + M_2 = b_1Q + b_2Q = (b_1 + b_2)Q \qquad (31)$$

In the price equation

$$p = (w_n/A)k \qquad (32)$$

the mark-up k governs the size of the surplus.

Distribution, i.e. the division of domestic income into ordinary or normal wages and the surplus (profits, land rents and labour (ability) rents) and the structure of normal wages, profits, land and labour rents, is a social ethical issue of immense complexity associated with the issue of distributive justice:

$$W/Y = 1/k \text{ and } (P + R)/Y = 1 - (1/k) \qquad (33)$$

In the long run, the *volume* of gross investment I is *governed* by trend GDP (Q) and its evolution, with Q, in turn, being determined by the whole socio-economic-cum-technological structure. (The *single* investment project depends, however, on more or less certain expectations about the future.)

$$I = (g + d)vQ = (g + d)K \tag{34}$$

($v = K/Q$ is the capital coefficient.)

Hence the long-period *volume* of gross investment I represents *derived or induced* demand; only the capacity effect of investment is taken into account in a situation in which overall long-period effective demand equals long-term aggregate supply.

Net trend investment (gK) is governed by the *long-period or trend* growth rate g of the *autonomous* variables, G and X (*see* for some implications Bortis 1997, pp. 155–75, 204–220). 'Replacement' investment (dK) depends on the depreciation ratio d, that is, the fraction of the total capital stock to be replaced for physical, economic and technological reasons. The coefficient d indicates, therefore, the extent of the technical dynamism of the entrepreneurs in the sense of Schumpeter, i.e. regarding the introduction of new techniques of production and of new products.

Saving (private and state saving, t being the tax rate)

$$S = sQ + tQ - G \tag{35}$$

adjusts to investment through changes in output. This is particularly evident if we consider ratios:

$$s + t - (G/Q) = (g + d)v \tag{36}$$

Given an equilibrium of the balance on current account, a higher output can be achieved only if government expenditure increases, or, if private consumption increases, because of a decline in the saving/income ratio s or in the tax/income ratio t. Government expenditures (or exports) are of particular importance because they set economic activity into motion. The level of government expenditures G greatly contributes to determining the scale of economic activity. This is evident from our basic relation, the supermultiplier relation, which can be derived from Equations (30) to (34).

$$Q = \frac{G + X}{z_s[1 - (1/k)] + \pi(b_1 + b_2) - (g + d)v} \tag{37}$$

$$z_s = 1 - c_s = s_s + t_s \tag{38}$$

Relation (37), the supermultiplier relation, shows how output Q and employment N are governed *in principle*. Hence this relation represents the pure theory of output and employment in a monetary production economy.

Definition (38) represents the leakage coefficient z_s, which indicates the fraction of the surplus over ordinary wages that is *not* consumed, the fraction consumed being c_s. Consequently, the leakage coefficient is the sum of the fractions of the surplus paid for taxes (t_s) and saved (s_s). Since the long-period consumption coefficient c_s and the long-period tax coefficient t_s are both determined by institutions – consumption habits and tax laws – the long-period saving propensity s_s is a *pure residual* varying with the normal level of output and employment, given the rate of profits as is implied in the mark-up (Bortis 1997, pp. 166–168). This is perfectly analogous to Keynes's short-period theory of saving but different from the Pasinetti equation where, given the level of employment, the savings propensity of the capitalists and the rate of growth determine the rate of profits in a Keynesian *Treatise on Money* way (*see* again Bortis 1997, pp. 166–168).

Following Hicks, Equation (37) may conveniently be called a supermultiplier relation 'which can be applied to any given level of [autonomous demand components] to discover the equilibrium level of output [Q] which corresponds to it' (Hicks 1950, p. 62). Hence the autonomous demand components, G and X, set economic activity in motion, similarly to the expenditure of rents by the landlords in Quesnay's extended *tableau économique* (on this see Oncken 1902, p. 394).

Once output and employment are determined through the supermultiplier relation (37), the output and employment scalar $1-u$ (definition 27) is also fixed. In principle, the normal quantities corresponding to a specific output and employment level obtain if the full employment quantity vector in the quantity system (21) is multiplied by the employment scalar. The determination of normal output and employment is equivalent to fixing the output and employment trend around which cyclical fluctuations occur (Bortis 1997, pp. 149–151). It has already been suggested that the position of the output and employment trend is of considerable socio-economic and political importance because this determines the extent of long-period – system governed – permanent involuntary unemployment. The latter is, in turn, an important element governing the social and political climate in a country.

Methodologically speaking, the supermultiplier relation (37) represents, as suggested already, the pure long-period Keynesian employment theory, picturing how output and employment are determined *in principle* by the various demand variables and parameters on the right-hand side of this equation (Bortis 1997, pp. 142–204). In a way, this relation is a metatheory – a metaphysical theory – of employment to determine what is – probably – essential about employment determination in a monetary production economy (*see* on this the methodological introduction in Bortis 2003a, pp. 411–415). Determination *in principle* of some socio-economic phenomenon attempts to capture the essential features of the causal mechanism at work, which are timeless and invariable. Moreover, in a pure or 'ideal-type' model, the *ceteris paribus* clause is automatically implied, which is to say that the predetermined variables on the right-hand side of the supermultiplier relation (37) are considered independent of each other. This, as a rule, will not be the case if some real-world situation is considered.

In principle, normal output Q, and hence trend employment N, are positively linked to the autonomous variables G and X, and to the gross investment–output ratio $I/Q = (g + d)v$. This ratio depends on the rate of growth of the autonomous variables $(G + X)$, g, which is also the rate of growth of long-period or normal output and employment, and upon the replacement coefficient d. In an open economy, the rate of growth of exports is crucial, as Nicholas Kaldor has always insisted upon (*see* on this Bortis 1997, pp. 155–156, 185–189, 190–198). The (Schumpeterian) d is an indicator of the technical dynamism of entrepreneurs. The effect of exports (X) on output and employment will be particularly strong if exports consist mainly of high-quality manufactured products with a large value added, i.e. a high content of direct and indirect labour (Kaldor 1985, pp. 57–79). However, normal output will be lower if, given exports X, the technological and cultural dependence on the outside world is strong, as would be reflected in large import coefficients b_1 and b_2, and if the terms of trade (π) are unfavourable, which would show up in a high value of π. Very importantly, normal output (Q) is negatively linked with the property share in income, $1-(1/k)$, and with the leakage coefficient, z_s, associated with this share; as a rule, z_s will be larger if the distribution of property income is more unequal. Given government expenditures and gross investment, a higher leakage out of income ($z_s[1-(1/k)]$) reduces effective demand because consumption is diminished. Fundamentally, unemployment occurs because the saving–income ratio, s_s $[1-(1/k)]$, exceeds the investment–output ratio, $(g+d)v$, at full employment. Full employment could be maintained only if private and/or public consumption were increased. A redistribution of incomes, i.e. raising the share of normal wages $(1/k)$, would lead to higher private consumption through enhancing spending power. In principle, a higher level of public expenditures, G, would require a tax increase: the tax rate, t_s, would have to be raised to preserve budget equilibrium, which would reduce the saving coefficient s_s. If these measures are not undertaken, output, employment and tax receipts will decline and, given government expenditures, budget deficits will occur. These will reduce the saving ratio until it equals the investment ratio at some long-period equilibrium level of output and employment involving persistent involuntary unemployment. Hence the negative association between distribution and employment emerges, because the property share and the saving and the leakage ratio associated with it are too high; and s_s and thus z_s will be the higher the more unequally property income is distributed. Thus, the notion of unequal income distribution has a double dimension: the property share is high, and property income is itself unequally distributed. This leads to a high leakage out of income, given by $z_s[1 - (1/k)]$ to which corresponds a reduced level of output and employment.

This crucial relationship between unequal distribution and involuntary unemployment represents, according to Schumpeter, the essence of the Keynesian Revolution: '[The Keynesian doctrine] can easily be made to say both that "who tries to save destroys real capital" and that, via saving, "the unequal distribution of income is the ultimate cause of unemployment." *This* is what the Keynesian Revolution amounts to' (Schumpeter 1946, p. 517). Indeed, Keynes held that the 'outstanding faults of the economic society in which we live are its failure to provide for full employment and its arbitrary and inequitable distribution of wealth and incomes. [Up] to the point where full employment prevails, the growth of capital depends not at all on a low propensity to consume but is, on the contrary, held back by it [and] measures for the redistribution of incomes in a way likely to raise the propensity to consume may prove positively favourable to the growth of capital' (Keynes 1936, pp. 372–373; on this *see also* Garegnani 1978/79). The inverse long-period link between employment and distribution is the crucial feature of the supermultiplier relation. On the empirical level, Galbraith and Berner (2001) represents an important effort to deal comprehensively, in a Keynesian spirit, with inequality, unemployment and development on a global level.

Links with Keynesian and post-Keynesian political economy – the classical–Keynesian synthesis

The preceding sections deal with principles, that is, with the fundamental forces governing prices and quantities in a classical–Keynesian view. As such, these sections exhibit aspects of the pure long-period classical–Keynesian model of production, value, distribution and employment, and as such picture the functioning of the socio-economic system. The technical–institutional system partly determines the behaviour of individuals and collectives because the system imposes restrictions upon behaviour.

For example, through the supermultiplier relation the system sets a restriction to all workers and employees: no more than (1−u)100 per cent of the workforce can find a job (definition 27 and relation 37);

however, *who* will be employed or unemployed depends on the *behaviour* of the various individuals. In the medium and the short run, behaviour of economic agents takes place within the – institutional – system, thus giving rise to specific behavioural outcomes that differ from the system outcomes (Bortis 1997, pp. 83–117). The issue of institutions and behaviour is, in fact, a central tenet in Bortis (1997).

Post-Keynesianism prominently deals with the behaviour of consumers and producers in the medium term, whereby behaviour is coordinated by the system, represented by effective demand. A significant example of this interaction is the double-sided relationship between profits and investment (Joan Robinson, Michal Kalecki): profits influence investment behaviour, and the level of investment governs profits. This gives rise to a theory of employment determination in the medium term, in fact, in the course of cyclical growth, with the income effect and the capacity effect of investment interacting (Bortis 1997, pp. 204–220). The cyclical variations of output and employment may go along with a specific 'pricing in the business cycle'. The domain of Keynesians is the determination of economic activity in the short term, where productive capacities are given and only the income effect of investment is relevant. Here, each investment project is associated with uncertainty and expectations, which, as a consequence, govern the short-period volume of investment, in contrast to the long-period investment volume, which is determined by the evolution of trend output and hence by the entire technical and institutional system. Finally, money and finance can be brought into the picture without any difficulty, starting, for example, from the concepts of industrial circulation and financial circulation in Keynes's *Treatise on Money* (Volume I, Chapter 15) and the whole of the *General Theory* (for a broad sketch *see* Bortis 1997, pp. 220–235). Hence classical–Keynesian political economy appears as a synthesis, an elaboration and an extension of Keynesian and post-Keynesian political economy.

4 Conclusion: a tribute to Luigi Pasinetti

Three of the very greatest political economists of the twentieth century – Maynard Keynes, Piero Sraffa and Luigi Pasinetti – have one important point in common. They rendered possible what seemed impossible through providing solutions to fundamental theoretical puzzles, while at the same time setting forth basic theoretical constructions that could be elaborated, linked together and put into a wider context. Maynard Keynes convincingly refuted Say's Law through transforming monetary theory into a coherent general theory of employment, interest and money (Bortis 2003b, Shackle 1967). Piero Sraffa's *Production of Commodities by Means of Commodities* and his introduction to Ricardo's *Principles* initiated a revival of classical political economy, specifically the classical approach to value and distribution, and solved the transformation problem which had discredited the Ricardian approach until the 1950s (Bortis 2002, Pasinetti 1977, Chapter V). Luigi Pasinetti, finally, set up the preconditions to bring together Keynes and Sraffa, separated hitherto by a theoretical abyss, at the level of fundamentals, creating thereby the analytical basis for classical–Keynesian political economy. This story has been recounted here.

Luigi Pasinetti's task was exceedingly difficult. Just let us recall what Joan Robinson wrote, in view of the cleavage between Keynes and Sraffa, in 1978: 'It is the task of the post-Keynesians to reconcile [Keynes and Sraffa] ... Post-Keynesian theory has plenty of problems to work on. We now have a general framework of long- and short-period analysis which will enable us to bring the insights of [Ricardo], Marx, Keynes, and Kalecki into coherent form and to apply them to the contemporary scene, but there is still a long way to go' (Robinson 1978, p. 18). In reality there was no such general framework at the time, only large pieces of original and excellent economic theory, and the way still to go was very long indeed. As emerges from these lines, it is fair and right to say that Luigi Pasinetti has covered most of the way, and certainly the most difficult, narrow and steep paths, closing thus that wide gap between Keynes and Sraffa. He made it that the rest of the way to go has become a broad and convenient avenue. Indeed, what remains to be done is to elaborate, to complete and to put into a wider context (for a first step, *see* Bortis 1997 and 2003a). The system of principles set forth in section 3 above on the basis of Pasinetti (1986a), which summarises, in a nutshell, his entire work, suggests that the analytical foundations worked out by Luigi Pasinetti are very solid and that the results in term of theories will be immensely fruitful.

It must be mentioned that, in addition to his tremendous constructive work, Luigi Pasinetti also played a crucial role in fundamental critical work. In fact, he initiated the capital theory debate of the mid-1960s between Cambridge, UK and Cambridge, MA (Garegnani 1970, Harcourt 1972) and did the most important work on the Cambridge (England) side. The capital theoretic debate was really a discussion at the level of fundamentals or of principles (Bortis 1997, pp. 281–293). As such, the results of this debate constitute a kind of watershed between the great approaches in economic theory – neoclassical/Walrasian and classical/Keynesian – as are set forth in Pasinetti (1986a). To reject its results means remaining in the neoclassical camp; accepting the results of the debate implies adhering to post-cum-classical–Keynesian political economy.

On the foundations Luigi Pasinetti has provided, it will be quite easy to erect a very solid system of classical–Keynesian political economy. This system of political economy represents, in our view, the economic theory of an intermediate way between what Luigi Pasinetti calls the extreme solutions, Liberalism (capitalism) and Socialism (with central planning), a middle way which could be called Social Liberalism, i.e. Liberalism on a social – 'fair' distribution and full employment – basis (Bortis 1997 and 2003a).

Luigi Pasinetti's outstanding achievements in pure theory put him into line with the very greatest political economists ever. Indeed, on the back of the (2004) paperback edition of *Modern Theories of Money*, edited by Louis-Philippe Rochon and Sergio Rossi, Geoffrey Harcourt writes the following: 'One dimension of Keynes's revolution was his insistence that money and finance be integrated with real factors right from the start of the analysis. This collection fits centrally in this tradition, as well as in the Post-Keynesian approach which combines the insights of the classical political economists Marx and Sraffa with those of Keynes, Kalecki and Pasinetti.' A tremendous tribute indeed, which, certainly, all post-cum-classical–Keynesian political economists may join!

REFERENCES

Bortis, H. (1997): *Institutions, Behaviour and Economic Theory – A Contribution to Classical-Keynesian Political Economy.* Cambridge UK and New York: Cambridge University Press.

(2002): Piero Sraffa and the revival of classical political economy, *Journal of Economic Studies*, vol. 29, no. 1, 74–89.

(2003a): Keynes and the Classics: Notes on the Monetary Theory of Production. In: Louis-Philippe Rochon and Sergio Rossi (eds) *Modern Theories of Money – The Nature and Role of Money in Capitalist Economies.* Cheltenham and Northampton, MA: Edward Elgar, pp. 411–74.

(2003b): Marshall, the Keynesian revolution and Sraffa's significance, *Journal of Economic Studies*, vol. 30, no. 1, 77–97.

Felderer, B. and Homburg, S. (2003): *Makroökonomik und neue Makroökonomik*, eighth edition, Berlin, Heidelberg, New York: Springer Verlag.

Galbraith, J.K. and Berner, M. (2001): *Inequality and Industrial Change – A Global View.* Cambridge University Press.

Garegnani, P. (1970): Heterogeneous capital, the production function and the theory of distribution, *Review of Economic Studies*, vol. 37, 407–36.

(1978/79): Notes on consumption, investment and effective demand, *Cambridge Journal of Economics*, vol. 2, 335–53 and vol. 3, 63–82.

Harcourt, G. (1972): *Some Cambridge Controversies in the Theory of Capital.* Cambridge University Press.

(1986): *Controversies in Political Economy: Selected Essays of G.C. Harcourt* (ed. by O.F. Hamouda). Brighton: Wheatsheaf.

Harcourt, G. (with O. F. Hamouda) (1992): Post-Keynesianism – From criticism to coherence? In: Claudio Sardoni (ed.) *On Political Economists and Modern Political Economy – Selected Essays of G.C. Harcourt*. London and New York: Routledge, pp. 209–32.

Kaldor, N. (1985): *Economics Without Equilibrium*. Armonk, NY: M.E. Sharpe.

Kalecki, M. (1971): *Selected Essays on the Dynamics of the Capitalist Economy.* Cambridge University Press.

Keynes, J.M. (1971/1930): *A Treatise on Money*, 2 vols, CW V and VI. London: Macmillan.

(1973/1936): *The General Theory of Employment, Interest and Money.* CW, vol. VII. London: Macmillan.

King, J.E. (2003): *A History of Post Keynesian Economics since 1936*. Cheltenham and Northampton, MA: Edward Elgar.

Lowe, A. (1976): *The Path of Economic Growth*. Cambridge University Press.

Oncken, A. (1902): *Geschichte der Nationalökonomie*, vol. I (only one volume published). Leipzig: Hirschfeld.

Pasinetti, L.L. (1977): *Lectures on the Theory of Production*. London: Macmillan.

(1981): *Structural Change and Economic Growth – A Theoretical Essay on the Dynamics of the Wealth of Nations*. Cambridge University Press.

(1986a): Theory of Value: A source of alternative paradigms in economic analysis. In: Mauro Baranzini and Roberto Scazzieri, (eds) *Foundations of Economics – Structures of Inquiry and Economic Theory.* Oxford: Basil Blackwell, pp. 409–31.

(1986b): Sraffa's circular process and the concept of vertical integration, *Political Economy – Studies in the Surplus Approach*, vol. 2, no. 1, 3–16.

Petty, W. (1662): *A Treatise of Taxes and Contributions*. London: N. Brooke; reprinted in *Economic Writings* (1899) (ed. by C. Hull), 2 volumes, Cambridge University Press; reprinted by Augustus M. Kelley (1963), pp. 1–97.

Ricardo, D. (1951): *On the Principles of Political Economy and Taxation* (ed. Piero Sraffa with the collaboration of Maurice Dobb). Cambridge University Press.

Robertson, D.H. (1956): *Economic Commentaries*. London: Staples.

Robinson, J. (1978): Keynes and Ricardo, *Journal of Post Keynesian Economics*, vol. 1, 12–18.

Rochon, L.-P. and Rossi, S. (eds) (2003): *Modern Theories of Money – The Nature and Role of Money in Capitalist Economies*. Cheltenham, Northampton, MA: Edward Elgar, pp. 411–74.

Roncaglia, A. (2000): *Piero Sraffa – His Life, Thought and Cultural Heritage*, London and New York: Routledge.

Schumpeter, J.A. (1946): John Maynard Keynes, 1883–1946, *American Economic Review*, vol. **36**, 495–518.

Shackle, G.L.S. (1967): *The Years of High Theory – Invention and Tradition in Economic Thought 1926–1939*. Cambridge University Press.

Sraffa, P. (1960): *Production of Commodities by Means of Commodities*. Cambridge University Press.

8 Growth theory, structural dynamics and the analysis of consumption

Davide Gualerzi

1 Introduction

Recent growth theory has focused on endogenizing the growth rate, overcoming the limitations implicit in a view of growth driven by exogenous factors. Although there is room to discuss in which sense we now have an endogenous growth theory and to what extent it explains more than previous theory, this has redefined the research agenda towards the analysis of knowledge and human capital accumulation, laying out the foundations of the production of these intangibles.

The attention paid to the composition of the growth process has remained, at best, a minor concern. A second characteristic of the approach is that while investment is now important for the growth rate, the usual assumption is made that the saving propensity and investment behavior are one thing. Thus, the question of effective demand does not arise. This, I would argue, further complicates the possibility of looking at issues of composition, although they are quite obvious when considering technical change and product innovation, as done by many growth theorists. Variety is considered as a factor in determining consumption spending, but the link to growth is not elaborated. The relevance of Pasinetti's structural dynamics for growth theory can be better understood focusing on these questions.

The analysis of consumption built into the structural dynamics approach is indeed one of its distinguishing features; the well-known consequence is an economic system whose structure changes on both the production and the demand side. A changing consumption composition becomes a crucial aspect of the growth process. This is based on a criticism of traditional consumer theory and the attempt to develop a theory of consumption suitable to the analysis of growth.

This chapter examines first the numerous questions for consumption theory raised by Pasinetti's structural dynamics, which involve issues in the history of thought and in economic analysis, as well as questions of empirical verification and historical evidence. In this respect it is interesting to consider how the question of new products disappeared and then re-emerged in consumer theory and how that compares with the consumption theory contained in Pasinetti's structural dynamics. Comparing these foundations with the capabilities approach of Amartya Sen, as done by Walsh (2003), highlights the main questions that stand in the way of *a dynamic theory of consumption*, anticipated in Pasinetti's analysis of the demand side.

The chapter argues that the issue requires focusing on two dynamic processes: the development of need and the development of commodities. That, however, implies an explicit discussion of the relationship of consumption patterns and investment in new products and new industries. Treating consumers neither as sovereign nor as mute agents, simply conforming to the norms of habit formation, is a decisive step to analyze a changing composition of consumption. But ultimately that drives the attention to the composition of the growth process and requires an articulation of the principle of effective demand in the long run.

The final section outlines how empirical investigation and historical evidence can be brought in to illustrate and discuss the process of change of consumption patterns. The suggestion is that of studying the stylized facts and the institutional setting defining specific phases of development of the 'consumption sphere' and, in particular, the impact of new technologies. This highlights a possible way to articulate the two levels of analysis that Pasinetti argues are necessary to bring forward the shift of paradigm contained in the Keynesian Revolution.

2 Consumer theory: wants and new products

The question of change in consumption is not directly confronted in most economic theory. Traditional consumer theory rests on a model of allocation; as such, it is static and has difficulties in accommodating change in the items of consumption. Its structure is largely defined by the overall goal of establishing a supply and demand determination of prices. This highlights the different role that consumption theory has in the basic structure of the main traditions of economic analysis. The classical tradition has focused mainly on production and distribution; it did not attempt to develop a theory of consumption as such, for reasons that would require a discussion of the notion of subsistence and its function in the classical system. The Keynesian tradition has mostly discussed consumption as a component of aggregate demand, consistently maintaining the focus on its contribution to spending, but did not much elaborate on its motivations, or on its internal structure and evolution. Therefore, changes in the consumption structure bring into focus the question of output composition, which remains mostly open in the classical and Keynesian theory and is instead entrusted to (given) consumer preferences in mainstream theory.

The question of consumption composition and product innovation has recently resurfaced under the heading of quality improvement and variety growth.[1] Recent developments have examined how variety sustained consumption spending (Bils and Klenow, 2001) and the reasons for its fluctuations (Parker and Preston, 2005). They do not discuss, however, the implications for growth. Their analytical structure hardly permits focus on the major forces of transformation, such as those relating to technology or consumer learning. We are therefore still at the beginning of the construction of what we might call a dynamic theory of consumption.

From the theory of wants to utility theory

Indifference curves and utility analysis rest on a very specific understanding of rationality and of consumer sovereignty. This is the source of many analytical problems, most fundamentally the relationship between observed variables, such as prices, income and demand, and unobserved variables, such as preferences. These analytical difficulties are only one aspect of the inadequacy of traditional consumer theory to guide the analysis of consumer behavior. As observed by Zamagni (1986), consumer theory has a specific analytical purpose that reflects the role of demand in the Neoclassical theory of value. Indeed, we are not dealing with an attempt to analyze the consumer and consumption patterns (Gualerzi, 1998) but rather with an analytical apparatus necessary to derive demand curves with the desired properties, so that they can concur with supply curves to determine equilibrium prices.

For the present purposes it is of great interest to note that, as pointed out by Lancaster (1966) and Ironmonger (1972), the approach based on utility maximization is a shift away from the notion of wants one finds in early marginalism. In the transition from the original focus on wants to the concept of diminishing marginal utility in Marshall, the discontinuity in the satisfaction of needs was lost. Discontinuity is indispensable in considering an order in the satisfaction of needs, which is the characteristic

[1] The renewed interest in the issue of new goods (Bresnahan and Gordon, 1997; Boskin Commission, 1996) stems mainly from the question of whether quality improvements are adequately taken into account by prices. The issue at stake is to measure quality improvement so as to have better measures of inflation (hedonic pricing) and therefore of growth.

of lexicographic models. The attempts by Lancaster and Ironmonger to improve consumer theory rest indeed on the discontinuity of wants.

Characteristics and the consumption technology

Responding to one of the most serious limits of the theory, Kevin Lancaster's characteristic model (1966, 1971) addresses the question of product innovation and differentiation. New products redefine continuously the domain of consumers' choice. In the traditional approach, 'any change in any property of any good implies that we have a new preference pattern for every individual' (1971, p. 4). It follows that 'we can do only two things: (i) ignore the changes, and proceed as if the new variant is the same good as before or (ii) regard the variant as an entirely new good, throwing out any information concerning demand behavior with respect to the original variant, and start from scratch' (p. 8).

This is so because utility indexes are associated directly to goods rather than to the 'characteristics' that make these goods the object of 'wants.' This has an important consequence. In early marginalism, especially in Menger, one can find the basis of 'the consumption technology approach' and of 'the diet problem' (pp. 9, 146). Hicks, Lancaster notes, drew explicitly the analogy with the entrepreneur choosing means to satisfy objectives, but abandoned the approach because of its 'technical difficulties.'

Characteristics are the objective properties, the common substance in otherwise different goods. It is what makes them valuable in their capacity to respond to wants. Therefore 'the relationship between people and things' is a 'two-stage affair. It is composed of the relationship between things and their characteristics (objective and technical) and the relationship between characteristics and people (personal, involving individual preferences)' (p. 7). Lancaster's objective is to put the 'characteristics model' at the core of demand theory, and show that 'product variations and new goods fit easily and naturally' (p. 10).

A linear consumption technology expresses the relationship between the characteristics vector and the goods vector and transforms the characteristics space into the goods space. Given prices, a good becomes part of the consumption basket if it lies on the efficiency frontier. Thus, traditional analysis appears as a special case of this more general approach, one in which 'the number of goods and characteristics is equal and the efficiency surface consists of a single facet' (p. 50). As in the case of goods, consumption of characteristics is proportional to income for all consumers with the same preference parameters. Given these parameters and income distribution, aggregate consumption will depend on the preference distribution.

'Operational use of the model requires identification of the relevant characteristics and data of the consumption technology. Neither of these requirements is yet easily met, partly because of the conceptual problems in identifying relevant characteristics and partly because the appropriate data have not hitherto been available' (p. 113). For one thing, characteristics should be less than products, in order to have an advantage for the analysis of product innovation and differentiation. *A priori* criteria and the effects of satiation and dominance, both implied by the notion of hierarchy of wants, are the foundation for such identification, which is ultimately corroborated by a 'revealed relevance' analysis based on empirical study of markets. An intermediate step is 'group analysis,' intended to define the boundaries within which substitution effects are likely to be strong. This is important because 'our model of demand behavior is ... a "fine structure" model, designed to explain market behavior with respect to goods defined in a very narrow sense ... this means that we are concerned with the spectrum of varieties or models within a broadly defined market, not with such aggregates as "food" or "automobiles" ... At the same time the consumer is facing a consumption technology in which any specific characteristic might be obtained from any good' (pp. 115–116).[2]

The consumption technology approach is grounded on goods' characteristic. The latter is 'an objective, universal property of the good (or activity)' so that 'personal reactions are reactions to the characteristic, not reactions about what the characteristic is' (p. 114). The 'objective' link characteristic–things allows for the identification of the consumption technology data. Assuming that there is enough information to identify characteristics, using the criteria mentioned earlier, we can infer individual preferences, the things–people relationship, based on what can be called a 'revealed relevance' mechanism: the market response will establish whether 'consumers appear to react to these characteristics or not' (p. 157).

The result is reformulating consumer choice as a linear programming problem. This approach has two major advantages. The first is 'being able to sail through the otherwise dangerous problems concerning new goods, model changes, and so on.' But more importantly it can 'take account of such things as negative effects and interactions,' which have implications for the evaluation of cost and benefit.

[2] Lancaster then continues: 'The first requirement for any attempt at operational use of the model, therefore, is to find the circumstances ... under which we can analyze part of the total consumption universe in a relative isolation from the remainder' (ibid.).

New commodities

Ironmonger (1972) also takes the question of new commodities and quality changes as a starting point for a re-examination of consumer theory.[3] His approach is centered on a consumption technology intended to satisfy 'various separate wants,' leading to the choice of an 'optimum budget … (which) is found to be a solution of a linear programming problem' (p. 12). There are some distinguishing elements that make this contribution more interesting for a theory of the evolution of consumer demand and innovation, be it the recognition of satiation effects, but most important, elaborating an independent role of new products in determining consumer demand.

Ironmonger's analysis rests not on characteristics but rather on wants separability. Wants arise from physiological and psychological needs. They are the object of satisfaction, rather than 'a single desire, happiness or utility' on which traditional theory has focused. Marshall, acknowledging the work of Menger, Jevons, and others, introduced wants and desires into economic theory. He then developed the notion of diminishing marginal utility in relation to satiable wants. Ironmonger observes that 'with the mathematical development of the theory of consumer behavior, stemming from the work of Pareto and Fisher in the 1890s, and in the 1930s associated with the work of Hicks and Allen and the rediscovery of the work of Slutsky, the distinction (with separable wants) was dropped completely and commodities were invariably regarded as satisfying a single want' (p. 11), i.e. utility. This, as Richard Stone points out in the book's foreword, 'leads him to emphasize discreteness and discontinuities, which can best be handled by programming methods.' The existence of separate wants 'is particularly relevant from the point of view of technical change in the commodities entering into the consumption process' (p. 13).

The objective is not simply incorporating the characteristics of new commodities into rational choice but examining how they define this choice. 'New commodities and quality changes in commodities can be brought out of the pond of consumer tastes so that tastes can provide a more constant frame of reference than before' (p. 13). The static nature of consumer theory is contained in the assumption that tastes are constant. But even without changes in the factors customarily taken to determine taste, such as age, sex, occupation, marital status, the 'number and nature

[3] He points out that 'the theoretical arguments have been left as originally written and no attempt has been made to compare or contrast these arguments with … the approach of Kelvin Lancaster' (p. 3). When Ironmonger is writing, the approach had been already presented in the *Journal of Political Economy* (1966).

of commodities are constantly changing' (p. 12). Ironmonger concludes that it seems desirable to have a theory which distinguishes between these two aspects.

New commodities add a dimension, independent from taste, income and prices, to the determination of consumer choice, which is pursued with the analysis of diffusion processes. The study of diffusion paths leads to new possibilities of empirical testing. Analyzing group behavior, it is possible to formulate hypotheses about the form of the diffusion curve, providing a picture of the relationship between new commodities and market demand; in the same way aggregation is used to identify the patterns of change for income levels (satiation) and prices. Ironmonger's contribution then focuses on the empirical study of demand. The diffusion processes are used to distinguish the effects of new products from those of the variables customarily taken into account in demand analysis, income and prices. He notes that 'there have been only a few explicit studies of the phenomenon of diffusion following introduction. In general, the main demand studies have steered away from these commodities' (p. 130).

Still, the consumption technology, and the optimization procedure associated with it, do not take us beyond comparative statics results. Although opening the way to consider wants, new commodities and social acceptability of evolving forms of satisfaction, the approach must ultimately make reference to wants and preferences as something given to the analysis. This is the problem with exogenous preferences – they make it possible and plausible to analyze consumers' choice independently from the economic process.

3 Pasinetti's structural dynamics and consumption theory

The most notable feature of Pasinetti's analysis of consumption is that it is part of a multisectoral approach to growth. This allows for a desegregated treatment of the demand side. Starting from a criticism of growth theory that neglects the question of structural change and the dissatisfaction with what Pasinetti calls the 'pseudo dynamics' of steady state models, his contribution lays out the foundation for a substantive analysis of the process of change of consumption structure and the framework for more theoretical and empirical investigation. Structural change is a fundamental question to be treated together with the analysis of growth; it involves both the supply and the demand side.

We have seen that traditional consumer theory rests on a model of allocation; as such it is static and has difficulties in accommodating change. Pasinetti's structural dynamics directs the attention precisely to the evolution of consumption patterns, as an aspect of the growth process. Therefore, the focus on the demand side leads to the consideration of the twin questions of change in consumption, which involves taste formation and learning, and new markets formation.

This is stressed by Pasinetti's main contention: full employment can be maintained only if demand composition changes. Spending must be redirected to new areas of consumption. This follows exclusively from the existence of technical change. Within 'natural dynamics' the solution of these two problems is entrusted to a consumption theory based on the generalization of the Engel curve and on consumers' learning. In this scheme, changes of demand composition are determined by income growth, technical change and consumers' learning.

It is then appropriate to examine first the criticism of traditional demand theory. Indeed, the possibility of a meaningful investigation of change in consumption, and development of a dynamic theory, rests on that criticism.

In Pasinetti's model the recognition of an order in the satisfaction of needs – already suggested by wants separability – implies that a certain level of consumption for a commodity must be reached if any other commodity can bring in any utility at all. That calls into question the notion of the rational consumer busy determining his preferred basket of consumption making marginal substitutions. Indeed, absolute utility depends not only on the amount but also on the order in which goods are consumed.

The criticism exposes the limits of a static approach based on utility maximization and rational behavior, indicating that factors other than relative prices can be far more important to determine choice. Indeed, Pasinetti argues that relative prices become important only when the level of demand is approaching saturation levels. Consequently, the notion of choice based on income dynamics, sequential satisfaction of need, reflecting biological but also social priorities, and the limits set by market saturation, suggest a picture of consumption and of consumers quite distinct from that of traditional theory.

The question, of course, is: what governs consumption, its structure and expansion? It is interesting to notice how naturally the question arises from within the model and also how little there is in the way of answering the question, despite the large literature on demand theory. What do we know about demand patterns' evolution? What theory do we have of such evolution?

Pasinetti argues that we know one thing about consumption expenditure: it does not expand proportionally. Actually, there is a well-known empirical regularity that indicates that there is a certain pattern of evolution endogenously determined by income growth.

The non-proportional growth of consumption expenditure is based on a generalization of the Engel curve. The Engel curve has been neglected because it creates a problem for utility theory: it does not fit its marginal substitution notion that never confronts the issue of saturation. Although Engel curves can be fitted into standard demand analysis (Deaton and Muellbauer, 1980), dealing with the problem exposes the difficulties of the dominant paradigm in front of well-established evidence on the pattern of economic development. The second foundation for a dynamic theory of consumption is learning. The process of learning is prior and more fundamental to consumer choice than the notion of rational behavior, which can guide choice only over a given set of products and at a given level of income. Furthermore, learning is likely to become more and more important as income increases. Mere rationality is the static counterpart of learning, as marginal utility is the static criterion opposed to need hierarchy.

4 Capabilities, need development and commodities

Structural dynamics and capabilities

An interesting way to look at Pasinetti's search for a dynamic theory of consumption is to consider structural dynamics in light of the approach based on capabilities presented by Amartya Sen. Interestingly, also Sen's theory of human capabilities follows from a dynamic perspective, that of development.

Sen is another critic of traditional consumer theory, the theory of the 'rational fools' (1977). He has pointed out that continuity of preferences is indispensable for the principle of substitution. However, once we abandon the example of trading apples for oranges and instead consider life styles, alternative systems of preferences individuals evaluate and choose from, the plausibility of the continuity assumption becomes far less obvious. He has also observed (1985) that preferences refer not to needs but rather to goods in the market, which are defined in a market economy by other economic agents. Moreover, needs can be satisfied by different types of goods, in different consumption forms (individual, family, social). It follows that there is a discrepancy between preferences and needs.[4]

The notion of 'subject capability' refers to what can be accomplished with the goods available. Though goods' characteristics are distinct from

[4] Gibbard (1986) has pointed out that Pareto ordinality focuses on satisfaction of preferences, not of needs.

capability, the latter accounts for the result obtained in terms of need satisfaction. In more general terms, rather than in the sense of axiomatic maximization, rationality can be redefined as systematic exploitation of information and reasoning.

The relationship between Pasinetti's structural dynamics and Sen's capabilities approach is discussed by Walsh within a larger account of the developments of classical theory (2003). Walsh quotes Pasinetti to stress how the question of change is at the center of the approach.[5] 'In the sense in which there can be said to be "equilibrium-" in his model, it is a *continually* changing equilibrium ... the assumption of *balanced* technical progress plus the uniform expansion of demand "are not only unlikely, they are impossible" (Pasinetti, 1981, p. 66)' (p. 371). This is why, he concludes, Pasinetti (1993, p. 107) has stressed the importance of a theory of consumers' choice in a dynamic context (p. 373).

With respect to the analysis of Sraffa, Walsh notices that Smith's notion of necessaries and conveniences, the consumption basics as he calls them (p. 374), can suffice to highlight that 'structural economic dynamics gives us new goods that do not remain wildly expensive luxuries – they may become new basics. And if they were made by new manufacturing processes, there are of course new technical basics, too' (ibid.).

'What then of the relationship between the evolving basics of a structural dynamic model and capabilities?' asks Walsh. 'I wish to stress from the beginning that the relationship is *not* a tight mapping ... but there *is* ... a significant relationship nonetheless' (p. 376). Leaving aside for the moment the problem of defining a list of capabilities,[6] the point is that 'a Pasinetti-type model presents a *truly dynamic process* (emphasis added) in which commodities arguably necessary to the realization of vital capabilities appear sequentially over time.' Actually, there are '*two* sequential aspects' in Pasinetti's model and they 'arise for different reasons' (ibid.). The first is from the recognition that 'human needs form a hierarchy, which can (and should) be addressed *sequentially*.' But there is also a '*technically* sequential property,' which stresses the lack of any necessary correspondence between commodities created by 'unbalanced growth' and need structure: 'Sometimes a technical discovery may occur

[5] Referring to Pasinetti, Walsh consistently speaks of transformational growth. This is quite appropriate in light of the main conclusion that there cannot be growth without structural transformation. Pasinetti, however, does not use the term, which is instead developed in several books by E.J. Nell, culminating in *The General Theory of Transformational Growth* (1998).

[6] Walsh quotes Sen as saying '[t]here can be substantial debates on the particular functionings that should be included in the list of important achievements and the corresponding capabilities' (Sen, 1999).

just when the need it can fulfill is becoming dominant, but of course there can be no guarantee in the structure of the model that it will be so' (p. 377).

Hierarchy of needs implies an ordering and the obvious one is that going bottom-up, from basic needs, such as those relating to survival, to 'superior' needs, leading to the realization of personality. Walsh quotes Bertram Schefold as saying '[t]here are certain hierarchies of needs, from basic need up to higher needs such as the need for self-fulfillment' (1990, p. 376). He concludes that 'Schefold (and Pasinetti) both assume that human nature reveals the presence of an *extreme* hierarchy of needs,' (p. 376) way beyond those of survival. Let's suppose that this is indeed the case and consider 'a strict hierarchy of human needs all the way from water and nutrients up to the creative needs of a great artist. Again, there is no reason to suppose that the sequential development of the *material basis for needs fulfillment* (emphasis added) laid out in the path of a Pasinetti model of structural dynamics would map closely onto this structure of need. Conveniences that could make life better would indeed be arriving on the scene, and a genuine enrichment of classical kind taking place, but not necessarily for every important aspect of life at once, nor for one after another in a special order of need' (p. 377). Nor is there any guarantee 'that a particular amount of a particular commodity will be necessary (or sufficient) to allow the fulfillment of a particular capability,' a point stressed by Sen. '*Sometimes* it will happen' (ibid.).

So, despite the fact that the notion of need hierarchy reaches well beyond survival and that capabilities open the way to consider what can be accomplished by individuals through different forms of consumption, the stumbling block remains the relationship between goods and need. Nor is the reference to capabilities, although clarifying the relationship between subjectivity and goods, of much help in this respect. The point is that both, need hierarchy and capabilities, imply a close relationship with commodities, in the sense of being fulfilled and, at the same time, of being revealed and made actual by them. In the latter sense they appear to depend on commodities, though this aspect is not much investigated.

The mapping problem

Walsh concludes that structural dynamics, and the evolving basket of consumption it implies, does not indicate a tight mapping to the list of capabilities, 'but surely a soil and a climate in which capabilities can flourish' (p. 377). However, focusing on the mapping problem highlights a problem internal to structural dynamics, i.e. the relationship between goods, or as Walsh calls it, the material basis of need fulfillment, and the need structure. There is a problem of technical feasibility, i.e. consistency with technical progress, and one of consistency of the means to the satisfaction of needs and the ascending pattern dictated by the needs hierarchy.

Pasinetti takes as a reference point the idea of market saturation, with learning on the part of consumers as the force driving consumption into new territory. Basic needs will be saturated first and, while they can be satisfied by better quality goods, this will inevitably lead to higher-level needs, so that new commodities will be added to the consumption basket. More so if learning is pervasive, as it is to the entire analysis.

Thus, a 'basic need' approach is built into the hierarchical pattern of need satisfaction, although quite clearly that does not imply a limitation on the kind of needs considered. Needs that are basic today might not have been such in the past. Indeed, structural dynamics implies a basket of necessaries and conveniences of an improved and more cultivated life (Walsh, 2003, p. 375). But then the problem arises of the relationship between these new commodities entering the standard of living of consumers and the underlying structure of need. And that is conceivably having an impact also on the fulfillment and development of human capabilities.

In fact, the lack of tight mapping exposes a more fundamental problem: not only is there no necessary correspondence between need, capabilities and the actual evolution of the means of consumption, other than that imposed by market saturation, but this relationship depends, it appears, on the commodities that the economic progress creates. This is the truly dynamic problem for a theory of consumption and it has not been solved by taking into account new products in consumer choice. The two sides of the issue are, on the one hand, the ordering built into the need structure, and on the other hand, an evolving set of commodities intended to satisfy needs.

Walsh's argument suggests considering commodities development beyond the logic that governs the structural dynamics of demand in Pasinetti's model. While it is then quite appropriate to point out that transformational growth will give us an evolving material basis for the fulfillment of need, that very evolution calls for an explanation.[7] The point is to dig into the process by which new commodities come into being and become means to need satisfaction.

It is now clear that need hierarchy, even if understood as a sequence starting from basic, survival needs up to the highest level of human self-realization, is not sufficient to explain consumption patterns' evolution.

[7] Indeed, embedded in a market economy based on capital is the orientation to change and innovation, a point stressed several times by Edward Nell (1998).

The law of non-proportional expansion of consumption expenditure, no doubt, plays an important role in it, but cannot further explain demand evolution. And yet, the reference to an evolving material basis emerges quite clearly as the condition for the sequential satisfaction of needs. Only the analysis of *commodities development* can give determinacy to a dynamic theory of consumption. The point is, it could be argued, that this material basis is not investigated within the process that structures consumption patterns.

Capabilities and need development

Need hierarchy does serve to establish the fundamental law of motion of the consumption structure and the difference with traditional consumer theory. And yet, the notion of need and need structure is not adequately investigated with respect to the very dynamic process that shapes consumption patterns. The reference to capabilities makes that more evident. To go beyond the notion of need as a given, and of the need structure itself as a hierarchical arrangement fundamentally given, we need a theory of need development.

In a basic need approach, needs can be fulfilled, not developed. The hierarchical arrangement implies a certain pattern for the satisfaction of higher-level needs that become areas of expansion of consumption spending. In this sense we could say that income growth reveals the structure of needs. But within this broad regularity we should search for the reasons that determine the forms taken by the satisfaction of needs, their effects on the volume of spending and the evolving structure of demand. These depend very substantially on product innovation and, more precisely, on consumption innovation (Gualerzi, 1998, 2001). Furthermore, the volume of spending and the choice of products, particularly new products, reflect a differentiation of consumers, i.e. an economic and social segmentation of the market, and in particular the distinction between consumers more capable and motivated to try new products and those who are not.

Capabilities move us a step forward because through them we can take into account what individuals, but also groups and possibly social classes, can accomplish with goods. It is then possible to look at the capabilities approach from another angle. A really interesting aspect of capabilities is how they allow us to speak of need, and in particular how they permit us to go beyond a basic need approach. How so?

The capabilities approach suggests that commodities are conditions, but their outcome depends on what one can make with them. It is a drastically different approach than that embodied in the diet problem, in which combinations of characteristics satisfy a given need, in a given need structure. If we think of capabilities as a way of referring to the subjective element in the interaction with commodities and an aspect of personality development, then capabilities become part of need development. It could be said that individuals, according to social rules and practices, define the feasibility of a form of need satisfaction, driven by their search for self-realization.

Thus, if we agree that the Pasinetti model depends very much on the structural dynamics of demand, then neither the neoclassical concept of preferences nor a theory of 'basic needs' might be sufficient to study such a transformation. Sen's theory of human capabilities can make the difference. It might allow for taking into account need development as it actually occurs, that is, by means of innovation of commodities and consumption practices. This defines also the proper space of commodities development within consumption theory. It should be observed that all of this follows from focusing on need development.

Need development depends on the development of commodities, which, together with social practices and consumer learning, define the forms of consumption. Not that the need for food or shelter matter for a dynamic theory of consumption, but rather a socially accepted, although differentiated, and technically feasible form of satisfaction of the need for food and shelter. The reason why it has proven to be impervious to traditional theory is possibly that it calls into question the traditional view of the consumer and of consumer choice (Gualerzi, 1998). But with the criticism of traditional theory offered by Pasinetti we have moved a long stretch away from that. An analytical development of the insights of Walsh into the relationship between Pasinetti's structural dynamics and Sen's capabilities approach is, then, quite possible within the larger perspective of the *consumption–growth relationship* and the transformation of the consumption sphere (Gualerzi, 2001).

5 Need development and developing commodities

The consumption–growth relationship

Why should we focus on the consumption–growth relationship? Which problems can we address that other approaches can't or only partially can? The main point is that this relationship is structured around the two dynamic processes which have emerged from the analysis above: need development and the process of developing new products. This allows for an analysis of consumption centered on the process of change.

In turn, that clarifies the relationship between consumption evolution and growth. The two problems so clearly raised by Pasinetti's model – changes in consumption patterns and new markets formation, can then be addressed in this framework.

The approach based on the consumption–growth relationship rests on the idea that the research on consumption patterns can bring forward new results if the traditional distinction between the analysis of consumption and that of growth is overcome and the focus shifts instead onto their mutually reinforcing effects. When the main aspects of this reciprocal determination are clarified, a more specific kind of investigation, and the search for empirical evidence, might become considerably easier. Furthermore, much of the knowledge on consumption that is developed in different fields of investigation can be given coherence and relevance within an economic scheme.[8]

Consumption expenditure cannot grow without change in the 'forms' of consumption, and change in a market economy depends on investment in developing commodities. In other words, we cannot speak of change of the forms of need satisfaction without new products and investment in these products; alternatively, we cannot have a theory of investment and output composition without a view of the growth of the market, which includes a view of its transformation, i.e. its structural development.

Indeed, new products do not fall from the sky. They are the object of planning and speculation on the part of firms, and developing commodities bear a close relationship to the effort to expand their market, which in turn is linked to the growth of the market as a whole. The development of new commodities requires investment that therefore shows a particular two-sided relationship with market growth: on the one hand, it contributes to effective demand as spending in R&D; on the other, it builds productive capacity to serve the market as it grows according to the path set by the product cycle. Through investment in what we can call market development, firms pursue their goal of self-expansion, at the same time contributing to the growth of the market as a whole.

Ultimately, change in consumption depends on a logic that goes beyond the consumption itself, to include several aspects of the growth process.

[8] Paraphrasing what Pasinetti says about a theory of technical change ('[it] would pertain to a much wider field than economics,' 1981, p. 67), one could argue that the scheme could better than others accommodate knowledge on consumption that otherwise would remain irrelevant to economic analysis.

Socially determined needs and the consumption sphere

To approach growth in this perspective requires a particular notion of need and need development. That is why we speak of socially determined needs.

We are indeed referring not to any notion of need belonging primarily to the sphere of nature, nor to a general notion of human and social needs, but rather to a specific notion of 'socially determined needs' (Levine, 1981, 1998). Socially determined needs suggest that an essential aspect of need is the possibility of development. Second, they stress that in a market economy need can be understood only in relation to commodities. After all, that is implied in the idea that any need, irrespective of its position in the need hierarchy, can be satisfied by higher-quality commodities and by adding new commodities to the consumption basket.

As opposed to subsistence needs, 'which are imposed on the individual' (Levine, 1981, Vol. II, p. 280), socially determined needs contribute to the individual's self-seeking and personal identity. It is precisely the freedom according to which needs are developed, which makes them impossible to determine *a priori*. This is in sharp contrast with the notion of needs 'by which the species renews itself within a determinate system of natural relations' (Levine, 1981, Vol. I, p. 45). While on the one hand indeterminate, and for this reason subject to development, they are on the other hand specifically determined, not by nature, or individuals as such, but rather by the social process shaping individual identity. Need development is, then, a constant stimulus to change and the potential for the expansion of the market.

The dynamic force implicit in the structure of production and consumption is the development and the multiplication of needs implied by *the constitution of the individual personality within a system of persons.* The development of need, latent in the idea of its social determination upon the basis of individuality, is, then, the potential exploited by firms and the basis for new market formation. The consumption sphere is the sphere of economic life that ensures the realization and development of socially determined needs, it is the economic space that can be exploited for purposes of market expansion. In a market economy, needs are satisfied by means of commodities, more specifically by a combination of commodities and consumption practices. This combination determines the forms of needs satisfaction. The transformation of the consumption sphere is therefore the result of the interplay of the processes of change originating both within the domain of personal identity and within industrial production. Its transformation follows from firms' logic of expansion and individuals' effort towards self-realization.

Consumption patterns and new markets formation

To clarify the process of determination that accounts for a) the evolution of consumption patterns and b) new markets formation, we have to consider the interdependence between the construction of socially determined individual identity through consumption and the drive to self-expansion of firms, based on their strategies of investment.

Change in the forms of needs satisfaction is the result of innovation in consumption; more specifically, individuals validate and establish new products as part of a form of need satisfaction devising the appropriate consumption practices, that is, 'discovering' the usefulness of products. In turn, new products are the most relevant aspect of firms' market development strategies, through which they pursue the goal of expanding their market. At the macro level these two processes determine the volume and direction of investment and the level and composition of consumption spending, therefore the structure and the rate of expansion of the market. In particular, autonomous investment determines not only the level of effective demand but also its composition. As a result, the system of socially determined needs is translated into a specific structure of consumption and a determinate stage of development of the consumption sphere. During this transformation new markets are created, because both new income is created and the structure of needs evolves. The development of needs acts as a force that, through change, can expand the market. In other words, change translates into the creation of markets through the development of the need structure.

This self-sustaining process of determination spells out the internal mechanism of endogenous growth; the expansion of aggregate circulation – the rate of growth of the system as a whole – depends on the intensity and success of the market development strategies.

The remarkable aspect of this mechanism is that the transformation of the consumption sphere may act again as a stimulus to change, since it recreates the conditions for more structural determination of the market and further expansion. When the structure of needs is manifested in a specific structure of consumption, the latter can act as the starting point for a new round of need development, mainly because of the potential implicit in the forms of satisfaction now established and the new interdependencies they reveal.

Transformation is indeed necessary for the growth process; it is driven by the social construction of need that shapes the consumption sphere. At the center of the process is the reciprocal determination of the structure of consumption and the structure of investment. Therefore, focusing on need development also permits clarification of the role of new products in the analysis of consumption, the issue discussed, although with partial results, by Lancaster (1966) and Ironmonger (1972). The question remained confined to the problem of change of the items of choice, it was not related to the problem of the pattern of change. If we focus on that, it turns out that it cannot be analyzed independently from the growth process, and in particular from investment in new products.

The consumption–growth relationship and the principle of effective demand

It is possible, then, to draw a general conclusion. The ultimate reason for framing the question of a dynamic theory of consumption within the consumption–growth relationship is that of finding a solid ground for an endogenous dynamics of transformation, that is, internalize that question into the analysis of the growth process driven by investment. Ultimately, changes in consumption patterns are part of the theory of effective demand and of a particular understanding of the operation of the principle of effective demand in the long run (Gualerzi, 2001, 2005).

Investment, i.e. firms' strategies of market development, redetermines through structural transformation the level and composition of output. Stripped to the bone, the mechanism outlined above says that the successful insertion of a new product in the consumption basket validates the underlying strategy that developed that innovation, modifying as a result consumption patterns. We have seen, in particular, that need development and development of commodities proceed on the basis of the same process transforming the consumption sphere. The dynamic theory of consumption sketched above rests on this mechanism, but the latter also articulates the particular long-run view of the principle of effective demand contained in the consumption–growth relationship. To that extent, it relates to the deeper level of analysis that Pasinetti associates with the shift of paradigm centered on that principle, the core of the Keynesian Revolution (Pasinetti, 2007).

The focus on new products is just a first step. It is indispensable in driving attention to investment and its effects in the long run. This is the question posed by the Harrod–Domar model, except the latter focused only on the level of investment and not on its composition. This overlooks changes in this composition aimed at the development of new industries and new products. Focusing exclusively on investment as creation of productive capacity, it implicitly contains the idea that growth could be just expansion of output, precisely what Pasinetti would call 'pseudo-dynamics.' A better story can be told about the growth process, one which rests on the particular role played by investment.

It appears plausible to maintain that investment sustains growth in the aggregate through the development of new industries and new products, although a question remains as to the size of the stimulus. New products can displace old ones, leaving open, at least in principle, the possibility of a zero sum game. This is contradicted by the additional expenditure that is necessary to develop these new products. But most fundamentally, the point is that new products act on need development, and that contains the possibility of developing new markets, well beyond the displacement of old products.

Thus, there is an ordering in the development of the material basis for need fulfillment and indeed it relates to the saturation of the markets serving certain needs. That 'ordering' comes from what can broadly be defined as product innovation, an essential aspect of markets in advanced industrial economies.[9] But product innovation must be seen in light of the process of need development. The latter is reflected in the transformation of the consumption sphere and follows from the firms' efforts to develop the market and the drive to self-realization of individuals. While consumption patterns' evolution, i.e. the very object of the theory of consumption, proceeds from that, it is governed by the level and composition of investment, therefore by the principle of effective demand.

6 Growth, consumption and institutions

Empirical analysis: stylized facts and institutions

Empirical evidence and observed long-term trends have an important role in the approach outlined above, although that requires some methodological clarification. The fundamental idea is that the basic mechanism manifests itself in the specific forms taken by consumption transformation and the underlying strategies that sustain it. Thus, empirical evidence can be used to illustrate and discuss the mechanism and the specific aspects of a certain phase of structural transformation. Actual dynamics can then be approached by focusing on the stylized facts and the institutional setting of that particular phase or cycle of expansion. This can narrow down the investigation to more limited goals in a second stage.

[9] This is quite consistent with the idea that 'the variation in the composition of consumption may well occur independently of the increase in income and of the changes in prices, as a consequence of the appearance on the market of newly invented goods and services' (Pasinetti, 1993, p. 40).

This use of empirical evidence and the facts of history is itself quite uncommon for economic analysis, at least for the traditional view of theory specifying testable propositions that are then proven correct or not by empirical analysis. It has also an important methodological consequence. It suggests how to articulate what Pasinetti regards as a second level of the analysis, concerning institutional dynamics.

In this respect, it might be useful to indicate the most pressing institutional problems for advanced market economies emerging from structural dynamics. One is clearly that of what we can call the institutions for full employment, that is, those institutions responding to the necessity of pursuing full employment as an explicit goal of policy. A second concerns the institutions appropriate to what, although still vaguely understood, is often called the knowledge economy, in light of, for instance, the problems raised by intellectual property and externalities. A third one may be indeed that of the institutional arrangements relevant to the transformation of the consumption sphere.

We can approach this last question from the point of view of which institutions are better suited to guide and govern, at least to some extent, this transformation and therefore also have an impact on the growth process. This would probably imply discussion of how consumption can evolve along socially desirable lines and which institutional setting is more conducive to efficiency and innovation. This is clearly too large an issue and is left to another discussion of structural dynamics. However, given the relationship between theory and evidence delineated above, one suggestion is immediate.

Learning, inequality, and patterns of consumption

Empirically observed trends of transformation of consumption patterns highlight the pattern taken by need development in a certain stage of development or cycle of expansion of the economy. That suggests grounding abstract notions, such as learning and consumption innovation, in the stylized facts and the socio-economic dynamics of a certain period. A useful way to address this aspect is to consider an overall phenomenon, such as the diffusion and increased sophistication of information and communication technologies (ICT), and to focus on its implications for learning and consumption.

Petit and Soete (Setterfield, 2002) have pointed out two major trends of transformation in the past two decades: the skill-biased nature of technological change, associated with the spread of new information and communication technologies, and the rise of income inequalities. On the one hand, the particular nature of technological change 'suggests a *new complementary* relationship between capital and skills' (p. 281); on the other, it implies a growing difference between workers who acquire these skills and those who do not. This is reflected in the structure of employment. Petit and Soete also indicate the link between learning at the level of production and learning on the part of consumers, suggesting that 'the divisions occurring in society in terms of the desire and ability of individuals or families to use new technologies are closely related to what is happening within working organizations' (p. 288).

The rise of new complementarities between the ever-increasing capabilities of information technologies and the learning process of users, and of consumers at large, suggests, then, that new problems may arise from an uneven process of skills acquisition. The dualism arising from the uneven process of acquisition of ICT-related skills, depending on age, education, occupation, besides individual inclinations, affects both the development of consumption patterns and the labor market, with the latter feeding back on the former.

This might be taken as an example of a more general problem. The boom and the bust of the 1990s' cycle of expansion in the US economy suggested that there are obstacles to the transformation of consumption driven by ICT, and by the Internet in particular. This technological frontier highlights opportunities and limitations for the development of needs and the creation of markets, but also less than desirable changes in consumption patterns. Empirical evidence on these aspects could help to better understand the obstacles standing in the way of the 'knowledge economy' often advocated by the European Community. In this respect there might be a problem of institutional development and/or a problem of appropriate social policies capable of addressing questions such as Internet addiction and the impact of virtual reality on personality structures and social behavior.

7 Concluding remarks

The relevance for growth theory of Pasinetti's structural dynamics is better understood taking into full account its contribution to the analysis of consumption. I have argued here that a dynamic theory of consumption based on those foundations requires analysis of the relationship with the growth process. To study a changing consumption composition, i.e. changing means and forms of need satisfaction and changing patterns of consumption expenditure, we need to focus on the composition of the growth process, therefore on investment directed to new products and new industries. That is better done focusing on the reciprocal determination of consumption and growth.

It is certainly not a coincidence that Pasinetti's theory of growth and structural change leads to study of consumption and that the critical views of consumer theory, such as that of Sen, arise from a dynamic context, that of economic development. The problem of the transformation of what Walsh appropriately calls the material basis for the satisfaction of needs highlights that two main development processes appear not yet satisfactorily analyzed: the evolving structure of need, and/or capabilities, and the development of new commodities. Though still at the level of the basic scheme, we now have a way of looking at these two processes as the key to the structure and evolution of consumption patterns and the rise of new markets, therefore addressing the two main questions posed by Pasinetti's model.

In Pasinetti, structural dynamics learning is the force that may keep final demand in line with the expansion of output warranted by productivity growth. This calls for an analysis of how learning actually occurs. In this respect one can notice that the focus of modern growth theory on the accumulation of intangibles has not much contributed to this goal, assuming more than analyzing the way in which they have become first movers of economic growth. The focus on the endogenous mechanism of growth connecting investment and consumption transformation seems a promising way to pursue also the empirical aspect of the research agenda on growth. Descriptive evidence would take theoretical relevance within an appropriate theory of transformation, which is open to refinements and modeling at different levels of analysis. The suggestion above is that of grounding the learning process on some actual dynamics driven by technological change, for example the pervasive effects of the spread of ICT. The reference to the stylized facts of a certain phase of development may be the key to give empirical relevance to phenomena such as consumption innovation. It may also define the framework for the question of institutional dynamics.

Ultimately, the new centrality of investment in determining the growth rates in modern growth theory can more than benefit from the attention directed to the demand side and issues of composition of the growth process. Structural dynamics, then, would have contributed in a fundamental way to redefining our understanding of growth in advanced market economies.

REFERENCES

Bils, M. and Klenow, P. 2001. 'The Acceleration of Variety Growth', *American Economic Review*, **91**(2), 274–280.

Boskin Commission. 1996. 'Towards a More Accurate Measure of the Cost of Living', Senate Finance Committee, Washington, DC.

Bresnahan, T.F. and Gordon, R.J. (eds.) 1997. *The Economics of New Goods*. The University of Chicago Press.

Deaton, A. and Muellbauer, J. 1980. *Economic Theory and Consumer Behaviour*. Cambridge University Press.

Gibbard, A. 1986. 'Interpersonal Comparisons: Preference, Good, and the Intrinsic Reward of a Life', in Elster, J. and Hylland, A. (eds), *Foundations of Social Choice Theory*, Cambridge University Press.

Gualerzi, D. 1998. 'Economic Change, Choice and Innovation in Consumption', in Bianchi, M. (ed.) *The Active Consumer: Novelty and Surprise in Consumer Choice*. London: Routledge.

2001. *Consumption and Growth: Recovery and Structural Change in the U.S. Economy*. Cheltenham, Northampton, MA: Edward Elgar.

2005. 'Consumption Composition: Growth and Distribution', in Balducci, R. and Salvadori, N. (eds) *Innovation, Unemployment and Policy in the Theories of Growth and Distribution*, Cheltenham, Northampton, MA: Edward Elgar.

Ironmonger, D. S. 1972. *New Commodities and Consumer Behaviour*. Cambridge University Press.

Lancaster, K.J. 1966a. 'A New Approach to Consumer Theory', *Journal of Political Economy*, 74(2), 132–157.

1971. *Consumer Demand: A New Approach*. New York: Columbia University Press.

Levine, David P. 1981. *Economic Theory*, Vol. I and II, London: Routledge and Kegan Paul.

1998. *Subjectivity in Political Economy. Essays on wanting and choosing*. London: Routledge and Kegan Paul.

Nell, E. 1998. *The General Theory of Transformational Growth*. Cambridge University Press.

Parker J. and Preston, B. 2005. 'Precautionary Saving and Consumption Fluctuations', *American Economic Review*, **95**(4), 1119–1143.

Pasinetti, L. L. 1981. *Structural Change and Economic Growth*. Cambridge University Press.

1993. *Structural Economic Dynamics*. Cambridge University Press.

2007. *Keynes and the Cambridge Keynesians: 'A Revolution in Economics' To Be Accomplished*. Cambridge University Press.

Petit, P. and Soete, L. 2002. 'Is a biased technological change fuelling dualism?' in Setterfield, M. (ed.) *The Economics of Demand-Led Growth. Challenging the Supply Side Vision of the Long-Run*. Cheltenham, Northampton, MA: Edward Elgar.

Schefold, B. 1990. 'On Changes in the Composition of Output', in Bharadwaj, K. and Schefold, B. (eds) *Essays on Piero Sraffa: Critical Perspectives and the Revival of Classical Theory*. London: Unwin Hyman.

Sen, A. 1977. 'Rational Fool: A Critique of the Behavioral Foundations of Economic Theory', tr. it. in Sen, A., 1986, *Scelta, benessere, equità*. Bologna: Il Mulino.

1985. *Commodities and Capabilities*. Amsterdam: North-Holland.

1999. *Development as Freedom*. New York: Knopf.

Walsh, V. 2003. 'Sen after Putnam', *Review of Political Economy*, **17**(1), 107–113.

Zamagni, S. 1986. 'La teoria del consumatore nell'ultimo quarto di secolo: risultati, problemi, linee di tendenza', *Economia Politica*, **III**, n. 3, December.

9 Luigi Pasinetti's structural economic dynamics and the employment consequences of new technologies

Harald Hagemann

1 Introduction: structural change as an essential feature of economic growth

Since the Industrial Revolution the long-run development of capitalist economies is not only characterized by growth of the national product but also by inherent changes in its composition, i.e. structural change. It could be very difficult empirically to separate genuine structural changes, i.e. alterations in composition that are permanent, from temporary changes due to cyclical fluctuations of the economy. From the very beginning Luigi Pasinetti has emphasized that structural change is inherently associated with modern economic growth processes.[1] Furthermore, he has often deplored the inadequacies of modern economic theory to investigate the role and consequences of technical change.[2] Having been influenced intellectually by the Cambridge School of Economics,[3] i.e. the Keynesian Revolution and the revival of classical political economics by Sraffa's foundation of neo-Ricardian economics, it comes as no surprise that Pasinetti's research in the last three decades also has focused on a modern analysis of Ricardo's machinery problem, i.e. the investigation of the employment consequences of new technologies.

Against the background of increasing unemployment in the Western world since the mid-1970s and the microelectronic revolution, as exemplified in the introduction of industrial robots in production, the spectre of technological unemployment has come centre stage again. The double-sided nature of technological change, which both destroys old jobs, firms and even whole industries on the one side and creates jobs, firms and industries on the other side, has revived old controversies between labour displacement pessimism and compensation optimism, which Schumpeter

[1] See Pasinetti (1965) for the analytical part of his dissertation.

[2] See, for example, his 1999 lecture 'Economic Theory and Technical Progress' to the Royal Economic Society Annual Conference in which he traces the roots of these inadequacies.

[3] See his recent study *Keynes and the Cambridge Keynesians* (Pasinetti 2007).

(1954, p. 684) once declared 'dead and buried'. The question of whether and under what conditions technological change will lead to persistent unemployment became the central theme of the new Chapter 31, 'On machinery', which marked 'the most revolutionary change'[4] in the third edition of Ricardo's *Principles*, published in 1821. There Ricardo modified his earlier view that the introduction of machinery is beneficial to all the different classes of society and instead took note that technical progress may cause unemployment, 'without being able to give a satisfactory explanation' (Pasinetti 1981, p. 230). According to Pasinetti, Ricardo was drawn to face the machinery problem due 'to its enormous practical relevance in an industrial society' (ibid.), as shown in the Luddite riots in the period 1811–1813 when workers smashed the new productivity-enhancing textile machines which had caused a greater displacement of labour. 'Unfortunately, economic theorists have never been adequately equipped to deal with this problem' (ibid.) of technological unemployment.

Although the subtitle *'A Theoretical Essay on the Dynamics of the Wealth of Nations'* of his landmark book (Pasinetti 1981) indicates a stronger Smithian flavour, we can thus identify a modern theoretical analysis of Ricardo's machinery problem as one of the main aims of Pasinetti's structural economic dynamics. In his *Structural Change and Economic Growth* (1981) and the subsequent book *Structural Economic Dynamics* (1993), in which he investigates the implications of human learning on the development through time of a 'pure labour' economy, it is Pasinetti's central concern to study the conditions which have to be fulfilled in order for the economy to keep full employment and full capacity utilization through time when it is exposed to dynamic impulses such as technological change, a growing population (changes in the ratio of active to total population or in the ratio of working hours to total time), and changes in consumers' preferences according to Engel's law. The equilibrium path through time is no 'steady state' with constant structural proportions, i.e. a semi-stationary growth path, but one where permanent changes in some basic magnitudes, such as the national product, total consumption and investment or overall employment, are continuously associated with changes in their composition. The dynamic movements of production, prices and employment are typical features of any modern economic system, independently of its institutional set-up.

In the following we first deal with the analytical perspectives of structural economic dynamics. The distinction between 'horizontal' and

[4] Sraffa (1951, p. LVII).

'vertical' structures, which is rooted in the tradition of economic theory and has been examined by various authors in recent literature, is also important for a deeper understanding and assessment of Pasinetti's contribution. Section 3 then focuses on Pasinetti's vertically integrated analysis, in which the structural dynamics of employment is the outcome of both the structural dynamics of technology and demand. In particular, the macroeconomic difficulty of achieving full employment through time is emphasized. We conclude in Section 4 with a discussion of comparative advantages of the horizontal versus the vertical approach in the analysis of technological and structural change. The controversial issue of whether technical change, which takes place at the industry level, is properly captured by a vertically integrated model in which different rates of productivity growth in the various vertically integrated sectors are exogenously given, will be addressed.

2 Structural economic dynamics: analytical perspectives

The role of the production structure of the economy comes into focus as soon as the problem of structural change arises, as in the analysis of the employment consequences of new technologies. In general, we have to distinguish two alternative approaches of economic activity, namely *horizontally* integrated and *vertically* integrated models of economic structure.[5] The strength of the horizontal or sectoral model, or the circular view of production, as developed by Quesnay, Marx, Leontief, Sraffa and von Neumann, lies in the consideration of interdependencies within the production process and the elaboration of the impact of process innovations on industrial structure. The vertical model, meanwhile, focuses on the time aspect of the production process and gives prominence to the need to ensure the availability of certain inputs as they are required in a succession of production stages over time (see Figure 9.1).

Classical economic theory had been distinctly macroeconomic because of its consideration of the pattern of interdependence between different sectors of economic activity. The sectoral composition of the economy, which already plays a central role in Quesnay's *Tableau économique*, comes into focus in Marx's schemes of reproduction. Horizontal constraints on capital accumulation are important in the analysis of an economy where the various sectors are either stationary or expanding at a uniform rate. However, authors such as Smith and Marx, despite the latter's emphasis on sectoral interdependencies, have also considered vertical constraints

[5] For a more detailed analysis *see* the contributions in Baranzini and Scazzieri (1990), Hagemann *et al.* (2003) and Landesmann and Scazzieri (1996).

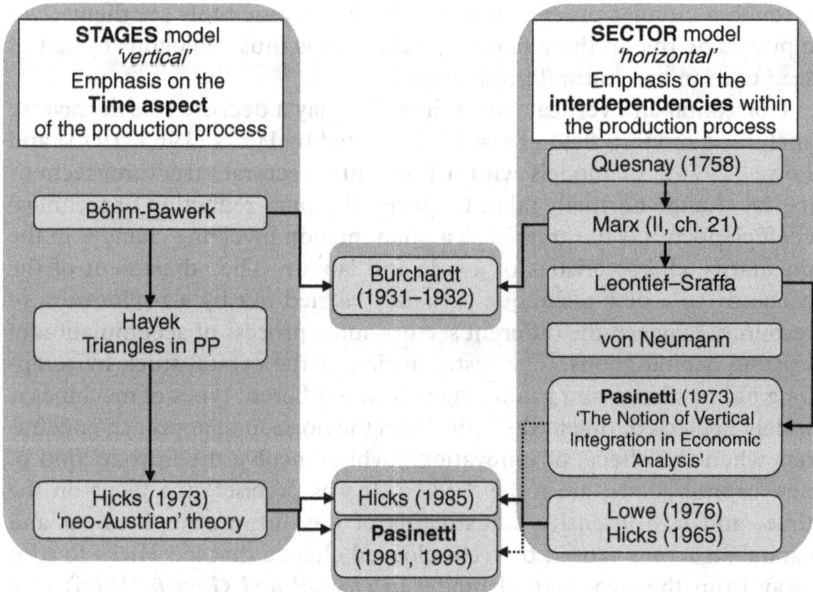

Figure 9.1 Structural economic dynamics: analytical perspectives

on capital accumulation which derive from the sequential nature of most production processes. It was, however, Böhm-Bawerk who first outlined the capital structure in terms of the construction time needed to bring about a given productive capacity of final products and to elaborate an analytical framework in which the transformation of the production structure is associated with a changing composition of the time profiles of the whole economic system. In Böhm-Bawerk's representation of the structure of production (later used by Hayek in his famous 'triangles' of *Prices and Production*), a sequence of original inputs of labour (and land) is transformed into a single output of consumable commodities. There is no distinction between fixed and circulating capital. Both types of capital are intermediate products or working capital. The production process is treated as unidirectional rather than circular.

It was Burchardt (1931–1932) who set out to compare, contrast and combine the schemes of the stationary circular flow in Böhm-Bawerk and in Marx, and thus provided the first synthesis of the vertical and the horizontal approach. He criticized the Austrian model for its inadequate treatment of the role of fixed capital in production. In an industrial system the physical self-reproduction of some fixed capital goods, which Lowe (1976) later called 'machine tools', is an important technological characteristic. They can be maintained and increased only through a circular process in which these machine tools are themselves inputs. The role of these fixed capital goods is thus analogous to that of seed corn in agricultural production.

Horizontal and vertical constraints also play a decisive role in traverse analysis, a modern field of research initiated by Hicks (1965, 1973) and Lowe (1976). In models with a horizontal sectoral structure, technological change normally takes the form of a pure reduction of technical coefficients but is not treated as a phenomenon involving changes in the qualitative characteristics of goods and labour. The adjustment of the economy to a new technique is mainly carried out by a reallocation of resources between the different sectors and a process of accumulation of existing capital goods. The restructuring of the capital stock by scrapping old machines and producing new and different types of machines is widely neglected, due to the difficulties the horizontal approach encounters when the effects of innovations, which involve the introduction of new capital goods, are to be studied. It was precisely the focus on the time- and cost-intensive adjustments of the output, employment and capital structure caused by technological change that led Hicks to turn away from the two-sectoral model in *Capital and Growth* (1965) to a vertical representation of the productive structure in *Capital and Time* (1973). There Hicks based his traverse analysis, mainly designed to give a modern theoretical treatment of Ricardo's machinery problem by which he had become fascinated from the late 1960s, on the concept of a neo-Austrian, vertically integrated production process, in which a stream of labour inputs is converted into a stream of consumption good outputs.[6] While abstracting from intersectoral interdependencies, it is a significant property of Hicks's neo-Austrian model that it brings intertemporal complementarities in the production process into sharp focus. Whereas he admitted that the Austrian method has problems in showing the effects of innovations upon industrial structure, as reflected in input–output relationships, Hicks saw the decisive advantage of his neo-Austrian approach in the ability to cope with the important fact that technological change nearly always involves the introduction of new capital goods.

> It is here undesirable that these goods should be physically specified, since there is no way of establishing a physical relation between the capital goods that are required in the one technique and those that are required in the other. The only relation that can be established runs in terms of costs, and of capacity to produce final output; and this is precisely what is preserved in an Austrian theory. (Hicks 1977, p. 193)

[6] For a more detailed analysis of Hicks's investigation of Ricardo's machinery problem *see* Hagemann (1994, 2008).

A similar interpretation is given by Pasinetti (1981, Chapter VI). While conceding that the input–output model gives more information on the structure of an economy *at any point in time*, Pasinetti emphasizes that, because of the changing coefficients *over time*, the vertically integrated analysis has a greater empirical significance for structural economic dynamics. Measuring capital goods in units of vertically integrated productive capacity of the final commodity 'has an unambiguous meaning through time, no matter which type of technical change, and how much of it, may occur' (p. 178). In contrast to Hicks's and Lowe's reinvestigations of Ricardo's machinery problem, Pasinetti does not elaborate traverse analysis but concentrates on the restrictive set of conditions which has to be fulfilled in order for the economy facing dynamic impulses to develop through time with full employment and full capacity utilization.

3 Vertically integrated sectors and the structural dynamics of employment

It is one of the great merits of Pasinetti's analysis of structural change that he has shown so clearly the double-sided nature of technological change, which so often is treated exclusively as a supply-side phenomenon. Pasinetti has integrated into his theoretical framework not only the demand aspect of technological change but also the interaction between the two sides. The factor ultimately responsible for structural change is technical progress as a result of learning. Increases in productivity lead to increases in per capita income. Yet even with increases in real income, consumers do not expand their demand for each existing commodity proportionally. Moreover, new products emerge as a corollary of technical progress. This generalization of Engel's empirical law, i.e. the integration of the structural dynamics of demand, plays an important role in Pasinetti's analysis. Indeed, Pasinetti emphasizes 'in the long run, it is the level of real income – not the price structure – that becomes the relevant and crucial variable' (1981, p. 78).

It is a characteristic feature of Pasinetti's structural economic dynamics that only final commodities are considered. 'No intermediate stage, and thus no intermediate commodity, will be explicitly represented. All production processes will be considered as vertically integrated, in the sense that all their inputs are reduced to inputs of labour and to services from stocks of capital goods' (1981, p. 29).

As time goes by, the various vertically integrated sectors experience structural dynamics of both their production and their costs (and thus equilibrium prices), with important consequences for the development of the demand for labour, i.e. it generates a certain *structural dynamics of employment*. If, with a constant labour supply, labour productivity in sector i grows with the rate ρ_i and demand for good i grows with the rate r_i, the sectoral demand for labour would only be constant in the special but unlikely case $\rho_i = r_i$. If r_i exceeds (is smaller than) ρ_i, sector i will expand (reduce) its demand for labour. With different rates of productivity growth and different sectoral rates of growth of demand, apart from the very special case in which demand grows in every single sector at exactly the same rate as labour productivity, reallocation of labour between the sectors will be necessary. Thus, a high level of employment can be maintained only with the necessary mobility of labour between sectors (and regions). Pasinetti's theoretical framework allows both expanding and declining industries to be observed in the process of structural change. When, in some sectors, the introduction of new technologies causes high rates of productivity growth which cannot be matched by a proportional increase in demand because some level of saturation has been reached, a decline in employment in these sectors cannot be avoided.

With a growing population, the economy must also enlarge its overall productive capacity continuously. Furthermore, a very definite relation between the rate of growth of sectoral demand and the amount of new investment has to be fulfilled in each sector. In order to maintain full employment over time, an effective demand condition and a capital accumulation condition must be satisfied. It is therefore very probable that, even if the economy starts from an equilibrium position with full employment of the labour force and full utilization of productive capacities, the structural dynamics which cause that position to change will not result in the maintenance of full employment by the endogenous mechanisms of the market system.

If we take Pasinetti's more complex economic system, in which production takes place by means of labour and capital goods needed to produce the final output,[7] then the *full-employment condition* amounts to

$$\underbrace{\sum a_{ni} \cdot a_{in}}_{1} + \underbrace{\sum (1/T_i) \cdot a_{nk_i} \cdot a_{in}}_{2} + \underbrace{\sum a_{nk_i} \cdot a_{k_in}}_{3} = 1 \qquad (1)$$

Here a_{ni} and a_{nk_i} denote the labour-input coefficients per unit of consumption good i respectively the corresponding capital good k_i produced,

[7] *See* Pasinetti (1981, pp. 35–43). In this model capital goods are produced from labour alone, whereas in the most complex model capital goods are also needed for the production of capital goods but still are specific for the corresponding consumption goods sector so that the various vertically integrated sectors are not interconnected, and no basic product in the sense of Sraffa exists.

a_{in} and a_{k_in} denote the demand coefficients per capita for consumption goods and the corresponding net investment, whereas a_{k_i} indicates the replacement coefficients. The average lifetime of capital goods in the vertically integrated sector i $(i = 1, 2, \ldots, n - 1)$ is $T_i = 1/a_{k_i}$. Overall, employment thus consists of the three components of:

- demand for labour in the production of consumption goods (1),
- demand for labour in the production of replacement investment (2), and
- demand for labour in the production of net investment (3).

The *capital accumulation conditions* for keeping full employment through time amount to

$$a_{k_in}(t) = (g + r_i(t)) \cdot a_{in}(t) \quad i = 1, 2, \ldots, (n-1) \tag{2}$$

where g denotes the rate of population growth. They require the fulfilment of the Harrod–Domar equation in every sector of the economy. These are necessary but not sufficient conditions.

Maintaining full employment over time also requires that the *effective demand condition*

$$\begin{aligned} &\sum a_{ni}(0) \cdot a_{in}(0) \cdot e^{(r_i - \rho_i)\cdot t} + \sum (1/T_i + g + r_i(t)) \cdot a_{nk_i}(0) \\ &\quad \cdot a_{in}(0) \cdot e^{(r_i - \rho_i)\cdot t} = \mu(t) \cdot \nu(t) \end{aligned} \tag{3}$$

must be satisfied. Whereas μ represents the participation rate, i.e. the ratio of active to total population, ν indicates the ratio of working hours performed to the total number of hours per period (year). The macroeconomic conditions depend both on technology and on the growth and composition of output.

From his analysis Pasinetti draws

> the important conclusion that the structural dynamics of the economic system inevitably tend to generate … *technological* unemployment. At the same time, the very same structural dynamics produce counter-balancing movements …, *but not automatically*. There is nothing in the structural evolution of technical coefficients on the one side and of per-capita demand on the other, as such, that will ensure … the maintenance of full employment. Therefore, if full employment is to be kept through time, it will have to be actively pursued as an explicit aim of economic policy. (Pasinetti 1981, p. 90)

In order to sustain full employment over time, society has to choose one of the following strategies or a combination of them:

- a Keynesian-type policy which will raise per capita demand for existing goods;
- the promotion of research and development of new goods. Since technological progress leads not only to an increase in

productivity but also to product innovations with high potential for an increase in demand, investment and employment, a more supply-side oriented policy of this kind aims at strengthening the latter tendency in order to compensate for the former;
- a policy of shortening the working week or reducing the participation rate. Within certain boundaries, technological progress allows society to choose between producing more and/or better goods and enjoying more leisure time.

It is the main merit of Pasinetti's investigation to have shown so clearly that full employment will be maintained only if the economy is able to implement a continuous process of structural reallocation of labour between the sectors, in accordance with the twofold effects of technological progress on labour productivity and the evolution of demand. The structural dynamics of employment causes serious problems for firms and individuals because it requires a very special pattern of investment behaviour and training as well as mobility between sectors (and regions) over time.

4 Productivity growth, input–output structures and vertically integrated sectors

As already indicated, the distinction between horizontal and vertical structures has remarkable implications for dynamic analysis. In a pathbreaking paper, Pasinetti (1973) examines the construction of a vertical structure from a set of interdependent activities and shows that a set of vertically integrated sectors, i.e. a single vertical structure, may be associated with any given circular economy. In particular, Pasinetti demonstrates that, under certain conditions, the analysis of growth processes requires a conceptual framework encompassing compositional shifts from one set of vertically integrated sectors to another, but not a change in the identity of individual sectors. Pointing out that the notion of vertical integration is implicit in the theory of value of the classical economists such as Ricardo, and looking at a vertically integrated sector as a compact way of representing a 'sub-system' (Sraffa 1960, p. 89) as it synthesizes each sub-system into a single labour coefficient and a single composite commodity, Pasinetti's 1973 paper on 'The notion of vertical integration in economic analysis' breathes fully the Sraffian spirit and is completely within the horizontal approach emphasizing the interdependencies within the production process.

For Pasinetti this does not change in his analysis of structural economic dynamics when priority is given to the vertical approach over the horizontal one, due to the breaking down of inter-industry relations which become different over time, since 'in order to give a vertically integrated sectoral model an empirical content, one must first of all collect data and fit them into an input–output table in the usual inter-industry way' (1981, p. 113). However, even sympathetic and knowledgeable commentators recognize that

> the focus on structural dynamics leads Pasinetti to a representation of the productive system which is sharply different from that characteristic of von Neumann, Leontief and Sraffa. ... Pasinetti chooses to concentrate on a limited number of vertically integrated sectors, each corresponding to a final commodity, and to avoid the explicit consideration of transactions between capital goods industries. The result is a conceptual framework permitting the author to obtain a set of neat, sometimes striking conclusions, without being disturbed by the physical and quantitative changes in the capital stock of an economic system under the influence of technical progress. (Scazzieri 1983, p. 77)

Pasinetti's work seems to have given stimulus to two different views of vertical integration: one where interdependence is still present and basic products in the sense of Sraffa exist, and one where interdependence has passed away. Thus Schefold probably was the first who noticed and criticized, in his review of Pasinetti (1981), that it is not legitimate to assume that the different rates of productivity growth in the various vertically integrated sectors are exogenously given. In so doing, he is forced to give up the general model containing basic products in favour of a special model in which, even in its 'more complex' version (involving capital goods for the production of capital goods), no basic products exist and, as such, the production process is not circular. Even when taking into consideration the fact that the diffusion of new technologies is often dependent on the existence of industries that are interrelated from the technological point of view, this approach excludes one important aspect of technological change: its industry-specific nature, which, as a general rule, implies that rates of productivity growth in the different vertically integrated sectors cannot be thought of as being independent of one another.[8] This important characteristic – that technological change takes place at the industry level and, in the case of basic products, indirectly affects all other sectors – is disregarded in vertically integrated sectors, but is at the very centre of input–output models. For example,

[8] *See* Schefold (1982, p. 549). Schefold repeats this critique in his review of Pasinetti (1993): 'But the rates of productivity growth in different integrated sectors are not really independent of each other, and if different rates are assumed arbitrarily, they may imply a negative rate of productivity growth at the level of "ordinary" industries' (Schefold 1994, p. 1936).

in the debate on the causes of the acceleration of productivity growth in the US economy since the mid-1990s, the most important studies come to the result that between 0.3 per cent and 0.5 per cent of the increase in macroeconomic labour productivity is due to the second channel of impact of the new information and communication technologies, which consists of the indirect effect of the application of the output of the ICT sectors as an input in other sectors.

It may have been the critique raised by Schefold *et al.* which has induced Pasinetti to generalize his analysis of vertical integration and to develop his concept of vertically hyper-integrated sectors.[9] These require the input–output data but use them differently to allow for differences in production periods and to comprise time-saving technical progress.

Whereas Lavoie (1997, p. 466) thinks it most likely that 'Pasinetti assumes that the rates of productivity growth in each vertically integrated sector are, by definition, the result of the rates of productivity growth in each industry' but comes to the conclusion that 'because basic commodities are neutralised, it [Pasinetti's vertically hyper-integrated sectors] generalises the presentation of the 1981 book instead of that of the 1973 article', Pasinetti consistently has pointed out, in private conversations and correspondence with Marc Lavoie and the author, that there can be only *one* view of vertical integration. He agrees with his critics that technical change is specific to the industry level and that changes taking place at the vertically integrated level are consequences of what happens at the industry level. He emphasizes

> that any technical change, taking place at the industry level, will indeed affect the changes in many (with irreducible matrices in all) vertically integrated sectors. It is however inappropriate to say that the various vertically integrated sectors are inter-dependent, because dependence does *not* run from one vertically integrated sector to another. What one should say is that they are all causally dependent (but through different channels) on the same technical changes that take place at the industry level.[10]

No doubt this interpretation is correct and could also be agreed by critics such as Schefold. The debate has clearly shown once again that it cannot be stated that of the two approaches to disintegrate production structures, the horizontal and the vertical one, one is superior and the other inferior. Both approaches have their comparative (dis)advantages. Whereas it is a strength of the horizontal approach to elucidate intersectoral

[9] *See* Pasinetti (1988, 1989) and Lavoie (1997).

[10] Luigi Pasinetti, letter to Marc Lavoie, 16 January 1995; copy sent to Harald Hagemann 25 January 1995.

interdependencies of production structures in growth equilibrium, it encounters some difficulties in dealing adequately with the exact time profile of the interindustry adjustment in the economy in the wake of dynamic impulses. This has caused Hicks to iterate between the two approaches. While following the horizontal route when embarking on his traverse voyages in Chapter XVI of *Capital and Growth* (1965), he shifted to a vertical representation of the productive structure in *Capital and Time* (1973) to analyze the employment consequences of new technologies, before finally taking a complementary perspective and exploring both routes in which the economic system can adjust when it faces horizontal or vertical rigidities, as comes out best in Chapters 13 and 14 of his *Methods of Dynamic Economics* (1985).

Whereas there are certain similarities in synthesizing the horizontal and the vertical approach between Hicks and Pasinetti, one should not exaggerate the analogies. The treatment of fixed capital goods as intermediate goods in the Austrian representation of the productive process is a strength and the Achilles heel at the same time. On the one hand, it allows dealing with new technologies which apply the emergence of new types of capital goods, as has been pointed out often by authors such as Amendola and Gaffard, who criticize the horizontal approach for its failure to deal with this important empirical fact. On the other hand, with the loss of circularity in Austrian models, other important empirical phenomena, such as the fact that technical progress predominantly takes place at the industry level, and that productivity growth in one sector affects productivity growth in other sectors where the output of the former sector is used as an input, are completely removed. Pasinetti's statements make it clear that he does not want to give up this perspective and that he remains on the Leontief–Sraffa route, emphasizing interdependencies within the production process. In giving a rationale of framing a dynamic analysis in terms of vertically integrated sectors, Pasinetti (1981, p. 117) thus stresses that 'static input–output analysis and dynamic vertically integrated analysis appear as mutually complementary and completing each other'. However, in the simplified vertically integrated relations which are constructed for the purpose of structural economic dynamics, the interdependencies of the underlying inter-industry relations sometimes get lost.

In his discussion of the possible solutions to the problem of technological unemployment, Pasinetti rightly argues that preventing the introduction or destroying the new machines is not the proper way out. He also criticizes the marginalist solution of decreasing wages for its negative effect on effective demand and heavily attacks Wicksell as the creator of the marginalist argument: 'If one follows this argument logically, one comes to the conclusion that a continuous process of technical progress is accompanied by a continuous process of decreasing wage rates! The conclusion is so absurd that it requires no comment' (Pasinetti 1981, p. 230). Perhaps a comment is required. Wicksell had often made clear that technical progress 'normally' leads to higher real wages.[11] However, this requires a process of capital accumulation which is counteracted by high population growth, as expressed in Wicksell's neo-Malthusian views. In his investigation of Ricardo's machinery problem, the passage Pasinetti refers to, Wicksell assumes a very special case of technical progress which implies a decreasing marginal productivity of labour, is connected with the co-existence of the old and new methods of production and, furthermore, is unconvincing in its abstraction from capital in production.

Let us conclude with Pasinetti's solution, which seems agreeable to a wider audience of economists as well as to the general public:

> The correct answer to the problem is clearly that of introducing the machines, of producing with them the same physical quantities as before with fewer workers, and of employing the workers that have become redundant in the production of *other* commodities, old and new. Or, alternatively, to increase for all the proportion of leisure time to total time. In this way productivity and total production and leisure time will increase; which will mean an increase in the real per capita incomes of the whole community. (Pasinetti 1981, p. 231)

REFERENCES

Baranzini, M. and Scazzieri, R. (eds.) (1990), *The Economic Theory of Structure and Change*, Cambridge University Press.

Boianovsky, M. and Hagemann, H. (2004), 'Wicksell on technical change, real wages and employment', in Bellet, M., Gloria-Palermo, S. and Zouache, A. (eds.), *Evolution of the Market Process: Austrian and Swedish Economics*, London: Routledge, pp. 69–93.

Burchardt, F. (1931–32), 'Die Schemata des stationären Kreislaufs bei Böhm-Bawerk und Marx', *Weltwirtschaftliches Archiv*, **34**, pp. 525–64, and 35, pp. 116–76.

Hagemann, H. (1994) 'Employment and machinery', in Hagemann, H. and Hamouda, O.F. (eds.), *The Legacy of Hicks*, London: Routledge, pp. 200–24.

(2008), 'Capital, growth and production disequilibria: on the employment consequences of new technologies', in Scazzieri, R., Sen, A.K. and Zamagni, S. (eds.), *Markets, Money and Capital. Hicksian Economics for the 21st Century*, Cambridge University Press, pp. 346–66.

[11] For a more detailed discussion of Wicksell's interpretation of Ricardo's machinery problem and the development of his views on technical change, real wages and employment, see Boianovsky and Hagemann (2004).

Hayek, F.A. (1931), *Prices and Production*, London: Routledge and Kegan Paul.
Hicks, J. (1965), *Capital and Growth*, Oxford: Clarendon Press.
(1973), *Capital and Time. A Neo-Austrian Theory*, Oxford: Clarendon Press.
(1977), *Economic Perspectives. Further Essays on Money and Growth*, Oxford: Clarendon Press.
(1985), *Methods of Dynamic Economics*, Oxford: Clarendon Press.
Landesmann, M.A. and Scazzieri, R. (eds.) (1996), *Production and Economic Dynamics*, Cambridge University Press.
Landesmann, M. and Scazzieri, R. (eds.) (2003), *The Economics of Structural Change*, 3 vols, Cheltenham and Northampton, MA: Edward Elgar.
Lavoie, M. (1997), 'Pasinetti's vertically hyper-integrated sectors and natural prices', *Cambridge Journal of Economics*, **21**, 453–67.
Lowe, A. (1976), *The Path of Economic Growth*, Cambridge University Press.
Pasinetti, L.L. (1965), 'A new theoretical approach to the problems of economic growth', *Pontificiae Academiae Scientiarum Scripta Varia*, Vatican City, **28**, 571–696.
(1973), 'The notion of vertical integration in economic analysis', *Metroeconomica*, **25**, 1–29.
(1977), *Lectures on the Theory of Production*, London and Basingstoke: Macmillan Press.
(1981), *Structural Change and Economic Growth. A Theoretical Essay on the Dynamics of the Wealth of Nations*, Cambridge University Press.
(1988), 'Growing subsystems, vertically hyper-integrated sectors and the concept of vertical integration', *Cambridge Journal of Economics*, **12**, 125–34.
(1989), 'Growing subsystems and vertically hyper-integrated sectors: a note of clarification', *Cambridge Journal of Economics*, **13**, 479–80.
(1993), *Structural Economic Dynamics. A Theory of the Economic Consequences of Human Learning*, Cambridge University Press.
(1999), 'Economic theory and technical progress', 'Economic Issues' Lecture, Royal Economic Society Annual Conference, Nottingham, 31 March.
(2007), *Keynes and the Cambridge Keynesians. A 'Revolution in Economics' to be Accomplished*, Cambridge University Press.
Ricardo, D. (1951), *On the Principles of Political Economy and Taxation* (first edn 1817; third edn 1821), Vol. I of *Works and Correspondence of David Ricardo*, edited by P. Sraffa with the collaboration of M. Dobb, Cambridge University Press.
Scazzieri, R. (1983), 'Economic dynamics and structural change: a comment on Pasinetti', *Rivista Internazionale*, **30**, 73–90.
Schefold, B. (1982), 'Review of Pasinetti (1981)', *Kyklos*, **35**, 548–50.
(1994), 'Review of Pasinetti (1993)', *Journal of Economic Literature*, **32**, 1936–7.
Schumpeter, J.A. (1954), *History of Economic Analysis*, London: Allen & Unwin.
Sraffa, P. (1951), *'Introduction' in The Works and Correspondence of David Ricardo*, Vol. I, Cambridge University Press, pp. XIII–LXII.
(1960), *Production of Commodities by Means of Commodities. Prelude to a Critique of Economic Theory*, Cambridge University Press.

10 The concept of 'natural economic system': a tool for structural analysis and an instrument for policy design

Roberto Scazzieri

1 Introduction

John Hicks, in his *Methods of Dynamic Economics* (1985), noted that '[a] method ... is a family, or class, of models. A model is a piece of theory, a theoretical construction, which is intended to be applied to a certain range of facts ... Models may thus be classified according to the facts to which they are intended to refer ... the particular grouping which I have in mind relates to the dynamic character of the model. I think we shall find that for that kind of grouping the term *method* is appropriate' (p. 1). If we follow Hicks's suggestion, it appears that there is a fundamental distinction in the theory of a dynamic economy between (i) contributions starting from given assumptions relative to the 'motion' of the economic system over time, and quite independently of the historical transformations that are associated with that motion, and (ii) contributions starting from given assumptions relative to the 'structure' of the economic system at any given time, and aimed at identifying the dynamic path which the economic system would follow on the assumption that certain features of the original structure would persist over time. What has been called the '"magnificent" dynamics'of the classical economists (*see* Baumol, 1959, p. 8) is a remarkable attempt to combine the analysis of the historical long-run with a specific set of constraining assumptions on certain structural or behavioural features taken to be constant within the relevant time horizon.[1] Subsequent research work has called attention to the

Some of the propositions of this chapter were originally presented at a seminar discussion at the Catholic University of Milan on 17 December 2005. The author is grateful to Prue Kerr, the Senior Visiting Fellow at the Institute of Advanced Study, University of Bologna, for careful reading and stimulating exchange of ideas. The usual caveat applies.

[1] In Baumol's description, the 'magnificent' dynamics 'has usually involved simple deduction from fairly broad generalizations, often in the nature of alleged psychological or technological laws. The magnificent dynamics may also be distinguished by the ambitious subject considered – the development of the whole economy over long periods' (Baumol, 1959, p. 8).

relevance of the hierarchy of motions, and to the relationship between the hierarchy of motions and the actual path followed by the economic system over time (*see*, for example, Simon and Ando, 1961; Simon, 1962; *see also* Landesmann and Scazzieri, 1996).

Luigi Pasinetti's *Structural Change and Economic Growth: A Theoretical Essay on the Dynamics of the Wealth of Nations* (1981) is probably the first explicit attempt to disentangle the two analytical strands mentioned above and to build a theory of 'magnificent dynamics' explicitly founded on that distinction. For that reason it is one of the great economics books of the twentieth century. It is firmly rooted in the tradition of classical economic theory and structural economics, yet it is distinct from most contributions in that tradition for its explicit discussion of a specific method of structural dynamic analysis. A characteristic feature of Pasinetti's approach is the idea that the theory of economic dynamics is a theory of the long run, that it is in the long run that the fundamental properties of the economic system can be identified, and that the economic theory of the long run is *necessarily* a theory of structural change. Such analytical features make Pasinetti's contribution a highly original exploration into a much vexed question of economic theory.

Institutional and technical changes have been characteristic features of long-run dynamics since ancient times. The speed of institutional and technical change has increased significantly at least since the industrial revolution in eighteenth-century Britain. The starting point of Pasinetti's investigation is the attempt to provide a theoretical explanation for the close association between high growth rates and high rates of structural change (that is, high rates of change in the composition of fundamental economic magnitudes). In short, Pasinetti's theoretical exploration starts off with a salient stylized fact of economic history (structural change) and attempts to provide an answer to the question of why the long-run relationship between fundamental magnitudes of the economic system makes it necessary for the economic system to change its basic structure. From this point of view, *Structural Change and Economic Growth* is an exploration into the theory of economic history. It is, however, a theory of economic history distinctly different from the one proposed by John Hicks in his 1969 book. The reason for this is that, differently from Hicks, Pasinetti maintains that the explanation of why structural change is necessary presupposes the identification of a long-run path of structural change that may be different from the historical path, yet may be essential in the explanation of why the latter took its specific course. Hicks's theory of economic history is an attempt to give reasons for historical dynamics in a specific combination of general and contingent causes. Pasinetti's theory of economic dynamics is an attempt to identify a particular benchmark, that is, a path of long-run change (natural dynamics) on which the necessary relationship between the rate of growth of the economic system and the rate of structural change is most clearly in view. This means that Pasinetti's theory of economic history gives emphasis to necessary dynamic linkages (most clear in the long run) and points to the *distance* between actual economic history and the natural long-run path as the key factor explaining the specific features of any given economic system in its evolution through time. In other words, Pasinetti comes close to acknowledging that, in most cases, the historical characteristics of any given path of economic dynamics are due to well-defined structural properties and to the way in which the realization of such properties may be modified by contingent factors. It is for this reason that economic dynamics is associated with structural analysis, which is considered as the investigation of fundamental properties common to dynamic paths under ideal conditions. Knowledge of ideal laws of change is taken to be a necessary prerequisite for the explanation of specific dynamic paths, as dynamic paths reflect both the abstract laws governing economic change and the contingent factors determining how distant any given state of the system will be from the corresponding ideal (or 'natural') state.

The structure of this chapter is as follows. Section 2 discusses the concept of a 'natural' economic system, its roots in classical economic theory and the distinctive character of this concept in Pasinetti's formulation. Section 3 examines the status of institutional assumptions and their relationship with the natural properties of any given economic system. Section 4 addresses the issue of normativity as it emerges from the distinction between the 'natural' and the 'contingent' characteristics of the economic system under consideration. Section 5 brings the chapter to a close by discussing possible applications of Pasinetti's conceptual innovation to the field of structural analysis and policy design.

2 Natural economic system and economic causality

The concept of 'natural economic system' is central to the architecture of Pasinetti's theory of long-run economic dynamics. As Izumi Hishiyama points out: 'It should be stressed that Pasinetti's "pure production" model . . . goes back to the classical point of view. And yet it presents a sort of "fundamental Tableau of the economic order" of the modern industrial economies in a dynamic context' (Hishiyama, 1996, p. 129). The concept of 'natural economic system' has clear classical roots, which Pasinetti himself identifies with long-period analysis and the possibility to detect, by means of it, a set of fundamental (relatively persistent) features of the economic systems (what classical economists such as Smith and Ricardo used to call 'natural' features). In spite of this classical influence (which is explicitly acknowledged), Pasinetti considerably extends and modifies the original classical conceptions.[2] In particular, Pasinetti's view of dynamic analysis derives from an original blending of the methods of dynamic analysis followed by François Quesnay and Adam Smith and is remarkably distant from the method adopted by David Ricardo.[3] Above all, Pasinetti's analysis in *Structural Change and Economic Growth* concentrates upon properties that are independent of any particular institutional set-up. In his view, such properties have the remarkable characteristic of being of a fundamental nature (they are considered to be *common* to all economic systems that have moved beyond the early stages of division of labour and productive specialization) *and* of remaining disguised when the economist focuses

[2] Mauro Baranzini and Geoff Harcourt have examined the route followed by Pasinetti since the early 1960s in his reformulation of the classical concept of natural economic system: '[I]n his well-known (1962) article "Rate of Profit and Income Distribution in Relation to the Rate of Economic Growth", Pasinetti was able, starting from Kaldor's income distribution theory, to define a "natural" rate of profit at the macroeconomic level, determined by the natural rate of growth of the system and the propensity to save of the "pure" capitalists' class ... A few years later ... Pasinetti was able to fix the concept of "natural" at the industry or sector level (and hence no longer at the macro-level) where there logically exist a whole series of "natural" rates of interest, at a stage which even precedes the process of capital accumulation' (Baranzini and Harcourt, 1993, p. 6). This process eventually led to the formulation of the natural system in *Structural Change and Economic Growth*, which is characterized by 'a clear distinction between the two levels of inquiry (the first "natural", the second "institutional")' (Baranzini and Harcourt, 1993, p. 7). Pasinetti's concept of the natural system has been described as 'an unfamiliar piece of "highly" classical economic theory' (Baranzini and Harcourt, 1993, p. 35). To elucidate the characteristics of that system, Heinrich Bortis has proposed a distinction between four different ways in which the concept of 'natural' may be relevant in economic theory: 'A first meaning ... relates to the forces of nature which are made use of by man (society) in the process of production ... A second meaning of "natural" relates to the broad organization of society as grounded on fundamental features of human nature that are invariant or change but very slowly ... The concept of a "natural" (reasonable) organization of society leads to a third meaning of "natural" which is also made use of in Pasinetti (1981), namely "natural" in the sense of "normative" implying, however, that the natural (reasonable) state of society is not brought about automatically by natural (inherent) forces ... Finally, a fourth meaning of "natural" emerges in relation with positive economics which aims at describing and explaining reality. Description may be based upon and explanation directed to the persistent and permanent aspects of reality while neglecting rapidly changing factors as linked to the vagaries of the market in the main' (Bortis, 1993, pp. 356–58).

[3] Both Quesnay's *ordre naturel* and Smith's natural progress in the development of the wealth of nations are important sources for Pasinetti's analysis of the dynamics of the natural economic system (*see*, respectively, Hishiyama, 1960, 1996; Negishi, 1985). On the other hand, Pasinetti carefully avoids taking Ricardo's view that the fundamental structure of natural dynamics, even if possibly concealed in the short run, will eventually become visible in the long run.

upon existing institutions and behavioural principles.[4] Pasinetti's dynamic analysis, as expounded in *Structural Change and Economic Growth*, is an attempt to analyze the long run in terms of fundamental economic forces and their interaction. Producers' and consumers' learning is considered to be the guiding factor of long-run dynamics. This means that economic dynamics is seen to be led by 'motive forces' that are themselves changing their composition and intensity as time goes on (thereby making proportional dynamics impossible). Against such a stylized background, Pasinetti examines 'natural' economic dynamics by adopting a method of analysis that is more Smithian than Ricardian in character. Ricardo's study of the long-run path of a capitalist economic system gives way to the study of the dynamic path that *should be* followed by any given economic system making full use of its productive potential (in terms of both its labour force and its capital equipment). It is important to realize that Pasinetti's natural dynamics is necessarily associated with the long run. In Pasinetti's own words, this is because the '"natural and primary" determinants are bound to make themselves felt in the long-run, whatever transitory short-run deviations there may be' (Pasinetti, 1981, p. 127). However, Pasinetti is also careful in distinguishing between the long-run evolution of any given economic system and its natural evolution. This is because the natural pattern of change 'is always there', independently of whether the existing economic system is able to follow its natural evolution or not. If that is the case, the identification of natural paths has intrinsically normative implications. Natural economic dynamics is concerned with the 'dynamic norm' that any given economic system should follow. Dynamic economic analysis brings about a *methodological shift* (from the abstract exploration of theoretical possibilities to the identification of concrete policy instruments and goals) provided the economist is able to discover the fundamental structural properties of the economic system, that is, the properties inherently associated with the way in which the economic system is constructed. These properties are the sources of normativity since the identification of the fundamental structure of any given economic system suggests a way to discover the potential of such a system, and thus also allows identification of 'structurally congruent' policy goals and instruments. (These are objectives and instruments adequate to the realization of the structural potential inherent in the economic system under consideration.)

[4] An early statement of the above distinction between the natural properties and the institutional features of any given economic system may be found in Pasinetti (1964–65).

To conclude, Pasinetti's theory of natural economic dynamics is an exploration in the field of pure economics, strictly speaking. This means that, after selecting a specific set of structural assumptions (essentially, a set of consumption coefficients and a set of labour coefficients), the logical implications of the initial set of assumptions are deduced without introducing any additional assumption, that is, without introducing any assumption not included in the original core. This point of view is associated with a fundamental rethinking of classical economic theory. This is because, while taking inspiration from the dynamic theories of Smith and Ricardo, Pasinetti argues for a radical reformulation of their theories in order to disentangle their structural core from institutional and behavioural assumptions of a particular type. In this way, Pasinetti's theory of the natural economic system is an attempt to turn the classical theories of Smith and Ricardo into a fully fledged pure (and *general*) theory of a production economy. This point of view has important methodological implications as to the use of economic theory in the identification of causal relationships. For Pasinetti represents the economic system by 'an analytical apparatus of amazing simplicity' (Bortis, 1996, p. 136), whose aim is not to describe real economic processes in their full complexity but to identify their most essential and indispensable components and relationships. This approach has a twofold implication for economic causality. First, it is assumed that simple causal relationships (presumably of the deterministic type) are circumscribed to the domain of the most fundamental properties (the 'natural economic system'). Second, it is conjectured that economic systems in their full complexity would be conducive to multi-layered causal relationships, which would often lead to uncertain outcomes. However, Pasinetti also identifies a precise connection between the former and the latter type of causality. This is because the natural economic system is not conceived as a fictive construction but as a true set of relationships distilled from economic reality. As a result, any existing economic system would show 'natural causality' at work to a greater or lesser extent. Indeed, the *distance* of any real economic system from the corresponding natural system[5] would itself be an important explanatory factor when trying to understand the actual performance of any given economic system under a specific institutional and behavioural regime. To conclude, Pasinetti's formulation suggests a flexible use of economic causality and presupposes the ability to move back and forth between the simple

[5] In the case of Pasinetti's pure labour economy, this would be the natural economy associated with a set of labour and consumption coefficients compatible with those observed in the actual economic system.

relationships of the natural economy and the complex relationships to be observed in economic reality (*see also* Baranzini and Scazzieri, 1990, pp. 248–50). This means that a pluralistic approach to causal relationships should be followed (*see also* Kerr and Scazzieri, 2006, for a further elaboration on this theme). Natural causality presupposes analytical simplification and the latter is consistent with the identification of causes that are *prima facie* independent of any specific context. On the other hand, 'real causality' (that is, the identification of causes directly relevant in explaining the actual performance of a particular economic system under given conditions) is clearly influenced by the context under consideration and its history. This distinction is remarkably close to John Hicks's distinction between 'static causality' (which he considered to be independent of time) and 'contemporaneous' or 'sequential' causality (which he considered to be inherently associated with the time dimension) (*see* Hicks, 1979). For Hicks's static causality shares with Pasinetti's natural causality the feature of being associated with permanent laws that are always in operation, independently of whether or not the context of observation makes them immediately visible. Yet Pasinetti's real causality is inherently historical in the sense that it presupposes a careful identification of context in time and of its pattern of change (*see*, in particular, Pasinetti, 1981, pp. 219–44 and Pasinetti, 1993, pp. 36–59). What makes Pasinetti's point of view highly distinctive is his attempt to connect natural causality with context-dependent causation by means of a normative standard. This means there is no presumption that the context of observation would make natural causality visible in a spontaneous way (not even in the long run). However, it is assumed that natural causality is always present and that appropriate behavioural or policy regimes can activate it. Natural causality is initially identified in terms of positive laws and independently of historical time. It is subsequently shifted to the domain of normative properties once the performance of the economic system under specific conditions is examined. In short, Pasinetti outlines a bridge between different types of causality that is also a bridge between positive and normative laws. We shall examine some implications of this point of view in Sections 3 and 4 below.

3 Institutional assumptions and natural properties

The starting point of Pasinetti's discussion of the natural system is the classical analysis of the 'primary and natural' determinants of value and distribution (Ricardo, 1951 [1817]). In this connection, however, Pasinetti makes clear that the natural system derives its identity not from any tendency of the economic magnitudes to attain certain long-run levels but from the analytical possibility of identifying structural conditions that are 'always there – even if it is not so much apparent – in the *short* no less than in the long run, whatever amount of temporary disturbances there may be' (Pasinetti, 1981, p. 127*n*; *see also* Section 2 above). This point may be easily overlooked but is quite essential in understanding the logic of Pasinetti's natural system. For it calls attention to the fact that, according to Pasinetti, the identification of a 'natural' system presupposes first of all the identification of a particular economic structure, that is, of a particular and relatively permanent set of relationships among economic magnitudes. It also presupposes recognition of the particular range of movements of those economic magnitudes that would maintain such variables consistent with one another over time.[6]

The above point of view is associated with a characteristically dual attitude to the scope and nature of economic theory. In Pasinetti's own words:

> Economic analysis as a whole [consists] of two distinct stages of investigation. The first stage is that of 'pure economic theory'. Here we find the objectively observable elements of the reality one wants to investigate, and which are essential to the economic scheme at the basis of our analysis. At this level, one has to highlight the necessary and persistent relationships of reality, leaving open to a subsequent stage the determination of all those alternative features, and especially those of an institutional character, which by their nature can be interchangeable. The second stage (that follows logically the first and leads to a 'complete economic analysis') is the one at which such interchangeable – and therefore alternative – features are introduced.
>
> I have labelled this latter stage as analysis of the institutional type, precisely because the principal objects of investigation become the different behavioural options of economic agents, both when they act upon the drive of individual motives and when they act with social intentions, or even when they are driven and regulated by public institutions. (Pasinetti, 2004, pp. 379–80, my translation; *see also* Pasinetti, 1994)

Pasinetti's natural system derives from the identification of fundamental relationships but is far removed from the idea that such relationships

[6] It is worth noting that Pasinetti's natural dynamics reflects a point of view remarkably close to that of the writers in the natural jurisprudence tradition. In particular, Pasinetti's point of view has certain features in common with that of early legal theorists such as Gaius and Ulpianus (second and third centuries respectively), according to whom there are aspects of natural law (such as those associated with the so-called *ius gentium*, or 'law of the peoples') that are neither associated with a real or a conventional state of nature nor immutable through time, but are themselves subject to vary by following a certain set of 'natural' attitudes and dispositions that may or may not be activated depending upon specific historical conditions (*see* De Gennaro, 2006).

would be somehow more apparent, or relevant, in the long run. This is because the natural system is a particular economic structure allowed to move over time by following its own 'internal logic', that is, by following the two conditions below: (i) the system should always satisfy the structural constraints associated with it; (ii) the system should make *full use* of the potential associated with the above structural constraints. For example, an industrial economy would be characterized by 'natural forces' such as 'an evolving technology, a growing population and an evolving pattern of consumers' preferences' (Pasinetti, 1981, p. 127). The internal logic of such an economy would imply that the system moves over time by satisfying two types of conditions ensuring full employment and full capacity utilisation: 'a series of sectoral new investment conditions, defining the evolving structure of capital accumulation; . . . a macro-economic effective demand condition, referring to total demand in the economic system as a whole' (ibid., p. 128). This point of view entails a sharp departure from the Ricardian analytical tradition and might suggest some proximity with the conceptual and methodological assumptions of Quesnay's *Tableau économique* (Quesnay, 1758). More generally, Pasinetti comes to conceive the natural system as a fundamental heuristic device, which would in principle allow both the identification of the potential for change inherent in any given system and the room left to economic reform in reducing the distance between the natural system and the existing economic institutions and practices.

The identity of the natural system is determined by two distinct sets of conditions: (i) the production coefficients and the per capita consumption coefficients associated with the existing (average) state of technology and the existing (average) composition of demand respectively; (ii) the consistency requirements to be met in order to achieve a 'satisfactory' compatibility among the fundamental magnitudes of the economic system under consideration. In particular, Pasinetti has argued that '[a]n economic system, at a given point of time, is said to be in a "satisfactory" situation when the existing labour force is fully employed and the existing capital goods are neither too abundant to remain idle nor too scarce to be insufficient to provide jobs for all the existing labour force' (Pasinetti, 1987, p. 994). He has also argued that '[a]n economic system is said to be moving "satisfactorily" through time when its dynamic movements maintain through time the full employment of the labour force and the full utilization of the productive capacity' (ibid.). If we consider a multisector dynamic model in which commodities are produced by means of labour and (produced) capital goods, the general condition for a satisfactory dynamics requires the fulfilment of two distinct types of necessary conditions: (i) waste should be avoided by ensuring that sectoral investment does not lead to idle productive capacity and also by ensuring that the available labour force is fully employed; (ii) 'artificial scarcities' should be avoided by ensuring that the growth of productive capacity in each sector does not fall short of the growth of the corresponding sectoral demand and also that the growth of the overall effective demand does not outstrip what the available labour force would be able to produce (*see* Pasinetti, 1987, pp. 995–96).

The natural economic system is constructed so as to meet the conditions for satisfactory growth (*see* above). As a result, it fulfils the basic requirement of *structural efficiency*, which concerns 'the relations among sectors and their relations with the economic system as a whole' (Pasinetti, 1987, p. 996). The simultaneous fulfilment of the no-waste condition and of the no-scarcity condition (*see* above) entails that the requirements for a natural dynamic path can be formulated in terms of 'exact equalities' (ibid.). The structural efficiency of the natural system and of its dynamic path has a family resemblance with notions of efficiency used elsewhere in the economic literature. However, the structural efficiency of the natural system is distinct from traditional concepts of Pareto-efficiency in so far as Pasinetti takes a reverse attitude to the relative 'priority' of final consumption goods versus labour and means of production. In his natural system, structural efficiency is defined by looking at ways to avoid both waste and scarcity in the utilization of labour and produced means of production. Pareto efficiency, meanwhile, is defined, within a multiple objectives framework, as a way to single out the maximal values of a particular objective function n when we take the values of the other $n-1$ objective functions as given (*see* de Finetti, 1937; *see also* Scazzieri, 2009). Pasinetti's natural system points to the logical possibility of defining efficiency purely in terms of structural compatibilities (the no-waste and no-scarcity condition) and independently of any explicit maximization exercise.

The study of relative prices and income distribution is an important field of application of Pasinetti's concept of natural economic system. He drops the Ricardian emphasis upon the long-run tendencies of prices and distributional variables (such as the rate of profits or the wage rate) and concentrates upon what would be required if such variables were to be consistent with the abstract requirements of the corresponding natural system. A striking instance of what Pasinetti's approach leads to is provided by his analysis of the causes of 'creeping inflation' and of the shortcomings of conventional monetary policy in dealing with it:

> If prices do not fall in those branches where productivity increases above average, then creeping inflation is the only way in which the economic system can maintain or try to maintain an efficient price structure. The conclusion is very

simple. When there are institutional obstacles to cutting prices in those branches of production where productivity is growing above average, a corresponding rise in the general price level of prices (creeping inflation) must be allowed in order to restore, or at least to move towards the restoration of, the natural (efficient) structure of the price system ... Constancy of [relative] prices and avoidance of inflation is a contradiction, if efficiency is to be kept in the economic system as a whole. It follows that, in such situations, any attempt by the central monetary authority to prevent the average price level from increasing (by limitations on credit or on the available quantity of money) can only result in putting the economic system under strain. (Pasinetti, 1981, pp. 221–22)

The distinction between natural features and institutional features is a characteristic element of Pasinetti's approach to the study of the dynamic possibilities open to any given economic system. Indeed, in some of his latest contributions, Pasinetti has introduced a 'separation theorem' showing how certain fundamental properties of the economic system may be taken as given across a range of different institutional set-ups (*see*, for example, Pasinetti, 2007). Income distribution is a field in which the distinction between natural properties and institutional constraints is most clearly in view (*see also* Scazzieri, 1983). This issue may be illustrated by considering the theory of natural rates of profit and of the natural rate of interest presented in *Structural Change and Economic Growth* (Pasinetti, 1981, pp. 128–55). Pasinetti argues that, in an economic system in which population grows at rate g and per capita demand for each final commodity grows at rate r_i $(i = 1, 2, \ldots, m)$, a natural dynamics (that is, a dynamic path allowing full employment of the labour force and full utilization of existing capital equipment) would normally require a *different* natural rate of profit for each productive sector (defined as the vertically integrated sector associated with any given final commodity). This 'own' natural rate of profit would be given for each sector by the sum of the rate of population growth g (common to all sectors) and of the rate of increase of per capita demand for the final commodity produced in that sector. This gives for each sector the corresponding natural rate of profit $\pi_i^* = g + r_i$ (*see* Pasinetti, 1981, p. 131). The logical requirement of a range of natural rates of profit is explained by the following argument (which Pasinetti associates with the case of an economy with stationary population and continually improving techniques):

If there are two commodities, i and j, both of which are expanding at the same per capita rate of growth $(r_i = r_j)$, both of which require exactly the same amount of labour to be produced, but such that the labour required by the first commodity is all direct, while the labour required by the second commodity is partly direct and partly first embodied into a machine; then for the community as a whole, when $r_i = r_j > 0$, the second commodity is more expensive to produce than the first ... Thus, the productivity of labour in terms of consumption good i and the productivity of labour in terms of consumption good j are exactly the same when $r_i = r_j = 0$; but the former is higher than the latter when $r_i = r_j > 0$. As a consequence, the price of j will have to be higher than the price of i by the same proportion ... as the corresponding productivity is lower. (Pasinetti, 1981, p. 130)

To put it another way, the very need to avoid any difference arising between the productivity of labour in terms of consumption good i and the productivity of labour in terms of consumption good j, combined with the need to expand productive capacity at a rate determined by the rate of growth of final demand for each sector, brings about the need for a set of natural rates of profit different from one sector to another. Such natural rates of profit are charges to be made 'in order not to violate the basic principle of equal rewards for equal amounts of homogeneous labour' (ibid., p. 132).

The same principle (equal rewards for equal amounts of homogeneous labour) allows the identification of a natural rate of interest on loans. This principle is independent of capital accumulation and may be expressed with reference to the debt–credit relationships of a pure labour economy (an economy in which commodities are produced by means of direct labour alone). Pasinetti identifies the natural rate of interest as 'a rate of interest which preserves intact through time the purchasing power of all loans in terms of labour' (ibid., p. 168). In principle, this criterion implies that the rate of interest on loans should be zero in terms of labour (as the same quantities of homogeneous labour should have exactly the same purchasing power at different time periods). The same condition implies that, whenever debt–credit relationships are stipulated in terms of a commodity h (produced in the economic system), the natural rate of interest $i^{\star}_h$ be positive and equal to the rate of variation of the unit wage σ_w (the rate of remuneration of labour) (so that $i^{\star} = \sigma_w$). The rationale for this is that one hour's labour at time t will by definition be equal to one hour's labour at time $t+1$ (thereby ensuring equality between labour embodied and labour commanded if the wage rate is chosen as *numéraire*). On the other hand, the value of any given loan is likely to change over time if the *numéraire* is any commodity h and the unit wage is continually increasing. In this case, the natural rate of interest $i^{\star} = \sigma_w$ will maintain 'unaltered through time all purchasing power relations in terms of labour' (ibid., p. 92). It is important to realize that the same normative criterion (a criterion derived from the fundamental structure of an economic system based upon the division and specialization of labour) brings about both a set of natural rates of profit (generally different from one sector to the other) and a single natural rate of interest (common to all debt–credit relationships in the economic system).

Pasinetti acknowledges that, under specific institutional assumptions, a tendency may arise towards equalization of the rates of profit on capital investment in the different sectors and towards equalization of such a (tendentially) uniform rate of profit with the (tendentially) uniform rate of interest on loans of similar risk. But it cannot in general be assumed that there is anything 'natural' in the equalization properties of rates of profit and rates of interest on loans. Indeed, the analysis of natural dynamic paths suggests that *differentiated* rates of profit (and a natural rate of interest determined independently of capital accumulation requirements) may be the rule as long as we stick to the pre-institutional level of investigation (ibid., pp. 128–31). But once we move to the institutional level of analysis, there is no guarantee that the specific institutional setting under consideration will be compatible with the structural conditions of the natural economic system. Indeed, it may be that 'some of the "natural" features of an economic system may be impossible to achieve within a particular institutional set-up' (ibid., p. 151). To see this, we may note that the need to achieve a range of sufficiently differentiated natural rates of profit might conflict with some of the most common institutional assumptions made by theoretical economists. This is because the 'fundamental principle of a capitalist economy that capital funds are to be left free to move from one sector to another' (ibid., p. 151) may be associated with a tendency towards 'equalisation of the rates of profit all over the economy' (ibid.). This situation is obviously incompatible with the condition of differentiated natural rates of profit across productive sectors. However, the economic system may still be able to achieve some of the properties of the natural state (such as economic growth with full employment of labour and full utilization of productive capacity) provided income distribution is adjusted accordingly. In particular, Pasinetti shows that the two fundamental macro-economic properties of the natural state (full employment of labour and full utilization of productive capacity) may be realized in the context of a capitalist economy with uniform rate of profit if, and only if, such a rate of profit is 'higher than . . . the weighted average of the sectoral "natural" rates of profit' (ibid., p. 152). In particular, the uniform rate of profit compatible with the two macro-economic conditions stated above is given by the following expression:

$$\pi_e = 1/s_c(g + r^*) \qquad (1)$$

where g is the rate of population growth, $r^\star$ is the weighted average rate of growth of per capita demand, s_c is the capitalists' propensity to save and π_e is the uniform rate of profit compatible with the macro-economic conditions of the natural state in the institutional set-up of a capitalist, perfectly competitive economy. It can be seen immediately that, as long as the capitalists' saving propensity s_c is lower than unity ($s_c < 1$), the uniform rate of profit π_e will be greater than the overall growth rate of the economic system (that is given by $g+r^*$).[7]

To sum up, Pasinetti's analysis points to an especially important use of the 'separation theorem' (*see* above) in the study of the conditions under which certain features of the natural economic system may be achieved (or approximated) even if the institutional set-up is not fully compatible with the natural system. In particular, his analysis makes clear that full employment of labour and full utilization of productive capacity may still be achieved under the conditions of a capitalist economy with a uniform rate of profit. However, this particular institutional set-up brings about an important change relative to the structural conditions to be satisfied by the economic system in the natural state. For in this case overall profits would have to be 'high enough' to allow the rate of profit to rise considerably above the overall growth rate of the economy. More generally, Pasinetti points to a new, important line of research into the properties of economic institutions. Different institutional set-ups may be especially effective in achieving different features (or objectives) compatible with the fundamental structural properties of the economic system. And the possibility to assess different institutional set-ups against the benchmark of the corresponding natural system provides the economist with an important tool for identifying the comparative advantages of alternative institutional set-ups. The distinction between the natural and institutional features of any given economic system allows the economist to assess economic and social institutions within a broad comparative perspective. This approach is unlikely to lead to definite conclusions 'valid for all times and places' (ibid., p. 154) as to 'the suitability of one type of institution or another' (ibid.). However, it may lead economists to acknowledge that '[d]ifferent institutional arrangements may turn out to involve different types of failures, and thus to have different advantages and disadvantages, or to work reasonably well at some stages and not so well at other stages of economic development and technological change' (ibid.). For example, as Pasinetti argues in *Structural Economic Dynamics*, 'the institutional task, that may be entrusted to the competitive market-price mechanism, of equilibrating

[7] It is worth noting that, in a uniform-profit rate economy, a capitalists' propensity to save significantly lower than 1 may greatly reduce the growth potential of the economic system relative to the corresponding natural economy. For example, if $g = 0.02$ and $r^* = 0.03$, a saving propensity $s_c = 0.5$ would increase π_e to 0.1 from an average natural rate of profit of 0.05.

the price structure ... is quite distinct from the institutional task ... of equilibrating the physical quantities. And the two should not be confused with each other' (Pasinetti, 1993, p. 124). This is primarily because '[t]he conditions that may be favourable to one institutional task may not necessarily coincide with the conditions that are favourable to the other. More specifically, if the market-price mechanism were to turn out to be particularly appropriate for one of the two tasks, that does not mean that it would also be *ipso facto* equally appropriate for the other' (ibid.).

This point of view suggests a particularly interesting route to institutional analysis in economic theory. This may be shown as follows. The analysis of economic structure sets out to identify the properties and constraints associated with any given economic system. However, the very concept of a natural economic system allows the economist to distinguish between two different levels of investigation: the 'natural' level of fundamental properties and constraints, and the 'historical' level of the properties and constraints that are associated with specific institutions and behavioural patterns, *but are not at all essential* as far as the fundamental structure of the system is concerned. A remarkable implication of this point of view is that, in general, any given economic system is associated with a hierarchy of structural levels (or levels of organization). The distinction between the 'natural' and the 'institutional' level of investigation calls attention to the multi-layered structure of any given economic system and is itself open to further refinement.[8] More generally, the above distinction paves the way to wide-ranging institutional policy, due to the combined influence of two analytical properties: (i) any given natural economic system is normally compatible with a *variety* of institutional set-ups; (ii) no 'historical' institutional set-up may realistically embody all features of the corresponding natural system. Institutional policy may be conceived as the attempt to transform institutional arrangements by introducing changes compatible with the degrees of indeterminacy that are associated with the internal hierarchy of the existing economic system (including the hierarchy between more fundamental and less fundamental institutions). It remains to be seen whether institutional policy should also be *guided* by the properties of the natural system. This brings to the fore the issue of the possible normativity of the natural system, which will be addressed in the following section.

[8] For example, Pasinetti himself has recently come to acknowledge the existence of a hierarchy *within* the institutional set-up of any given economic system, thereby distinguishing between 'fundamental' institutions and institutional arrangements of a secondary and more dispensable nature (*see* Pasinetti, 2007).

4 Sources of normativity

Pasinetti's *tour de force* in *Structural Change and Economic Growth* will be remembered as an impressive achievement in the fields of both analytical economics and economic methodology. In the latter case, Pasinetti has perhaps been the first theoretical economist to explicitly explore the normative implications of structural analysis at the 'natural' level. In this connection, he maintains that 'when it is granted that it is possible, on purely logical grounds, to (conceptually) build up the framework of a natural economic system, it becomes inevitable to think that it must be one of the aims of any society to bring the actual economic structure as near as possible to the one defined by the natural economic system; i.e., to organize itself, to devise institutional mechanisms, such as to make the actual economic quantities permanently tend towards their "natural" levels on dynamic paths' (Pasinetti, 1981, p. 154). The above statement implies that, according to Pasinetti, the conceptual framework of the natural economic system possesses inherent normative properties. His later work has examined in greater detail the sources of this normativity, and has highlighted that the normative properties of the natural economic system derive from the very way in which such a system has been constructed (*see* above; *see also* Scazzieri, 1996). The concept of a natural economic system derives from classical economic theory. At the same time, Pasinetti's natural system derives from a process of analytical simplification with respect to classical theories. This is a process by which the corpus of classical theory is, so to speak, 'stripped down' to its essentials, or to its minimal core. In a bold application of the philosophical principle known as 'Occam's razor' (*entia non sunt multiplicanda*), Pasinetti moves away from the behavioural and institutional assumptions of Smithian and Ricardian theory. In particular, he moves away from the institutional assumption of a decentralized, private ownership economy and still finds a meaningful core of structural properties.

In *Structural Change and Economic Growth* and in Pasinetti's later works we meet one important reason for the normativity of the natural system. For the natural system is a *prototype structural system* stripped of inessential behavioural and institutional properties. Therefore, the natural economic system is not a descriptive tool, nor is it a tool aimed at explaining in a direct way the actual workings of the real economic system. Natural dynamics, stripped of most of the behavioural and institutional assumptions introduced by the classical economists, leads to a normative theory precisely because it becomes a benchmark against which the actual workings of any given economic system may be assessed. If the natural economic system has desirable properties (for instance, full employment), we may take it as a standard of reference that we may wish to approximate. It is worth noting that the *normative* utilization of the natural system is different from the *heuristic* utilization of that system considered at the end of the previous section. As we have seen there, the logical relationships between magnitudes within the natural system allow the economist to discover (i) which institutional arrangements would be necessary in order to arrive at certain features of the natural system under an institutional set-up that does not allow the full 'implementation' of the natural system itself, and (ii) which institutional tradeoffs would have to be faced when trying to fulfil different institutional tasks in a setting dissimilar from the natural system.

The above set of questions is made possible by the very distinction between the natural system and the economic system described in its full complexity. In addition to that, the identification and analysis of the natural system allows a deeper level of investigation, since the natural system suggests a possible standard for institutional policy. As we shall see below, this property is due to the very process by which the natural system may be constructed. This may be shown as follows. In *Structural Change and Economic Growth* (1981), as well as in *Structural Economic Dynamics* (1993), Pasinetti derives the natural system from the 'deep structure' of the real economic system. He points out that any existing economic system is a complex hierarchical arrangement of different organizational layers and that any such system could be stripped down to its essentials, that is, to that set of characteristics in the absence of which it would cease to work as a functioning economy.[9] The natural economic system is the kernel of any 'real' economic system in the sense that its functions must be fulfilled, directly or indirectly, by any concrete institutional set-up existing under specific historical circumstances. Of course, not all institutional arrangements would be equally effective in view of the functions that the natural system brings to light. For example,

[9] The interpretation of Pasinetti's natural system may be facilitated by the consideration of his view of the economic system as a special case of Herbert Simon's 'hierarchy' of interrelationships within a complex system (*see* Simon, 1962). In Pasinetti's case, the economic system is considered as a hierarchical arrangement of pre-institutional and institutional layers, and the logical device of the natural system is a way to single out a 'most fundamental' layer of organization. The hierarchical criterion allows Pasinetti to ask which features the 'less fundamental' organizational layers should take in order to be fully consistent with the natural system. In Pasinetti's framework, that means asking which set of institutional features would bring about an economic system fully consistent with the corresponding natural system across all the different layers of its own organization. The same criterion allows Pasinetti to ask which specific institutional arrangements should be introduced in order to achieve certain properties of the natural system (such as full employment) within an institutional set-up in which the logical relationships of the natural system cannot be fully realized.

certain arrangements might be more successful to attain full employment and less successful to implement a structure of relative prices consistent with relative costs of production. The natural system is a prototype economy whose structure points to a set of necessary conditions that should be directly *or* indirectly satisfied. An ideal institutional set-up would match the structural requirements of the natural system in a direct way. This means that there would be an immediate and, in a sense, 'most effective' correspondence between the functions to be performed in the natural system and the tasks actually carried out by means of the existing institutional set-up. In general, however, we would have to deal with an 'imperfect' set of institutional arrangements. This means that the correspondence between ideal functions and actually performed tasks might be loose and far from efficient (as ideal functions, in most institutional arrangements, would not be performed in the best and most effective way).

The above conceptual framework suggests at least two different routes along which the natural economic system lends itself to normative use. First, the natural system may be conceived as a benchmark economy in which the fundamental economic functions are performed in the simplest possible way. This makes those functions clearly visible and allows an assessment of the way in which the same functions are carried out through the full institutional and behavioural complexity of the existing economic system. The natural economic system, by 'unveiling' what fundamental economic functions are, makes it possible to evaluate the effectiveness of existing arrangements. Second, the natural system may be conceived as an ideal economy that, even if it is identified at the pre-institutional level, has nonetheless clear institutional implications. Certain institutional set-ups allow better than others the emergence of features associated with natural economic dynamics. This entails that the natural economic system may be considered as a benchmark guiding institutional change (and institutional reform) towards the implementation of its structural properties. In either case, the consideration of the natural system suggests manifold ways in which the real economy could take advantage of the possibilities of improvement intrinsic to its own constitution. But this requires economists and policy makers to be bold enough to envisage a variety of institutional arrangements and behavioural patterns (these would often be institutions and behaviours quite different from the ones prevailing in the economic system under consideration). The utilization of the natural economic system as a normative prototype suggests that the search for a satisfactory economic system might take as a target (to be approximated through institutions and policies) a benchmark that is not outside the actual economic system (for example, a target associated with an exogenously determined social welfare function) but is to be discovered inside such a system, provided we are prepared to look deeply enough into its structure.

The discovery that there are normative properties inherently associated with the natural economic system (as a structural prototype) suggests a radically new standpoint in the analysis of economic structure. It also suggests a new method in the identification of institutional policies that may be envisaged in order to approximate a satisfactory economic system in a fairly accurate way.

5 Concluding remarks

Pasinetti's theory of the natural economic dynamics has certain features in common with other contributions to analytical economics that have sought to identify the abstract properties economic systems may have when those systems are examined by focusing upon certain structural (or long-term) relationships independently of behavioural characteristics and institutional constraints. From this point of view, there is a family resemblance between Pasinetti's theory of natural dynamics and contributions to the theory of maximal growth such as those of Jan von Neumann (1937) and Alberto Quadrio Curzio (Quadrio Curzio, 1986; Quadrio Curzio and Pellizzari, 1999). These contributions take a certain set of interrelated production processes as their starting point and examine in which way the structural constraints associated with such processes may influence the economic system's maximum rate of expansion. Individual or collective decisions may influence the economic system's actual performance but not its growth potential at any given time.

There is an even closer resemblance between Pasinetti's theory of natural dynamics and the contributions of Adolph Lowe to the understanding of the relationship between the 'instrumental' and the 'positive' analysis of growth paths (Lowe, 1964, 1976). Pasinetti, similarly to Lowe, makes a distinction between the dynamic path that could be envisaged on the basis of certain structural conditions and macroeconomic goals (these are close to Lowe's 'goal-adequate' trajectories) and the actual path followed by the economic system under given historical and institutional constraints. In spite of the resemblance to the abovementioned theories, Pasinetti's concept of the natural economic system has a distinct character. This is primarily because of his emphasis upon the internal hierarchy of any given economic system and his claim that such a hierarchy points to an essential structural asymmetry between different components of the economic system. The simplest possible set of economic interrelationships is the 'kernel' of the economic system, and its properties exert an influence across all the other organizational layers of that system. As we have seen, the natural system may exert a dual influence upon the economic system considered in its full complexity. Under special conditions, the institutional set-up reflects the structural properties of the natural system in a direct way, so that there is no need of further institutional adjustment. In general, however, existing institutions are far removed from the natural system. In this case, the necessary conditions to be met in order to attain certain desirable features of the natural dynamic path (such as full employment) may require a complex institutional adjustment. This means that certain functions of the natural system may be carried out in a seemingly roundabout way, that certain tradeoffs between different objectives (such as full employment and price stability) could be envisaged, and that any actual path of institutional change may or may not bring the economic system closer to the requirements of the natural system.

As we have seen, the very distinction between a structural benchmark associated with certain desirable properties and the actual economic system suggests a normative utilization of the concept of a natural economic system. However, it is important to bear in mind that Pasinetti's natural system is neither 'primitive' nor especially removed from economic reality – the relationships of the natural system may or may not be immediately visible. However, such a system exerts a permanent influence upon the performance of the economic system at any given time (*see* above). This point of view has important consequences for economic policy in general and for institutional policy in particular. Knowledge of the natural properties of any given economic system may provide useful guidelines to policy along two distinct tracks. First, the natural system could function as an *ideal benchmark* to be approximated through appropriate institutional arrangements, so as to bring the 'less fundamental' layers of the organizational hierarchy of the economic system as close as possible to its kernel of 'more fundamental' properties and relationships. Second, the natural system could function as a *control device* by means of which to check the mutual consistency of policy objectives within a particular institutional set-up and the adequacy of existing (or envisaged) institutional arrangements in view of stated policy objectives. In either case, the natural system may be an important instrument for policy design. But its role is quite different in the two cases. Using the natural system as an ideal benchmark entails a concentration of attention upon the theoretical design of institutional arrangements rather than upon the timing, bottlenecks and constraints associated with the actual functioning of any given set of social institutions. Alternatively, using the natural device as a control system entails a concentration of attention upon the existing institutional arrangements, the analysis of the adequacy of such arrangements, and the identification of the boundaries within which institutional change may realistically take place. The former track presupposes the readiness to conceive major transformations of existing institutions and suggests a fundamentally optimistic view of policy design. The latter track suggests a more guarded attitude to institutional change and looks at design principally as a route to the 'fine tuning' of existing institutions in order to reduce the cost of achieving given policy objectives through seemingly imperfect and not fully appropriate arrangements.

REFERENCES

Baranzini, M. and Harcourt, G.C. (1993) 'Introduction', in M. Baranzini and G. C. Harcourt (eds.), *The Dynamics of the Wealth of Nations. Growth, Distribution and Structural Change. Essays in Honour of Luigi Pasinetti*, Basingstoke and London, Macmillan; New York, St Martin's Press, pp. 1–42.

Baranzini, M. and Scazzieri, R. (1990) 'Economic Structure: Analytical Perspectives', in M. Baranzini and R. Scazzieri (eds.), *The Economic Theory of Structure and Change*, Cambridge University Press, pp. 227–333.

Baumol, W. (1959) *Economic Dynamics: an Introduction, with a contribution by Ralph Turvey*, New York, Macmillan (1st edn 1951).

Bortis, H. (1993) 'Reflections on the Significance of the Labour Theory of Value in Pasinetti's Natural System', in M. Baranzini and G.C. Harcourt (eds.), *The Dynamics of the Wealth of Nations. Growth, Distribution and Structural Change. Essays in Honour of Luigi Pasinetti*, Basingstoke and London, Macmillan; New York, St Martin's Press, pp. 351–83.

(1996) 'Structural Economic Dynamics and Technical Progress in a Pure Labour Economy', *Structural Change and Economic Dynamics*, 7 (2), 135–46.

de Finetti, B. (1937) 'Problemi di "optimum"' (Optimum problems), *Giornale dell'Istituto Italiano degli Attuari*, **8**, 48–67.

De Gennaro, A. (2006) *I diritti in Occidente. Diritti individuali e filosofia politico-sociale occidentale* (*Rights in the West. Individual Rights and Western Socio-political Philosophy*), Bologna, Bononia University Press.

Hicks, J. (1969) *A Theory of Economic History*, Oxford, Clarendon Press.

(1979) *Causality in Economics*, Oxford, Basil Blackwell.

(1985) *Methods of Dynamic Economics*, Oxford, Clarendon Press.

Hishiyama, I. (1960) 'The *Tableau Economique* of Quesnay – its analysis, reconstruction and application', *Kyoto University Economic Review*, **30** (April), 1–46.

(1996) 'Appraising Pasinetti's Structural Dynamics', *Structural Change and Economic Dynamics*, 7 (2), June, 127–34.

Kerr, P. and Scazzieri, R. (2006) *'Between Theory and History: Causality in Economics', Workshop Plurality in Causality*, Institute of Advanced Study, University of Bologna, 12 May.

Landesmann, M.A. and Scazzieri, R. (eds.) (1996) *Production and Economic Dynamics*, Cambridge University Press, pp. 318–20.
Lowe, A. (1964) *On Economic Knowledge: Toward a Science of Political Economics*, New York and Evanston, IL, Harper and Row.
(1976) *The Path of Economic Growth*, Cambridge University Press.
Negishi, T. (1985) 'A Reconstruction of Smith's Doctrine on the Natural Order of Investment', in T. Negishi, *Economic Theories in a Non-Walrasian Tradition*, Cambridge University Press, pp. 23–34.
Pasinetti, L.L. (1964–65) 'Causalità e interdipendenza nell'analisi econometrica e nella teoria economica' (Causality and interdependence in econometric analysis and economic theory), *Annuario dell'Università Cattolica del S. Cuore*, Milan, pp. 233–50.
(1981) *Structural Change and Economic Growth. A Theoretical Essay on the Dynamics of the Wealth of Nations*, Cambridge University Press.
(1987) '"Satisfactory" versus "Optimal" Economic Growth', *Rivista internazionale di scienze economiche e commerciali*, **34** (10), October, 989–99.
(1993) *Structural Economic Dynamics. A Theory of the Economic Consequences of Human Learning*, Cambridge University Press.
(1994) 'Economic Theory and Institutions', in R. Delorme and K. Dopfer (eds.), *The Political Economy of Diversity – Evolutionary Perspectives on Economic Order and Disorder*, London, Elgar, pp. 34–45.
(2004) 'Sraffa e la matematica: diffidenza e necessità – quali sviluppi per il futuro?' (Sraffa and mathematics: diffidence and necessity. Which ways forward?), in *Piero Sraffa*, Accademia Nazionale dei Lincei, Attidei Convegni Lincei, n. 200, 373–83.
(2007) *Keynes and the Cambridge Keynesians*, Cambridge University Press.
Quadrio Curzio, A. (1986) 'Technological Scarcity: An Essay on Production and Structural Change', in M. Baranzini and R. Scazzieri (eds.), *Foundations of Economics. Structures of Inquiry and Economic Theory*, Oxford and New York, Basil Blackwell, pp. 311–338.
Quadrio Curzio, A. and Pellizzari, F. (1999) *Rent, Resources, Technology*, Berlin, Heidelberg, New York, Springer.
Quesnay, F. (1758) *Tableau économique, Versailles*. (Also published as *Quesnay's Tableau économique*, edited, with new material, translations and notes by M. Kuczynski and R.L. Meek, London, Macmillan; New York, A.M. Kelley for the Royal Economic Society and the American Economic Association, 1972.)
Ricardo, D. 1951 [1817] *On the Principles of Political Economy and Taxation*, vol. I of *The Works and Correspondence of David Ricardo*, edited by P. Sraffa with the collaboration of M.H. Dobb, Cambridge University Press for The Royal Economic Society.
Scazzieri, R. (1983) 'Economic Dynamics and Structural Change: A Comment on Pasinetti', *Rivista internazionale di scienze economiche e commerciali*, xxx (1), January, 73–90.
(1996) 'Introduction. Pasinetti's Structural Economic Dynamics: A Symposium', *Structural Change and Economic Dynamics*, 7 (2), June, 123–5.
(2009) 'The Feasibility of Normative Structures', in M.C. Galavotti (ed.), *Bruno de Finetti. Radical Probabilist*, London, College Publications pp. 129–52.

Simon, H. (1962) 'The Architecture of Complexity', *Proceedings of the American Philosophical Society*, **156** (6), December, 122–37.
Simon, H. and Ando, A. (1961) 'Aggregation of Variables in Dynamic Systems', *Econometrica*, **29** (2), April, 111–38.
von Neumann, J. (1937) 'Uber ein ökonomisches Gleichungssystem und eine Verallgemeinerung der Brouwerschen Fixpunktsatzes', in *Ergebnisse eines Mathematischen Kolloquiums*, vol. viii, Vienna, pp. 73–83. (English translation as 'A Model of General Economic Equilibrium', *Review of Economic Studies*, 1945–6, vol. 13.)

11 Structural change and invariable standards

Takashi Yagi

1 Introduction

In the structural change process, the relationships among the various changes in the production structures, in commodity prices, in distribution, in the aggregate income and in the aggregate capital may be complex. The changes of productivity and the changes in distribution will be two major problems in considering the process of structural change and economic growth. It will be crucial to consider the choice of standard to grasp not only price and wage changes but also changes in such aggregates as income, distribution and capital. We will start by examining the relationship between the changes in productivity caused by the shift in production techniques and the changes of prices and wages by using the system with no surplus. Then we will consider the problems caused by the changes in distribution by using an enlarged Sraffian price system (evaluation system).

Pasinetti (1981, 1993) introduced the notion of the dynamic standard commodity to analyze the changes in prices and wages. The dynamic standard commodity is defined as a composite commodity whose rate of productivity change is equal to the weighted average of the rates of growth of productivity of the entire economy. It has an important property that, if it is chosen as standard, the general price level is kept constant over time. In structural dynamics, the choice of numéraire commodity is crucial to the analysis of changes of commodity prices and also to the analysis of changes in the general price level. Unless the dynamic standard commodity is chosen as numéraire, the general price level will change. Pasinetti (1993) calls the inflation caused by the choice of other numéraire than the dynamic standard commodity structural

The author would like to thank Professors G.C. Harcourt, H. Kurz, L.L. Pasinetti and B. Schefold for their helpful comments. The author is grateful for the financial support of the Grant-in-Aid for Scientific Research of the Japan Society for the Promotion of Science (Research Project 17530137, Category (C)).

inflation. The notion of structural inflation is defined by the difference between the productivity change rate of the numéraire commodity chosen and the weighted average of the rates of growth of productivity of the entire economy. If we denote the rate of change of labour productivity of numéraire commodity by $\rho^{(h)}$, the weighted average rate of social productivity change by ρ^* and the rate of structural inflation by σ_S, the structural inflation rate σ_S is defined by the difference between $\rho^{(h)}$ and ρ^*, i.e. $\sigma_S = \rho^{(h)} - \rho^*$. Therefore, in the case of $\rho^{(h)} \neq \rho^*$, the general price level will not be constant if commodity h is chosen as numéraire. The structural inflation is avoided only when the dynamic standard commodity is adopted as numéraire. Thus structural inflation will occur in the context of structural dynamics if any commodity other than the dynamic standard commodity is adopted as numéraire. The choice of numéraire is crucial to general price changes.

By introducing the notion of structural inflation, the idea of real income becomes ambiguous. It may be necessary to reconsider the notion of real income, because even if the value of net product is measured in some physical terms of a commodity or a composite commodity other than the dynamic standard commodity, the aggregated value of net product will have some effects of structural inflation. This fact brings about a problem of measurement or redefinition of real income. In present economic textbooks, the distinction lies between nominal income which is measured in nominal money, and real income which is measured in terms of some real unit of a commodity or a composite commodity. However, from the point of view of structural dynamics, even if income is measured in terms of some real unit of product, it has an effect of structural inflation. Therefore income can be classified in three ways: nominal income, 'real' income with structural inflation, and truly real income measured in terms of the dynamic standard commodity. If wage and commodity prices are measured in truly real terms, the general price level will be kept constant. The problem in distinguishing between 'real income' with structural inflation and 'truly real income' measured in terms of the dynamic standard commodity will relate to the search for an invariable standard of value by Ricardo. This distinction is the role of the dynamic standard commodity.

However, it is difficult to compute the dynamic standard commodity. This difficulty can be said to lie between solving the index number problem and finding an invariable standard of value. In the structural dynamic model, the dynamic standard commodity is a composite commodity whose composition must change with the evolution of the economic system. The basket of goods will vary at different time periods in the context of structural dynamics. But even if its composition varies through time, the values of the dynamic standard commodity at different times should be compared in order for it to be an invariable standard of value.

The classical economists had no idea of developing index numbers and they pursued an invariable standard of value. Modern economists, meanwhile, have no interest in pursuing an invariable standard of value to measure prices and wages, and might be content with the measurement in terms of numéraire or some index number. In order to visualize the dynamic standard commodity, it is necessary to solve two different problems: one is to find a standard to keep the general price level constant, the other is to compare different compositions of a heterogeneous composite commodity of different time periods. The latter problem is that of index number. In this chapter we will explain new ideas based especially on the ideas of Sraffa's (1960) standard commodity (or standard system), Pasinetti's (1981, 1993) notion of the dynamic standard commodity and Hicks's (1981) productivity indexes.

2 Sectoral and social productivity change

The quantity system and the sectoral productivity change

In this section, we will consider a production system with no surplus in order to define the sectoral and social productivity in physical terms. Pasinetti (1981, 1993) constructed a structural dynamic model in continuous time. However, we will consider a discrete time period, Period 1 and Period 2, in order to make the problems transparent. The number of commodities is assumed to be n. It is assumed that there is no introduction of new commodities. The notations of given data of Period 1 and Period 2 are shown as follows.

Notations of given data

$\mathbf{A}^1$, $\mathbf{A}^2$: the (transposed) Leontief input coefficient matrix of each period. The input coefficient matrixes are assumed to be a semi-positive and indecomposable matrix, $\mathbf{A}^1 \geq 0$, $\mathbf{A}^2 \geq 0$, $\mathbf{A}^1 \neq \mathbf{A}^2$.

L_A^1, L_A^2: the actual total labour of each period, $L_A^1 > 0, L_A^2 > 0$.

L_S^1, L_S^2: the standard total labour or in short standard labour of each period, which is normalized by the actual total labour L_A^1. They are calculated as $L_S^1 = (1/L_A^1)\, L_A^1 = 1,\ L_S^2 = (1/L_A^1)\, L_A^2$. Then we have $L_S^2 = L_S^2/L_S^1 = L_A^2/L_A^1$.

$\mathbf{l}_A^1, \mathbf{l}_A^2$: the Leontief labour input coefficient vector corresponding to the actual total labour L_A^1, L_A^2 respectively, $\mathbf{l}_A^1 > 0$, $\mathbf{l}_A^2 > 0$.

$\mathbf{l}_S^1, \mathbf{l}_S^2$: the standard labour input coefficient vector corresponding to the standard total labour L_S^1, L_S^2 respectively, $\mathbf{l}_S^1 > 0, \mathbf{l}_S^2 > 0$. The standard labour input coefficient vectors are calculated as $\mathbf{l}_S^1 = (1/L_A^1)\mathbf{l}_A^1, \mathbf{l}_S^2 = (1/L_A^1)\mathbf{l}_A^2$.

$\mathbf{x}^1, \mathbf{x}^2$: the actual output vector of each period, $\mathbf{x}^1 > 0, \mathbf{x}^2 > 0$.

$\mathbf{y}^1, \mathbf{y}^2$: the actual net product vector of each period, $\mathbf{y}^1 = \mathbf{x}^1[\mathbf{I} - \mathbf{A}^1] > 0, \mathbf{y}^2 = \mathbf{x}^2[\mathbf{I} - \mathbf{A}^2] > 0$.

$\mathbf{q}^1, \mathbf{q}^2$: the output vector of the standard system of each period, $\mathbf{q}^1 > 0, \mathbf{q}^2 > 0$. The vectors $\mathbf{q}^1, \mathbf{q}^2$ are an eigenvector of the matrix $\mathbf{A}^1, \mathbf{A}^2$ respectively and they are assumed to satisfy $\mathbf{q}^1\mathbf{l}_S^1 = \mathbf{x}^1\mathbf{l}_S^1 = 1$, $\mathbf{q}^2\mathbf{l}_S^2 = \mathbf{x}^2\mathbf{l}_S^2 = L_S^2$. We assume $\mathbf{q}^1 \neq t\,\mathbf{q}^2$ (t: positive scalar).

$\mathbf{s}^1, \mathbf{s}^2$: the standard net product vector of each period, $\mathbf{s}^1 = \mathbf{q}^1[\mathbf{I} - \mathbf{A}^1] > 0, \mathbf{s}^2 = \mathbf{q}^2[\mathbf{I} - \mathbf{A}^2] > 0$. By assumption, $\mathbf{s}^1 \neq t\,\mathbf{s}^2$ (t: positive scalar)

The produced means of production can be reduced to the indirect labour inputs by calculating the vertically integrated labour coefficient vector. If we denote the vertically integrated labour coefficient vectors corresponding to the standard labour coefficient vectors $\mathbf{l}_S^1, \mathbf{l}_S^2$ by $\mathbf{v}_S^1, \mathbf{v}_S^2$, then they can be represented as

$$\mathbf{v}_S^1 = [\mathbf{I} - \mathbf{A}^1]^{-1}\mathbf{l}_S^1 \tag{1}$$

$$\mathbf{v}_S^2 = [\mathbf{I} - \mathbf{A}^2]^{-1}\mathbf{l}_S^2 \tag{2}$$

From the above notations and the vertically integrated labour coefficient vectors of (1) (2), the standard total labour of each period is represented respectively as[1]

$$L_S^1 = \mathbf{x}^1\mathbf{l}_S^1 = \mathbf{y}^1\mathbf{v}_S^1 = \mathbf{s}^1\mathbf{v}_S^1 = 1 \tag{3}$$

$$L_S^2 = \mathbf{x}^2\mathbf{l}_S^2 = \mathbf{y}^2\mathbf{v}_S^2 = \mathbf{s}^2\mathbf{v}_S^2 \tag{4}$$

[1] From the definition of **y** and the definition of the vertically integrated labour coefficient vector, we have

$$\mathbf{x}\mathbf{l}_S = \mathbf{x}[\mathbf{I} - \mathbf{A}][\mathbf{I} - \mathbf{A}]^{-1}\mathbf{l}_S = \mathbf{y}\mathbf{v}_S$$

From the definition of **s** and **q**, we have

$$\mathbf{x}\mathbf{l}_S = \mathbf{q}\mathbf{l}_S = \mathbf{q}[\mathbf{I} - \mathbf{A}][\mathbf{I} - \mathbf{A}]^{-1}\mathbf{l}_S = \mathbf{s}\mathbf{v}_S$$

Then we have the Equation (3) (4).

From this, we can consider that the vertically integrated labour coefficient vectors can be regarded as the indicator of division of labour.

We will define the labour productivity by the vertically integrated labour coefficient. The inverse of $v_S{}^{(j)}$, the jth component of $\mathbf{v}_S$, represents the physical productivity of labour of commodity j, i.e. $\lambda_S{}^{(j)} = 1/v_S{}^{(j)} (j = 1, \ldots, n)$. Thus the sectoral productivity of labour of commodity j of each period can be represented as

$$\lambda_S^{1(j)} = 1/v_S^{1(j)} \tag{5}$$

$$\lambda_S^{2(j)} = 1/v_S^{2(j)} \tag{6}$$

In order to define the rate of sectoral productivity changes, we will take Period 2 as the base year. If we denote the rate of productivity change of commodity j (the sectoral productivity change rate of commodity j) by $\rho^{(j)}$, then it can be defined by[2]

$$\rho^{(j)} = (\lambda^{2(j)} - \lambda^{1(j)})/\lambda^{2(j)} = 1 - \lambda^{1(j)}/\lambda^{2(j)} = 1 - v_S^{2(j)}/v_S^{1(j)} \tag{7}$$

It should be noticed that the definition of the sectoral productivity change rate $\rho^{(j)}$ itself is given by the given data $[\mathbf{A}^1, \mathbf{l}_A^1, L_A^1; \mathbf{A}^2, \mathbf{l}_A^2, L_A^2]$ or $[\mathbf{A}^1, \mathbf{l}_S^1; \mathbf{A}^2, \mathbf{l}_S^2]$, irrespective of the composition of output.

Measurement of social productivity change

The next problem is to find out the weighted average of the rates of growth of labour productivity of the entire economy. Pasinetti (1981, 1993) calls this the 'standard' rate of growth of productivity of the economic system. It may be a difficult task to find an appropriate indicator of the social productivity change rate, or the 'standard rate' of growth of productivity. In order to measure the social productivity change rate, we must get some appropriate index number, because we are considering a multisector model and the net product of the economy is composed of a heterogeneous commodity bundle. Hicks (1981) suggested two different productivity indexes: the real cost approach and the opportunity cost approach. He considered the labour coefficients as the price weights for his productivity index. In Hicks (1981), labour coefficients indicates a given technique of each period and the total labour of each period is given exogenously. The index number of the real cost approach is constructed by the actual bundles

2 If Period 1 is chosen as the base year, the rate of productivity change of commodity j (the sectoral productivity change rate of commodity j) $\hat{\rho}^{(j)}$ can be defined by

$$\hat{\rho}^{(j)} = (\lambda^{2(j)} - \lambda^{1(j)})/\lambda^{1(j)} = \lambda^{2(j)}/\lambda^{1(j)} - 1 = v_S^{1(j)}/v_S^{2(j)} - 1$$

of commodities produced under given production conditions. The index number of the opportunity cost approach is constructed by the bundle of commodities which can be potentially producible by the given production condition and the actual total labour. The opportunity cost approach will enlarge the applicability of cost approach and enable us to construct more productivity indexes.

As for the price vectors to construct index numbers, we can make use of the vertically integrated labour coefficient vectors $\mathbf{v}_S^1, \mathbf{v}_S^2$. As for the quantity vectors to construct index numbers, according to Hicks (1981), both the actual net product and the potentially producible net product can be eligible as the quantity weights. Therefore, not only the actual net product vectors $\mathbf{y}^1, \mathbf{y}^2$ but also the standard net product vectors $\mathbf{s}^1, \mathbf{s}^2$ are eligible as quantity weights. In order to calculate the standard net product vectors $\mathbf{s}^1$, $\mathbf{s}^2$, we need only the input coefficient matrixes, the labour coefficient vectors and the quantities of actual total labour, i.e. a set of data $[\mathbf{A}^1, \mathbf{l}_A^1, L_A^1; \mathbf{A}^2, \mathbf{l}_A^2, L_A^2]$. By using the standard net product vectors $\mathbf{s}^1$, $\mathbf{s}^2$ for quantity weights, we can focus upon the difference in techniques of different periods. The standard net product vectors are preferable for the construction of a productivity index because the composition of the standard net product has a direct connection to the technique and has no influence from the differences in demand composition. In addition, the standard net product vectors $\mathbf{s}^1$, $\mathbf{s}^2$ have a preferable property as standard in the Sraffian price system when the rate of profit is positive (*see* Section 4 below).

We will use Fisher-type index numbers because in our model the Fisher-type indexes bring about the quite interesting result that the inverse of the Fisher-type price index becomes equal to the Fisher-type output index divided by the labour input index. Let us denote the price index of Fisher type by P_{sv}, the output index of Fisher type by Q_{sv}, the input cost index by C_{sv}. If a set of data $[\mathbf{A}^1, \mathbf{l}_A^1, L_A^1; \mathbf{A}^2, \mathbf{l}_A^2, L_A^2]$ is given, we can obtain the data set $[\mathbf{s}^1, \mathbf{s}^2, \mathbf{v}_S^1, \mathbf{v}_S^2]$. Then the indexes will be represented as[3]

$$P_{sv} = \sqrt{\frac{\mathbf{s}^1\mathbf{v}_S^2}{\mathbf{s}^1\mathbf{v}_S^1} \cdot \frac{\mathbf{s}^2\mathbf{v}_S^2}{\mathbf{s}^2\mathbf{v}_S^1}} \qquad Q_{sv} = \sqrt{\frac{\mathbf{s}^2\mathbf{v}_S^2}{\mathbf{s}^1\mathbf{v}_S^2} \cdot \frac{\mathbf{s}^2\mathbf{v}_S^1}{\mathbf{s}^1\mathbf{v}_S^1}} \qquad C_{sv} = \frac{\mathbf{s}^2\mathbf{v}_S^2}{\mathbf{s}^1\mathbf{v}_S^1} \tag{8}$$

From (3) (4), we have

$$L_S^2 = \frac{\mathbf{s}^2\mathbf{v}_S^2}{\mathbf{s}^1\mathbf{v}_S^1} \tag{9}$$

[3] The index numbers constructed with a set of data $[\mathbf{y}^1, \mathbf{y}^2, \mathbf{v}_S^1, \mathbf{v}_S^2]$ have the same formulation as those from (8)–(12).

From (9), the indexes of (8) can be rewritten as

$$P_{sv} = \sqrt{\frac{\mathbf{s}^1\mathbf{v}_S^2}{\mathbf{s}^2\mathbf{v}_S^1} \cdot L_S^2} \qquad Q_{sv} = \sqrt{\frac{\mathbf{s}^2\mathbf{v}_S^1}{\mathbf{s}^1\mathbf{v}_S^2} \cdot L_S^2} \tag{10}$$

We will call P_{sv} the Standard price index and Q_{sv} the Standard output index. From the theory of index numbers, the relationship between C_{sv}, P_{sv}, Q_{sv} becomes

$$C_{sv} = P_{sv} \cdot Q_{sv} \tag{11}$$

From (8)–(11), we can define the productivity index as

$$\Lambda_{sv} = 1/P_{sv} = Q_{sv}/L_S^2 = \sqrt{\frac{\mathbf{s}^2\mathbf{v}_S^1}{\mathbf{s}^1\mathbf{v}_S^2} \cdot \frac{1}{L_S^2}} \tag{12}$$

We will call Λ_{sv} the Standard productivity index, or more precisely the Standard physical productivity index. The Standard productivity index takes out the effect of social productivity changes resulting from the difference in the structures of division of labour from equations (3) and (4). It should be stressed that Λ_{sv} is defined both by $1/P_{sv}$ on the price side (or cost side) and by Q_{sv}/L_S^2 on the quantity side, and therefore Λ_{sv} is considered as a useful measure of the productivity change rate of the entire economy. The reason we use the Fisher-type index number is so that we can derive the double definitions of Λ_{sv} of (12) (*see* Yagi (1998, 2007)).

If we take Period 2 as the base year, the rate of social productivity change will be represented as

$$\rho_S^* = (\Lambda_{sv} - 1)/\Lambda_{sv} = 1 - 1/\Lambda_{sv} \tag{13}$$

If we take Period 1 as the base year, the rate of social productivity change will be represented as

$$\hat{\rho}_S^* = \Lambda_{sv} - 1 \tag{14}$$

In the following, we will use both definitions of productivity change rate, ρ_S^* and $\hat{\rho}_S^*$.

Effective labour and standard income

From (12) we can represent the standard output index as follows:

$$Q_{sv} = \Lambda_{sv} L_S^2 \tag{15}$$

The right member is the product of the Standard productivity index and the standard labour. This is the same as the definition of effective labour which is considered in the case of Harrod-neutral technical progress. It will be convenient to denote the effective labour by

$$L_E^2 = \Lambda_{sv} L_S^2 \tag{16}$$

In our model, the effective labour is determined by the Standard productivity index and the standard labour. From (15) (16), we have

$$Q_{sv} = L_E^2 \tag{17}$$

The standard output index is equal to the effective labour.

Corresponding to the effective labour L_E^2, the effective labour coefficient vector will be defined as

$$\mathbf{l}_E^2 = \Lambda_{sv} \mathbf{l}_S^2 \tag{18}$$

Then the effective labour is represented by

$$L_E^2 = \mathbf{x}^2 \mathbf{l}_E^2 = \Lambda_{sv} \mathbf{x}^2 \mathbf{l}_S^2 \tag{19}$$

From (3) (4) (19), we obtain

$$\mathbf{x}^2 \mathbf{l}_E^2 = \Lambda_{sv} L_S^2 \mathbf{x}^1 \mathbf{l}_S^1 \tag{20}$$

This means that the effective labour of Period 2 can be compared with the standard labour of Period 1. Equation (20) is an important basis for our intertemporal comparisons.

The vertically integrated labour coefficient vector given by the effective labour coefficient vector $\mathbf{l}_E^2$ can be defined as

$$\mathbf{v}_E^2 = [\mathbf{I} - \mathbf{A}^2]^{-1} \mathbf{l}_E^2 \tag{21}$$

The relation between $\mathbf{v}_E^2$ and $\mathbf{v}_S^2$ is represented by

$$\mathbf{v}_E^2 = \Lambda_{sv} \mathbf{v}_S^2 \tag{22}$$

From this we have

$$\mathbf{s}^2 \mathbf{v}_E^2 = Q_{sv} = L_E^2 \tag{23}$$

From (3) (20) (23), we have

$$\mathbf{s}^2 \mathbf{v}_E^2 = \Lambda_{sv} L_S^2 \mathbf{s}^1 \mathbf{v}_S^1 \tag{24}$$

This is quite an interesting result. Although the standard net products are composed of heterogeneous commodities and though the production technique changes from $[\mathbf{A}^1, \mathbf{l}_A^1]$ to $[\mathbf{A}^2, \mathbf{l}_A^2]$, the standard net products can be compared with each other because the aggregated values of the standard net products are measured in terms of labour. The difference in the aggregated values of the standard net product comes from two factors: Λ_{sv} and L_S^2.

3 Prices and wages in the system with no surplus

A simple price system

Let us consider the intertemporal comparisons of prices when the rate of profit is equal to zero. A set of given data is $[\mathbf{A}^1, \mathbf{l}_A^1, L_A^1; \mathbf{A}^2, \mathbf{l}_A^2, L_A^2]$. Let us denote the price vector of Period 1 by $\mathbf{p}_S^1$, that of Period 2 by $\mathbf{p}_S^2$, the wage rate of Period 1 by w_S^1, that of Period 2 by w_S^2. Then we have the price systems of each period respectively as

$$\mathbf{p}_S^1 = \mathbf{A}\mathbf{p}_S^1 + w_S^1\mathbf{l}_S^1 \tag{25}$$

$$\mathbf{p}_S^2 = \mathbf{A}\mathbf{p}_S^2 + w_S^2\mathbf{l}_S^2 \tag{26}$$

These price vectors will be rewritten as

$$\mathbf{p}_S^1 = w_S^1\mathbf{v}_S^1 \tag{27}$$

$$\mathbf{p}_S^2 = w_S^2\mathbf{v}_S^2 \tag{28}$$

Each price system has n independent equations and $(n+1)$ variables.

Case 1: commodity h *as numéraire*

If we take commodity h as numéraire, the price of h will be set equal to unity as

$$p_S^{1(h)} = p_S^{2(h)} = 1 \tag{29}$$

Let us denote the price vectors and the wage rates expressed in terms of commodity h respectively by $\mathbf{p}_h^1, \mathbf{p}_h^2, w_h^1, w_h^2$. Then they will be defined as

$$\mathbf{p}_h^1 = \mathbf{p}_S^1/p_S^{1(h)}, \quad \mathbf{p}_h^2 = \mathbf{p}_S^2/p_S^{2(h)}, \ w_h^1 = w_S^1/p_S^{1(h)}, w_h^2 = w_S^2/p_S^{2(h)} \tag{30}$$

Then from (27) (28) (30) we have

$$\mathbf{p}_h^1 = w_h^1\mathbf{v}_S^1 \tag{31}$$

$$\mathbf{p}_h^2 = w_h^2\mathbf{v}_S^2 \tag{32}$$

Let us denote the rate of change of the price of commodity h by $\sigma^{(h)}$, the rate of change of the price of commodity i by $\sigma^{(i)}$, the rate of change of the wage by σ_w, the rate of change of productivity of commodity h by $\rho^{(h)}$

and the rate of change of productivity of commodity i by $\rho^{(i)}$. Under the condition of $p_S^{1(h)} = p_S^{2(h)} = 1$ of (29), we have

$$\sigma^{(h)} = p_h^{2(h)}/p_h^{1(h)} - 1 = 0 \tag{33}$$

$$\sigma^{(i)} = \rho^{(h)} - \rho^{(i)} \tag{34}$$

$$\sigma_w = (w_h^2 - w_h^1)/w_h^1 = \rho^{(h)} \tag{35}$$

In this case, the general price level does not necessarily become constant.

Case 2: labour commanded

If the wage rates of both periods are equal to unity, then the rate of change of the wage will become equal to zero, i.e.

$$w_S^1 = w_S^2 = 1 \tag{36}$$

$$\sigma_w = 0 \tag{37}$$

And if we denote the price vectors under the condition (36) by

$$\mathbf{p}_w^1 = \mathbf{p}_S^1/w_S^1 \tag{38}$$

$$\mathbf{p}_w^2 = \mathbf{p}_S^2/w_S^2 \tag{39}$$

These vectors are measured in terms of physical unit of labour. When the rate of profit is equal to zero, the price systems (27) (28) become

$$\mathbf{p}_w^1 = \mathbf{v}_S^1 \tag{40}$$

$$\mathbf{p}_w^2 = \mathbf{v}_S^2 \tag{41}$$

Since the vertically integrated labour coefficient vectors can be compared with each other, the price vector of Period 2 can be compared with that of Period 1. From (7), the rate of change of the price of commodity i will be represented by

$$\sigma^{(i)} = p_w^{2(i)}/p_w^{1(i)} - 1 = v_S^{2(i)}/v_S^{1(i)} - 1 = -\rho^{(i)} \tag{42}$$

The general price level becomes

$$P_{sv} = 1/\Lambda_{sv} \tag{43}$$

If we denote the rate of change in the general price level by σ_S, then we have

$$\sigma_S = P_{sv} - 1 = 1/\Lambda_{sv} - 1 \tag{44}$$

Therefore, from (13) (44), we have

$$\sigma_S = -\rho_S^* \tag{45}$$

In the present case, the general price level will decrease at the rate of social productivity change.

Finally, the value of the standard net product of Period 2 becomes

$$\mathbf{s}^2\mathbf{p}_w^2 = L_S^2 \tag{46}$$

Case 3: the effective wage

Let us define the effective wage by the product of the standard productivity index and the standard wage, i.e.

$$w_E^2 = w_S^2 \Lambda_{sv} \tag{47}$$

Let us denote the price vector of Period 2 by $\mathbf{p}_E^2$ and define it by

$$\mathbf{p}_E^2 = \mathbf{p}_S^2 \Lambda_{sv} = w_S^2 \Lambda_{sv} \mathbf{v}_S^2 \tag{48}$$

The general price level P_E^2 corresponding to the price vector $\mathbf{p}_E^2$ will become

$$P_E^2 = (1/\Lambda_{sv})\Lambda_{sv} = 1 \tag{49}$$

In this case, the general price level is constant from Period 1 to Period 2.

This is the case where the wage grows at the standard rate of productivity change of the economy. Let us denote by w_E^2 the effective wage of Period 2 which grows at the rate of $\hat{\rho}_S^*$ of (14). The condition will be given by

$$\sigma_w = \hat{\rho}_S^* \tag{50}$$

Under the condition of $w_S^1 = w_S^2 = 1$, the rate of change of the wage σ_w will be represented by

$$\sigma_w = (w_E^2 - w_S^1)/w_S^1 = \Lambda_{sv} - 1 \tag{51}$$

The rate of change of the price of commodity i will be represented by

$$\sigma^{(i)} = \hat{\rho}_S^* - \sigma^{(i)} \tag{52}$$

Finally, the value of standard net product will become

$$\mathbf{s}^2\mathbf{p}_E^2 = \Lambda_{sv} L_S^2 \tag{53}$$

Case 4: effective labour

If we use the effective labour coefficient vector, by multiplying (28) by Λ_{sv}, we have

$$\mathbf{p}_E^2 = w_S^2 \mathbf{v}_E^2 \tag{54}$$

In this equation, the wage rate w_S^2 means the wage which will be paid for one unit of effective labour (L_E^2). If we want to obtain the wage rate which will be paid for one unit of standard labour (L_S^2), we should rewrite the price system (54) as

$$\mathbf{p}_E^2 = \frac{w_E^2}{\Lambda_{sv}}\mathbf{v}_E^2 \tag{55}$$

The wage rate w_E^2 means the wage which will be paid for one unit of standard labour (L_S^2). In this case, the general price level P_E^2 will be represented by

$$P_E^2 = (1/\Lambda_{sv})\Lambda_{sv} = 1 \tag{56}$$

The general price level is constant from Period 1 to Period 2. The value of standard net product will become

$$\mathbf{s}^2\mathbf{p}_E^2 = \Lambda_{sv}L_S^2 \tag{57}$$

Sraffa's standard commodity and Pasinetti's dynamic standard commodity

From the above analysis, we can conclude that if the value of the standard net product is set equal to unity, then the general price level will decrease at the rate of the social productivity change given by the Standard productivity index. Also, if the value of the standard net product is set equal to the effective labour, then the general price level will become constant. These results bring us to the proposition that, in the system with no surplus, in order to keep the general price level constant, the value of the standard net product should be kept equal to the effective labour. From (53) or (57), we have

$$\mathbf{s}^2\mathbf{p}_E^2/L_S^2 = \Lambda_{sv} \tag{58}$$

The left member of (58) is the value of standard labour embodied in the standard net product. It means the value of the standard net product produced by means of one unit of standard labour. It can be called the value productivity of the standard net product. In the system with no surplus, the condition to keep the general price level constant can be considered as the condition that the rate of change of the value productivity of the standard net product is set equal to the social productivity change rate $\hat{\rho}_S^*$.

Pasinetti (1993) admits the difficulty of computing the dynamic standard commodity and states: 'It is not easy to visualize such a composite commodity' (p. 71). This difficulty may lie in a mixture between the difficulty in solving the index number problem and the difficulty in finding an invariable standard commodity. First, it may be difficult to calculate the social productivity change rate (the weighted average of the rates of productivity change of the entire economy), in order to keep the general price level constant. Second, it may be difficult to find the composition of the dynamic standard commodity at different times for the purpose of comparison. However, from the above discussions, to visualize the dynamic standard commodity in our model, we can define the dynamic standard commodity as follows:

$$\hat{\mathbf{s}}^2 = \mathbf{s}^2 / \Lambda_{sv} L_S^2 \tag{59}$$

In our present model, the dynamic standard commodity of Period 2 is defined as the standard net product of Sraffa (1960) divided by the standard labour L_S^2 and by the Standard productivity index Λ_{sv}. In Period 1, since both the standard labour L_S^2 and the Standard productivity index Λ_{sv} are set equal to unity, the standard net product is considered as the dynamic standard commodity of Period 1. In Period 2, the standard condition to keep the general price level constant can be represented as

$$\hat{\mathbf{s}}^2 \mathbf{p}_E^2 = 1 \tag{60}$$

The value of the dynamic standard commodity $\hat{\mathbf{s}}^2$ is constant from Period 1 to Period 2 even if the composition of the dynamic standard commodity varies from $\mathbf{s}^1$ to $\hat{\mathbf{s}}^2$ and the price vector varies from $\mathbf{p}_S^1$ to $\mathbf{p}_E^2$. Under the condition (60), the price vector $\mathbf{p}_E^2$ becomes the vector of the real prices because the general price level is kept constant.

4 Invariable standard for distribution

The Sraffa system

Now we proceed to consider the system with a surplus. Let us denote the rate of profits by r, which is assumed to be uniform all over the economic system. Moreover, let us denote the maximum rate of profit by R. Then the rate of profit will take real numbers ranging from 0 to R ($0 \leq r \leq R$). Similarly, a uniform rate of wage (post factum) is assumed to be prevailing in the economy. It is indicated by w_S. The Sraffian price system given by the standard labour coefficient vector $\mathbf{l}_S$ can be represented as

$$\mathbf{p}_S = (1 + r)\mathbf{A}\mathbf{p}_S + w_S \mathbf{l}_S \tag{61}$$

From the equation system (61), we can derive the linear wage curve

$$r = R(1 - w_S) \tag{62}$$

This is the equation of the famous linear wage curve. Let us make clear the following two important properties. First, it is important that under condition (62), the difference between the actual income $\mathbf{y}\mathbf{p}_S$ and the standard income $\mathbf{s}\mathbf{p}_S$ corresponds to the profit which comes from the difference between the actual capital and the capital of the standard system (standard capital). From this the standard income $\mathbf{s}\mathbf{p}_S$ can be considered as a useful proxy for the actual income $\mathbf{y}\mathbf{p}_S$ and works as a helpful reference.

Let us explain this point. We can define the actual capital as $\mathbf{m}_y = \mathbf{xA}$ and the standard capital as $\mathbf{m}_S = \mathbf{qA}$. Then, if we use the notations of the price vector measured in terms of the standard net product as $\mathbf{p}_{sp} = \mathbf{p}_S/\mathbf{s}\mathbf{p}_S$, and the notation of the wage measured in terms of the standard net product as $w_{sp} = w_S/\mathbf{s}\mathbf{p}_S$, from (61) and $\mathbf{q}\mathbf{l}_S = \mathbf{x}\mathbf{l}_S$ (see Notations), we can derive the following equation[4]

$$\mathbf{y}\mathbf{p}_{sp} - \mathbf{s}\mathbf{p}_{sp} = r(\mathbf{m}_y\mathbf{p}_{sp} - \mathbf{m}_S\mathbf{p}_{sp}) \tag{63}$$

This equation means that the difference between the actual income $\mathbf{y}\mathbf{p}_{sp}$ and the standard income $\mathbf{s}\mathbf{p}_{sp}$ is equal to the profit obtained by the capitalist from the difference of $(\mathbf{m}_y\mathbf{p}_{sp} - \mathbf{m}_S\mathbf{p}_{sp})$. From this result, the linear wage curve (62) can be applied to the analysis of the actual economy if we neglect the profit which comes from the difference of $(\mathbf{m}_y\mathbf{p}_{sp} - \mathbf{m}_S\mathbf{p}_{sp})$.

Second, we have an interest in the value of standard labour embodied in the standard net product (the value productivity of the standard net product) under the condition (62). From (61) we can derive the following equivalence[5]

$$\mathbf{s}\mathbf{p}_S/\mathbf{x}\mathbf{l}_S = 1 \Leftrightarrow r = R(1 - w_S) \qquad \textit{for all } r : 0 \leq r < R \tag{64}$$

[4] From (61), we can derive the following equation:

$$\mathbf{y}\mathbf{p}_{sp} = r\mathbf{m}_y\mathbf{p}_{sp} + w_{sp}\,\mathbf{x}\mathbf{l}_S$$

Also for the standard system, we have

$$\mathbf{s}\mathbf{p}_{sp} = r\mathbf{m}_s\mathbf{p}_{sp} + w_{sp}\mathbf{q}\mathbf{l}_S$$

Since $\mathbf{q}\mathbf{l}_S = \mathbf{x}\mathbf{l}_S$ by definition (see Notations), by subtracting the latter equation from the former equation, we can obtain Equation (63).

[5] From (61), we have

$$\mathbf{q}(\mathbf{I} - \mathbf{A})\mathbf{p}_S = (r/R)R\mathbf{q}\mathbf{A}\mathbf{p}_S + w_S\mathbf{q}\mathbf{l}_S$$

From this we have

$$(1 - r/R)\mathbf{s}\mathbf{p}_S = w_S\mathbf{x}\mathbf{l}_S$$

From this we can derive Equation (64).

In this case, the value of standard labour embodied in the standard net product becomes equal to unity. But now let us put it as

$$\mathbf{sp}_S/\mathbf{xl}_S = v_L \tag{65}$$

where v_L is the value of labour. Then we consider the enlarged price system (61) with (65). There are $(n+1)$ equations and $(n+3)$ unknowns (r, w_S, $\mathbf{p}_S$, v_L). And under the condition (62), from (64) (65), we can derive the following:

$$v_L = 1 \Leftrightarrow r = R(1 - w_S) \qquad \textit{for all } r : 0 \leq r < R \tag{66}$$

Therefore we can consider that, under the condition (62), the price vector is normalized by the condition v_L=1. The price vector will become

$$\mathbf{p}_v = \mathbf{p}_S/v_L = (1 - r/R)[\mathbf{I} - (1 + r^1)\mathbf{A}]^{-1}\mathbf{l}_S \tag{67}$$

This price vector is measured in terms of unit of standard labour.

Evaluation system for two periods comparison

Let us proceed to consider the two periods case, and denote the rates of profit by r^1, r^2, the wage rates by w_S^1 and w_S^2 and the value of labour by v_L^1 and v_L^2. When a set of data $[\mathbf{x}^1, \mathbf{A}^1, \mathbf{l}_A^1; \mathbf{x}^2, \mathbf{A}^2, \mathbf{l}_A^2]$ or $[\mathbf{A}^1, \mathbf{l}_A^1, L_A^1; \mathbf{A}^2, \mathbf{l}_A^2, L_A^2]$ is given, the model can be shown as follows:

$$[\textbf{Evaluation System}] \qquad \begin{aligned} \mathbf{s}^1\mathbf{p}_S^1 &= v_L^1\mathbf{x}^1\mathbf{l}_S^1 \\ \mathbf{s}^2\mathbf{p}_S^2 &= v_L^2\mathbf{x}^2\mathbf{l}_S^2 \\ \mathbf{p}_S^1 &= (1 + r^1)\mathbf{A}^1\mathbf{p}_S^1 + w_S^1\mathbf{l}_S^1 \\ \mathbf{p}_S^2 &= (1 + r^2)\mathbf{A}^2\mathbf{p}_S^2 + w_S^2\mathbf{l}_S^2 \end{aligned}$$

In this system, if the rates of profit (r^1, r^2) are given exogenously, there will be $(2n+2)$ independent equations and $(2n+4)$ unknowns $(w_S^1, \mathbf{p}_S^1, v_L^1, w_S^2, \mathbf{p}_S^2, v_L^2)$. If the condition of standard for each period is given, the above system will become determinate. Let us consider the case of $R^2 \leq R^1$. In this system, the following proposition will hold.

Theorem In the above Evaluation System, the value of labour of Period 1 is equal to the value of labour of Period 2 if and only if

$$r^1 = R^1(1 - w_S^1) \textit{ and } r^2 = R^2(1 - w_S^2) \tag{68}$$

where $0 \leq r^1 < R^2$ and $0 \leq r^2 < R^2 \leq R^1$.

Proof From price equations of the above Evaluation System, we have

$$(1 - r^1/R^1)\mathbf{s}^1\mathbf{p}_S^1 = w_S^1\mathbf{x}^1\mathbf{l}_S^1 \tag{69}$$

$$(1 - r^2/R^2)\ \mathbf{s}^2\mathbf{p}_S^2 = w_S^2\mathbf{x}^2\mathbf{l}_S^2 \tag{70}$$

Therefore, for all r^1 of $0 \le r^1 < R^2$ and for all r^2 of $0 \le r^2 < R^2 \le R^1$, we have

$$v_L^1 = 1 \Leftrightarrow \mathbf{s}^1\mathbf{p}_S^1 = \mathbf{x}^1\mathbf{l}_S^1 \Leftrightarrow r^1 = R^1(1 - w_S^1) \tag{71}$$

$$v_L^2 = 1 \Leftrightarrow \mathbf{s}^2\mathbf{p}_S^2 = \mathbf{x}^2\mathbf{l}_S^2 \Leftrightarrow r^2 = R^2(1 - w_S^2) \tag{72}$$

Then, for all r^1 of $0 \le r^1 < R^2$ and for all r^2 of $0 \le r^2 < R^2 \le R^1$, we have

$$v_L^1 = v_L^2 = 1 \Leftrightarrow r^1 = R^1(1 - w_S^1)\ \textit{and}\ r^2 = R^2(1 - w_S^2) \tag{73}$$

From this, Theorem is verified.

Q.E.D.

Let us consider that the price system of Period 2 is given by the effective labour coefficient vector $\mathbf{l}_E^2$. By multiplying both members of the price system of Period 2 of the above Evaluation System by Λ_{sv}, we have

$$\mathbf{p}_E^2 = (1 + r^2)\mathbf{A}^2\mathbf{p}_E^2 + w_S^2\mathbf{l}_E^2 \tag{74}$$

Under the condition (68), the prices and wages of both periods are measured in terms of unit of effective labour. The reduced forms of $\mathbf{p}_v^1, \mathbf{p}_{Ev}^2$ are represented as

$$\mathbf{p}_v^1 = \mathbf{p}_S^1/v_L^1 = (1 - r^1/R^1)[\mathbf{I} - (1 + r^1)\mathbf{A}^1]^{-1}\mathbf{l}_S^1 \tag{75}$$

$$\mathbf{p}_{Ev}^2 = \mathbf{p}_E^2/v_L^2 = (1 - r^2/R^2)[\mathbf{I} - (1 + r^2)\mathbf{A}^2]^{-1}\mathbf{l}_E^2 \tag{76}$$

The price vector of (76) is measured in terms of unit of effective labour and therefore can be compared with the price vector of (75).

Under the condition (68), for all r^1 of $0 \le r^1 < R^2$ and for all r^2 of $0 \le r^2 < R^2 \le R^1$, we have

$$\mathbf{s}^1\mathbf{p}_v^1 = \mathbf{x}^1\mathbf{l}_S^1 \tag{77}$$

$$\mathbf{s}^2\mathbf{p}_{Ev}^2 = \mathbf{x}^2\mathbf{l}_E^2 \tag{78}$$

Then, from (20) (77) (78), we have

$$\mathbf{s}^2\mathbf{p}_{Ev}^2 = \Lambda_{sv}L_S^2\mathbf{s}^1\mathbf{p}_v^1 \tag{79}$$

This equation represents the physical output comparison when the rate of profit is positive. It should be noted that the value of $\mathbf{s}^2\mathbf{p}_{Ev}^2$ is constant even if the rate of profit varies. It is given by the effective labour L_E^2.

The effective wage curve

By multiplying both members of $\mathbf{s}^2\mathbf{p}_S^2 = \mathbf{x}^2\mathbf{l}_S^2$ of (72) by Λ_{sv}, we have

$$\mathbf{s}^2\mathbf{p}_E^2/L_S^2 = \Lambda_{sv} \tag{80}$$

By this condition, the value of standard income per standard labour is constant even if the rate of profit varies. This is the same condition as (58). Contrary to (58), in this case, the general price level will not be constant when the rate of profit varies (*see* p. 261). The condition (80) is the invariable standard condition for distribution. And therefore, this is the condition for the linear wage curve.[6]

In (74), the wage rate is represented by w_S^2, which is the wage payable for one unit of effective labour. Let us change the wage variable from w_S^2 to w_E^2. The effective wage rate w_E^2 is the wage which can be paid for one unit of the standard labour of Period 2. Because of $w_E^2 = w_S^2\Lambda_{sv}$, the price system (74) will be rewritten as

$$\mathbf{p}_E^2 = (1 + r^2)\mathbf{A}^2\mathbf{p}_E^2 + \frac{w_E^2}{\Lambda_{sv}}\mathbf{l}_E^2 \tag{81}$$

Corresponding to this price system, we can derive the following linear wage curve:

$$r^2 = R^2(1 - w_E^2/\Lambda_{sv}) \tag{82}$$

The condition of the effective wage curve of (82) will be given by (80). As for the effective total wage ($W_E^2 = w_E^2 L_S^2$), we have

$$r^2 = R^2(1 - W_E^2/\Lambda_{sv}L_S^2) \tag{83}$$

Moreover, since the wage share is given by $\omega^2 = W_E^2/\mathbf{s}^2\mathbf{p}_E^2 = w_S^2\Lambda_{sv} L_S^2/\Lambda_{sv}\mathbf{s}^2\mathbf{p}_S^2 = w_S^2$, we have

$$r^2 = R^2(1 - \omega^2) \tag{84}$$

When we consider the effective wage curve of (83), the value of the standard net product (the standard income) is given by (78). These effective wage curves are shown in Figure 11.1.

Ricardo gave up measuring the absolute values; he was concerned only with the problem of the comparison of relative share of distribution.

[6] Harcourt (1972, p. 40) put forward an interesting assumption: 'For all rates of profit from zero to its maximum, the value of total net product is equal to the maximum total wage obtained when the rate of profit is zero.' As seen in (78), for our effective wage curve, we are considering the same as Harcourt's assumption by setting the standard income equal to the effective labour.

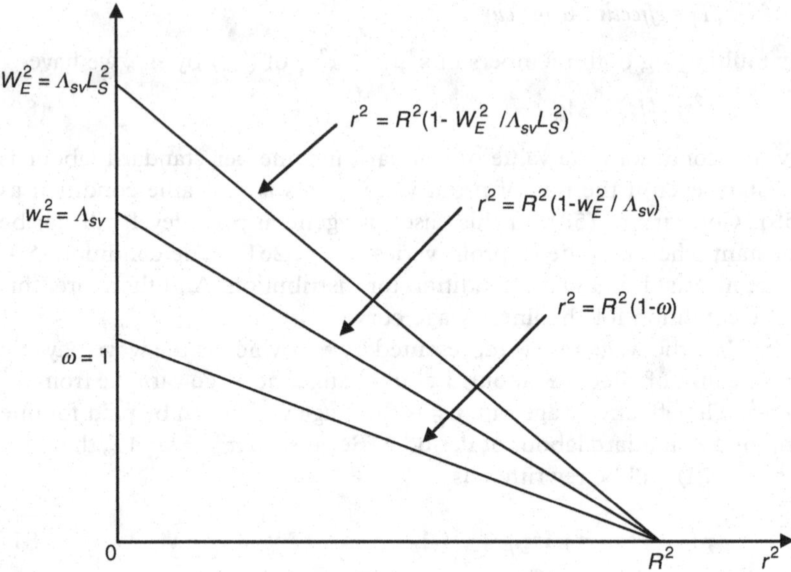

Figure 11.1 Effective wage curve

With our effective wage curves, we can do absolute comparisons of wages. The relationships between w_E^2 and w_S^1 can be represented as

$$w_E^2 = ((R^2 - r^2)/R^2)/((R^1 - r^1)/R^1)\Lambda_{sv} w_S^1 \tag{85}$$

Finally, corresponding to the effective wage curve, we can obtain the value of capital of the standard system. Since this becomes equal to $1/R$, the value of capital of Period 2 will be represented as

$$\mathbf{m}_S^2 \mathbf{p}_E^2 = \frac{\Lambda_{sv}}{R^2} \tag{86}$$

It should be noted that, if we consider the effective wage curve, the value of capital is kept constant as the rate of profit varies.

5 Invariable standard for the general price level

Distribution effect to the general price level

Let us consider the case that the prices and wages of both periods are measured in terms of the unit of standard labour. Under the condition of (68), the reduction equations, or the reduced forms of $\mathbf{p}_v^1, \mathbf{p}_v^2$, are represented as

$$\mathbf{p}_v^1 = \mathbf{p}_S^1/v_L^1 = (1 - r^1/R^1)[\mathbf{I} - (1 + r^1)\mathbf{A}^1]^{-1}\mathbf{l}_S^1 \tag{87}$$

$$\mathbf{p}_v^2 = \mathbf{p}_S^2/v_L^2 = (1 - r^2/R^2)[\mathbf{I} - (1 + r^2)\mathbf{A}^2]^{-1}\mathbf{l}_S^2 \tag{88}$$

These price vectors are measured in terms of the same unit of labour. The total labour of the economy can be represented by

$$\mathbf{s}^1\mathbf{p}_v^1 = L_S^1 = 1 \tag{89}$$

$$\mathbf{s}^2\mathbf{p}_v^2 = L_S^2 \tag{90}$$

By using the price vectors of (87) (88), let us consider the index numbers. The weight vectors for index numbers are given by [$\mathbf{s}^1$, $\mathbf{s}^2$, $\mathbf{p}_v^1$, $\mathbf{p}_v^2$] and a set of the given data is $[\mathbf{A}^1, \mathbf{l}_A^1, L_A^1; \mathbf{A}^2, \mathbf{l}_A^2, L_A^2]$. For the index numbers of this case, let us denote the price index of Fisher type by $P_{sp(r^1,r^2)}$, the income index of Fisher type by $\Omega_{sp(r^1,r^2)}$ and the input cost index by $C_{sp(r^1,r^2)}$. Then they will be represented as

$$P_{sp(r^1,r^2)} = \sqrt{\frac{\mathbf{s}^1\mathbf{p}_v^2}{\mathbf{s}^1\mathbf{p}_v^1} \cdot \frac{\mathbf{s}^2\mathbf{p}_v^2}{\mathbf{s}^2\mathbf{p}_v^1}} \quad \Omega_{sp(r^1,r^2)} = \sqrt{\frac{\mathbf{s}^2\mathbf{p}_v^2}{\mathbf{s}^1\mathbf{p}_v^2} \cdot \frac{\mathbf{s}^2\mathbf{p}_v^1}{\mathbf{s}^1\mathbf{p}_v^1}} \quad C_{sp(r^1,r^2)} = \frac{\mathbf{s}^2\mathbf{p}_v^2}{\mathbf{s}^1\mathbf{p}_v^1} \tag{91}$$

From (89)–(91), these indexes can be reduced to a simpler form as follows:

$$P_{sp(r^1,r^2)} = \sqrt{\frac{\mathbf{s}^1\mathbf{p}_v^2}{\mathbf{s}^2\mathbf{p}_v^1} \cdot L_S^2} \quad \Omega_{sp(r^1,r^2)} = \sqrt{\frac{\mathbf{s}^2\mathbf{p}_v^1}{\mathbf{s}^1\mathbf{p}_v^2} \cdot L_S^2} \tag{92}$$

From the theory of index numbers, the relationship between $C_{sp(r^1,r^2)}$, $P_{sp(r^1,r^2)}$, $\Omega_{sp(r^1,r^2)}$ becomes

$$C_{sp(r^1,r^2)} = P_{sp(r^1,r^2)} \cdot \Omega_{sp(r^1,r^2)} \tag{93}$$

In our model, however, from the above, we can obtain the following relationship:

$$\Lambda_{sp(r^1,r^2)} = 1/P_{sp(r^1,r^2)} = \Omega_{sp(r^1,r^2)}/L_S^2 = \sqrt{\frac{\mathbf{s}^2\mathbf{p}_v^1}{\mathbf{s}^1\mathbf{p}_v^2} \cdot \frac{1}{L_S^2}} \tag{94}$$

In (94), the productivity change is calculated both from the cost side by $1/P_{sp(r^1,r^2)}$ and from the quantity side by $\Omega_{sp(r^1,r^2)}/L_S^2$. It should be stressed that $\Lambda_{sp(r^1,r^2)}$ is obtained by the given production techniques $[\mathbf{A}^1, \mathbf{l}_A^1, r^1, L_A^1; \mathbf{A}^2, \mathbf{l}_A^2, r^2, L_A^2]$. In order to make a distinction between $\Lambda_{sp(r^1,r^2)}$ and Λ_{sv}, we will call this index $\Lambda_{sp(r^1,r^2)}$ the Standard value productivity index μ.[7] It measures the social productivity changes in value terms. $\Lambda_{sp(r^1,r^2)}$ is independent of the composition of demand. From (12) (94), we have the price index

$$P_{sp(r^1,r^2)} = \frac{1}{\Lambda_{sp(r^1,r^2)}} = \frac{1}{\Lambda_{sv}} \frac{\Lambda_{sv}}{\Lambda_{sp(r^1,r^2)}} \tag{95}$$

The term $\Lambda_{sv}/\Lambda_{sp(r^1,r^2)}$ represents the effect of distribution to the general price level. Thus we denote the term $\Lambda_{sv}/\Lambda_{sp(r^1,r^2)}$ by

$$\xi(r^1, r^2) = \Lambda_{sv}/\Lambda_{sp(r^1,r^2)} = P_{sp(r^1,r^2)}/P_{sv} \tag{96}$$

In the case of $\Lambda_{sp(r^1,r^2)} \neq \Lambda_{sv}$, there is some effect of distribution to the general price level. It is quite interesting that the changes in the general price level between $\mathbf{p}_v^1$ and $\mathbf{p}_v^2$ are determined by the social productivity change measured by the standard productivity index Λ_{sv} and the distribution effect to the general price level defined by $\xi(r^1, r^2)$.

Real wage and real prices

Now let us consider the real values obtained by dividing $w_S{}^2, \mathbf{p}_S{}^2$ by the Standard price index $P_{sp(r^1,r^2)}$. If we denote the real wage by $w_R{}^2$ and the real price vector by $\mathbf{p}_R^2$, we can define them as follows:

$$w_R^2 = w_S^2/P_{sp(r^1,r^2)} \tag{97}$$

$$\mathbf{p}_R^2 = \mathbf{p}_S^2/P_{sp(r^1,r^2)} \tag{98}$$

These values mean the real values because they are denominated by the price index. From (47) (74) and (97)–(98), we have

$$w_R^2 = w_E^2/\xi(r^1, r^2) \tag{99}$$

$$\mathbf{p}_R^2 = \mathbf{p}_E^2 \,/\, \xi(r^1, r^2) \tag{100}$$

Also we have

$$\mathbf{s}^2\mathbf{p}_R^2 = \Lambda_{sp(r^1,r^2)} L_S^2 \tag{101}$$

[7] In the case of $\mathbf{s}^1 = t\,\mathbf{s}^2$, we have $\xi(r^1, r^2) = 1$ and $\Lambda_{sp(r^1,r^2)} = \Lambda_{sv}$.

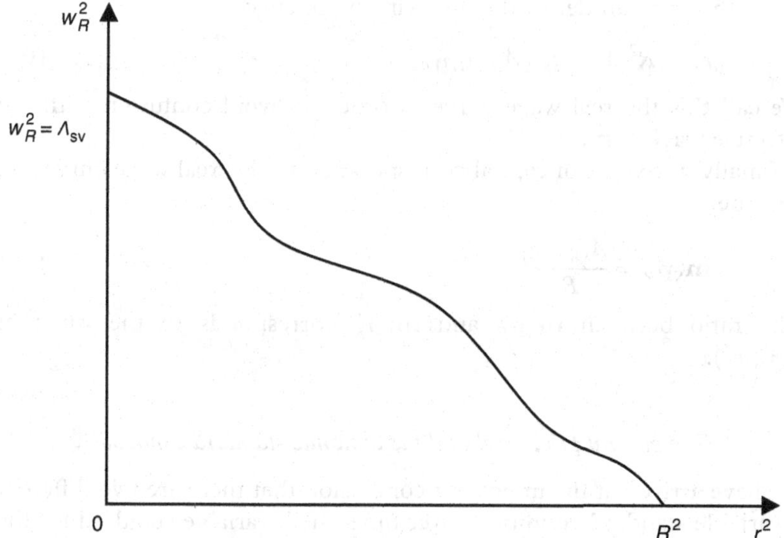

Figure 11.2 Real wage curve

Corresponding to $\Lambda_{sp(r^1,r^2)}L_S^2$, let us define

$$\mathbf{l}_R^2 = \Lambda_{sp(r^1,r^2)}\mathbf{l}_S^2 \tag{102}$$

From this, we have

$$\mathbf{x}^2\mathbf{l}_R^2 = \Lambda_{sp(r^1,r^2)}L_S^2 \tag{103}$$

In (101), the labour which is equal to the value of the standard net product varies as the rate of profit changes. Dividing the price system of Period 2 by $\Lambda_{sp(r^1,r^2)}$, we have

$$\mathbf{p}_R^2 = (1+r^2)\mathbf{A}^2\mathbf{p}_R^2 + w_S^2\mathbf{l}_R^2 \tag{104}$$

In this case, the general price level will be kept constant because the general price level corresponding to $\mathbf{p}_R^2$ will become

$$P_R^2 = P_{sp(r^1,r^2)}/P_{sp(r^1,r^2)} = 1 \tag{105}$$

Then let us consider the wage curve. If we rewrite the price vector (104) as

$$\mathbf{p}_R^2 = (1+r^2)\mathbf{A}^2\mathbf{p}_R^2 + \frac{w_R^2}{\Lambda_{sp(r^1,r^2)}}\mathbf{l}_R^2 \tag{106}$$

From this, we can derive the following wage curve:

$$r^2 = R^2(1 - w_R^2/\Lambda_{sp(r^1,r^2)}) \tag{107}$$

We call this the real wage curve in order to avoid confusion with the effective wage curve.

Finally, the value of capital corresponding to this real wage curve will become

$$\mathbf{m}_S^2\mathbf{p}_R^2 = \frac{\Lambda_{sp(r^1,r^2)}}{R^2} \tag{108}$$

The ratio between $\mathbf{m}_S^2\mathbf{p}_E^2$ and $\mathbf{m}_S^2\mathbf{p}_R^2$ corresponds to the value of $\xi(r^1, r^2)$.

The general price level and the dynamic standard commodity

We have arrived at the important conclusion that there are two different invariable standard conditions over time: the invariable standard for the general price level and the invariable standard for distribution through time. As seen in (80), the condition $\mathbf{s}^2\mathbf{p}_E^2/L_S^2 = \Lambda_{sv}$ can be considered as the invariable standard condition for distribution. In order to keep the general price constant, the condition of standard will become

$$\mathbf{s}^2\mathbf{p}_R^2/\mathbf{x}^2\mathbf{l}_S^2 = \Lambda_{sp(r^1,r^2)} \tag{109}$$

The ratio between (80) and (109) will also correspond to $\xi(r^1, r^2)$.

From (109), we can define the dynamic standard commodity to keep the general price level constant as follows:

$$\tilde{\mathbf{s}}^2 = \mathbf{s}^2/\Lambda_{sp(r^1,r^2)}L_S^2 \tag{110}$$

The condition $\mathbf{s}^2\mathbf{p}_R^2 = \Lambda_{sp(r^1,r^2)}L_S^2$ can be rewritten as

$$\tilde{\mathbf{s}}^2\mathbf{p}_R^2 = 1 \tag{111}$$

Under the condition (111), the general price level becomes constant and the rate of inflation becomes equal to zero. But in this case, the wage curve does not become linear. Therefore the condition $\tilde{\mathbf{s}}^2\mathbf{p}_R^2 = 1$ is not the invariable standard for distribution.

6 Concluding remarks

We have examined the complex features of the relationships among the various changes in the production structures from $[\mathbf{A}^1, \mathbf{l}_S^1]$ to $[\mathbf{A}^2, \mathbf{l}_S^2]$, in commodity prices, in distribution, in the aggregate income and in the aggregate capital. The analysis in this chapter will be close in relevance to the interests of the classical economists, especially Ricardo. We have shown a method for considering this problem by combining the ideas of Sraffa (1960), Pasinetti (1981, 1993) and Hicks (1981). The notions of the effective wage curve and the real wage curve may be crucial to the theory of capital.

REFERENCES

Harcourt, G.C. (1972), *Some Cambridge Controversies in the Theory of Capital*, Cambridge University Press.

Hicks, J.R. (1963), 'The measurement of capital in relation to the measurement of other economic aggregates,' in Lutz, F.A. and Hague, D.C. (eds.) *The Theory of Capital*, London, Macmillan.

(1981), 'Valuation of Social Income III,' in Hicks, J.R., *Wealth and Welfare*, Oxford, Basil Blackwell.

Pasinetti, L.L. (1973), 'A notion of vertical integration in economic analysis,' *Metroeconomica*, **25**, 1–29.

(1977), *Lectures on the Theory of Production*, Columbia University Press.

(1981), *Structural Change and Economic Growth*, Cambridge University Press.

(1993), *Structural Economic Dynamics*, Cambridge University Press.

Sraffa, P. (1960) *Production of Commodities by Means of Commodities*, Cambridge University Press.

Yagi, T. (1998), 'Alternative theories on the evaluation of real national income,' written in Japanese, in Egawa, M., Tomono, N., Uemura, T. and Yagi, T. (eds.) *Keizaigaku No Shosou: Essays in Honor of Professor Toshinosuke Kashiwazaki*, Gakubunsha, Tokyo.

(2000), 'The structure of *Production of Commodities by Means of Commodities*,' written in Japanese, in Kataoka, H. and Matsumoto, M. (eds.) *Gendai Keizai Ronsou: Essays in Honor of Professor Toshio Ono*, Gakubunsha, Tokyo.

(2007), '"Invariable Measure of Value" and Contemporary economics,' Nishikawa, J., Yagi, T. and Shimizu, K. (eds.) *Reconstructing Social Science*, Akashi Shoten, Tokyo.

Part III

Epilogue: structural dynamics as part of the 'unfinished revolution'

The final part of the book offers a direct exchange between two economists – Robert Solow and Luigi Pasinetti – who played a major role in the construction of post-war economic growth theory. Through their contributions, both Solow and Pasinetti expressly proposed to place their discussion on structural dynamics in the more general framework of macroeconomic theory. This is why they agreed to begin their respective contributions with their recent exchange at the Accademia dei Lincei in Rome on Pasinetti's book on *Keynes and the Cambridge Keynesians*, also published by Cambridge University Press in 2007.

During the preparation of the present volume, when asked to contribute, both Solow and Pasinetti felt that their exchange could be the best way to emphasise how different analytical foundations can generate divergent views as well as a common interest in structural dynamics. They suggested that the editors should publish these successive comments in the present volume, each comment being expanded with a special addendum specifically devoted to the issue of structural dynamics. The editors proposed to Professors Solow and Pasinetti to leave the content of all the answers they gave to the audience. To facilitate the general understanding of this final section, the context in which the exchange took place as well as the commentators' names have been deliberately omitted.

On Pasinetti and the unfinished Keynesian Revolution

Robert M. Solow

Defending the neoclassical position, whatever that is, is not really my main business here today. We are here to talk about Luigi Pasinetti's very interesting book (Pasinetti: 2007).

The *General Theory of Employment, Interest and Money*, Keynes's great work of 1936, is a difficult book because it contains several different themes. It is not always clear that the different themes are compatible with one another, so the book is very hard to summarize or to give to beginning students to read. I think Luigi Pasinetti's work shares some of that quality; there is more than one thing going on and it is not always clear – at least not always clear to me – exactly how the several themes fit together.

I am going to focus my discussion on one of those themes: 'A Revolution in Economics to be Accomplished.' Luigi Pasinetti argues that the Keynesian Revolution was left incomplete and that the Cambridge Group (and a part of the book consists of very affectionate and very nicely written portraits of members of the Cambridge Group) was trying to complete it, but did not succeed. Professor Pasinetti's own project is in fact to contribute to completing the Keynesian Revolution. I don't remember that he ever says very clearly, or even not very clearly, exactly what the Keynesian Revolution was and how it is incomplete, what the remaining gap is.

What arises from the pages of the book – and Will Baumol touched on this – is that the Keynesian Revolution was somehow opposed to more or less everything in orthodox economics, in what is today called neoclassical economics. Without further details, it is almost as if we were trying to agree to meet somewhere in Rome and I asked you where, and you said, not in the Piazza Colonna. Yes, I understand that, but it doesn't help me very much about where exactly to go.

This is the text of the revised and adapted comments read by Professor Solow at the Accademia dei Lincei (Rome, 28 November 2008), to which an 'afterword' by Solow (*see* next page) has been appended.

I am going to take a very particular view. I am going to state what I think Keynes's *General Theory* accomplished. I am going to agree that it is incomplete, but I think that it is perhaps inevitably incomplete for a reason that I will describe. Third, I am going to maintain that the Cambridge Group was not really engaged in completing it, but that others were, and not in the direction that Professor Pasinetti prefers.

You should keep in mind all the time that I am exactly what Joan Robinson called a 'bastard Keynesian.' Joan Robinson intended that label as a devastating insult, to make the bastard Keynesians ashamed of their origins and of their actions. But I rather like the label and I adopt it cheerfully. I am sure that if I were a Freudian I would be a bastard Freudian; and if I were a Marxian I would be a bastard Marxian; and so I am indeed a bastard Keynesian.

In my view, Keynes freed macroeconomics from its dependence on market clearing, especially, but not only, in labor markets. In the older view, in the view that Keynes opposed, there were indeed what Pigou called lapses from full employment. They had to be explained mainly by temporary deviations of prices and wages from their proper values. Keynes, in opposing this, argued that those lapses were persistent and normal and could not be expected to cure themselves. Of course, Keynes argued in the *General Theory* much else besides, but that, it seems to me, was the main point of the Keynesian Revolution.

Keynes, by the way, thought that he had worked out that a modern economy could be in equilibrium with unemployment, meaning that there were no internal forces at all tending to move it out of that state. Most modern economists, including bastard Keynesians like me, think that Keynes did not quite make good on that assertion. He simply lacked the analytical tools. Long after the *General Theory*, several economists showed how particular not wholly implausible assumptions – but not wholly plausible either – could indeed in principle give rise to an under-employment equilibrium. These were mostly assumptions about expectations. When you set your mind to it, it is not hard to visualize situations in which, if there are almost universally pessimistic expectations about the immediate future, actions will be taken which indeed bring about the pessimistic state and thereby confirm the pessimistic expectations. But in the same situations, if for some reason universal expectations had been optimistic, they would have given rise to actions which would have brought about a better state and thus confirmed the favorable expectations. But those are rather special assumptions and I don't want to direct attention to them now.

Most of us bastard Keynesians think that this failure to provide a tight notion of equilibrium with unemployment is unimportant. The Keynesian revolution survives quite well if the restoring forces in an under-employment disequilibrium, say, are so weak and so slow that it would take unacceptably long for a satisfactory equilibrium to be restored; and if there are fiscal and monetary policies available to the state that would shorten the period and drastically reduce the social cost. For a bastard Keynesian like myself, the Keynesian Revolution would then have won the battle, and indeed that is what I think is the case.

For long enough periods of time, disturbances occur frequently enough that aggregate output is determined by aggregate demand with persistent excess supply of output. Other possibilities exist, of course, but that is the one that one wants to focus on. That is my idea of what the Keynesian revolution was: the direction of macro-economic thought to situations in which aggregate output, not necessarily in every market, is limited on the demand side, and thus there is persistent excess supply at the aggregate level. That battle, to my mind, was won, and I never had any hesitation about that.

Like any good intellectual revolution, the Keynesian one opened up large vistas of useful research on the behavior of consumer spending, on the behavior of business investment spending, on the mechanisms by which monetary policy and fiscal policy can affect aggregate demand, and therefore output, when output is limited by effective demand. There is room for research on the behavior of labor markets, and credit markets, on portfolio choice, on the role of expectations, on wage formation and price formation.

You will see from what I have said that the Keynesian Revolution will never be complete because behavior and institutions in our societies change. They evolve. And what are the correct answers, or at least reasonable answers, to those questions now or five years ago may be inadequate answers five years from now. I hope small armies of young economists will be engaged in trying to bring the Keynesian Revolution up to date. But – and this is where I differ very strongly from Professor Pasinetti – almost all of this work of extending and completing and embedding the Keynesian Revolution has been carried out by bastard Keynesians. In fact, I do not myself see that the Cambridge Group was carrying on Keynes's work in any genuine way. Similarly, I am inclined to question whether there is much of a connection between Keynesian ideas and classical economics, if by classical economics we mean economics free of demand-side considerations.

Professor Pasinetti's interest in classical economics seems to come from a belief that demand considerations are bound up with social institutions in a way that supply-side considerations are not. So the supply-side considerations can therefore be described as 'natural.'

I am not really convinced by this distinction, neither its reality, nor its significance, because, on the production side, productive efficiency is already an institutional consideration. Robinson Crusoe's decisions are a mixture of technology and preferences. In fact, once we get away from the realistically uninteresting case of one primary factor and no technological substitutability, choice plays about as big a role on the production side as it does on the consumption side. The motives and information and rules of thumb of firms are just about as important as utility functions and other such things for consumers, so the productions side is not at all free of institutional influences. There's nothing natural about the classical model.

We take up here another question. In the latter part of the book Luigi Pasinetti seems to want to draw a related distinction along these lines: that if it is not the fundamental cause of the failure of orthodox economics, it is at least the symbol of the failure of orthodox economics that it is somehow the economics of an exchange economy with the quantities of goods produced already given. So it provides only an elaborate working out of the consequences of market exchanges, whereas the unfinished part of the Keynesian Revolution will somehow give proper primacy to the production side of the economy and be an economics of production.

I have to say that I really do not understand this distinction. I remember dimly from the 1960s that it was one of those oracular statements that Joan Robinson used to make which were intended to end discussion, not to begin it, but in fact I don't think it is accurate. When I was sitting in my office at MIT making notes for this discussion, I could not find my copy of Arrow and Hahn's book on competitive general equilibrium. (I had presumably lent it years ago to a student who is now teaching in California, or something of that sort.) But I did find my copy of Gerard Debreu's *Theory of Value*. When I opened it I discovered that in Debreu's book, the chapter on the theory of the producer comes before the chapter on the theory of the consumer. The notion of the production set is prior in his discussion to the study of markets.

Then I managed to put my finger on another old book from my younger days, Jacob Mosak's book on *General Equilibrium Theory and International Trade*, and there I found exemplified exactly what had always seemed to me to be the case: the prominence given in orthodox treatments of general equilibrium to the pure exchange case is a purely pedagogical device. The idea was that it is easier to solve, to demonstrate to the students, or to oneself for that matter, how equilibrium theory works out, if the supply of goods is already given. Then if you now add a production side to the economy, you have all that earlier work available to be used as a sort of lemma in producing a theory that involves the production side as well. When I opened Mosak's book I found that he had done exactly that and said that it was what he was doing. He treats the pure exchange case first, he says, because then it will be easier, once we have these results in our pockets, so to speak, to allow for the production side. He then goes on in the very next section of the book to elaborate his international equilibrium with production. So I really don't think that any such distinction characterizes the difference between orthodox economics, neoclassical economics and the new Keynesian economics to come.

It is interesting that, as I read Professor Pasinetti's book, I found that the most interesting and exciting pages in it are precisely the pages in which he is talking about his own work, not about the unfinished Keynesian Revolution as a drama of some kind. I think that Professor Pasinetti's own work on what he calls structural dynamics, on essentially how to extend the study of macroeconomic dynamics to incorporate the structural changes – some endogenous, perhaps most endogenous, but at least some still exogenous – in an analytical framework that is capable of looking at the evolution of capitalist economies. I am wholeheartedly in favor of that. And there Luigi Pasinetti has some important predecessors. Hollis Chenery, for instance, my old friend from graduate student days, was trying to do exactly that in his analysis of developing economies long ago, but without the elegance and without the analytical detail that Professor Pasinetti is able to bring to bear.

Another very distinguished and able economist, Leif Johansen, the Norwegian, wrote a Ph.D. thesis which was a multisectoral model of economic growth in which he too proposed to try to provide a framework in which structural changes can be embedded naturally and analytically. I am all in favor of this. I think that is exactly an open question. I think it has very little to do with the Keynesian Revolution, but has everything to do with improving our analysis of an evolving capitalist economy.

To give you a concrete example – and as a bastard Keynesian I am a great believer in concrete examples – I think that modern analyses of economic growth have paid too little attention to the distinctions between the production of goods and the production of services. It is very odd for me to be saying that, since I have spent a certain amount of time trying to explain to over-enthusiastic non-economists that goods and services are both examples of economic goods and that they obey many of the same laws, have many of the same incentives. But in fact there may very well be systematic empirical differences in the capital intensity of goods production and the capital intensity of production of services. And there may very well be differences in the pace and role of technological change in the service industries and in the goods industries. This is a case of structural dynamics and today Luigi is one of the few economists who is paying serious attention to such things. But it is not in any way related to the Keynesian Revolution.

Let me summarize the world as seen by a bastard Keynesian. There was a Keynesian Revolution. It was the Keynesian Revolution most of us know and love. It focused the attention of the profession on the macroeconomic importance of aggregate demand and argued that aggregate output often was limited by aggregate demand; that policy mechanisms in periods of excessive unemployment and idle capacity should be aimed at increasing aggregate demand. Those lessons are still with us. They are in yesterday's newspaper and I hope in tomorrow's newspaper in the European Union, in the United States, in the People's Republic of China, and everywhere. I think that was a true revolution. It was much opposed at the time. I think it remains and will always remain to be completed because we will never – I presume never – come to the end of the evolution of the forces that govern aggregate demand and the way labor markets and commodity markets and service markets translate those things into behavior that we observe from time to time.

Now I will say one word about how all this fits with neoclassical growth theory, with which I seem to be associated. I don't know how many people in this room have read that 1956 paper of mine which determined so much of my career, as I did not realize it would at the time I was writing it. If you have read it and if you have read it to the end, you will remember that after about two-thirds of the text, there is a section that begins with words something like the following. Everything so far has been the neoclassical side of the coin and now we have to talk about the Keynesian aspects of the problem, the fact that growth paths for capitalist economies are very rarely paths of continuous equilibrium at full employment. Indeed they are not. But there is a puzzle, and this is another puzzle that perhaps is an uncompleted part of the Keynesian Revolution. It relates to something else which is an emphasis that I endorse and have endorsed in the past. I think that the economics of the medium run is terribly important and not worked out for the following reason. While it is true that the growth paths of capitalist economies are never paths of continuous full employment, full utilization equilibrium, it is true as a matter of historical fact that it would be reasonable to describe those paths as fluctuations around a trend, with most of the time the fluctuations contained within fairly narrow bounds – a couple of percent, three or four percent on either side of the trend path, defining what Axel Leijonhufvud once called the corridor around that path.

Only rarely – the Great Depressions of the 1890s in the US, the 1930s in the world at large, and one doesn't want to guess about the next few years (one no longer has to guess) – are there very large divergences from that path. I always thought (and that is what I think you would read into that 1956 paper, if you read it through to the end with some sympathy) that the goal of neoclassical growth theory was simply to try to understand the forces that underlay the trend. It's not at all engaged in the problem of describing actual paths, because actual paths consist of successions of short runs. What is lacking, and where I think the medium run is of such fundamental importance, is how to knit together those two things. Keynes after all wrote in the *General Theory* as if the stock of capital were constant. He was explicit about that. Investment is taking place, but it is small relative to the existing stock of capital. So he would treat the stock of capital as exactly constant. In the long run obviously one cannot do that, since one of the obvious, undeniable, visible aspects of growth paths is that the stock of capital rises.

How does one make the analytical connection between the short run and the long run? In other words, what happens in the medium run when we can no longer treat the stock of capital as a constant, but we have somehow to carry on an analysis of aggregate demand and aggregate supply?

I have made a couple of attempts at that; other people have, too. I don't think that that problem is solved and I hope one can continue to try to solve it. I am afraid that the tendency amongst very modern macroeconomists (I cannot know what takes place in Italian universities, but I can tell you that if this discussion were taking place at the University of Minnesota in the US, the student body would be totally uncomprehending) is that they would regard every moment not only in the long run or in the medium run but in the short run as well, as an example of full macroeconomic equilibrium. This strikes me as madness. But I am just an old bastard Keynesian, after all.

First afterword: Pasinetti on structural dynamics

Robert M. Solow

The preceding remarks originated in a discussion, at the Accademia Nazionale dei Lincei, of Luigi Pasinetti's *Keynes and the Cambridge Keynesians*. Naturally, then, it consists mostly of comments on the work of the Cambridge Group and on the significance Pasinetti attaches to that work. The developments dedicated to structural dynamics are rather limited in the preceding exchange: an expression of strong support of the basic idea, a reference to earlier strands of work on multisector growth models and patterns of economic development, and the concrete suggestion that analyzing the sources and consequences of the well-documented shift from goods to services in modern economies is an excellent example of structural dynamics waiting to be undertaken. I should have seized that occasion to emphasize that the shift seems to be a response to the relatively high income elasticity of demand for services such as education, recreation, travel, food preparation and health care, and therefore a clear example of the need to think about demand side and supply side together. I would like to add a few more general remarks here.

I cannot imagine how anyone could be 'against' the goal of a structural dynamics. Multisector growth models and one-sector growth models are complements, not rivals. The main reason for pursuing one-sector and two-sector analysis is transparency. The role of certain fundamental principles, like the central importance of diminishing returns to factors of production that can be accumulated, or the role of biased technological progress, is easier to understand in a fully aggregative context. But the way these principles work themselves out in practice may need to be studied in an explicitly multisectoral model. The same is true of basic demand-side influences, like different income elasticities of demand. Long-run variations in the composition of aggregate output are visible to the naked eye. They need to be understood.

This would hardly need saying to anyone who thinks of macroeconomics as a pragmatic discipline, not an ideological opportunity. In precisely that spirit I want to suggest one more currently salient issue about which an empirically validated structural dynamics would almost surely have useful things to say.

I have in mind a rather less clear-cut example. There are hints in the past decade or so that the wage share of national income may have fallen relative to the property share. Since the measured 'wage share' includes a return to human capital, and the human-capital component itself may have been increasing, the share of 'raw' labour may have decreased more sharply. In the US at least, however, the measurement of income shares has been strongly affected, and may have been distorted, by the growth of the financial services industry, which may be transitory rather than 'structural'. Suppose, however, that there does indeed turn out to be something of a long-run character to explain.

Then once again a multisector, multi-factor growth model would be the natural vehicle. Relative shares in national income are weighted averages of sectoral shares in value added. Long ago I wrote an article that showed, using fairly primitive methods, that much of the apparent time-series stability of relative income shares could be accounted for simply by this averaging process. A full explanation would have to account both for shifts in the intra-sectoral distribution of value added and for endogenous and exogenous shifts in the sectoral weights. Something might need to be said about both factor substitution elasticities within sectors and demand-side substitution elasticities among sectoral outputs. There may be other, more purely macroeconomic, forces at work. Incorporating them in a multisector growth model would force an explicit formulation of any such forces that is in any case desirable.

I remember a joke from my childhood. Scholars of many different nationalities are shown an elephant and asked to write a brief essay about it. The German writes An Outline of an Introduction to a Treatise on the Fundamental Nature of the Elephant, the Frenchman writes on L'Elephant et l'Amour, the Pole writes on The Elephant and the Polish Question, and so on. The point I am trying to get across is that structural dynamics is a natural extension of ordinary economics and worth continued attention, not some exotic addendum to be attached to near-irrelevant special interests.

Growth and structural change: perspectives for the future

Luigi L. Pasinetti

In his contribution to the present volume, Professor Solow has chosen to reproduce his own discussion at the Lincei Academy on my book (Pasinetti, 2007) with an 'Afterword', bringing out the link between the legacy of the Cambridge Keynesians and structural dynamics. I propose to do the same here. This seems to me to be the best way to respond to the Editors' invitation to contribute, i.e. to offer my own 'Reply' to the discussion with an 'Afterword' appended to it.

To begin with, let me say how grateful I am to Professor Solow for taking the sting out of Joan Robinson's original 'devastating insult', as he has taken it, and proudly defining himself a 'bastard Keynesian'. Admirable! But not yet enough, I think, to take full advantage of his generous stand. He says: *'I don't remember that [*Pasinetti*] ever says ... exactly what the Keynesian revolution was about and how it is incomplete, what the remaining gap is'*, after stating: *'Keynes's great work of 1936, is a difficult book because it contains several different themes. It is not always clear that the different themes are compatible with one another, so the book is very hard to summarize or to give to beginning students to read. I think Luigi Pasinetti's work shares some of that quality; there is more than one thing going on and it's not always clear – at least not always clear to me – exactly how the several themes fit together'* (*see* above).

I take this as a great compliment, for which I am thankful. It may incidentally also give some substance to my repeated remarks on the 'lack of communication' in the Cambridge Group. Yet I cannot take it in the literal sense. I think it is a very nice way of saying that he does not agree with me.

This is a modified version of the final 'Reply to Criticism' read at the Round Table on Pasinetti, 2007, at the Accademia Nazionale dei Lincei, 28 November 2008, to which an 'Afterword' by Pasinetti (*see* pp. 283–7) is now appended. References to specific pages of the book (Pasinetti, 2007) are simply given by stating the page numbers in round brackets. They are preceded by llp only when some ambiguities might arise. I have used *italics* for quotations from the Comments of the Participants, but kept Roman type for quotations from my own book.

There are plenty of references to the 'Keynesian Revolution' in the book, as one may gather even simply by using the long list appearing in the Index (with all its variations, *see* Pasinetti, 2007: 375–6); or the Table of Contents, and particularly Chapter VIII, where there appears a whole specific section ('The ideal task of Keynesian economics', in ibid: 269–273) which is framed with the purpose of specifying the substance of what, in my view, the Keynesian Revolution should aim at. And all this, even without mentioning other relevant references, such as the three recent conferences[1], which both Professor Solow and I attended, where I presented papers precisely on this issue. So much have I been concerned, as to begin my *Preface* by immediately stating: 'The "Keynesian revolution" only succeeded half-way . . . In terms of economic policy its successes were immediate [and these are indeed the aspects to which Professor Solow refers, in stating *his* view of the Keynesian Revolution, but] in terms of economic theory [and this is the part that Professor Solow leaves aside], Keynes's original ideas failed to achieve wide acceptance. Economic science essentially continued to do "business as usual", i.e. with a Walrasian engine at its core' (ibid: xiii). Most probably, the crucial discriminating point is precisely here (with the 'Walrasian engine at its core'). This is what Hicks did, explicitly, in his immensely popular IS-LM Keynesian model (Hicks, 1937). It is again the point from where Franco Modigliani started (by his own explicit statement) in his famous 'Liquidity Preference' article (Modigliani, 1944). It is basically the view of the Keynesian Revolution that is presented by Professor Solow here. Incidentally, this may also explain why, in a rough language, so alien to Solow's kindness (but not unusual in Joan Robinson), the replacing of Keynes's *theory* with that of Walras, and simultaneously accepting the Keynesian unemployment economic policies – justified, by the various authors, with a whole series and variety of attempts[2] – could not but be perceived (by the daughter of a Major General!) as generating 'bastard' offsprings. Solow's kindness now eliminates the unpleasant aspect. But the disagreement remains. For me, a genuine 'Keynesian revolution' cannot be confined to temporary measures aimed

[1] I am referring to the conferences on: 1) Hicks (*John Hicks: One Hundredth Anniversary Workshop*), Bologna, October 2004; 2) Modigliani (*Franco Modigliani – Tra teoria economica e impegno sociale*), Lincei Academy, Rome, February 2005; 3) Modigliani again (*International Conference on Franco Modigliani*), New School, New York, April 2005.

[2] As is well known, Hicks was at the very origin of all this series of 'bastard Keynesian' interpretations. Interestingly enough, Hicks himself (1980–1981) finally repudiated his IS-LM 'Keynesian' model, and very strongly so. To stress his change of mind, he decided to change his name! (*See* Pasinetti, 2007: 44n, and also 2008.)

at saving a sinking ship in times of mass unemployment. Much else should be at stake.[3]

This issue leads me straight to the second point of disagreement. This refers to my presentation of the historical development of economic thought as following a succession of two relevant, contrasting, paradigms: one associated with the investigations of the process of exchange (relying on subjective individual preferences and the principle of optimum allocation of given resources) and the other associated with the investigations of the process of production (and relying on objective technical relations in production and on the principle of human learning).

I originally developed this contrast in a work (Pasinetti, 1986) in which I investigated the ways in which the subjective and the objective *theories* of value (as opposed to pre-theoretical approaches) have emerged in the history of economic thought, and how they can be placed at the basis of the two mentioned (opposed) paradigms, in a way similar (though not entirely coincidental, due to our moving in the field of the social sciences) to that suggested by Thomas Kuhn (1970) in his well-known work on the way 'scientific revolutions' have taken place in the history of science.

I feel Professor Solow may have underestimated the importance of this distinction. I should like to stress that I have repeatedly and at length given my reasons for making it. Some authors, however, make, in my view, excessively accommodating concessions to the objections made to the above-mentioned distinction, thus risking to lose the enormous analytical interpretations and possibilities that such a logical framework makes possible.

I find it significant that Professor Solow should refer precisely to the formalization given by Jacob Mosak – namely the one which I myself originally used in my own work – to acknowledge the logic and clearness of a model of pure exchange. But he attributes it to being a device for didactical purposes. I think my counter-arguments on this point are much stronger. I have defined explicitly at the very beginning (Pasinetti, 2007: 19–20) the criterion that one should adopt to single out the features characterizing what can be called the basic model of each paradigm. As I specify, they should be those features, and only those features, that the basic model 'cannot do without'. It is logic, not didactical expedience,

[3] Let me simply recall Keynes's concluding sentences of the *General Theory* (p. 372): 'The outstanding faults of our economic society are its failures to provide full employment and its arbitrary and inequitable distribution of wealth and income', to which I added: 'Presumably both at the national and at the international level, ... and with ... the dramatic problem of the appalling widespread poverty in the middle of plenty' (Pasinetti, 2007: 235).

that must be considered in order to define what is the basis characterizing the structure of each paradigm. And on this basis, the gap between the two paradigms appears astonishingly huge. I found it interesting to recall on this point how strongly Piero Sraffa felt, when commenting on the gap that separates the approach of the Marginalists from that of the Classics (the two major representatives of the two above-described, contrasting, paradigms). He used the words 'abysmal gulf' (ibid: 195).

Yet I did not confine myself to relying on arguments of logic only. I thought it necessary to look deeply into the facts and thus I thought it appropriate to insert factual arguments in the form of a rather extended excursus on the 'historical background of economic analysis' (ibid: 250–255), in which the clear emerging of the two paradigms, on the *historical* scene, is presented with a fully thought-out explanation and rationale.

Professor Baumol should have no fear on this point. There is no 'prohibition' on my part on the pursuit of other approaches to investigate particular aspects, provided they are inserted in the appropriate way. The production paradigm, unlike the pure preference paradigm, is developed with a plurality of degrees of freedom (*see* further hints below). There is no reason to reject one paradigm, as such, as 'wrong', with respect to the other. Both are given a justification, but with reference to different and appropriate historical phases in the evolution of economic analysis. And in the historical phase that we are living in at present, the pure preference paradigm has become terribly insufficient.[4]

One clear reason why it has become insufficient may indirectly be seen from the standard defence of mainstream economics (rational expectations included) displayed by Professor Bertola.[5] This is surprising to me, at a time when most economists are having serious doubts about 'modern economics'.[6] It is even more surprising at a meeting like the present one, in which the defence of neoclassical theory has very wisely and explicitly been avoided also by Professor Solow (see the beginning of his contribution).

It is possible, to judge from what Giuseppe Bertola writes, that he may not have looked at the third part of my book with the concentration that it would have needed. He starts from the sub-title of the book and a bit too quickly tries to deal with it by an intelligent reference. Of course – he

[4] Let me briefly recall, e.g., the ways in which I conclude my *Book Two* (Pasinetti, 2007: 237) or the section on the 'methodological reductionism of neoclassical economics' (ibid: 263).

[5] Bertola's comment is not printed in the present book.

[6] See, as a significant example, the leading editorial, and cover page, of *The Economist*, 24 July 2009.

says – the Keynesian model is incomplete. It *must* be incomplete. '*In 1931, Gödel proved that every logical system has to be intrinsically self-referential and incomplete: not only must something be assumed but much else must remain logically undecidable.*'[7] By all means, Gödel's proof was a remarkable step forward, in logic and philosophy. It refers to *all* logical systems as such, not – as in my case – to the way in which alternative logical systems may develop in history. However, I must say, I find Professor Bertola's citation a splendid one. I am only surprised that he does not seem to realize that it applies perfectly well to the general equilibrium model, which he is so innocently defending. The reason simply is that such a model is – or it is aimed to be – a *closed* model. And, as all closed (or would-be closed) axiomatic models, it is indeed subject to Kurt Gödel's famous undecidability proof. Had Professor Bertola paid a little more accurate attention to my *Book Three* – which is the most engaging part of my work – he would surely have realized how concerned I have been with the thorny problem of the complexity of the industrial world, for which I am presenting the newly proposed paradigm (Pasinetti, 2007: 274–79, 307, 323–30). He would surely have come across what I have called the *separation theorem*. By it, I make the proposal to *separate* 'those investigations that concern the foundational bases of economic relations … from those investigations that must be carried out at the level of the actual economic institutions' (ibid: 275). Only some readers have in fact paid explicit attention to this (I think) *important* aspect of my model. Baumol tries a rather eclectic attempt – *We need them all* – he says of all attempts. In principle, of course, I agree. I am *not against* any specific approach, provided that it is used appropriately. Even less am I advocating any prohibition! I have tried my best to sketch out a logical framework for ordering the investigations of complex

[7] The reference given by Bertola is to a popular writing on *Gödel, Escher, Bach – An Eternal Golden Braid.* But I think that Gödel (1906–1978) was such an exceptional mind as to deserve some more specific references, especially to a mostly Italian audience. When I was a Research Fellow of Nuffield College in Oxford (at that time, considered the centre of British philosophical thought) I had, on the Gödel theorem, long conversations with my friend-philosopher Evandro Agazzi, later to become a professor of the history of science (specifically physics). To the remarkable *Gödel Theorem,* he devoted the major part of his principal work (Agazzi, 1961) – a good reference, I think. I may also mention, to the interested economists in the present audience, that Gödel offers a curious parallelism with the case of Sraffa *and* his admirers. During roughly the same years when Sraffa was bringing to completion his book *Production of Commodity,* Gödel (at Princeton) was bringing to completion his *Mathematical Proof of the Existence of God* – a modern, axiomatic (non-religious) version of St Anselmus's (1033–1109) ontological proof of God's existence. Gödel's admirers (like Sraffa's) have since done an enormous amount of work to trace and collect the complex scribbled notes, many times rewritten, through which Gödel arrived at his final result (*see* Gödel, 2006).

phenomena (ibid: 267–69). Perhaps my reply to what I call the *third objection*, to my *separation theorem*, as is anticipated and specified in my book (ibid: 327–28), seems to go in Baumol's direction. The logical framework of what I call 'the natural system' – very much unlike that of the general equilibrium model – is *not* closed. Many things have to be decided from outside it – not because of Gödel's theorem, which does not concern this aspect, but owing to its own logical characteristics.

Let me finally come to a few brief comments on some specific questions. I was first asked to what extent, in my mind, do 'natural' and normative coincide. A complete answer would require going into long details, and my method of referring to specific pages of the book would not be so effective in this case. The shortest answer I can think of is to say that the two concepts overlap to a great extent, but do not coincide. It is easy to think of relations that are 'normative', but do not belong to the 'natural system', and equally well of relations that belong to the 'natural system' but are not necessarily (or exclusively) 'normative'.

The second question is more intriguing. Professor Baumol was asked if he would be prepared to utilize the phrase 'magnificent dynamics', that he coined a long time ago, in connection with the paradigm which I proposed. Professor Baumol has avoided, perhaps wisely, picking up the question. But – interestingly enough – it is again Professor Solow who has become involved with it, even if in an indirect way. The term *'magnificent dynamics'*, as is well known, was coined by Baumol (1951) with reference to the grand dynamics of the Classics, of Marx, of Schumpeter and of Harrod (indeed the first economist to extend Keynes's theory to the long run). It is at least legitimate for us to begin by asking: does Solow's neoclassical growth model belong to Baumol's category? I think the answer is no, as Solow himself explains: *'While it is true that the growth paths of capitalist economies are never paths of continuous full employment, full utilization equilibrium, it is true as a matter of historical fact that it would be reasonable to describe those paths as fluctuations around a trend, with most of the time the fluctuations contained within fairly narrow bounds – a … corridor around that path.'* This is a tricky proposition. It seems to me an attempt to get away from the criticism I made (Pasinetti, 2007: 231n), which points out that Solow's growth model (1956) is logically consistent only in a hypothetical world of *proportional dynamics*, i.e. in a world with a single commodity (or at most a composite commodity with absolutely *constant* composition through time), which – I point out – can never be the case in economic systems with technical progress. This may also be the point at which Professor Solow has come to realize the relevance of my work on *structural dynamics*, as he nicely states. I should be so glad to find him consistent one step further, by accepting that his proposition that '*the Keynesian revolution will never be complete because behaviour and institutions in our society change. They evolve*' contains a contradiction. *Revolution* and *evolution* are antithetic terms. The real way to avoid these contradictions is to accept my *separation theorem:* a break (a *revolution*) with respect to neoclassical *theory*, and a set of investigations of the appropriate (evolving) *institutions.* Indeed, in agreement with Professor Solow, though in a different direction, I sincerely do '*hope small armies of young economists will engage in trying to bring the Keynesian revolution*' to its accomplishment.

Nevertheless, at the end of this discussion, it is encouraging for me to realize that the two different directions just hinted at (Solow's and mine) may not be so entirely divergent as might at first appear, after all. It is comforting for me to discover that there is an overlapping area in our evaluations – the one concerning *structural economic dynamics* – on which we seem to entertain similar convictions as to its relevance, and therefore as to its being a really important field of research for younger generations of economists to concentrate on. I am sure Solow's position on this is so pre-eminent and inspiring for the *armies of young economists* as to make me more than happy to be able to join him.

Second afterword: the significance of structural economic dynamics

Luigi L. Pasinetti

I am glad Professor Solow has decided to participate in the present *Collection of Essays* by deciding to reproduce here his contribution to the recent Lincei Academy discussion on my latest book, and most of all by making a crucial addition to it – namely an afterword devoted to *structural economic dynamics*. This makes it only too logical (as explained above, p. 276) that I should myself follow his example by reproducing my 'Reply to criticisms' in the same discussion, and similarly by adding the present afterword on the same subject.[1]

The question at stake is not a minor one. It is in fact a fundamental question, as it goes down to the very significance of the type of analysis that can be carried out with a one-sector-model approach associated with Solow's neoclassical growth model versus the significance of the structural economic dynamics approach associated with my own work.

The crux of the matter is revealed by the proposition with which Solow opens the substantial part of his afterword. Writes Solow: 'I cannot imagine how anyone can be "against" the goal of structural dynamics. Multi-sector growth models and one-sector growth models are complements, not rivals. The main reason for pursuing one-sector and two-sector analysis is transparency. The role of certain fundamental principles . . . is easier to understand in a fully aggregative context. But the way these principles work themselves out in practice may need to be studied in an explicitly multi-sectoral model' (see p. 274 this volume).

These sentences shed light precisely on the major point of contrast between Solow's one-sector model approach and the approach to structural economic dynamics which I have been pursuing in my works. There are, of course, many differences between the two approaches,

[1] The references are R.M. Solow 'On Pasinetti and the unfinished Keynesian Revolution' and L.L. Pasinetti 'Reply to Criticisms', in the *Proceedings* of the Accademia Nazionale dei Lincei, Rome: *Round Table* of 28 November 2008, on Luigi Pasinetti's book: *Keynes and the Cambridge Keynesians – a 'revolution in economics' to be accomplished* (Cambridge University Press, 2007).

because of the different theoretical *paradigms* from which they stem. But there is one major contrast on which I shall concentrate here – it concerns the specific topic of *structural dynamics*.

I want to argue that the structural dynamic approach to growth is not merely complementary to the one-sector approach. It goes much beyond complementarity, to such an extent that, when we consider the passage of time, the one-sector approach becomes incompatible with structural analysis.

Essentially, the two approaches embody two different *visions* of the industrial world. The *vision* behind structural dynamics originates from the consideration of a permanently *evolving* economic system. The *vision* behind the aggregate model of traditional growth theory embodies a static, or at most a stationary, view of the economic system, and the reason is that it is inherently incapable of absorbing any change in time of the structure.

At a first glance, a multi-sector model may look like a simple, more detailed, specification of the one-sector model. And hence the analysis of the structural dynamic type might at first appear as complementary to the traditional aggregate growth model. But in fact this apparent impression is false.

Any multi-sector model is characterized by having, at any given point in time, a particular *structure*. The size of the aggregate output of the economic system will, of course, turn out to be a *weighted* average of the outputs of the various sectors, the weights being given by the sectoral *proportions*, with respect to aggregate output, of the quantities of each good demanded as a consumption good and/or as an intermediate commodity for the production of (all) goods. This structure of the whole system derives from technology on the one side and from demand on the other side. But both technology and demand together will shape a structure which is *specific to a specific point of time*. When we introduce time, the whole structure will in general change; and as a consequence the whole complementarity between the two approaches will break down. Notice that it will break down on the side of the aggregate, *not* on the side of the structural, view.

We could, of course, imagine an economic system that *grows* in absolute terms, while maintaining *relative* quantities absolutely constant. In my 1981 book, I have shown that there are three highly hypothetical cases in which this can happen. I have called them the three cases of *proportional dynamics*. They are:

1. The case of population growth at constant returns to scale.
2. The case of uniform technical progress in all sectors and equally uniform expansion of demand for all goods and services.

3. The case in which, in each single (vertically integrated) sector, the rate of growth of productivity is exactly equal to the rate of growth of per-capita demand, so that the two rates of growth cancel each other out inside each single sector.

These three cases are precisely those cases that must be taken as implicitly assumed by traditional economic theory when talking of growth, if we want to give logical consistency to such a theory. But such a type of growth would simply be an expansion at constant proportions (a kind of blowing up) of the (supposedly optimum) position assumed to have been achieved by the economic system, at the initial point of time. It would really be hard to attribute any significance to such a type of (proportional) dynamics. In fact, in such cases, it would not even make much sense to set up a multi-sector growth model, since we could simply compare total aggregate quantities, perfectly knowing that the whole structure within them remains constant.

If we are going to pay any attention to the criterion, which Professor Solow has always advocated, of empirical relevance, we should obviously rule out these three cases as failing to give any relevant representation of the real world. But if we rule out these cases, we are left with an economic system whose structure *evolves* through time, with productivity and demand growing at different rates from sector to sector and independently of one another. In this context, it will indeed make sense to talk of dynamics – of a *true* dynamics – in which not only the absolute but also, and most importantly, the *relative* magnitudes are continually evolving.

It is within a context of this type that the *interaction* of the unequal evolution of technology and of the inevitably complex evolution of the *composition* of consumption of goods and services gives rise to the *structural* dynamics of quantities, of prices and of sectoral employment. As a laborer, each single individual contributes to a very specialized part of the division of production tasks in each single sector, but as a consumer, he/she demands in principle the goods produced by all sectors of the whole economic system. Almost paradoxically, it can be shown that there exists a genuinely *macroeconomic* equilibrium condition that must be satisfied overall. Obviously, it will be the task of the institutions of the economic system to govern the interaction between individual efforts and consumption choices so as to drive the economic system to the fulfilment of such macroeconomic condition (which, as I have shown, turns out to be the equivalent of Keynes's effective demand/full employment condition).

I think I have been able to give the clearest version of such a macroeconomic condition by using a simple pure labor model. The results have been summarized in a few sentences which can be found in my 2007 book (p. 285), and which may be usefully synthesized as follows.

One must notice the essentially macroeconomic nature of the overall equilibrium condition, not so much because of the sum of the *m* sectors but more fundamentally because all sectors are linked – even when there are no inter-industry relations – by the effect of the overall demand. Each worker may contribute to a very tiny fraction of the production of a particular good (a sectoral contribution), but at the same time, with his/her family, will contribute to the demand for virtually *all* the goods and services produced in the economic system. Through this channel, owing to the all-embracing effect of overall demand, the set of all production processes forms a *true* economic 'system'. Such a condition is indeed a single relation, but it concerns the *whole* economic system. In this way it becomes a single truly macroeconomic relation, independent of the number and structure of the sectors and irrespective of all the movements of both technology and of consumers' demand.

I trust the reader will see, in this context, that the only approach capable of resuming a genuine dynamic analysis in economic growth models is not simply that of introducing time but of introducing time in a *relevant* way. This implies introducing a *continually evolving structure* of the economic magnitudes, as time goes on.

This is the gist and purpose of structural economic dynamics.

REFERENCES

Academia Nazionale Dei Lincei (2009), 'Reply to criticisms' from 'Round Table on Luigi Pasinetti's book: *Keynes and the Cambridge Keynesians – a 'revolution in economics' to be accomplished'*, *Proceedings* (*Rendiconti degli Atti dell'Academia Nazionale dei Lincei – Classe di Scienze Morali, Storiche e Filologiche*), series no. IX, Volume XX (2009), Number 4 (2010), pp. 767–830.

Agazzi, E. (1961), *Introduzione ai Problemi dell'Assiomatica*, Milan: Vita e Pensiero.

Baumol, W.J. (1951), *Economic Dynamics – An Introduction*, London: Macmillan.

Gödel, K. (2006), *La Prova matematica dell'Esistenza di Dio*, Turin: Bollati Boringhieri.

Hicks, J. R. (1937), 'Mr. Keynes and the "Classics" – a Suggested Interpretation', in *Econometrica*, **5**, 2, 147–59.

(1980–81), 'IS-LM: an Explanation', *Journal of Post Keynesian Economics*, IV, **3**, 139–55.

Keynes, J.M. (1936), *The General Theory of Employment, Interest and Money*, London: Macmillan.

Kuhn, T.S. (1970) *The Structure of Scientific Revolutions*, 2nd edn, University of Chicago Press.

Modigliani, F. (1944), 'Liquidity Preference and the Theory of Interest and Money', *Econometrica*, **12**, 1, 45–88.

Mosak, J.L. (1944), *General Equilibrium Theory in International Trade*, Monograph 7, Bloomington, IN: Cowles Commission.

Pasinetti, L.L. (1981) *Structural Change and Economic Growth – A Theoretical Essay on the Dynamics of the Wealth of Nations*, Cambridge University Press.

(1986), 'Theory of Value – a Source of Alternative Paradigms in Economic Analysis', in Baranzini, M. and Scazzieri, R. (eds) *Foundations of Economics. Structures of Enquiry and Economic Theory*, Oxford, Basil Blackwell, pp. 409–31.

(2007), *Keynes and the Cambridge Keynesians. A 'Revolution' in Economics to be Accomplished*, Cambridge University Press.

(2008), 'Hicks's "Conversion" – from J.R. to John' in: Scazzieri, R., Sen, A. K. and Zamagni, S. (eds) *John Hicks: One Hundredth Anniversary Workshop*, Cambridge University Press, pp. 52–71.

Solow, R.M. (1956), 'A Contribution to the Theory of Economic Growth', *Quarterly Journal of Economics*, **70**, 1, 65–94.

Index